Woman Playing the Lute.
Chinese, style of Wei
Dynasty, 386–557. Red-
dish earthenware, poly-
chromed, 9 inches high.
New York, The Metro-
politan Museum of Art,
Gift of Mrs. Edward S.
Harkness, 1934.

Heinrich Frauenlob Directing Minstrel Performance. Fourteenth century.
Manesse Manuscript of German Minnesingers. Heidleberg Library.

THE HERITAGE OF
MUSICAL STYLE

HOLT, RINEHART AND WINSTON, INC.

NEW YORK CHICAGO SAN FRANCISCO ATLANTA DALLAS
MONTREAL TORONTO LONDON SYDNEY

Donald H. Van Ess

STATE UNIVERSITY OF NEW YORK AT BROCKPORT

THE HERITAGE OF
MUSICAL STYLE

TO MY MOTHER

Library of Congress Catalog Card Number: 73-101138
SBN: 03-081241-0
Printed in the United States of America
0123 17 98765432

Cover: *Woman Playing the Lute*. The Metropolitan Museum of Art

Book Design: Marion D. Needham

PREFACE

This book is intended for the introductory course in music—often called Introduction to Music or Introduction to Music Literature, and still widely known by its original name, Music Appreciation. Also, the book can be used in courses in the humanities.

The Heritage of Musical Style has evolved from the author's deep conviction that the great treasures of music, as of the other fine arts, are not confined to one or two epochs but are to be found in all periods of civilization. Moreover, the style of music—its form, underlying ideas, and its rhythmic, melodic and harmonic characteristics—is closely related to the prevailing culture of each epoch. Thus, the present text provides a broad perspective of man's achievements in music, and emphasizes how a knowledge of the cultural background of music can be an important factor in the enrichment of the musical experience of the listener. The keystone is the *conceptualization* of essential elements of music into basic styles or musical ideas—culled from each period and presented against the intellectual and artistic background of each cultural epoch. In this way, the reasons for the growth, practices, and styles of music come more clearly into focus.

Since the volume has been planned and organized to be used by the general reader, the student in the liberal arts curriculum, and possibly music students taking an introductory course for majors, several approaches are possible in using this text. The general reader will find the first chapter, "Meaning in Music," to be a helpful foundation for the chapters that follow. Depending on the amount of time and the background of the class, the student or his instructor may choose either to cover the first chapter in a thorough, systematic way or use it only as a reference in reading later chapters. The music major with a knowledge of the fundamentals may omit the chapter and commence with Chapter 2 (The Greco-Roman Era).

The book is organized historically but makes no attempt to cover every facet of music history, and detailed descriptions of techniques, composers and periods have been omitted whenever possible in favor of definitive summaries of these aspects. Ancient and medieval music, for example, is treated briefly but succinctly to enable the reader to move on to later periods relatively early in the course. Also, some of the later chapters reflect the author's desire to present familiar examples rather than the obscure and the unusual.

Two helpful guides for the general reader are to be found in the Appendix: a Glossary of basic theory and musical forms, and a Pronunciation Guide for names of artists, musicians, and musical terms.

The present publication also includes a companion workbook (*A Listener's Guide to the Heritage of Musical Style*) and a collection of five, twelve-inch stereo recordings correlated with the text and workbook.

Based upon the assumption that esthetic enjoyment is enhanced by knowledge of the musical work, the accompanying workbook contains abbreviated scores in which thematic material is presented in single line form. The fundamentals of music notation are discussed in the first chapter of the textbook; helpful suggestions and basic techniques for using the abbreviated scores are presented in Chapter 1 of the workbook.

In addition to line scores, the workbook contains helpful listening guides to understanding the basic styles of each period; it also includes listening forms for the recorded examples, and review exercises. The listening forms may be completed in class (where listening facilities are limited) or be assigned outside of class.

The number of listening assignments can, of course, be extended or decreased, depending on the needs of the class. Also, certain early chapters may be given less emphasis to permit more extensive examination of later chapters that involve more resources for listening.

The humanities philosophy that serves as the foundation of this book, has a particular significance that needs to be underscored. Perhaps it is better to say the humanistic spirit itself needs to be *reaffirmed*, since there seems to be more than a casual relationship between the chaos of our time and the loss of human values as exemplified in some forms of art.

Study of the arts could provide the needed restoration of the humanistic spirit by bringing to the foreground the creative powers of man as represented in his painting, architecture, literature, and sculpture. Music especially occupies a key role in our renewal of the humanities. Artistic experiences, centered around noted works of music, not only bring enjoyment but also furnish a basis for forming tastes and standards. Hopefully, such experiences will help us separate greatness from mediocrity and see beyond changing fashions of taste.

In addition to the publishers and individuals who granted me permission to reproduce musical examples, photographs, and text, I wish to thank the following for generous assistance: Richard Wilbur, Wesleyan University, for the translation of *Correspondences* by Charles Baudelaire; Annie Knize, for the photograph of Anton Webern; Joseph Jenks, State University of New York, for translations of old English selections; Samuel Brick, University of Florida, for reading the manuscript in its early stages; Robert Gemmett, State University of New York, for the photograph of Beckford's Fonthill Abbey; and typists Rita Burrell and Kathryn De Wolf for their splendid help.

I also wish to acknowledge the excellent assistance of the staff of Holt, Rinehart and Winston including Alice Trimmer, music editor, and especially Ruth Chapman for her skillful and tasteful editorial guidance.

Brockport, N.Y., 1970   *DONALD H. VAN ESS*

CONTENTS

THE HERITAGE OF
MUSICAL STYLE

1

MEANING IN MUSIC

PRELIMINARY CONSIDERATIONS: THE ELEMENTS OF MUSIC

Through the humanities . . . we may come to know the excitement of ideas, the power of imagination and the unsuspected energies of the creative spirit.

Report of the Commission on the Humanities

Undoubtedly the most important objective in listening to music, as with any experience in the arts, is simply personal enjoyment. However, what we are seeking through our study of the fine arts is a significant kind of musical enjoyment that will have real depth and substance and a lasting value in our lives. Our goal is true esthetic enjoyment, which results from an understanding of the composer's art and a feelingful response to the expressive elements of music such as melody, harmony, rhythm, and form. Esthetic enjoyment, then, may be defined as a pleasurable experience of relatively lasting importance involving intellectual perception and emotional response. It is, obviously, derived from meaningful listening experiences based on music of merit. Musical works of value, no matter what the period—the Renaissance, the classical, or the contemporary period—generally exhibit certain characteristics such as craftsmanship, logical order, intelligent use of available materials and human feeling. Moreover, these works provide meaningful musical experiences for the listener; they affect us inwardly, arrest our attention, move us emotionally, and compel us to hear them again and again. And lastly, they provide us with a more complete view of life, with its moments of joy, sorrow, deep religious thought, love, and death—in short, life's struggles and fulfillments.

To what source do we turn to find the music that will fulfill many or all of these requirements? To a particular period? To one composer? Through the study of the collective achievements of Western man in the fine arts we may find the rich sources of ideas and experiences that have continually inspired man since the Great Age of Greece. And through the study of these works we may discover values that are enduring and meaningful and that will in turn give our lives needed direction and purpose. Consequently, our musical listening and study will embrace a wide range of musical forms and styles and center upon representative works of the various historical periods. The ultimate aim of this endeavor is the development of musical taste, a taste that will be far-reaching in scope and that will recognize the commonality of the arts.

Perceptive Listening   Enjoyment may be derived in a wide variety of ways as we listen to music. For example, a highly skilled performance of a technical passage may evoke a feeling of amazement and awe. Or, pleasant moments may arise while hearing a full, resonant harmony, a climactic ending of a symphony or may be derived from hearing a highly inventive drummer in a modern jazz ensemble. These are some of the broad aspects of musical enjoyment—they are comparable perhaps to selected highlights or passages in a novel or drama. Understandably, if we focus our attention only on these aspects we have missed the plot or the central ideas of the musical composition or novel.

This leads to several questions the interested listener will ask: What is it that I am supposed to be concentrating on in the composition? Is the composer merely filling space with colorful sounds or is there any unifying idea that I should hear which will help me to obtain a fuller enjoyment in listening? In short, the serious listener wants to know the *meaning* of the work, that is, what the composer has intended to be expressed or understood.

How is meaning embodied in tones? The answer is to be found in an examination of the art itself. First, music is primarily an art of tonal design or structure. Unlike painting, the design is not presented in complete form but rather as it is sounded. Music unfolds in time in much the same way as prose and poetry. Although the vehicle for communicating meaning is different (tones as opposed to words), music shares the same cognitive principles as verbal language. For example, in both music and literature, certain "key" ideas (themes in music and sentences in literature) hold our attention and lead us to anticipate further developments. Moreover, just as recognition, retention, and recall are required in tracing the unfolding plot of a novel, music likewise demands the same perceptive powers as a theme is restated or varied in the course of a musical composition. Meaning, then, in tonal art, is embodied in the composer's ideas —the themes or significant series of tones upon which a composition is based. They are the uniting thoughts or ideas that give logic and coherence to the musical creation; they are the focal points of our attention, the plot, so to speak, that is woven into a tonal fabric.

As we hear a musical composition performed we also react emotionally. Certain feelings or moods are evoked as we hear a powerful climax sounded by the brass or percussion or a peaceful, pastoral section played by the flutes. Thus, music perception may be said to involve both a cognitive response (identification of themes and musical elements) and emotional response (reaction to tonal sensation). Since the latter is in the province of unmeasurable feelings, we must seek cognitive grounds for learning about music. The emotional aspect of perception is equally important; it will be enriched by a greater depth of understanding of tonal art and with increased experience in listening.

Music is made up of many component elements (melody, harmony, rhythm, and so on) that are a part of the total creative expression. The comprehension of these elements will require practice in listening. To illustrate, after several hearings of a certain work, the novice listener will begin to differentiate interesting features in addition to thematic material, such as tempo or speed of music, types of instruments and voices, and rhythmic patterns, to name a few. The principal objective—*perceptive listening*—is attained when the formal structure (the organization of the thematic ideas within a musical form) is understood and the various elements (harmony, rhythm, melody, instruments, and so on) are identified and experienced as part of the whole.

Fundamentals of Musical Notation

By nature, music is susceptible to a wide range of personal interpretations evoked by tonal sensation. As a result, unless there is an awareness of what to listen for, the composer's ideas and their elaboration may, to the uninitiated, be replaced by visions of fantasy or become lost in a diffusion of sound. What is needed to avoid these common pitfalls is an understanding of the fundamentals of notation and the elements of music. This knowledge will permit the listener to follow the main melodic patterns in this book and the line scores contained in the accompanying workbook. Furthermore, a study of these preliminary but vital aspects will enable the reader to discuss intelligently the basic techniques as he encounters them in this survey of music history.

Musical notation includes: (1) a set of lines and spaces referred to as the great staff, (2) note symbols, (3) meter symbols, and (4) symbols and terms for expression.

The Great Staff   The great staff consists of eleven lines with a space between each line. Each line has a given letter name as does each space, A, B, C, D, E, F, G, A, and so on; also, each consecutive line and space is referred to as a "step."

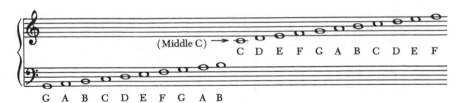

The Great Staff

The middle line, or "middle C," separates the great staff into two segments or ranges of sound: the high range indicated by the *treble clef sign* (𝄞) encompassing the soprano and alto parts, and the low range indicated by the *bass clef sign* (𝄢) encompassing the tenor and bass parts. *Leger lines and spaces* are added lines and spaces below the staff and above. These are to be used if a musical passage is to extend beyond the range of the bass clef or treble clef.

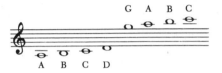

Leger Lines

Music for the keyboard instruments (piano and organ) is normally written on the great staff. Music designed for other instruments and human voices is written in either the treble or bass clef, depending on the range of the instrument or voice. The treble clef is used for higher-pitched instruments or voices such as flute, clarinet, soprano voice, and so on. The bass clef is for lower-pitched instruments or voices such as the trombone, tuba, and bass voice.

Vertical lines drawn through the staff are called *bar lines* which separate the notes into *measures*. The practice of using bar lines for this purpose began in the sixteenth century. Double vertical lines as found in modern music designate a sectional division or the ending of a composition. Repeat signs (double bar combined with two dots) signify that the preceding section (or section enclosed in these signs) is to be repeated.

Examples of Bar Lines

Note Symbols   The relative duration in time of a musical tone, that is, its note value, is indicated by the shape of the written note. Also, each note has its corresponding *rest* symbol to indicate the measurement of silence. The whole note (𝅝) is the note of longest duration, and following in a decreasing order of time value, or duration, are the half note (𝅗𝅥), quarter (♩), eighth (♪), sixteenth (𝅘𝅥𝅯), and so on. Below is a table of common notes and their rest equivalents.

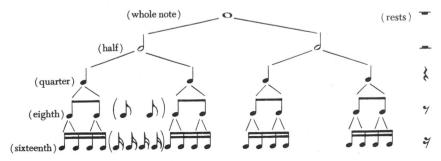

Table of Note Values and Rests

A dot placed after a note prolongs it by half again its duration, thus:

Increasing the Duration of Notes

A *tie* (♩‿♩) is a curved line connecting two notes of the same pitch into a continuous sound. A *fermata* (𝄐) indicates a momentary holding of a tone. Some articulation signs include the *accent* (♩), which means that a slight additional force or stress is to be given a note, and the *dot* (♩), which indicates that the note is to be played very short. A curved line beneath or over a series of notes signifies that they are to be played *legato*, meaning smoothly, in a connected manner.

Meter Symbols Appearing at the beginning of a piece of music (just after the clef sign or after the key signature if one is present) is a *meter* or *time signature* consisting of two numbers that indicate the meter of the music. The upper number represents the number of beats or pulses in each mea-

Duple Meter

Triple Meter

Compound Meter

sure, and the lower, the type of note value that is to receive one beat. For example, $\frac{3}{4}$ meter means that the basic beats or notes are quarter notes (lower figure), and there are three beats or counts in each measure. Meters are classified as duple ($\frac{2}{2}$, $\frac{2}{4}$), triple ($\frac{3}{2}$, $\frac{3}{4}$, $\frac{3}{8}$), quadruple ($\frac{4}{2}$, $\frac{4}{8}$, $\frac{4}{4}$ [also written as C]), and compound ($\frac{6}{4}$, $\frac{6}{8}$, $\frac{9}{8}$).

Symbols such as ♯ and ♭ appearing just before a note are called *accidentals* or *chromatics*. The ♯ (sharp sign) indicates that the written note is to be raised in pitch one-half step, for example from C to C♯; the ♭ (flat sign) designates a lowering of the pitch one-half step, for example from B to B♭; a ♮ (natural) is used to cancel out a chromatic sign present in a measure, that is, to restore a note to its original pitch. The grouping of flats or sharps at the left-hand side of the staff designates the *key* of the music, that is, a certain number of sharps or flats placed together on the staff. The matter of keys and scales is taken up in subsequent pages.

Symbols and Terms for Expression   By means of various terms and markings the composer may indicate the desired (1) tempo or speed of the music, (2) level of dynamics or volume, and (3) the general mood or feeling. Some of the common expression markings are as follows:

TEMPO	*VOLUME*	*MOOD*
Largo (very slow)	pp = very soft	dolce (sweetly)
Lento (slow)	p = soft	cantabile (in a
Andante (moderate)	mp = moderately soft	singing
Allegretto (quite fast)	mf = moderately loud	manner)
Allegro (fast)	f = loud	pesante (heavy)
Presto (very fast)	ff = very loud	marziale (march-
Ritard (rit.) = to	(to increase	like)
slow up	volume)	maestoso (with
Accelerando (accel.) =	(to decrease	majesty)
to speed up	volume)	
	sf = heavy accent	

The Elements of Music

Over the centuries, various ways of manipulating tones have been devised for the purpose of obtaining a greater range of musical expression. Thus we find that the composer may alter or change the tone or tones as to color (*timbre*), speed (*tempo*), intensity (*volume*), highness or lowness (*pitch*), and duration (*rhythm*). Or, on a higher level, he may arrange the tones successively into *melody*, simultaneously into chords or *harmony*, or combine several melodies into *counterpoint*. These are the component elements of music, the materials from which a musical composition is created. Let us examine these elements in greater detail.

Timbre   Each instrument and voice has a distinct tone color or timbre, as determined by the physical structure of the sound-emitting source. For example, the oboe has a rather reedy and somewhat nasal quality that is largely attributed to the double reed in the instrument's mouthpiece.

Tempo   The speed of music may vary from extremely slow (designated by the term *largo*) to very fast (*presto*). We perceive the tempo in the *beat*, that is, a steady recurring pulsation felt in varying degrees in almost all music. In modern times an attempt has been made to classify the degrees of tempo by the use of the metronome invented in 1815. The tempo marking for "largo," for example, ranges from 40 to 60 beats per minute; "presto," on the other hand, has from 168 to 208.

Volume   The intensity of the tone may range from very soft (indicated by *pp*) upwards through infinite shadings to very loud (*ff*). Volume markings first began to appear in the late sixteenth century. Volume may be changed gradually, either increased (marked *crescendo* in printed music) or decreased (*diminuendo*).

Pitch   The relative height or depth of a sound, that is, its pitch, is determined by the rate of vibration of the sound-producing medium. The lowest pitch on the piano is 27½ vibrations per second, the highest, 4186. The practice of pitch notation (staff lines and symbols) dates back to the Middle Ages. A standardized system of tuning all tones in the scale equally was not established until the eighteenth century. In 1939 the international pitch standard was set at A = 440 vibrations per second.

Rhythm   Rhythm, which may be defined as a feeling of forward motion, is the lifeblood of all music. Rhythm results from the repetition of a pattern of notes of differing time value. As the series is played, the notes having a slightly longer duration (♩ ♩ ♩ ♩ or ♪. ♪ ♪. ♪) tend to receive a greater stress than notes of short duration. This pattern of "stress-release" provides music with a forward, propelling movement, an effect also present in architecture, where a series of columns or spaces create visual rhythm.

Melody   A melody (or *theme*) is a series of successive tones arranged into a logical pattern. Themes may vary in length from several tones to many measures. Further discussion of melody follows.

Harmony   The technique of combining tones to form chords is referred to as harmony. We hear chords as tones juxtaposed upon one another, hence, harmony is the *vertical* aspect of music (that is, tones sounded simultaneously) as opposed to melody, which is the *horizontal* aspect of music (tones sounded in succession).

Counterpoint   The technique of combining two or more melodic lines is called counterpoint or *polyphony* (pron. po-lif-o-nee).

Texture   The particular manner in which tones are arranged in musical space is called texture. The three types of texture are: *monophonic* (only one melody or part), *polyphonic* or *contrapuntal* (two or more melodies or parts sounded together), and *homophonic* (a single melody and chords).

Melody and Its Components

> Melody is the most essential of . . . the elements, not because it is more immediately perceptible but because it is the dominant voice of the music. . . .
>
> Igor Stravinsky, *Poetics of Music*

The constituent parts of melody, those features that determine the character and effect of the melody, include the following: (1) the contour, which may be smooth (tones moving up or down the scale from one scale step or tone to an adjacent tone), or angular (wide leaps or *intervals* present between tones); (2) rhythmic pattern (the particular arrangement of note values); (3) compass (the distance or interval from the lowest to highest note in the melody); and (4) the inner progression of tones, which may be *diatonic* (the melody remaining within the key, no accidentals present), or *chromatic* (accidentals used). The following melodic example will illustrate these points.

Sonata, Op. 49, no. 2, Ludwig van Beethoven (1770–1827)

1. Contour: smooth, mostly step movement used.
2. Rhythmic pattern: ♩. ♪ ♩ ♩. ♪ ♩ Meter: triple.
3. Compass: F♯ to E, or a compass of seven tones.
4. Inner progression: mainly diatonic, but chromatic in measure 7.
5. Other features: the character of the melody is dancelike; the melody is divided into two smaller units or *phrases*, the first of which ends in measure 4.

Phrase and Cadence A never-ending succession of tones, like a continuous, unbroken series of words, is monotonous and unmeaningful to the listener. Thus, in order to create order out of the vast tonal spectrum available, the composer divides the tonal material into melodic units called *phrases.* Phrases vary in length from one musical epoch to another. For example, in the Renaissance they tended to be long and flowing, while in the classical period they were of shorter length and had more clearly defined endings.

Pope Marcellus Mass, Giovanni da Palestrina (1525–1594)

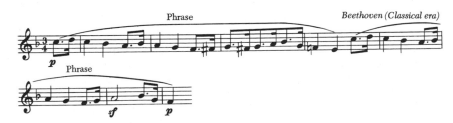

Andante favori, Ludwig van Beethoven

Various kinds of musical punctuation called *cadences,* are used by the composer to set off phrases from one another. For example, note in the two melodies by Beethoven (see above and below) that a momentary pause occurs at the end of the first phrase. This is comparable to a comma in punctuation and is called a *half cadence.* Observe the definite close or stop at the end of the melody. This effect is equivalent to a period, and is referred to as a *complete cadence.*

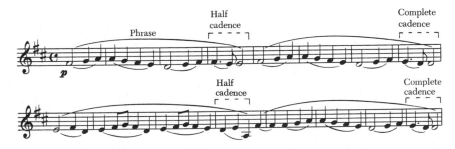

Melody from Beethoven's Symphony No. 9

Scales and Modes The theoretical basis of melody is the *scale,* a series of tones arranged in an ascending or descending order. Each period in music history is usually associated with a particular type of scale system, either *modal, tonal* (major and minor scales), or *chromatic.* To illustrate, music prior to about 1600 (the Greek, medieval, and Renaissance periods) employed archaic forms of scales called *modes;* thus, this time in music history is generally referred to as the Modal Age. Music composed between 1600 and 1900 (the baroque, classical and romantic periods) was generally constructed in the major and minor keys and scales. Because of the key-oriented system, this portion of music history is called the Tonal Age. The composers of our modern era, at least up to the mid-century point, have made extensive use of themes or series freely drawn from the chromatic scale. Due to the tendency of many present-day composers to employ the tones of the chromatic scale with complete freedom, that is, without regard for key relationships, some writers have regarded the first part of the twentieth century as an atonal period. However, we will find that many scales and different styles and methods of composition prevail in contemporary music.

The various scale systems—the major and minor, the ancient modes, and the chromatic—are the basic building materials of Western music and therefore require a brief explanation. To begin with, we should clarify two terms that are closely related: *key* and *scale.* "Key" refers to a particular group or family of tones in which a piece of music is written. "Scale" is the group of tones in the key arranged in order from lowest to highest. Furthermore, all the tones in the scale or key are held together by their relationship or gravitation to one tone, called the *keynote.* It is from this fundamental tone—the starting and ending tone of the scale—that the key or scale derives its name.

There are twelve major and twelve minor keys and scales. The major and minor scales are composed of whole and half steps, that is, tones and semitones that are readily perceived by examining the structure of the piano keyboard. In the following piano diagram, whole steps are present between all white keys except E-F and B-C (where black keys are missing). Half steps, then, are located between E-F, B-C, and any white key and an adjacent black key.

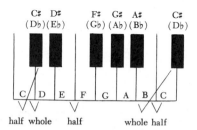

Diagram of Piano Keyboard

By playing all of the white keys (starting on C) in succession, we may produce the C major scale. All twelve major scales have the same pattern of whole and half steps as the C major scale: half steps appear between the third and fourth and seventh and eighth degrees of the scale; the remaining tones are a whole step or whole tone apart. The major scale has a bright-sounding effect that was generally favored by the composers of the classical period of the late eighteenth century.

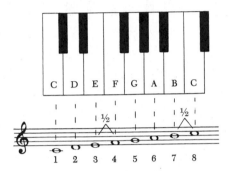

The Major Scale and Relationship to the
Piano Keyboard

A major scale can be built upon any tone. But in order to retain the whole- and half-step pattern, it becomes necessary to add sharps or flats for those keys other than C major. For example, we may construct a scale on the note "F" by adding a note to each successive line and space; however, a flat will be needed at the fourth degree in order to make the necessary half step between the third and fourth degrees. Instead of placing the flat in the body of the music, it is customary to put the flat sign at the left-hand side of the staff, and thus the single flat sign identifies the key signature for F major.

Incomplete F Major
Scale

Complete F Major
Scale

Although there are several types of minor scales, the common harmonic form will perhaps best illustrate the minor scale structure and effect. It is called the harmonic form because it is the preferred type for constructing harmony in the minor key. Notice in the following example that the minor scale has a different pattern of whole and half steps than the major scale. This arrangement of tones gives the minor scale a rather somber quality, which was generally preferred by the composers of the romantic period.

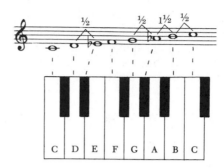

The Minor Scale (Harmonic Form) and Relationship
to the Piano Keyboard

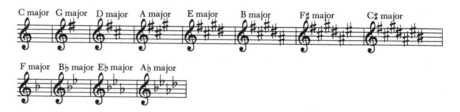

The Twelve Major Keys

The whole- and half-step scheme in each of the *ancient modes* is different from that of the major and minor scales. The basic difference to be noted is in the whole step between the seventh and eighth tones in most of the modes, a structural characteristic that accounts for the quaint and archaic sound generally associated with the modes.

Another marked difference between the modes and scales can be noted in the feeling of finality as the last tone of the series is sounded: there is a much stronger pull, or gravitation, from the seventh to the eighth tones in the scales, due to the half step that appears before the final tone in all major and minor scales.

Modes were employed in the Greek civilization, and were eventually passed on to medieval musicians who organized a series of eight modes (the so-called *Church modes*), which were in common use from the Middle Ages to the late Renaissance. They were as follows: Dorian, Hypodorian, Phrygian, Hypophrygian, Lydian, Hypolydian, Mixolydian, and Hypomixolydian. These modes will be treated more fully under music of the Middle Ages.

The Dorian Mode

The *chromatic scale* is composed of twelve different tones arranged in half-step intervals throughout, as follows:

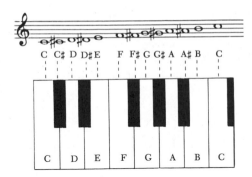

The Chromatic Scale and Relationship to the
Piano Keyboard

Other types of scales that have been used by contemporary composers include the *whole-tone scale,* in which all the tones are a whole step apart—for example, C D E F♯ G♯ A♯ C; and the *pentatonic scale,* which consists of five tones—for example, D♭, E♭, G♭, A♭, and B♭. Both of these scales were widely used by the impressionist composers Debussy and Ravel. These and other synthetic scales will be discussed in Chapter 10.

Harmony

The theoretical basis of harmony is a series of *intervals.* An interval may be defined as the distance between two notes, and is expressed in terms of the number of scale steps that exists between the two notes. For example, from C to G is a *fifth* (C D E F G), from C to E is a *third* (C D E). When the notes are sounded simultaneously it is referred to as a *harmonic interval,* and when sounded successively, as a *melodic interval.* The smallest interval[1] generally used in Western music is the half step or *minor second:* C to C♯, E to F, B to C, etc. The distance of two half steps is called the *interval of a major second:* D to E, C to D, F to G, E to F♯, etc. The terms *major* and *minor,* when applied to intervals, simply mean "larger" or "smaller." The fundamental types of intervals include the following:

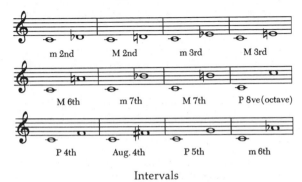

m 2nd   M 2nd   m 3rd   M 3rd

M 6th   m 7th   M 7th   P 8ve (octave)

P 4th   Aug. 4th   P 5th   m 6th

Intervals

[1] Smaller intervals, such as quarter steps, have been used by some twentieth-century composers, notably Béla Bartók.

The simplest type of chord is the *triad,* made up of three different tones, each an interval of a third apart. Chords or triads are derived by grouping a series of tones on each step or degree of the major and minor scales. Prior to about 1900, chords were generally constructed of tones placed a *third* apart; in the modern era other intervals, such as fourths and fifths, have also been used.

I   ii   iii   IV   V   vi   vii°   I

Triads in the Key of C Major

The *tonic* (I) is the chord of rest, usually the ending chord in traditional music. The other chords or triads represent a greater degree of activity or tension, and they, particularly the *dominant* (V), progress or gravitate to the tonic chord. The I, IV (*subdominant*), and V are the primary chords upon which much of our traditional music is based. And since they contain between them all the notes of the scale, they alone may be used to harmonize practically any melody. The next example illustrates how these primary chords may be employed in a harmonization of Henry Carey's *America.*

America with Simple Chord Accompaniment

Dissonance and Consonance Consonance results from an agreeable blending of two or more tones, producing a state of repose or rest; dissonance, from a combination of tones producing a feeling of tension and unrest. The intervals that are generally considered to be dissonant include the major second (C to D), minor second (E to F), and major seventh (C to B). Chords that contain these intervals are followed by consonant chords, or, more specifically, the dissonant notes are *resolved* by moving to more consonant combinations of tones. The intervals considered to be consonant include the major third (C to E), minor third (C to E♭), perfect fifth (C to G), major sixth (C to A), minor sixth (C to A♭), and octave (C to another C eight steps higher).

Each period in music history has had its particular esthetic principles concerning the use and treatment of dissonance. To illustrate, in the Renaissance (1400–1600) composers normally followed procedures that softened or modified the dissonant effect. Two methods that were widely employed included the *suspension* and the *passing note.* A suspension is a dissonant note that is tied over from a preceding chord and then resolved by moving down a step to become a part of the underlying harmony or chord. The passing note is a dissonant note that "passes" on the weak beat (that is, on the second or fourth beat of the measure) from one consonant note to another.

Two Methods of Treating Dissonance in the Renaissance
(1400–1600)

Following the Renaissance, certain dissonant notes gradually became accepted as regular members of chords. The *dominant seventh chord* (V7) (consisting of a triad plus an additional note a minor third higher) was the first of these new dissonant chords to become established in the musical practice of the eighteenth century. In the late nineteenth century other types of sonorities began to appear, such as the ninth, eleventh, and thirteenth chords, which were constructed by piling additional thirds above the basic triad.

Various Types of Chords

Counterpoint

The essential ingredients of counterpoint include (1) the independence of each melodic line or part rhythmically and melodically, and (2) a congruous harmonic effect resulting from the simultaneous sounding of the various melodic lines. In the following example of counterpoint, two folk-song melodies are combined. The bottom part has a rhythmic pattern and a melodic movement quite different from the top part (*Frère Jacques*), and yet, even though each part is relatively independent, both "fit" together harmonically.

Simple Example of Counterpoint

Contrapuntal Devices   When the composer creates in the contrapuntal style he is concerned with two basic problems: first, the maintenance of linear or horizontal movement among the various melodic lines, and secondly, the invention of interesting musical techniques or devices that will be suitable for the horizontal arrangement of tones. One such technique—a kind of "follow the leader" that has been used for centuries—is called *imitation* and is of two fundamental types: (1) *strict* or *canonical imitation*, in which one part is imitated exactly by another part following in close succession; and (2) *free imitation*, in which only several measures or even a few notes of the first part, or *leader*, are copied by a second part.

Imitation in a Traditional Song

Imitation in a Two Part Invention by J. S. Bach

MEANING IN TONAL RELATIONSHIPS

In works of art sensations are most profoundly and richly clarified through some deliberate and explicit pattern.

Irwin Edman, *Arts and the Man*

Musical Forms and Internal Organization of Tonal Ideas

Thus far we have been concerned mainly with the preliminary aspects of music—the mechanics of notation and the tonal materials that the composer has at his disposal. At this point we will direct our attention to the composer's methods of working with tonal ideas.

It was stated in the opening pages that meaning is to be found in the composer's ideas and their musical treatment. Thus, of paramount importance is the ability of the listener to identify the thematic ideas and to understand how they may be arranged in a musical context. Of first concern is the mold or pattern into which the composer organizes his thematic material; this mold is called the *musical form.* Each period is to be identified by its common musical forms. Some musical forms, such as the motet, mass, folk song, hymn, and madrigal, are primarily for the vocal medium. Others, such as opera, cantata, and oratorio, are for a mixture of instruments and voices. The purely instrumental forms include the symphony, sonata, fugue, concerto, suite, and toccata, to name a few. (See Glossary for definitions.)

Within these forms the composer arranges his thematic material syntactically, that is, into meaningful relationships. Just as letters or words do not represent meaning until brought into relationship with other letters or words, musical meaning does not become possible until the tones are ordered into a definite pattern and the pattern or theme is related to another pattern. Tones cannot be written in a completely random fashion any more than words can be stated in a disorganized way. Thus we find that music, like language, has its own "built-in" immutable law of order. Each period, moreover, has a different set of esthetic principles in regard to the ordering of these tones into complete melodies and harmony.

If order is the prime mover, so to speak, inherent in all musical art, and tones do not contain designative or verbal meanings as in spoken language, then meaning must be sought in the "life" of the tones, in their growth and development. To the composer, the tones are not data but tonal concepts—they have meaning in terms of relationships. Also, it must be kept in mind that some music carries an additional source for enhancing the meaning of the work, such as words (as in folk songs or art songs) or program notes (as in symphonic poems) provided by the composer. These secondary or in some cases primary sources of meaning should be studied thoroughly when encountered in our survey of music in history.

A Definition of Musical Thinking

The type of musical intellection required then of the listener may be defined as the process of following a discourse of tonal patterns (themes), which are arranged or presented discursively as in language. In other words, they are stated, restated, or undergo metamorphosis within a framework called the musical form, such as the sonata, concerto, symphony, and so on. The processes of memory and recall are employed in tracing the movement of the theme or themes. The reader must bear in mind that the listening experience is not a matter of cold, logical analysis but rather that of following empathically the life of tonal ideas as they grow, experience tension and resolution, and reach their final goal.

It may be helpful to outline a few of the fundamental ways in which thematic ideas may be treated in a composition; they are as follows: (1) thematic juxtaposition, (2) thematic variation, (3) thematic imitation, and (4) thematic development.

Thematic Juxtaposition In the first type, *thematic juxtaposition*, the main theme (A) is counterbalanced by a different theme (B) (this relationship may be diagrammed A B), or, more frequently, the main theme is juxtaposed before and after a new theme (A B A) or between the appearances of several new themes (A B A C A, and so on). Typical musical forms in which this type of musical syntax is commonly found include the folk song, folk dance, popular ballad, rondo, march, dance suite, and quite frequently in the second and third movements of the symphony and sonata of the classical period.

English Folk Song (Example of Thematic Juxtaposition)

Thematic Variation The character of the theme is changed with a series of successive alterations to the melody, or to the rhythm, tempo, and so on. Typical forms in which this type of syntax or musical organization is commonly found include theme and variations, passacaglia (a series of variations appearing over a repeated bass theme), and occasionally in the second movement of the classical symphony. The theme and variations principle first came into prominence during the fifteenth century.

Theme and Variations from Second Movement of the "Surprise Symphony" by Joseph Haydn

Thematic Imitation The theme is imitated by one or more instruments or voices in close succession. Typical forms in which this type of organization is commonly used include the round (*Row, Row, Row Your Boat*), canon, fugue, mass, and motet. Notice in the next example (a two-part invention by J. S. Bach) that the theme is first stated in the treble clef of the keyboard and then, after a time lapse of two measures, is imitated by the bass. Usually the imitation is at a different pitch level than was the original presentation of the theme.

Example of Thematic Imitation, Two Part Invention in
D Minor by J. S. Bach

Thematic Development This type of syntax or organization involves a "working out" or elaboration of a theme. It is usually found in the first and last movements of the symphony and the sonata of the classical period. The composer selects one or more characteristic features from his theme (such as a pronounced rhythmic or melodic figure) and alters and repeats it in a number of different ways. The figure or motive may be passed back and forth from one instrument to another (antiphonally), undergo a series of key changes (modulations), or be given a new chordal or harmonic accompaniment. Beethoven, in the first movement of his Symphony No. 5, bases the entire development section upon a four-note rhythmic pattern that is "tossed about" antiphonally between the various instruments of the orchestra.

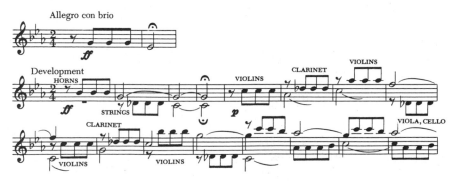

Example of Thematic Development, from Symphony No. 5
by Ludwig van Beethoven

Several qualifying remarks are necessary here. This listing of the four basic ways of organizing tones is not meant to be an exhaustive summary. For one thing, not all periods employ the four methods. For example, the second type, thematic variation, did not become generally employed until about the sixteenth century, and the third type, thematic imitation, not until about 1300, when the art of counterpoint had been advanced considerably. And, finally, it should be borne in mind that the construction and relationship of musical ideas becomes more subtle and abstract as we move forward in music history.

THE PERCEPTION OF MUSICAL STYLES IN HISTORICAL PERIODS

Style is defined as a distinguishable ensemble of . . . certain characteristics of works of art which are more or less stable in an artist, an era or a locale.

James S. Ackerman, *A Theory of Style*

The Common Musical Language of an Epoch   Once the listener has grasped the basic concept of meaning in music—that tonal figures represent ideas—we are then ready to move to the last phase, and that is the perception of musical styles.

Music is not a universal language; if it were, the complicated microtone system of India would be readily understood by the West and the cerebral techniques of some of our modern composers would be likewise directly comprehended by the Eastern mind. The only universal element in music, outside of the governing law of order and the power of music to evoke general states of emotion, is simply tone.

The shaping of tones into a meaningful pattern is an art that varies from epoch to epoch, country to country, and from one composer to another in the same era. However, within each epoch there is a commonality of style that permits the music historian to group together certain traits into what may be called the common musical language. It is a language in that there are certain scales and chords, and ways of combining them into complete melodies and harmonies that are used and understood by the majority of the musical artists in a particular period or region.

The comprehension of this common musical expression is our principal objective at the introductory level of study. By knowing the characteristics of the various periods, the serious student will be able to listen intelligently to any representative work in the principal periods of music history; in summary, he will know what to expect in terms of *musical style*. In our study musical style encompasses the preferred scales, modes, chords, rhythmic patterns, musical forms, and the basic characteristics of melody, harmony, and counterpoint.

Music: An Intrinsic Part of Civilization   Plato regarded music as one of the prime movers, an ultimate truth that lies at the very beginning of the universe and through which order is brought into the world. In looking back over the more than two thousand years of music, it is interesting to note that music has been woven through all of Western civilization, serving as a unifying element at all levels of society and as a medium for expressing individual and collective feelings and aspirations. It is difficult if not impossible to account for the permeation of music in Western culture. It may be explained by the curious dualism present in tonal art: the emotive power of tones (the power to evoke emotions or feelings) and the intellectual appeal provided by tonal patterns and structures.

Much music in the early periods had a functional purpose: to mold character, to enhance the religious setting, to provide military signals, and to provide music for the dance. The gradual shift to the principle of pure esthetic enjoyment, that is, the enjoyment of music as an art in itself presented in concert form, evolved as society took hold of new ideas and attitudes about the world and man. Thus, at the very core of our study is the importance of understanding the social and intellectual undercurrents—these are the wellsprings for the distinctive musical impulse of the period. Furthermore, by employing the intellectual history approach to our study, we may add more depth and meaning to listening experiences, for we will gain some idea of the sources of musical expression and perhaps feel some of the excitement of the times and its embodiment in the artwork itself. This procedure should contribute to the formulation of knowledgeable opinions and the development of musical taste covering a wide variety of styles and periods.

2

THE GRECO-ROMAN ERA

A PRELIMINARY OVERVIEW OF MUSIC HISTORY

> . . . it is the spirit of the East that never changes.
> It has remained the same through all the ages
> down from the antique world. . . . This state
> and this spirit were alien to the Greeks.
> Edith Hamilton, *The Greek Way*

Retrospect Examined in its broadest outlines, the development of music in Western culture has principally centered around the gradual evolution of three modes of musical expression: the rhythmic, the melodic, and the contrapuntal. There is much conjecture as to the origins of the first two types of expression. The nascent stages of musical art—the human desire to evoke a pattern of sounds into melody and especially the impulse to move in rhythm—must have been known to earliest man. Although we have learned much concerning the musical characteristics of primitive societies, there can be only speculation as to the musical attainments of man before the dawn of Western civilization.

In the eastern Mediterranean, beginning about 4000 B.C., there arose a high form of musical expression, as evidenced in the archeological findings of Egyptian musical artifacts and instruments. Historically, however, our attention is first focused on the Greek civilization (1200–146 B.C.), since here we find considerable evidence of scholarly inquiry into melody and rhythm and the philosophical basis of music. Here, then, are the roots of modern-day musical thought.

Douris. *Instruction in Music and Grammar in an Attic School.* Red-figured painting on the exterior of a kylix. *c.* 470 B.C. State Museums, Berlin

To complete our preliminary overview we finally note the emergence of a simple type of counterpoint called *organum* (A.D. 850). This crude technique of combining several strands of melody provided tonal art with a new dimension—a depth or fullness of sonority. This innovation, plus a system of notation devised by the early church musicians, opened the way to a contrapuntal method of writing music, that is, part music, which made possible all group performance practices known in the modern world. The Renaissance was the turning point in musical art—when the techniques of counterpoint and harmony were greatly expanded and when the widespread patronage by the Church and court marked the arrival of music as a high art form.

The newness of these important techniques, and indeed music as an organized art, is more fully understood when we place some of the major musical developments into their proper historical perspective. In the accompanying chart of the main periods of music, it will be seen that music as an intellectual expression, embodying certain accepted compositional principles and forms, is relatively new, and in fact the youngest of the arts in the Western world. The periods thus summarized in the chart will serve as landmarks for our exploration of music in Western culture.

THE MAIN PERIODS OF MUSIC HISTORY

CHRO-NOLOGY	EPOCH	PRINCIPAL CONTRIBUTIONS	REPRESENTATIVE COMPOSERS OR THEORISTS
1200–146 B.C. (Greek) 146 B.C. 476 A.D. (Roman)	Greco-Roman	Greek: Beginnings of music theory, scales, and tuning systems, philosophy of music. Roman: brass instruments, military music.	Pythagoras, Plato, Aristotle, Ptolemy
250–1150	Romanesque	Organization of the Church liturgy, codification of chant, notation and organum	Pope Gregory, Boethius, Odo of Cluny, Guido of Arezzo
1150–1400	Gothic	Advancement of polyphony and sacred musical forms, rise of secular music, first musical setting of mass	Pérotin, Léonin, Machaut, Landini
1400–1600	Renaissance	Epitome of choral polyphony, rise of instruments, and chamber music	des Prez, Palestrina, Gabrieli, di Lasso, Byrd, Morley
1600–1750	Baroque	The beginnings of the orchestra, opera, oratorio, concerto forms, fugue, the suite	Monteverdi, Corelli, Vivaldi, Bach, Handel
1740–1800	Rococo and Classical Era	The symphony, sonata form, concerto, string quartet, opera	Haydn, Mozart, Beethoven
1800–1900	Romantic Movement	Piano piece, art song, program symphony, symphonic poem, music drama	Beethoven, Schubert, Schumann, Chopin, Liszt, Berlioz, Brahms, Wagner, Bruckner
1880–1918	Impressionism	Piano music, symphonic poem.	Debussy, Ravel
1900–	Twentieth Century	Expressionism, Neoclassicism, Neoromanticism	Schoenberg, Berg, Bartok, Hindemith, Stravinsky, Webern

EASTERN MUSICAL CULTURE
AND INFLUENCE

Although the emphasis of this study is upon Western music and art, a brief synopsis of Eastern music and its relation to our musical tradition is needed to complete the perspective of music history.

Over the ages, Eastern musical concepts have been a constant source of interest and inspiration to the Western musician. In the nineteenth century the influence was mirrored in Rimski-Korsakov's orchestral works, which derived much of their brilliance and color from exotic Oriental percussion effects. Even Mozart and Beethoven in the classical era were drawn by the magnetism of Eastern melody and rhythm. But it is the twentieth-century composers who seem to have shown the greatest attraction to the mystic incantations of the East. Beginning with Debussy and Ravel early in the century, others, like Bartók and Hovhaness, have incorporated the spirit and technique of Eastern music into their work.

Indian Musical Instruments. Left: Tabla Drums. Center: Tambura. Right: Sitar.

Japanese Musical Instruments. Left: Koto. Center: Taiko Drum. Right: Shamisen
Illustrations on both pages from *Exploring Music, the Senior Book* by Beth Landis,
Holt, Rinehart and Winston, 1969.

Historically, the most important Eastern contributions were made in instrumental music in the medieval period. During that period many instruments were gradually absorbed into Western music, including the trumpet, buzine (large type of trumpet), oboe, small drum, triangle, cymbals, tympani or kettledrums, bells, and various stringed instruments.

Strangely, Eastern music, like its art, has remained static over the centuries. For example, Chinese music of today has still many of the principal instruments that were used around 1000 B.C., such as chimes and zither. The countries of the near East, Arabia, Persia, and Turkey, still use instruments that date from the tenth century: long-necked fiddle, pear-shaped lute, and sistrum, among others. India, in the same way, has retained its complicated system of scales and microtones since A.D. 500—nearly fifteen hundred years of the same theory and esthetic.

Conversely, Western art has passed through many shorter periods or cycles of artistic change, each possessing certain distinctive style characteristics in all of the arts (see accompanying chart of periods). Furthermore, Western instruments have from time to time been improved and modified. While it is true that since the nineteenth century very few changes have been made, recently, of course, a great deal of experimentation has been carried on in the electronic media.

Music of India: Comparison of East and West

The current interest in Eastern art centers chiefly about the fascinating melodic and rhythmic character of Indian music, the roots of which extend back to about 3000 B.C. The tones chanted in the sacred verses at the dawn of civilization have echoed down through the centuries. Even today the spirit continues into the world's concert halls through the superb performances of renowned "classical" Indian musicians (such as Ustad Ali Akbar Khan and Pandit Chatur Lal, respectively distinguished performers of the *sarod* and *tabla*).

Eastern music, in contrast to the multi-instrumental timbres of the West, generally emphasizes the more subtle sounds of two fundamental groups of instruments: the stringed variety and percussion. Chief among these in the performance of the highest form of Indian music are the *sarod, sitar, tabla,* and *tambura.*

The *sarod,* a long-necked instrument, has a gourdlike sound box and a total of twenty-five strings, ten of which are plucked with a piece of coconut shell. The remaining fifteen vibrate sympathetically when the instrument is played. The *sitar,* a large-bodied stringed instrument, has a broad neck and seven strings. The melody is generally played on the last string, the others providing a soft, dronelike effect through sympathetic vibration.

Accompanying the solo instrument (sarod or sitar), is the *tabla* consisting of two small drums played with the fingers and other parts of the hand. The tabla's main functions are to provide the metrical pattern or rhythmic background and to compete in a give-and-take fashion with the solo instrument (either the sarod or sitar) as the music gains increased momentum and excitement. The final member of the classical Indian ensemble is the *tambura,* a non-melodic instrument of four strings which supplies a hypnotic drone effect.

Since about A.D. 500 attempts have been made to codify principles of Indian music theory which include complicated scalelike patterns called *ragas* and rhythmic configurations called *talas.* The raga is a melodic pattern of seven notes, out of which a musical performance gradually unfolds. In a way it is comparable to a theme that is improvised in modern jazz. The raga's distinctive quality is derived from the particular intervallic arrangement of the tones in the series. Especially prominent in these exotic patterns are the microtone intervals which are smaller than our Western half step.

An Example of an Indian Raga (Todi, a Morning Raga)

At the outset of the performance, the tabla performer selects a certain rhythmic pattern or *tala* which is to be played throughout. Each tala is identified by a designated number of beats; for example, the Dadra has a rhythmic cycle of six beats divided 3, 3, the Rupak has a cycle of seven, divided 3, 2, 2, and a more complicated pattern such as the Jhaptal has a cycle of ten divided 2, 3, 2, 3. $(\underset{1}{1}\text{-}\underset{2}{2},\ \underset{3}{1}\text{-}\underset{4}{2}\text{-}\underset{5}{3},\ \underset{6}{1}\text{-}\underset{7}{2},\ \underset{8}{1}\text{-}\underset{9}{2}\text{-}\underset{10}{3})$

In the beginning stages of the performance the percussionist merely outlines the basic tala. Gradually as the music unfolds the drummer super-imposes elaborate rhythmic effects over the tala pattern (again as in modern jazz). Here perhaps is the essence of Indian music—a rhythmic intricacy which is unrivaled by the Western world in its subtlety and endless invention. Its characteristic feature is the use of complicated cross-rhythm or *polyrhythm.*

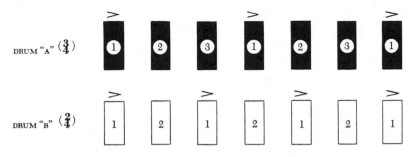

Illustration of Cross-Rhythm: Drum "A" sounds a triple metrical pattern against the duple pattern of drum "B." The accents (>) indicate normal metrical stress.

Polyrhythm is the term given to the simultaneous occurrence of two or more different rhythms. Imbued with an unusual rhythmic sense, the tabla performer, for example, may create polyrhythm by beating duple patterns on one drum against triple on the other drum. An even more involved form of polyrhythm arises from an interplay between the tabla and the sarod or sitar. With the heightened spontaneous improvisation of the tabla and the sarod, individual creative paths are explored resulting in phenomenal cross-rhythms which separate and converge in an uncanny fashion.

In contrast to our musical art (with the exception of certain forms of improvised jazz and authentic folk song expression), Indian music is neither written nor read, it is improvised, that is, created spontaneously. The only aspect of their art that has been written down is the theoretical. Music is transmitted from generation to generation in an oral (rote) manner as with our folk song and jazz tradition.

Indian music is monophonic (one part or melody, no harmonic accompaniment) as compared to the predominantly homophonic and contrapuntal textures in Western art. Moreover, it is an expression that is contemplative and meditative, evoking deep spiritual feelings among the native Indian listeners. These effects stem from various aspects of the performance, mainly from the particular raga which is used. Each raga has a different personality, so to speak; some are very somber and serious, others are happy and very playful.

Ironically, although Indian art is improvisatory and spontaneous, its fundamental principles of organization (raga and tala) and performance practices have remained essentially static over the centuries. Western music, on the other hand, is more directly linked with the listener, perhaps because of the Western mind's desire for known, remembered, recalled patterns of tones, in short, a predilection for form and structure as opposed to the spontaneous, unstructured expression of the East. The reader will observe that Western music seems to be more directly dependent upon the listening audience and subject to dynamic shifts in style from one epoch to another, reflecting the *zeitgeist* or spirit of the age.

In conclusion, the power of Eastern musical art rests with the unknowable, the exotic, the intangible. The power of the Western musical expression has in the past two thousand years been derived from a basically objective or rational point of view—from form and ideas that can be codified and communicated. This point of view is attributed to the Greeks, the founders of the Western musical heritage.

GREECE: ARTISTIC BACKGROUND

From whatever different sensations the arts may derive, from touch or vision or hearing—on to whatever the artists may project their visions, on statues, or murals or melodies—they are one in spirit and meaning.

Curt Sachs, *The Commonwealth of Art*

Before turning to the art and music of the Greeks, several principles that will serve as a guide in our survey of music history need to be mentioned. Essentially, a study of music, as with painting, sculpture, architecture, and literature, is meaningless when divorced from the human element and condition that created and nurtured it. An omission of Beethoven's hearing affliction from a discussion of his later works would be as illogical as bypassing the underlying religious motives in fifteenth-century Flemish music and art. The arts tend to reflect the intellectual and spiritual conscience of each epoch. They corroborate in their own distinctive way—through tone, word, pigment, or stone—man's attempt to transcend his small world and to preserve his highest thoughts and aspirations in some form or pattern for present and future esthetic contemplation.

This human trait, which extends as far back as the Egyptian civilization and is generally experienced in varying degrees in all of the arts during an epoch, has taken different forms and attained great artistic heights in particular periods. The Gothic cathedrals, the symphonies of Haydn, Mozart, and Beethoven in the classical era, the paintings of the Italian High Renaissance, and the sculpture and architecture of the Great Age of Greece stand as testimony of this trait to express and preserve the profound and the sublime. Because of this tendency toward a commonality in the arts and because a greater understanding is generally gained from relating the visual and tonal arts, a particular humanistic approach for our study of music seems to be in order. Therefore, beginning with the general artistic trends and influential social and intellectual currents in each epoch, our study will then proceed to a specific consideration of musical art—its composers, forms, and general characteristics of style.

Classicism of the Great Age   Of the various periods of the Greek civilization, that of the Great Age (480–323 B.C.) is the most significant intellectually and artistically. Musically it is important as the originating point of many Western concepts in music theory (such as scales, intervals, and tuning) and esthetic ideas concerning the art and practice of music. At no other time has so much greatness been compressed into such a brief period and so widely dispersed in all of the arts and humanities. The Great Age was the time of the sculptures of Myron, Phidias, and Praxiteles, the construction of the Parthenon, and the writings of Plato and Aristotle and the plays of Sophocles. Of utmost importance in regard to our study is the fact that the sculpture and architecture and esthetic thinking from this epoch clearly symbolize the characteristics of *classicism*—a recurring attitude or temper in Western music and art.

Classicism began to emerge in the first phase of the Great Age, roughly 480–460 B.C. The sculptures mark a radical departure from the earlier stiff and unlifelike figures toward freestanding, three-dimensional forms bearing strong traces of *idealism*. That is, the artist attempts to make the ideal form of man by eliminating certain blemishes usually found in the human figure and by abstracting certain facial features, such as the nose and forehead. There appears to be an over-all noble and rational posture both inwardly (as shown in facial expression) and outwardly. Three noted examples of sculpture from this era include The *Charioteer of Delphi, Discobolus* by Myron, and the *Zeus (Poseidon?)*.

The artistic style of the second phase of the Great Age, the classical period of Greek art, 460–323 B.C., exhibits the climax of artistic idealism— the epitome of rational order both in mind and body. Disclosed in the words of the contemporary artist Ilissos is an indication of the technical perfection now attained and an expression of the artist's concern for inner balance or self-control. He writes: "All means of art have been brought to full development but they are used to express the figure's inner life and not as ends in themselves." This was also the age of the construction of the Parthenon and Erechtheum in Athens and the formulation of the famous *canon of proportions* by Polyclitus: "Beauty consists in the proportions not of the elements but of the parts." Applied to sculpture, this concept meant that the correct proportion of finger to hand, forearm to upper arm, and all other parts of the anatomy must be maintained. This and other esthetic principles emphasizing clarity, control, and beauty of line represent the guiding attitude of the epoch. This "classical" view is implicit in such works as the *Doryphorus* by Polyclitus and the Parthenon sculptures supervised by Phidias, and in the esthetic writings on music by Plato and Aristotle. Their work in this realm will be taken up in subsequent pages.

The Waning of Idealism   The classicistic principles of the Great Age— balance, moderation, clarity, proportion, and control—gradually declined.

Ictinus and Callicrates. The Parthenon, the Acropolis, Athens. 447–432 B.C.
Alison Frantz

The demoralizing defeat of the Athenian army by the Spartans in the Peloponnesian Wars (431–404 B.C.) drained idealism and intellectual vigor. The eventual decline of Greek life can be seen in the ensuing disorganization of the city-states and the conquest of the Hellenic world by Alexander the Great. In the fourth century the serene idealism of the fifth century gave way to skepticism and unrest. Clearly disappearing were the qualities of wisdom, judgment, and moderation. Underlying these changes was the influence of the rising middle class, and particularly the philosophy of the Sophists, which stressed materialism and the pursuit of knowledge for utilitarian purposes. From this social and intellectual climate emerged a strongly felt pull toward realism and emotionalism, expressed in the arts of the fourth century. This trend is exemplified in sculpture by the dreamy *Hermes* and the *Cnidian Aphrodite* by Praxiteles, and musically in the movement toward virtuosity and vulgar taste among the masses. The change in artistic taste was brought to complete fruition in the Hellenistic period of Greek art, 323–146 B.C.

Hellenistic Art: Realism In general, Hellenistic art is strongly emotional, and instead of soaring idealism we find *realism*—as man actually is, with his sorrows and anxieties. The appeal to the purely sensual is seen in the numerous nude Aphrodite sculptures; moreover, the waning of the universal ideal image is shown in the demand for numerous personal portraits. The field of music was likewise affected, for we note that the popularization and vulgarization of musical art is frequently lamented by philosophers and historians in the fourth century B.C.

With the taking of Carthage by the expanding Roman Empire in 146 B.C. we come to a dividing point between two great civilizations and two world views—the idealism of the Greeks and the professionalism of the Romans. Unfortunately, the record of Roman artistic development is largely to be seen as a mirror of Greek culture. But, while lacking creative power, the Romans at least copied and dispersed the Greek legacy of music, art, and intellect throughout the Western World.

Summary The artistic style of the fifth century B.C. (the Great Age) symbolizes the classical temper; that of the fourth century, the romantic. These two modes are of particular importance since it will be seen that much of Western music and art has experienced a constant cyclic fluctuation between these two opposing artistic poles—Ethos and Pathos. Following the age of antiquity, the first major appearance of classicism occurred in the Italian High Renaissance (1450–1550) and then in the neoclassical era (1750–1800). Romantic trends were strong in the Baroque (1600–1750) and in the romantic age (1800–1900).

MUSIC IN GREEK LIFE

Mythological and Historical Origins of Music According to Greek mythology, music was created by Zeus (the divine ruler of all the gods at Mount Olympus) with the earthly Mnemosyne, who was the symbol of memory. Eventually there were nine daughters or muses of Zeus, each of whom presided over one of the arts and sciences: Calliope (heroic poetry), Clio (history), Erato (lyric and amatory poetry), Euterpe (music), Melpomene (tragedy), Polyhymnia (sacred lyric), Terpsichore (dance), Thalia (comedy), and Urania (astronomy). Contrary to modern usage, the term *mousike* (music) in actual Greek life did not refer to an autonomous art form but was generally applied to a combination of poetry, music, and dancing. Of these, poetry was considered the most important, music was the accompaniment, and dance was an integral part of the total expression.

Concerning the history of Greek music, we learn that the lawmaker Lycurgus (c. 800 B.C.), in organizing the city-state of Sparta, decreed the provision of music education for the youth of the state regardless of their sex, age, or status. The great statesman of Athens, Solon (c. 594 B.C.), also ordered musical instruction for free Athenians as a means of forming moral stability and effective citizenship. In the primary levels of education, music was at first taught by the *grammatist*, who also provided instruction in reading, writing, and literature. Later, special music schools were provided where elite Greek boys received instruction from the *citharist*. The music study was not specialized but included training in singing and playing (lyre, kithara, and aulos), dancing, and verse, with particular emphasis placed on the musical rendition of the works of great Greek lyric poets.

Some insight into the musical life of Greek countrymen is provided by one of the most informative writers of antiquity, Atheneaus, who lived about A.D. 200. In his collection of writings on Greek culture, entitled

Time Line: Greek Music	
9th cent. B.C.	*Iliad* and *Odyssey*
6th cent.	Pythagoras: musical intervals
4th cent.	Plato: *The Republic* Aristoxenus: *Harmonics* Euclid: *Systema Talaion*
2nd cent. A.D.	Ptolemy: reduction of Greek modes to 7

Girl Playing the Aulos. From Greek altar (the "Ludovisi Throne"), fifth century B.C. Alinari-Art Reference Bureau

Deipnosophistai (Sophists at Dinner), he describes in considerable detail the musical life of Greece, and quotes from numerous ancient Greek historians such as Polybius and Herodotus. The following extract throws considerable light on folk practices.

> The earliest Arcadians carried the art of music into their entire social organization, so that they made it obligatory for boys and men up to thirty. The boys from infancy up are by law practiced in singing hymns and paeans in which they celebrate their national heroes and gods. After these they learn nomos of Timotheus . . . and dance them annually in the boys' contests and men in mens' contests . . . and throughout their lives they do not employ imported entertainers as much as their own talents . . . what is more they practice marching songs with aulos accompaniment . . . they drill themselves in dance and display them in the theatre annually with public expense . . . Music appeases surliness for by stripping off a man's gloominess, it produces good temper and gladness becoming to a gentleman. This is why Homer introduced the gods making use of music in the first part of the *Iliad.* For after their quarrel over Achilles, they spent the time listening 'to the beautiful phorminx that Apollo held and to the muses who sang with beautiful voice.' For that was bound to stop their bickering and faction. It is plain therefore, that while most persons devote this art to social gatherings for the sake of correcting conduct and of general usefulness, the ancients went further and included in their customs and law the singing of praises to the gods by all who attended feasts, in order that our dignity and sobriety might be retained . . . music did not at the beginning make its way into feasts merely for the sake of shallow and ordinary pleasure . . .[1]

Greek Aulos

The widespread interest in choral singing is perhaps the most striking characteristic of Greek musical practice in the ancient world. Both men and women took part in performing at contests called *agons*. Several noted agons were held in connection with the Panathenean and Dionysian celebrations at Athens. We know very little about this music except for the generic names of musical forms performed by the musicians: the *nomos*, which was the esteemed form sung by the professionals, and its counterpart, the *instrumental nomos*, played by a soloist on the *kithara* or *aulos*. The latter instrument is a double-reed type that, except for its V-shape, bears some resemblance to the oboe. The kithara is shaped like a small harp. (These and other instruments are treated in subsequent pages.)

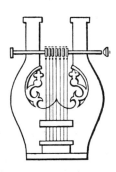

Greek Kithara

The Apollonian and Dionysian Cults   The roots of the two opposing ideals, classicism and romanticism, as was mentioned earlier, stem from style cycles in Greek art. They are further exemplified in the ancient Greek cults, the Apollonian and Dionysian. Apollo, the god of manly youth and beauty, was also the guardian of the nine muses. A combination of amazing strength, he was, as we note in Homer's works, capable of "producing

---

[1] Oliver Strunk, *Source Readings in Music History* (New York: W. W. Norton and Company, Inc., 1950), pp. 51–53.

sweet sounds with his bow strings and of healing the wounds of the heart." Thus, the instrument attributed to Apollo in Greek mythology is the lyre. This is borne out in numerous references in Greek literature and in a number of vase paintings depicting Apollo with the lyre. The cult of Apollo believed that music possessed a noble power, capable of purifying and elevating the mind. Hence, the qualities of balance, moderation, and emotional control were stressed.

Another side of man's nature, the emotional and passionate, found personification in the Dionysian cult, which favored an uninhibited, frenzied, and oftentimes sorrowful musical expression. Songs were sung to honor their esteemed god, Bacchus, the god of wine. Their favored instrument was the shrill aulos.

The Oneness of Music and Poetry   The ancient Greeks viewed music as being united with the spoken word; in fact, lyric poetry referred to poetry sung to the lyre accompaniment. Moreover, we learn that the great fifth-century dramatist Aeschylus reputedly originated tragedy at the Dionysian rite by assigning a dialogue to an actor (leader) and a chorus. This is the earliest record that we have of a performance by a group of singers or choral group. The chorus, which came to be an integral part of tragedy, numbered approximately twelve, and its functions included performing prefatory sections, accompanying, and, in addition, providing a commentary on the action in the tragedy. Indeed, music was, in the hands of the dramatists, intensified speech.

The reciprocal influence worked yet another way. The ordered rhythmic patterns that Aristotle speaks of were based on poetic meters such as the *iambic,* having a short stress followed by a long (. —), the *pyrrhic* (. .), the *trochee* (— .), the *dactyl* (— . .), the *anapest* (. . —), and *spondee* (— —). These were combined into various patterns. Although not employed in the same notational system as our modern method, these rhythmic patterns provided the basis for the evolution of modern rhythmic figures. For example, later on, in the medieval period, iambic became a short note followed by a note of longer value: ♪♩ ; the pyrrhic: ♪♪ ; the trochee: ♩♪ ; and the spondee: ♩♩ .

PHILOSOPHY OF MUSIC

Greek musical concepts are firmly rooted in a rational basis. This is understandable, since the Greeks applied reason to all facets of life, including science, politics, philosophy, and art. Beginning as early as the sixth century B.C., the scholarly inquiry of the Pythagoreans into the highest disciplines, music and mathematics, laid the foundations of arithmetic, geometry, and acoustics. In the latter field, mathematical theories were employed to determine the principal intervals of music.

The Grecian concepts of music were greatly expanded by Plato (427–347 B.C.) and Aristotle (384–322 B.C.). At the very base of the musical thinking of these intellectual giants of the Great Age are the contrasting philosophical attitudes of *idealism* and *realism.* The two world views may be more clearly understood when we note that Plato was a mathematician, a poet, and a lofty idealist, in short, of an artistic bent, while Aristotle was a scientist or materialist. In substance, Plato's idealism centered around the belief that the mind was superior to the senses, and, moreover, that science dealt with the changing natural world and not with "ideas," which are eternal. Knowledge is acquired only through the power of reason freed from sense experience and opinion. To Plato, music is one of the ultimate truths that lie at the very beginning of the universe. Through mathematics, of which music is an integral part, man approaches his goal—the contemplation of the eternal rather than the transitory. Hence, music occupies a paramount position in Plato's ideal society, because music by its very nature not only represents the order of the universe but demonstrates an inner order needed for the soul. In *The Republic,* Plato thus devotes considerable discussion to the esthetic values of music in relation to the education of youth.

Realism as purported by Aristotle, on the other hand, placed full emphasis upon scientific inquiry, that is, upon the validation of a theory by actuality. As a biologist he was more interested in the material world than Plato, although his excursions into metaphysical thought prove him to be quite as mystical as his teacher Plato. His regard for the real objects about us that we can feel and see led him consequently to treat music as a natural phenomenon rather than as a metaphysical object, as did Plato. Thus his views on music in the *Politics* are primarily related to specific and objective uses of music in education.

Plato and the Esthetic Role of Music Plato's philosophical writings on music fall into two categories: metaphysical and esthetic. The former is represented mainly in *Timaeus* and the latter in *The Republic.* Although it is not our intention to discuss *Timaeus* in any detail, a brief summary is needed to show the great heights to which abstract thinking involving numbers and music was carried by the ancients. In *Timaeus,* Plato envisions how the divine Maker created the universe out of the four elements, water, air, earth, and fire, and regulated it by musical proportions. Following the creation of the world soul that governs the four elements, Plato relates how the Maker divided and distributed the world soul throughout the entire cosmos on the basis of musical ratios. This is done by dividing the soul into parts that have the relationships of the tones of a gigantic scale. The divisions are obtained by using the ratio 1:2 (octave), 2:3 (fifth), 3:4 (fourth), and so on. Eventually these intervals are filled in with succeeding subdivisions of the scale. After imposing order upon the world soul through musical proportions, it is split into two halves and each formed into a circle, one becoming the sphere of the stars, another, which is subdivided into seven other circles, the individual orbits of the seven planets. The heavenly motions of the soul combined with the four elements constitute the complete cosmos.

It is little wonder that Plato, in *The Republic,* gave music a paramount position in the educational plan for the nation's youth. Essentially, music was to be employed as an esthetic factor in the shaping of moral and ethical character. The "order" inherent in certain forms of music was, according to Plato, to be equated with an ordered soul, the state of which was achieved through certain modes and forms of music, which would affect the soul by imposing their essence of logic, harmony, balance, and emotional control. Plato's theory concerning the affective power of music is called the *doctrine of ethos*. In this connection he states that the Dorian mode is to be used in education since it is indicative of courage and temperance, and hence would strengthen the personality.

The Phrygian is also admirable because it exemplifies freedom and peace. On the other hand, the Ionian and Lydian modes should be banished from the state, since they are too relaxed and expressive of sorrow. A central point made by Plato in *The Republic* is that there should be an inner balance, or homeostasis, within the individual. This, he believed, could be accomplished by training in music and gymnastics; the former would tend to temper or govern man's physical energy, the latter his emotional energy. However, he felt that music has a greater function than gymnastics, for he wrote that music education should begin first in early childhood, then be followed by gymnastics. He justifies this view by stating that music's affective power becomes perceived by the soul, and a good soul improves the body but a good body does not improve the soul. Music education, if properly planned, has the power to penetrate the soul of the educated and, as a result, can make the individual more graceful and refined.

Aristotle and the Liberal Art of Music   Although less a materialist than we are led to believe, Aristotle steered somewhat away from a metaphysical discussion of music, preferring to make some rather objective comments on the place and importance of the art in education. In the *Politics* he states that music contributes to the development of youth on three grounds: moral, intellectual, and social. Most emphatically, music is not to be thought of as a useful subject, as is the case with certain manual skills, but instead as a *liberal art* among the several branches of study (reading-writing, gymnastics, drawing, and music). Music performance, Aristotle believes, is desirable for youth, since it will enable them to express informed opinions on musical style and value when they attain adulthood. He says, however, that performing experiences in education must be held in proper balance, since he does not sanction professional music training. The reason: the professional practices for the sake of others, not for his own improvement. Hence, the aulos and kithara must be omitted from the educational plan, since they are instruments of the specialists or professionals.

Aristotle was quite explicit on the therapeutic value of music. In the *Politics* he refers to two techniques that in modern times are known as *homeopathic* and *allopathic* methods of treatment. In regard to the first method (homeopathic) he writes: "If insanely overwrought persons listen to enthusiastic melodies that intoxicate their souls, they are brought back to themselves again, so that their catharsis takes place exactly like medical treatment."[2] In the second method (allopathic), the form of treatment is different from the symptoms; thus the ill are soothed by impressing upon their disorganized souls the perfectly ordered ratios of music.

Together, the theories of Plato and Aristotle laid the foundation for two modern intellectual disciplines—esthetics and the psychology of music. The doctrine of ethos, the concept that certain modes or forms of music could affect the personality, was later adopted by the first medieval universities and had for a time an important position in medical training. Moreover, these principles have found widespread application in present-day psychotherapy.

THE OUTLINES OF MUSIC THEORY

The picture of the development of music theory in the ancient world is complex. This is due, in part, to the numerous second- and third-hand interpretations of the early theories by later post-Greek theorists. It is possible, nonetheless, to piece together information from several original sources to show that the Greeks did indeed furnish the theoretical basis for Western music. The evolution extends from Pythagoras in the sixth century B.C. to Ptolemy, the last Greek theorist, who lived in the second century A.D.

Pythagoras: The Founder of Music Theory

The intervals of the musical scale were mathematically determined by Pythagoras or his disciples about the end of the sixth century B.C. The instrument or device upon which acoustical experiments were carried out was called the *monochord*. According to medieval drawings it consisted of a string or strings stretched across the surface of a wooden sound box and a movable bridge to permit the "stopping" of the string at any desired point. The octave was found to have the ratio of 2:1. For example, if two strings of equal density, length, and tension are placed side by side and the second "stopped" at a point one-half of its length, the difference in pitch of the two strings would be an octave. This relationship is expressed in the proportion 2:1. The other intervals of the scale were determined in similar fashion: the fifth (ratio of 3:2; that is, the second string would have a vibrating length two-thirds that of the first), the fourth (4:3), the third (5:4), the second (6:5), and so on.

Pythagorean Intonation   The Pythagorean intonation, one of several tuning systems used in the ancient world, was another significant invention by the Greek mathematicians, probably as early as the fifth century. The main point in regard to this tuning system is that the pitches of the various

---

[2] Curt Sachs, *The Rise of Music in the Ancient World* (New York: W. W. Norton and Company, Inc., 1943), p. 253.

tones were derived from a succession of perfect fifths (C G D A E, and so on) which were reduced to one and the same octave (C D E F G A B C). In this system of tuning the intervals of the octave, fifth, and fourth resemble our modern tuning; however, the third (C E) was much wider than our present-day interval. This interval was classified as dissonant (*diaphonia*) by Greek theorists and also by medieval musicians. Apparently the interval of a third was not generally employed until the old Pythagorean intonation was abandoned. Certainly the avoidance of the third in much medieval part music, to about 1300, gives credence to this view. Concerning the consonant (*symphonia*) intervals, we find the octave, fifth, and fourth classified as such by the Greek writers.

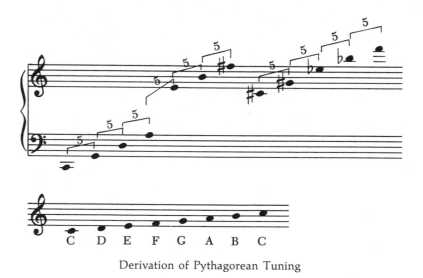

C   D   E   F   G   A   B   C

Derivation of Pythagorean Tuning

The Three Genera: Rise of the Modal System

Many historians are not in agreement as to when the modal system began. The modes, of course, were eight-toned scales or patterns (somewhat like our modern scales) that furnished the raw tonal material for musical composition and performance. The beginnings seem to stem from the early four-stringed Greek lyre, whose four strings provided a four-tone pattern, or *tetrachord*, the outer tones of which were separated by an interval of a fourth. Although the total gamut of tones was very limited on this primitive instrument, musicians were probably adept at making subtle changes of tones within the tetrachord, thus increasing the tonal possibilities.

By the fourth century B.C., theorists began to codify the musical practices that had probably been in existence for many years in the Greek territories. One of the first theorists was Aristoxenus who, about 350 B.C., outlined in his *Harmonics* three different tone arrangements (*genera*) that could be used with the four-toned pattern, or tetrachord. The tetrachord, he states, could be of either a *diatonic, chromatic,* or *enharmonic* genus. The diatonic genus consisted of two tones followed by a semitone; the chromatic, of a tritone and two semitones; and the enharmonic, an interval of a major third, or ditone, followed by two quarter tones.

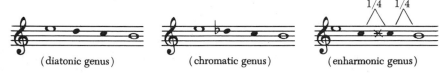

(diatonic genus)   (chromatic genus)   (enharmonic genus)

The Three Genera

The genera nomenclature has continued, with some modification, up to the present day: diatonic referring to a progression of tones within the scale or key, chromatic to a progression of tones foreign to the key or scale, and enharmonic to two tones having a different spelling (F♯–G♭) but of the same pitch. Curiously, the Greeks gradually abandoned the more complicated and subtle enharmonic and chromatic genera (which were probably inherited from their Eastern neighbors), and adopted the diatonic genus. This genus, which is of course made up of half and whole steps, became the foundation for all Western scales. According to Sachs, the Greek musicians had completed their transition to the diatonic genus by the second century A.D. Perhaps if the Eastern styles had been present in substantial form at the time of the early Church fathers, Western music might have followed the microtone scale systems similar to those in use in the Orient.

The Modal System   A further advancement of Greek music theory came with the idea of combining two or more tetrachords together in succession to form larger scales or modes. The earliest complete scale of eight tones was derived by connecting two tetrachords either *conjunctly* (the last note of one was also the first of the other), or *disjunctly* (a whole step separates the two tetrachords). The invention of the large fifteen-stringed *kithara* reputedly established a comprehensive scale-plan known as the *Systema Telaion* (*Greater Perfect System*) found in the writings of Euclid, dated approximately 325 B.C. Now the gamut of tones was increased to fifteen, covering two octaves and an added tone:

Tetrachord

The Greater Perfect System

About A.D. 150, Ptolemy, the last important Greek theorist, reduced the complex grouping of scales that had been in vogue for several centuries to seven, each having eight tones:

MODE	RANGE
Mixolydian	b–b
Lydian	c–c
Phrygian	d–d
Dorian	e–e
Hypolydian	f–f
Hypophrygian	g–g
Hypodorian	a–a

The modes, which were mentioned so frequently in the writings of Plato and Aristotle and eventually codified by Ptolemy, formed the basis of much of the music performed in the Roman Catholic Church from about the fifth to the sixteenth century.

Musical Examples Fortunately, we do have several extant fragments of Greek music. Some were written out on papyrus and others etched in stone. The ancient musicians employed a crude method of notation, consisting of letters taken from the Greek alphabet. Lacking, of course, in the notational system were the lines of the modern staff and symbols for indicating time values; moreover, the letters did not designate a definite pitch but only pitch in relation to the other tones. The letters were used to represent the different strings of the lyre or kithara; also, certain letters tipped sideways designated tones to be flatted or raised in pitch. Below is the transcribed version of the *Skolion of Seikilos* (a drinking song), with its original letter notation.[3]

Skolion of Seikilos

The few extant musical fragments that have been made available through the musicological research of Curt Sachs and others show rhythmic simplicity, repetition, conjunct melodic motion, limited range of tones, and a monophonic texture.

[3] William Starr and George Devine, *Music Scores Omnibus* Part I © 1964 Englewood Cliffs, N.J.: Prentice-Hall, Inc., 1964. By permission of the publishers.

Musical Instruments Used   The heritage of several Greek instruments extends back into the Egyptian civilization. The *aulos,* usually pictured in Greek art as a double-pipe instrument and known to be equipped with a double reed, is to be seen in early Egyptian reliefs. This is also true of the lyre, harp, small finger cymbals, and castanets. From about the ninth to the fifth century B.C., the early lyre is generally depicted as a small instrument with four strings, and, from the fifth century on, it is seen as having nine to twelve or more strings. The *kithara* is a heavier and larger instrument consisting of a wooden sound box, numerous strings, and stout arms that support the tightly strung hemp strings.

The Greek *aulete* (aulos performer) is occasionally shown with a capistrum, or cheek bandage, which evidently provided greater control of tone and volume. The eminent musicologist Curt Sachs believes that the early aulos had four finger holes on each pipe. The two pipes were connected to form a large "V." These early models played three types of modes or scales, the Dorian, Phrygian, and Lydian. The later models, about the fifth century B.C., were evidently capable of playing a wider variety of modes and had a more elaborate fingering system.

Professional competitions involving aulos performers were common in the later period of the Greek civilization. A precursor of these popular festivals has been traced to the Pythian Games at Delphi in 586 B.C. It is reported that one aulos player performed the *Pythic Nome,* a five-movement composition that was the musical version of Apollo's fight with a dragon. Each part or movement had a descriptive title such as "Challenge," "Iambic" (the actual fight), "Song of Praise," and "Victory Dance," according to the historian Pollux, writing in the second century A.D.

This event might be interpreted as the beginning of "program music," that is, music based on or suggestive of a literary or artistic reference. Later, in the nineteenth century, we will find that the programmatic principle is extensively used by such composers as Schumann, Liszt, and Berlioz.

In addition to the lyre and kithara and percussion instruments such as small cymbals, clappers (castanets), and tambourine, the only other instruments generally depicted are the *syrinx* and the *salpinx.* The syrinx, or panpipes, consisted of several gradated pipes fastened together; the salpinx, on the other hand, was a large wind instrument shaped like a long trumpet. Although not made of a metallic substance (several pieces of ivory were fitted together), it possessed the same basic acoustical system as the modern brass instrument; that is, the tone was produced by the player's lip vibrating against the crude mouthpiece. A more advanced development of brass instruments and playing did not, however, take place until the time of the Romans.

Oddly enough, the only indication of ensemble music, if we may use the term loosely, is to be found in several vase paintings. One such work, a relief on the *Borghesian Vase,* shows a group of festive performers with an aulos, castanets, two lyres, and a tambourine. It is doubtful that these instruments played harmony parts as such; however, it does seem conceivable that several instruments were combined in unison, that is, all playing the same melodic part.

A Procession of Kithara and Aulos Players from Curt Sachs, *Our Musical Heritage*, Prentice-Hall, Inc., 1948

PRINCIPAL CONTRIBUTIONS IN THE HUMANITIES—THE GREEK EPOCH

MUSIC

Pythagoras (d. 407 B.C.), devised ratios of musical intervals
Aristoxenus (lived c. 350 B.C.), *Harmonic Elements* (on music theory)
Euclid (lived c. 325 B.C.), *Systema Telaion* (two octave modes)
Ptolemy (lived c. A.D. 150), reduced modes to seven in number

PHILOSOPHY

Pythagoras (d. 507 B.C.), applied mathematical theorems to the universe, birth of philosophy
Socrates (d. 399 B.C.), devised the Socratic method
Plato (d. 347 B.C.), *Republic, Timaeus, Phaedo*
Aristotle (d. 322 B.C.), *Politics, Poetics, Metaphysics*
Pyrrho (d. 270 B.C.), Sophist
Zeno (lived c. 270 B.C.), founder of Stoicism

ART

Myron (d. 450 B.C.), *Discobolus*
Polyclitus (d. 440 B.C.), *Doryphorus*
Parthenon, completed 433 B.C.
Phidias (d. 432 B.C.), supervised Parthenon sculptures
Erechtheum, 405 B.C.
Praxiteles (d. 330 B.C.), *Hermes, Cnidian Aphrodite*
Dying Gaul, c. 325 B.C.
Lysippus (d. 320 B.C.), *Apoxymenos*
Laocoön, completed c. 1st-2nd cent. B.C.

LITERATURE

Homer (lived c. 850 B.C.), *Iliad* and *Odyssey*
Hesiod (lived c. 700 B.C.), *Works and Days*
Aeschylus (d. 456 B.C.), *Agamemnon*
Pindar (d. 438 B.C.), *Odes*
Sophocles (d. 406 B.C.), *Oedipus the King*
Euripedes (d. 406 B.C.), *Hippolytus*
Aristophanes (d. 380 B.C.), *Lysistrata*

HISTORICAL EVENTS

3000–1200 B.C.	The pre-Hellenic age, Greece inhabited by Minoans
1200 B.C.	Troy, last Minoan stronghold, falls, beginning of the Hellenic period
800–461 B.C.	Rise of city-states
461–429 B.C.	Pericles rules at Athens
431–404 B.C.	Peloponnesian War
400 B.C.	Athens defeated by Sparta, decline of democracy
346–337 B.C.	Macedonia conquers Greece
336–323 B.C.	Conquests of Alexander the Great
323 B.C.	Beginning of the Hellenistic period
146 B.C.	Carthage falls to the Romans

ROMAN CONTRIBUTIONS

Culturally Rome was an assimilator rather than a creator of unique forms in the Greek sense.

Bernard S. Myers, *Art and Civilization*

The Professionalism of Rome   The horde of Romans that invaded Carthage in 146 B.C. spread northward and eventually covered the British Isles, Europe, and as far east as Constantinople. This immense military and social organization spanned over nine hundred years, beginning about 500 B.C.

and extending to A.D. 476 when the structure, internally and externally decayed, finally fell. One principal reason for the downfall of an empire that prided itself on achievements in law, government, and military leadership, was the presence of a hollow materialism. Ironically, this attitude, which gave rise to empire building, was also the source of inner decay. Professionalism as opposed to idealism framed the background for political, intellectual, and artistic endeavors. Consequently, musical activities and performances were in the hands of specialists rather than the people.

The creative efforts of the Romans, understandably, seem almost insignificant when placed alongside the achievements of the Greeks. Several underlying differences, which will help to explain why the Romans did not excel artistically, should be mentioned.

The Greeks employed rationalism to solve philosophical, scientific, and artistic problems; the Romans, in contrast, were more practical in their application of reason. Absent from their civilization are the great original works of sculpture and architecture hewn in the spirit of humanism and idealism. Instead, we find numerous state centers for the amusement of the masses. The materialism of the Romans is also evident in their creation of a vast military power, in the formulation of the *Pax Romana,* which they disseminated through the Western world, and in the popularity of the Stoic philosophy.

Stoicism   Of the various philosophical attitudes prevalent in Rome at the height of the Empire, Stoicism probably had the widest following, indeed, if not total acceptance by the educated Romans as a way of life. It originated with the Greek Zeno of Citiium (c. 270 B.C.) who believed that virtue is the sole good, as an end in itself, and not as a means toward a higher good. Basically, it meant that man should, if need be, unflinchingly endure hardships and repress feelings and the demands of the body. Since the course of nature is completely determined by natural laws, man must face the reality that events will continue to happen again and again.

Although Zeno's Stoicism became modified and enriched with the changing epochs of the Empire, its essential principles were strongly reflected in the writings of such great personalities as Nero's philosopher and adviser, Seneca (c. A.D. 3–65), who accepted Stoicism as a religion, and even as late as Marcus Aurelius (A.D. 121–180), the last Roman Stoic.

Roman Stoicism clearly provided an atmosphere of ideas that were conducive to the development of a social order founded on duty and simplicity. Man, who is considered to be a part of an immense social organization, must accept his responsibilities and be unaffected emotionally by happenings, since they are all a part of the organized system. Ironically, the Stoic view that had contributed to several centuries of empire building became corrupted by luxury and cynicism in the last decades of the Republic.

Several passages from the writings of one of the last leading Roman Stoics, Marcus Aurelius, will illustrate some of the principal ideas of this philosophy which continued into the waning years of the Empire.

Every moment think steadily as a Roman and a man to do what thou hast in hand with perfect and simple dignity, and feeling of affection, and freedom, and justice; and to give thyself relief from all other thoughts.

. . . Nor can I be angry with any kinsman, nor hate him. For we are made for cooperation, like feet, like hands, like eyelids, like the rows of the upper and lower teeth. To act against one another then is contrary to nature; and it is acting against one another to be vexed and to turn away. What, then, is that which is able to conduct a man? One thing, and only one—philosophy. But this consists in keeping the spirit within a man free from violence and unharmed, superior to pains and pleasures, doing without a purpose, nor yet falsely and with hypocrisy. . . . And finally waiting for death with a cheerful mind, as being nothing else than a dissolution of the elements of which every living being is compounded. But if there is no harm to the elements themselves in each continually changing into another, why should a man have any apprehension about the change and dissolution of all the elements? For it is according to nature, and nothing is evil which is according to nature.

I have mentioned, there remains that which is peculiar to the good man, to be pleased and content with what happens, and with the thread which is spun for him . . . (from the *Meditations*)

Artistic Temper   In the above selections and in other Stoic writings, considerable emphasis is placed upon the importance of simplicity, the repression of emotions and feelings, directness of action, and respect for law and cooperative effort; in short, upon a cold, detached view of life. Indirectly, many of these traits are manifested in the forms of Roman art created during the Augustan age and later. These achievements were mainly in the realm of engineering design and construction, in which utility of purpose replaced personal expression, and strength and simplicity ruled supreme. Whereas Greek art was motivated by idealism, the Roman works were fostered by materialism; moreover, where the Greeks favored civic sculpture and architecture, the Romans were dedicated to state art. There is one positive side to be mentioned. Roman art inspired the modern attitude of functionalism and massiveness. Furthermore, their development of engineering principles such as the true arch, the vault, and the dome, and the employment of concrete, contributed to the creation of monumental projects, including canals, paved roads, aqueducts, and amphitheatres.

Roman Music: Instrumental Contributions   Just as in the field of art, Roman musical ideas were based mainly on the accomplishments of the Hellenes. Music theory, most all of their instruments with the exception of brass, and performance practices—all can be traced to the Greeks. In contrast to their predecessors, who developed an indigenous form of musical expression in choral singing and poetry, the Romans depended largely on professional musicians.

Colosseum, Rome. A.D. 72–80. Long axis 620', short axis 513', height 160'. Carl Frank

There is considerable evidence to the effect that the Romans made great strides in the construction and usage of brass instruments. The art and skill of trumpet making, which had its roots in ancient Egypt, evidently came into Roman hands from the Hebrews and Etruscans. This is verified by the Arch of Titus, constructed by the Romans following their conquest of Jerusalem in A.D. 70. Depicted on this arch are various objects the Romans took from Hebrew temples, including a trumpet of the same design as the ancient Egyptian models.

Roman usage is prominent in the history of brass instruments. Besides continuing the ancient cylindrical trumpet dating back to the Egyptians, they expanded the tonal range of brass instruments with their development of several conical forms of different pitch. Used extensively by the Roman legions spread throughout the Continent as well as the British Isles, these forms undoubtedly influenced the design of later instruments. Furthermore, Roman instruments used in public auditoriums and for the military represent early attempts to band brass instruments together.

Roman instruments consisted of four distinctive species: the *tuba, cornu, bucina,* and *lituus.* The basic designs for these instruments were, with the exception of the bucina, borrowed from the Etruscans. The chief identifying features of the tuba include a long, straight body made of bronze and a small bell at one end. This instrument, which measured about four feet in length, was constructed of several sections fitted together to form a straight cylindrical tube. Its mouthpiece was detachable, and mainly conical rather than cup-shaped. Evidently the instrument was combined with the cornu for musical performances, as shown in Roman mosaics and art reliefs.

A Roman Cornicen

The cornu consists of a large "G"-shaped tubing supported by a wooden brace. Like the tuba it was made of bronze; however, it was mainly conical, as opposed to the cylindrical form of the tuba. The cornu was carried over the shoulder of the Roman soldiers, thus antedating the twentieth-century helicons and sousaphones by two thousand years. The third Roman instrument, the bucina, remains in obscurity. Although there are inscriptions that differentiate the *bucinator* (bucina player) from the *cornicen,* there is, unfortunately, no certain representation of the bucina in the Roman world. The final instrument, the lituus, according to remaining instruments, embodied a cylindrical bronze pipe approximately five feet in length with a bell shaped into a hook.

Performance Practices   Findings reveal that the Romans grouped brass instruments together for public performance in the amphitheatre and for the military, and that they favored large ensembles, in which hundreds of players participated. For example, the writer Seneca of the first century A.D. reported that during one spectacle a vast number of lyre performers were seated on the stage and many more occupied seats in the audience. The accompaniment, he relates, included a multitude of brass instruments dispersed throughout the auditorium with organs and auloi on the stage. The organ mentioned by Seneca was probably the *hydraulis,* which, according to Willi Apel, was invented by the Greeks about 250 B.C. Water was used as a means of providing hydraulic pressure, which was activated by several men operating hand pumps.

The Romans continued the Greek practice of music festivals and competitions. The emperor Carinus, in A.D. 284, presented the citizens of Rome with a series of games at which one hundred trumpets played together (probably of the lituus or tuba class). In addition, one hundred players of the horn (probably the cornu) took part in the giant spectacles. These contests were also a part of the Olympic Games, which had originated with the Greeks much earlier. From the many reports of Roman historians who describe the trumpet tones as being raucous, it would seem that the Romans had a penchant for volume. From the historian Pollux we learn that the Greek trumpeter Archias proclaimed the Olympic Games three times without bursting his cheeks or blood vessels. Also, the ancient reports tell us that a certain Herodorus of Megra was victor at the Olympic Games ten times. So great were his lungs that he could not be heard with safety unless at a great distance.

Gladiatorial Contest, showing orchestra with hydraulic organ, tuba, and cornu players. Mosaic from Zliten, North Africa. A.D. *c.* 70

Summary

The roots of our present-day system of music are to be found principally in the ancient world of Greece and Rome. The Greek scholars not only produced a theory of music that has continued for over two thousand years, but they were also the first to seriously consider the role of music in education. Their achievements in music and art have always been a source of strength and vitality to each new epoch of history. The underlying force behind many of their accomplishments in art, music, literature, drama, and philosophy was an unquenchable intellectual curiosity within the framework of humanism.

The Romans inherited much of the greatness of their predecessors. However, this inheritance became manifested in a materialistic way of life, which produced in turn a need for a musical art diametrically opposed to the Greek ideals. However, in their own particular way the Romans fostered musical development in the instrumental field, which, if permitted to grow, perhaps could have given the Middle Ages a wealth of instrumental music. Instead, the rise of Christianity brought with it a new form of musical expression, which remained as the dominant musical style for over a thousand years.

PRINCIPAL CONTRIBUTIONS IN THE HUMANITIES: THE ROMAN EPOCH

MUSIC

No Roman theorists until Boethius (c. A.D. 500), the mediator between the ancient and Western world. No extant music; however, many references to music by historians and philosophers. Beginnings of brass instruments and ensemble performances.

PHILOSOPHY

Cicero (106–43 B.C.), *De Officiis* (Stoic)
Lucretius (c. 95–55 B.C.), *On the Nature of Things* (Epicurean)
Seneca (c. 3 B.C.–A.D. 65), Practical Ethics (Stoic)
Pliny (A.D. 23–79), Pantheism
Marcus Aurelius (A.D. 121–180), *The Meditations* (Stoic)
Sextus Empiricus (c. A.D. 200–250), Skepticism
Plotinus (A.D. 205–270), Neoplatonism

ART

Numerous copies of Greek sculpture
Originality mainly in Roman portraiture
Corinthian column popular
Monumental engineering feats (Appian Way, aqueducts)
Arch of Trajan, Arch of Titus
Colosseum begun A.D. 70
Pantheon begun A.D. 118, completed 126
Pont du Gard aqueduct

LITERATURE

Lucretius (c. 95–55 B.C.), *On the Nature of Things*
Vergil (70–19 B.C.), *The Aeneid*
Horace (65–8 B.C.), *Odes*
Livy (59 B.C.–A.D. 17), *History of Rome*
Ovid (43 B.C.–A.D. 17), *Metamorphoses*
Apuleius (fl. c. A.D. 169), *The Golden Ass*

HISTORICAL EVENTS

146 B.C.	Greece under Roman rule
58–50 B.C.	Julius Caesar invades Gaul and Britain
46 B.C.	Julius Caesar becomes dictator
4 B.C.	Birth of Jesus
A.D. 33	The crucifixion of Jesus
54	Nero Emperor of Rome
64	First persecution of Christians
313	Edict of Milan, Christians granted equality
330	Constantinople established as new capitol of the Empire
455	Rome sacked
476	End of the Roman Empire

3

THE ROMANESQUE PERIOD

(250–1150)

THE CULTURAL CORNERSTONES
OF THE MEDIEVAL PERIOD

The fantastic proportions of Romanesque architecture . . . the distortions of the human body
in its sculpture . . . were all evidence of a rejection of the natural order of things and its
replacement by the supernatural.
                    William Fleming, *Arts & Ideas*

The Rise of Christianity   The term *Patristic Period* designates the time of
the founding of the Christian Church by the early ecclesiastics, about A.D.
250–600. During this era, a time when urban areas, learning centers, and
trade disappeared, the Church fathers not only preserved formal thought
but developed the principal foundations of the Christian Church, including
its doctrine, ritual, and government. As the Church grew, it became an
organization of unity that filled the gap left by the disintegration of Rome.
Consequently, the course music followed in the Middle Ages was largely
determined by the Church-centered society, the views of its devout leaders,
and existing social and cultural conditions.

To briefly review the events leading up to the work of the founding
fathers, it should be borne in mind that the Roman Empire was approaching its zenith at the time of the crucifixion of Jesus, A.D. 33. Moreover,
not until A.D. 313 did the Roman state finally condone the presence of the
followers of Christianity. The memorable event of that year was the recognition of the Christians' rights and equality under the famous edict
issued by the the Roman emperor Constantine. Now the way was clear
for the movement to bring cohesion into the vast and highly fragmented
community of worshipers.

In addition to the rise of Christianity, the medieval world also witnessed the gradual decay and eventual dissolution of the Empire in the fifth century. The impact of the loss of a unified social order was indeed great. In a disorganized manner, men fled the onslaught of the roaming barbarians and replaced the large-scale system of order by tribal communities. It is no wonder that the arts did not develop rapidly in such unfertile soil.

The retreat of the Romans from the British Isles in the fourth century was an inglorious contrast to the invasion of 55 B.C. The loud and stirring wind instruments that centuries earlier had announced the Roman conquerors were discarded in the gigantic withdrawal. Remnants of these Roman instruments later appeared in English artifacts and in the armies of the English king, Richard the Lionhearted, during the Crusades. Hence, there were some vestiges of ancient instruments and music theory upon which the new world could build, although this musical heritage was very slight. The meager amount of music that did survive was largely the result of the monastic movement begun by the Benedictines in 529. What little was known of Greek theory and Christian Church music was kept alive through the efforts of these and other devout intellects.

The Outlines of Early Medieval Philosophy   The meaning of the sacred music composed during the Middle Ages is closely bound with the views of the founding fathers. The prevailing philosophy of the early Middle Ages is generally referred to as *mysticism.* The reason, of course, is that the world hereafter and not the present physical world was the central topic in the writings of these churchmen. St. Augustine (354–430), who was largely responsible for organizing the Church theology into a single cohesive form, had been a Neoplatonist before he became a Christian. His philosophy, which draws upon the work of Plato and the teachings of Christ, served as the foundation of the Church's doctrine until Aquinas's application of Aristotelian principles in the late Middle Ages. In the *City of God,* St. Augustine writes that all great cities in time finally decay except the permanent city of God; moreover, he states that the physical world is a city of sorrows, beyond which there is eternity. A significant characteristic of mysticism is the juxtaposition of faith and reason that Augustine postulates as the doctrine of illumination; the mind, he states, can understand because it is prepared by God, and, moreover, faith precedes reason.

It is not our intention to delve into the complexities of St. Augustine's philosophy; at best all we can do within the limits of our study is to cull together some cogent principles that seem to be indicative of the intellectual trend of the period. These may be summarized briefly: (1) the Church is supreme and infallible; (2) man's objective on earth is to prepare for the life hereafter; and (3) the physical world is considered inconsequential and not to be studied seriously. Thus, medieval philosophical thought denied the value of imagination and inquiry into the surrounding physical world, since the beginning and end of all knowledge was to be found in the Scriptures. The use of formal principles of reasoning (logic) within the religious context, rather than the investigation of fact or nature, became the rule.

Beneath the vast complex of metaphysical thought there were, however, some signs of a desire to question the existing doctrine and social order. Peter Abelard (1079–1142), a foremost logician and dialectician, was perhaps the first Church scholar to methodically and logically examine the doctrines upon which ecclesiastical authority rested. His method of inquiry (in *Sic et Non*), that of comparing the Scriptures and the views of the Church fathers on basic theological questions, pointed up discrepancies between the two sources and hence showed weaknesses in the very foundations of medieval thought. His approach to gaining knowledge may be summarized in these words: By reason I will understand that which I have accepted by faith; furthermore, by doubting and inquiry we perceive truth. The *nominalists,* led chiefly by William of Ockham early in the fourteenth century, continued this spirit of critical examination and gradually ushered in the humanistic philosophy with its emphasis upon *men* rather than universal Man, democracy rather than hierarchy, worldliness and industrialism rather than contemplation of God, and freedom rather than unity.

Medieval Artistic Ideals   The intellectual climate briefly described above constituted the framework in which early medieval society took shape and the artist and musician created. The Church, headed by a pope and an extensive hierarchy, was the ruling organization and center of all life in the Middle Ages. It was, moreover, a wealthy power block with controlling interests in the vast feudal system. Consequently, the Church was looked upon by all men as the gigantic fortress—a protectorate or guardian—of society, in which man lived, worked, and worshiped. The imprint of this spiritual climate and Church-dominated order was clearly stamped into the creative output of the musician and artist. The religious atmosphere, though limiting the scope of subject matter, provided the means and inspiration for many of the greatest artistic achievements in the Western world. In fact, we will find that the imposed limitations in the field of music, ironically, unleashed a creative outlook that transcended the initial ideas behind its adoption by early churchmen.

Romanesque, the principal artistic style of the early Middle Ages, began about A.D. 500 and reached its culmination in European church architecture, 1000–1100. It was an amalgamation of early Christian, Byzantine, and native barbarian styles, which were altered by existing artistic and social conditions in each geographical region. The Romanesque seems to have been basically an outgrowth of the Roman basilica and particularly the rounded arch form developed by the Roman builders. In addition to the rounded arch, the Romanesque churches are characterized by their thick, massive walls, heavily vaulted ceilings, small windows, and long hall running the full length of the edifice, flanked on either side by a series of small archways. The greater weight of the vertical masonry called for extensive side props, thus creating a heavy ponderous effect, particularly true in the earlier Romanesque churches.

Examples of this style include the Basilica of Sant' Ambrogio in Milan, the Cathedral at Pisa, and Notre Dame at Poitiers. Much of the sculpture of this age reflects the same asceticism as the architecture, and the façades of many Romanesque structures were decorated with distorted

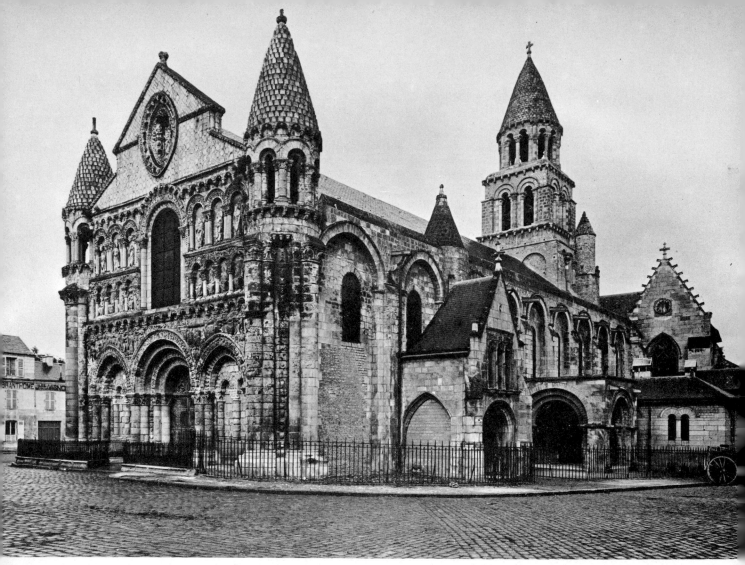

Notre Dame la Grande, at Poitiers, eleventh century. Archives Photographiques, Paris

and unlifelike figures. In contrast to the Greek sculptures of the Great Age, these are lacking in proportion and human expression; moreover, they seem to mirror a cold, severe attitude that denies the humanistic qualities of this world for the mystic realm of life to come. Likewise, we will find that the sacred music of the Romanesque age possesses the same austere, mystical, and solemn quality.

THE RISE OF MUSIC IN THE CHRISTIAN RITUAL

The Views of the Early Christians on Music The proliferation of Christian believers, spread throughout Europe and as far east as Constantinople, presented a diversified cultural background from which various musical and ritualistic elements were drawn by the Church fathers. Since Christianity began as a sect within the Jewish faith, it is not surprising that many of the Hebrew practices were adopted by the churchmen. For example, the *Mass* was derived in part from the Jewish synagogue ritual known as the *synaxis*. In addition, the function of the *cantor* (principal solo singer), certain melodic formulae, and procedures for singing the psalms were retained by the founders of the Church. However, the musical organization of the service and indeed the principal features of the liturgy itself emerged very slowly.

The broad outlines of the Mass were not completed until about the fourth or fifth century; moreover, the codification of the chant (the official church melodies) was not carried out on a significant scale until about the end of the sixth century. Thus, the road to the final clarification of music's role within the service was far from direct. Clearly, the old Greek doctrine of ethos—that music had the power to shape ethical character and to steel the personality—did not fit into the scheme of thought. Instead, music was assigned a dual functional role, as a means for inducing religious feelings among the Christian worshipers and as a vehicle for transmitting the word of God. These principles are found in the writings of such early Churchmen as Clement of Alexandria, St. Basil, and St. Augustine.

In the *Exhortation to the Greeks*, the Greek scholar and Christian convert, Clement of Alexandria (d. c. 215) criticizes the existing pagan interest in the crude mythological stories and demonic tragedies. In extolling the virtues of turning away from paganistic rites, he implores the Greeks to turn to the "new song," which under cover of metaphor refers to the word of God. He writes as follows:

> For my own part, I cannot bear the thought of all the calamities that are worked up into tragedy; as yet in your hands the records of these evils have become dramas, and the actors of the dramas are a sight that gladdens your heart. . . . , let us wreathe them, if you like, with ivy, while they are performing the mad revels of the Bacchic rite, and shut them up satyrs and frenzied rout and all, . . . Aye, and this Eunomus (musician) of mine sings not the nome of Terpender or of Capio, nor yet in Phrygian or Lydian or Dorian; but the new harmony, with its eternal nome that bears the name of God. This is the new song, the song of Moses. There is a sweet and genuine medicine of persuasion blended with this song. . . . See how mighty is the new song! It has made men out of stones and men out of wild beasts. They who were otherwise dead, who had no share in the real and true life, revived when they but heard the song.[1]

Another prominent figure during the Patristic Period is St. Basil (d. 379) whose liturgy is still used in the Eastern Church. In his *Homilies*, this early theologian moves away from the metaphorical views of Clement and subscribes to a more definitive usage of music in the liturgy. This line

[1] Oliver Strunk, *Source Readings in Music History* (New York: W. W. Norton and Company, Inc., 1950), pp. 59–63.

Time-Line: Romanesque Music	
313 A.D.	Edict of Constantine
413	St. Augustine: *The Confessions*
500	Boethius: *De Musica*
590	Gregory I Pope to 604
850	*Musica Enchiriadis*
1000	Guido 4-line staff
1100	St. Martial School
1150	Notre Dame School begins

of thought leads directly to the greatest of the founding fathers, St. Augustine, who was instrumental in establishing music on a permanent basis within the Roman Catholic Church. St. Basil has the following important remarks to make on music:

> For when the Holy Spirit saw that mankind was ill-inclined toward virtue and that we were heedless of the righteous life because of our inclination to pleasure, what did he do? He blended the delight of melody with doctrines in order that through the pleasantness and softness of the sound we might unawares receive what was useful in the words, . . .[2]

Further insight into how and why the Churchmen finally chose an expression that was to dominate all of Europe's cathedrals for centuries is provided in the writings of St. Augustine:

> When I call to mind the tears I shed at the songs of Thy Church, at the outset of my recovered faith, and how even now I am moved not by the singing but by what is sung, when they are sung with a clear and skillfully modulated voice, I then acknowledge the great utility of this custom. Thus vacillate I between dangerous pleasure and tried soundness; being inclined rather ... . to approve of the use of singing in the Church, that so by the delights of the ear and weaker minds may be stimulated to a devotional frame.[3]

Since the Bible contained a large number of references concerning the use of music it was, apparently, less a problem of justifying its inclusion in the Christian ritual than it was to determine the quality or type of expression. What the founding fathers desired were the dignified, somber and reverent sounds of the ancient psalms stemming from the Jewish liturgy, mingled with elements from Greek and Byzantine culture. Moreover, since the remains of pagan instrumental music were all too prevalent in the dying Roman world, it is no small coincidence that the ordered spiritual expression found in sacred vocal music was widely encouraged.

The Codification of Chant and Ritual Music   The official liturgical melodies that served the various forms of early medieval music (such as the mass, hymn, or psalm) employed in the ritual of the Roman Catholic Church are called either *chant, plainsong,* or *Gregorian chant.* Much of the chant from the Middle Ages has been preserved in the *Liber Usualis,* a standard collection used in the present-day Catholic Church. The musical style of these hundreds of sacred melodies includes a non-pulsatile rhythm, melodic simplicity, a sequence of tones based on the ancient modes, and a range of approximately eight tones.

---

[2] *Source Readings in Music History,* p. 65.
[3] From the *Confessions* (c. 413); in *Basic Writings of Saint Augustine,* translated by J. G. Pilkington and edited by W. J. Oates (New York: Random House, Inc., 1948).

Gregorian Chant, Antiphon:
Salve Regina, Mode I

Although many ecclesiastics took part in the massive task of collect-
ing and organizing the chant during this period, two prominent names
have come down to us in history: St. Ambrose, Archbishop of Milan from
374 to 397, and Gregory, Pope from 590 to 604, under whose papacy the
chant was collected and standardized for the liturgy. So great were his
efforts that his name became synonymous with the chant.

There were several sources from which the plainsong or chant gradually filtered into the hands of the codifiers: from Spain came the *Mozara-
bic chant* (much of which was deposited there by invading Visigoths from
Syria and Byzantium in the fifth century), from France the *Gallican*, from
Milan the *Ambrosian* (named after St. Ambrose), and, of course, there was
the great terminal itself, Rome.

It should be clear to the reader at this point that much of the ritual
music that came to be accepted was from a highly diversified and colorful
background. For example, we know that the tradition of the East is based
upon microtones, subtle pitch nuances and ornamentation. Therefore, the
chant that came from Byzantium was probably shorn of its particular
adornments by the musical scholars of the Church. Also the Greek influence was extremely significant since it is known that Greek was the chief
liturgical language during the early centuries of Christiandom; the extant
hymns from the first three centuries are in Greek. Furthermore, the Jewish tradition played a great part in the actual plan of the liturgy, for we
note the adoption of the following Hebrew practices: daily prayer hours,
the recitation of Biblical passages by a soloist, and responsorial and antiphonal singing of psalms (*psalmody*). *Responsorial psalmody* referred to a ques-
tion-answer repartee between soloist (priest) and congregation, and
antiphonal psalmody to successive exchanges of verses of the psalms by
two choruses. The Hebrew idea of *cantor*, or principal solo singer, also
became established along with the *schola cantorum* (Rome, fifth century),
which was a school for training both men and boys as musicians for the
Church.

Gradually, as the liturgy was formed into a regularized pattern, certain parts took on significant meaning. Two principal classes of service evolved in the early centuries: the eight *Offices*, or *hours*, which are celebrated daily at designated hours, and the *Mass*, a commemoration of the Lord's last supper. The Mass became the chief musical form for composers of the medieval and Renaissance periods. It consists of two parts: the *Ordinary*, the unvarying portion used from day to day, and the *Proper*, which changes according to the occasion. The five parts of the Ordinary are the *Kyrie, Gloria, Credo, Sanctus,* and *Agnus Dei*.[4] The Proper includes a large number of special parts such as *hymns, introits, graduals,* and *communion*.

MUSIC THEORY AND PHILOSOPHY

Musica Disciplina Music theory in the modern sense generally refers to the techniques of musicianship that are studied by every music student, such as notation, harmony, counterpoint, harmonic analysis, and orchestration. To the medieval musician, music theory referred to the scientific, philosophical, and speculative explanation of musical phenomena. Such a course of study would include the investigation of the numerical ratios of vibrating strings, tuning systems, the derivation of scales from numerical proportions, and the harmony of the universe.

The early scholars were less interested in studying music as an independent art form (*musica sonora*) than with treating music as a tool (*musica disciplina*) for understanding the mysteries of physical and spiritual realities. *Musica sonora* or *ars musica* did not emerge until about 1000, when musicians began to think more in terms of music for its own sake, to devise improved methods of notation, and to explore the possibilities of piling tones upon one another into what became *organum*. Some of the reasons for the rather late appearance of *musica sonora* are to be found in the educational practices and philosophies of the early Middle Ages.

Music was regarded by the medieval student as a discipline in the seven liberal arts, an ancient Roman system of education that became the standard plan in medieval higher learning. The seven liberal arts consisted of two branches: the *trivium* (grammar, rhetoric, and dialectic), and the *quadrivium* (geometry, mathematics, astronomy, and music). The term "liberal" generally referred to studies that would lead man to intellectual maturity and free him from the domination of the senses. The seven liberal arts that constituted the first level of "general" studies were followed by philosophy and finally the study of theology, the epitome of the curricular strata.

It is interesting to note that the trivium comprised the subjects that would lead to the mastery of language and verbal communication—the more practical skills needed for teaching, preaching, and discourse. The quadrivium, on the other hand, was composed of studies that reached beyond utilitarian needs and dealt with the abstract world of ideas. Music, then,

[4] See Glossary for texts of the Ordinary of the Mass.

A Demonstration of the Monochord. From a twelfth-century miniature. National
Library, Vienna

in this realm, was regarded as a scientific discipline and not as an autonomous art form imbued with distinctive tonal qualities and structure.

Although early medieval educational practices and theory did not
include *musica sonora*, we should not assume that the age was devoid of
practical music, since the Church was, of course, the center of all musical
development. Here, even though music played a functional role, its growth
was fostered through the establishment of the *schola cantorum*, the codification of chant, and the assigning of music to an important position in the
liturgy.

Boethius: Mediator Between Ancient and Western Worlds   The first important scholar of music following the Greek civilization was the Roman Boethius (d. 524), who in addition to his main treatise on music, *De Institutione Musica*, contributed a massive philosophical undertaking, *The Consolations of Philosophy*. The liberal versus illiberal division of education described by Aristotle finds a more definitive exposition in musical terms in Boethius's *De Institutione Musica*. The basic premise is the complete rule of reason over physical skill. Thus every scholarly study and art has by nature a more honorable position than a craft in which the hands rather than the mind are employed. The application of this tenet to music becomes obvious: the science of music that is based on reasoning is more admirable than performance.

He then classifies musical activity into three groups: (1) the musician concerned with instruments, (2) the musician who invents songs, and (3) the one who judges the work of the instrumentalist and the song composer. The third class (as with Aristotle) constitutes the highest realm of music, since it possesses the power of reason and judgment, whereas the other two classes are mere handmaidens or servants to the intellect. Clearly, the analytical power of the mind is superior to the faculty of hearing (one of the senses), which is subject to error. Thus Boethius is not interested in the sensuous nature of a musical tone but in the acoustical factors that cause its appearance. Boethius' principal effort in the theory of music was the assigning of Latin letters to each of the tones in the ancient Greek Greater Perfect System. However, the last link in the evolution of the lettering of the octave was not completed until Odo of Cluny, a theorist at Rhiems (c. A.D. 900), who lettered the scales in the modern cyclic pattern as follows: A B C D E F G A B C D E F G.

The Classification of Modes: Authentic and Plagal   Many innovations took place about the year 1000, indicating most definitely that *ars musica* was gaining greater momentum. One important development took place with the completion of the eight ecclesiastical modes by Hermannus Contractus (c. 1013–1054) who added the Hypomixolydian mode to the existing seven ancient Greek modes. About this same time the eight modes were divided into two groups: the *authentic* (Dorian, Phrygian, Lydian, and Mixolydian) and their counterparts the *plagal* modes, which were located an interval of a fourth below the corresponding authentic modes and given the prefix of "hypo." (Hypodorian, Hypophrygian, Hypolydian, and Hypomixolydian). Modes were identified by number rather than by name during the medieval period. In the following chart of the medieval modes, the bracketed notes represent the *finals;* the D indicates the dominant of each mode.

In selecting a particular mode as the basis for composing a melody, two factors would be borne in mind: first, the musical range of each mode differed (with the exception of the Dorian and Hypomixolydian, which were the same), and secondly, each mode differed as to the pattern of whole and half steps (again, with the exception of the Dorian and Hypomixolydian). The beginning and ending note of the mode was called the *final,* comparable to the keynote or tonal center in modern music. The final was

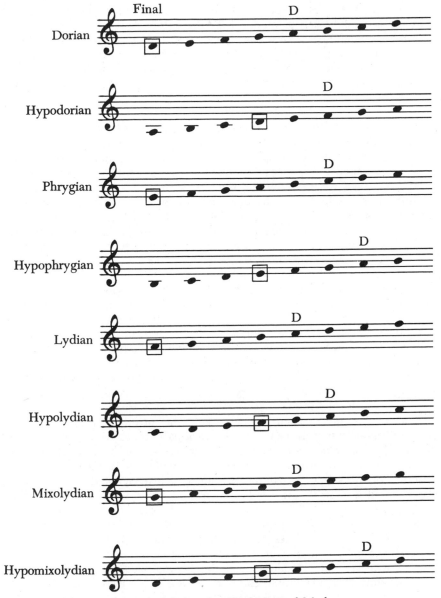

The Eight Medieval or Ecclasiastical Modes

the same for the authentic mode and its corresponding plagal mode. Al-though the tones of the modal melody gravitated to the final, a secondary tonal center called the dominant, or *reciting tone* (indicated by a D above), was also stressed within the body of the melody.

Generally, a mode may be identified in actual music by determining the ending note of the melody and the range of the melody: if the notes remain within the octave span of the finals (Dorian: D to D, for example), it is the authentic type of mode; if it falls below, it is the plagal variety. The modes remained in common practice until about the end of the Renaissance, when they were gradually replaced by major and minor scales, which had evolved from the modes by the increasing infiltration of added sharps and flats. (Lydian with a B♭ is a major scale; Mixolydian with F♯ is a major scale, and Hypodorian with G♯ is a minor scale.)

The Development of Notation to 1225   The music manuscripts from the early Middle Ages show the gradual formation of a rather crude system of notation referred to as *neumatic notation.* The background of these neumes may be sketched briefly. Scholars are not in agreement as to their exact origin; however, we do know that the Greeks made use of similar signs to indicate pitch inflections. These precursors of the neumatic system of notation consisted of three types: the *grave* (＼), which indicated a fall in pitch; the *acute* (／), a rise in pitch; and the *circumflex* (∧), a rise and fall. It has been suggested that these signs were used to give an idea of the melodic direction in such works as the *Iliad* and the *Odyssey,* which were actually sung by the Greeks.

The later forms of the neumes, which began to appear in Byzantium about A.D. 800, consisted of a variety of shapes and forms which were placed above the text. No staff lines or bar lines were employed at this early date. Rather than indicating a specific pattern of tones, the neumatic notation merely served to remind the church musician (who probably had the music memorized) of the general rise and fall of the melody to be sung to the Latin text beneath. Among the chief forms of symbols employed were the *punctum* (■), *virga* (／), *clivis* (∩), *podatus* (∨), *scandicus* (∴／), and *climacus* (∧\.).

A further advancement appeared with the introduction of "heighted" neumes, about the ninth century. The various neumes were placed above the text in a scalelike pattern to indicate more clearly the general rise and fall of the melody. Another important innovation is to be found in the addition of the single horizontal red line which designated the pitch "f." Later, about A.D. 1000, another line, usually yellow, was added. This line indicated the pitch "c," four steps or tones below "f." The combination of lines helped to establish a guide for determining more exact pitch relationships. The colored lines eventually gave way to the letters F and C, which were placed at the beginning of each line and designated these pitches respectively. Still later, the letter G was used and this eventually became, through considerable elaboration, the treble clef sign.

Concomitant with the rise of the staff of four lines, (generally attributed to Guido of Arezzo [c. 1000], there occurred several changes in the old neumatic symbols. Composers began employing heavy, black, square and diamond-shaped notes with the four-line staff, and by 1200 this system, which we may call *square notation,* or *plainsong notation,* became universally accepted, remaining in common practice until about 1300. Interestingly, it is still used by the Roman Catholic Church (see example

below). Although this new method of notation did designate the rise and
fall of pitch, it did not specify the time value of each symbol—a problem
to be solved by later theorists.

Be- ne- di-ca-mus Do -   -   -   -   -   -   -   -   - mi - no._____

Plainsong Notation

ORGANUM

Origins With the establishment of the essential features of liturgical
music by about the ninth century, Church musicians sought new modes
of expression within this somewhat closed and stabilized body of official
music. Two avenues of invention became favored among church musicians,
beginning about the ninth century: (1) the addition of a few (later many)
words and/or music to portions of existing chant; these additions are
called *tropes* and *sequences,* and (2) the expansion of musical texture from
one line of melody (*monophony*) to several (*organum*).

Organum[5] has, as its primitive distant relative, a phenomenon that
occurs when any group or congregation joins together to sing. The un-
trained voices will sing at the particular level that is most satisfying to
each individual. The result is a crude form of pseudo-singing called *heterophony.* Perhaps this type of group singing has been common to all societies
since the beginning of time. The Greek civilization used a similar method
called *magadizing,* that is, singing in octaves. This technique received its
name, apparently, from the obscure Greek harp, the *magadis,* which had
its strings tuned in octaves. We should also bear in mind that England
showed a propensity for part music at an early date. Giraldus Cambrensis,
the twelfth-century historian, reports widespread performance of part music
among the people of the British Isles. Although undoubtedly prevalent
among the people on an informal basis, part-singing or organum did not
appear as a formal intellectual endeavor until about the ninth century.

This monumental change in musical creativity was marked by the
introduction of an anonymous treatise entitled *Musica Enchiriadis* (*Hand-
book of Music*) about 850. The work outlines several ways of singing together, called *organum.* In the first method, one voice sings the chant melody
and, simultaneously, another voice sings a melody at an interval of a
fourth or fifth below. In this method, which is called *parallel organum* be-

[5] *Organum* is the collective name given to all early (medieval) forms of
composition in which two or more parts or melodies are combined.

cause the voice parts move in the same ascending-descending pattern, it was permissible to have a third or even a fourth voice added at the octave or fifth below the basic chant melody:

Parallel Organum, ninth century

The second method calls for both voices to begin on the same pitch (in unison) and gradually move away from one another and then return to the unison. This procedure allowed one voice to become partially "free" as a result of the *oblique* movement of the two parts. Note in the example below the point just before the unison is reached. This juncture, which is called the *occursus* (marked by an X) is the rudimentary beginning of the cadence, that is, the point where the musical phrase comes to a momentary or permanent rest. On the basis of usage, the early medieval composers apparently considered the intervals of consonant value to be the unison, fourth, fifth, and octave; the second also appears frequently in these manuscripts. The interval of a third, due to its "wide" tuning under the still continuing Pythagorean system, was probably too dissonant-sounding and hence not generally used.

"Free" or Oblique Organum

Later, in the eleventh century, greater freedom is found in the movement of the voice parts. This trend is to be noted in the treatise, *Micrologus* (c. 1040) by Guido of Arezzo. By employing both contrary and oblique motion, considerable independence of movement entered into each part:

Eleventh Century Organum (from the *Micrologus*)

The oldest collection of *organa* (plural for *organum*) is the *Winchester Troper*, from the Winchester Cathedral of the eleventh century. It is for two voices and written in "heighted neumes," that is, the neumes are placed at different levels to simulate a scale line. Although there were several monasteries established in England (as early as A.D. 600) where the *cantus Romanus* (plainsong or Gregorian chant) was studied, the organum techniques probably worked their way into the British Isles from France. Interestingly, after the supremacy of Rome, France held the lead in musical art, and continued in this position until the Netherlands became the leader in the fifteenth century.

Tropes, Sequences, and Liturgical Drama   The word *trope* refers to the device of adding new music or words (or both) to existing chant. Inherent in the idea are several innovations that are historically and artistically significant. In addition to fostering the creative spirit, troping also demonstrated the first attempt to extend a brief musical form, in this case, a chant, into a larger and longer work. Clearly, the Church musicians were trying to experiment and discover ways for creating more interest in the simple sacred melodies. The simultaneous juxtaposition of one or several melodic lines above or below a given chant (*cantus firmus*) was another manifestation of this creative surge.

Specifically, the word *trope* referred to the practice of interjecting original music between portions of the chant melody. Later, both new music and words were interpolated. Troping, apparently, had its beginnings about the ninth century with Notker Balbulus (d. 912) and came to be used with almost all parts of the Mass and of the Office. When words were added they were generally placed in segments of the melody that had a long melismatic line, that is, where many notes were sung to one syllable in the text.

A common example is to be found among the so-called Kyrie tropes, in which several words such as *fons bonitatis* (fountain of goodness) are interpolated between the two original words of the Kyrie: *Kyrie—fons bonitatis—eleison,* and set to the original melody in the chant. Curiously, this practice led to the use of extended sentences and even complete poems placed between two words of the official text. As a matter of fact, secular elements made considerable inroads into the sacred realm via this procedure.

Sequence, on the other hand, originally was the practice of adding extended texts to the final closing portion of the alleluia, a point where the performer would sing one syllable to a very ornate melodic line. Beginning about the ninth century, Church musicians added new words to these textless endings, and eventually the elaborately composed sequences broke away from the alleluia portion of the mass and became independent compositions. The Church later abolished the practice of tropes and sequences with the Council of Trent in 1560.

Some mention should be made of the origins of the sacred music drama, which is also to be traced to the troping principle. Just as Greek drama was born out of the liturgical rites of Dionysus, so too did Christian liturgical drama emerge from the ritual of the Catholic Church. Evidently, the tenth century (or even earlier) was the starting point of the germinating idea: the prefacing of the Introit of the Mass for Easter by a short dialogue, which was sung and accompanied by dramatic action. One of the earliest extant liturgical dramas is the *Play of Daniel*, which emanated from Beauvais, France, about 1150. The dramatic idea takes two main directions in the later centuries: a secular direction with the birth of opera around 1600, and a sacred course with the emergence of the oratorio, also in the same era.

LITURGICAL MUSICAL CENTERS: ST. MARTIAL AND NOTRE DAME

The Shift from South to North   Up to about 1000, the Mediterranean area was the principal center for musical study, indeed for all intellectual endeavor. The founding of the northern monasteries in France and England after 500 precipitated the gradual geographical shift in the pursuit of knowledge that eventually became centered in the Gothic cathedrals and then finally, about 1200, in the new universities.

Two centers of music study prior to the universities were the St. Martial monastery at Limoges from the tenth to the twelfth century, of particular importance in the latter century; and the School of Notre Dame at Paris, which contributed significantly during the latter part of the twelfth and thirteenth centuries. If the early developments of music theory and chant are to be largely attributed to the Church scholars, we must also credit them with the rise of music as a composed art (*musica sonora*). The sacred idiom, incidentally, dominates the field of composition until the fourteenth century, when secular musical expression begins to vie for honors in the creative realm.

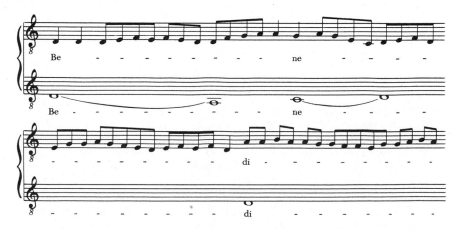

St. Martial Organum

St. Martial Organum   The reader may recall that the earliest type of organum consisted of two or more lines of music moving simultaneously. Aside from purely esthetic reasons, perhaps a lack of a definite system of notation made the simultaneous movement of voices from one *puncta* (point or note) to another imperative. Certainly this procedure would tend to keep the voices together. Outside of some simple variation of movement of the lines (contrary, parallel, and oblique) the artistic expression remained rather limited. However, the manuscripts of the St. Martial school (1100–1150) indicate a new trend in the technique of musical composition. Here observe the conventional two-part organum; however, the upper part now has many notes moving in a florid style, while the lower part consists of a chant melody in long sustained tones. This elementary but important change gave greater melodic interest to the upper voice and separated the parts into two somewhat independent strands of sound.

The lower voice part was called the *tenor*, from the Latin *tenere*, meaning to hold. Its function might be compared to the foundation of a medieval cathedral, since it furnished the principal base of Gregorian chant moving in slow, solemn "blocks" of sound. Above soared an added part called the *duplum*. Just as the Gothic structures now began to rise from heavy foundations to towering pinnacles, so too did music begin to emulate the same style in the latter part of the twelfth century. Gradually, in the ensuing generations, we will see two, three, and more parts piled above the cantus firmus. This technique of adding melodic parts upon one another is referred to as *successive counterpoint*.

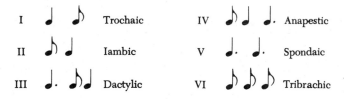

The Rhythmic Modes

The Notre Dame School   The second leading center of music, the Notre Dame School in Paris, headed by Léonin in the late twelfth century and followed by Pérotin (to be discussed in the next chapter), opened the way for the rise of music as a distinct art form. For now, instead of the free metrical style of the St. Martial School, musicians had a rhythmic system that, though very simple, permitted a greater variety in each part and freed the tenor part from its rather rigid and lifeless role. The new system, which brought a greater degree of order into musical composition, is called the *rhythmic modes*, and consists of six rhythmic patterns derived from the ancient Greek poetic meters.

By employing a particular type of *ligature* (as the black squarelike notes were now called) and a certain order of ligatures, the composer could inform the singer as to the rhythmic mode to be followed. A creative composer thus could write one voice part in Mode I, a second in another mode, and so on. Moreover, to break up the monotony, several different modes could be used in succession. Most all of these modes were written in triple meter, the preferred metrical scheme for sacred music up until the fourteenth century.

Léonin was one of the earliest composers to actually create a large body of musical works using the new rhythmic technique. His main contribution is a gigantic corpus of liturgical music called the *Magnus Liber Organi* (*The Great Book of Organum*), of some hundred works such as alleluias, graduals, and responsories for the church year. Frequently existing side by side in these pieces are Léonin's two fundamental stylistic traits. In the first, which we may call the *organal style,* the tenor sings the Gregorian chant melody in long sustained notes while the top part has a sweeping melodic line of considerable length. In the second style, his *discantus* (or measured) style, both parts are written in the new rhythmic modes. In addition to the two-part texture and the alternating discantus and organal style, we find octaves, fifths, fourths, and unisons as the prominent harmonic intervals; note also in the following example the use of long, sweeping melodic lines.

From Léonin's Organum

EARLY MEDIEVAL SECULAR MUSIC

Derivation and Description of Secular Music   We have noted thus far that the sacred realm contributed the first scholars of music and also the theoretical writings that provided a basis for medieval musical practice. To the ecclesiastics, musical art represented a dignified and solemn means for expressing religious faith and devotion. The principal method for achieving this end was through the somber and carefully ordered chant based on the ancient modes. To the roaming minstrel, in contrast, musical performance was an expression of his love of life and the physical world as opposed to the mystical. The itinerant entertainers' method of expression was, likewise, poles apart from the ecclesiastics'—namely through the lilting song and instrumental accompaniment. Whereas the Church scholars gave the Western world the intellectual foundations for musical art, the minstrels contributed and kept alive the melodic and rhythmic spirit of tonal art drawn from life itself.

The history of minstrelsy goes back to the Roman *mimes,* roaming musicians and *recitatists* who spread word of current events, recited historical and poetic works, and performed on various instruments such as the lyre and aulos. In the Middle Ages, the minstrel movement, which undoubtedly stemmed from the mimes, received its first foothold among the peripatetic scholars prior to the founding of the universities. One such motley band of students and entertainers of the tenth century was known as the *goliards,* whose music, as with most minstrels, was founded on poems of an amatory or satirical nature.

In contrast, the French *jongleurs* of the twelfth and thirteenth centuries were professional musicians, including both men and women, who traveled from village to village and castle to castle ekeing out a tawdry existence by providing entertainment, which included dancing, acrobatics, singing, and instrumental performance. Their repertory covered the vernacular epic songs called the *chansons de geste,* of which the *Song of Roland* is the most famous. Their contemporaries, the *troubadours* from southern France and the *trouvères* from northern France, continued the secular art under a more dignified manner, since they were mainly noblemen of considerable poetic skill. The total output of these French secular groups was indeed great: some 2000 troubadour poems and 250 notated melodies, combined with about 400 trouvère poems and 1400 melodies, are extant. The main vocal forms into which these melodies were arranged include the *chanson de geste, rondeau, virelai, ballade,* and the *lai,* which was derived from the sequence additions to the Gregorian chant. The *estampie* was their principal dance form, apparently played upon *vielles* or wind instruments such as *recorders.*

Trouvère Song: *Or la truix*

The German counterpart of the French poet-musicians were *minne-singers,* active from the twelfth to the fourteenth century. Among the noted minnesingers were Walther von der Vogelweide (d. 1230), Neithard von Reuenthal (d. 1240), and Heinrich Frauenlob (d. 1318). In many ways their art resembles that of the trouvères and troubadours, for we find considerable emphasis on chivalric love lyrics and songs of a devotional, epic, and political character. A large number of the minnesinger songs are characterized by their churchly effect, resulting from the use of church modes, religious text, and a slow and stately rhythm set in duple meter. In the fifteenth century the minnesinger tradition was carried on by the *meister-singers.*

Minnesinger Song: *Willekomen Mayenschein*

The Rise of English Minstrels   The beginning of minstrelsy in England seems to date from the Norman Invasion of 1066, when the Norman forces under the command of William the Conqueror moved into battle accompanied by a band of musicians. One of the minstrels, named Taillefer, led the van of warriors and, according to the poetic source, advanced into combat singing the *Song of Roland.* From this and other similar literary and historical references we may assume that one of the principal functions of the minstrel was to bolster the fighters' morale with spirited music. It is likely, moreover, that various instruments that were developed on the Continent were introduced on English soil as a result of the Norman inhabitation. One such instrument, the *buzine* (a medieval trumpet of Eastern origin) was used quite extensively in the invasion, for there is frequent mention of this instrument in the poetic narratives about the Battle of Hastings (1066).

The French cultural influence upon England in the years following the invasion was significant in many other respects. Not only did French become the accepted language for a period of time, but French literature, music, and art also enjoyed a dominant position in English life. This impregnation of French culture was due in large measure to the French minstrels, who moved to England in increasing numbers in the employ of the nobility. England, however, did not begin to show progress in indigenous vocal musical art until her language was developed into a literary form in the fourteenth century.

Another event that gave increased impetus to minstrelsy in England occurred in the latter part of the Crusades—when the minstrels on the Continent came under severe attack by the Church and local law authorities and were forced to disband their traveling groups. Many of them established permanent residence in large European towns and formed guilds. Some went to England, where they rapidly expanded into two categories of minstrels that existed until the sixteenth century: the itinerant or independent class, and the dependent musicians attached to a court or household. Both contributed greatly to the rise of English ensemble music.

The repertory of the early English minstrels included, apparently, the bulk of French secular tunes, such as the *virelai, rondeau,* and *estampie.* The latter, a dance form that originated in France during the late twelfth century, is represented in several English manuscripts dated about 1200. These are characterized by a two-part polyphony, a lively rhythmic pattern, clear cadential endings, symmetrical phrases, and an instrumental character resulting from the unvocal melodic skips and repeated note patterns.

Estampie

Summary   The style characteristics of early medieval secular music include: (1) a marked pulsatile rhythm; (2) an increasing emphasis upon the use of the Lydian mode, which has the same sound as the modern major scale; (3) secular text material in the vernacular instead of Latin; (4) considerable melodic repetition; and (5) the regularization of phrases into definite forms.

MEDIEVAL INSTRUMENTS TO 1200

Introduction   The instruments dating from pre-1200 are indeed a far cry from their modern counterparts. Aside from exterior shape and general contour, the only similarity exists in their method of tone production, either blown, struck, plucked, or bowed. A more definitive way to classify the methods of tone production is through the use of the terms *aerophones,*

Medieval instruments, Spain late twelfth century: harp, lute, organistrum, psaltery, psaltery, vielle. Arthur Kingsley Porter, *Romanesque Sculpture of the Pilgrmage Roads*. 1923. Marshall Jones

chordophones, idiophones, and *membranophones.* Under the classification of aerophones appear the wind instruments, which are of three types: (1) lip-vibrated instruments in which the lip vibrates against a mouthpiecelike opening—for example, the trumpet; (2) reed-vibrated (a reed is set into vibration)—for example, the oboe; and (3) flue-blown (an air column is set into motion)—for example, the flute. The second category (chordophones) consists of stringed instruments; the third (idiophones) of struck instruments, such as the gong; and the last group (membranophones) of percussion instruments with membranes stretched across the surface, such as the timpani.

Actually, before 1500 the instruments were in a primitive and formulative stage—a time when their musical potential was being shaped through a long succession of utilitarian functions, such as signaling, night watch, and tactical use in the military realm. Gradually over the centuries their character and purpose became more clearly focused, until, finally, in the fifteenth century, definite signs of instrumental groupings began to appear. This transition—from a heterogeneous conglomeration to a homogeneous ensemble—is the rudimentary beginning of the modern chamber ensemble, band, and orchestra. However, this foothold was not attained until the instruments had reached a higher level of technical development and the cultural and social atmosphere was conducive to the further growth of instrumental art.

Chordophones In the following example dating from the eleventh century, the medieval harp being played by King David is a little larger than the Greek kithara and generally consisted of about fifteen strings. It apparently made its first appearance in the medieval world among the Celtics living in the northern regions of England and Ireland. Modern scholars do not believe that the classical civilizations of Greece and Rome were familiar with bowed string instruments. The general view held by music historians is that these instruments were brought to Europe from Asia by immigrating tribes. The modern violin apparently evolved from the bowed *vielle.* This instrument, also shown in the example, is held between the

King David and Musicians. Top: harp, below: bells, cornett, vielle, and positive organ. Donald Jay Grout, *A History of Western Music*, Copyright © 1960 by W. W. Norton & Company, Inc., and J. M. Dent & Sons, Ltd.

knees in a vertical position and bowed with the right hand. The generic name for all these primitive violin forms is *vielle* or *fiedel;* later in the Renaissance they are called *viols.*

Aerophones Mention should be made of several problems that have considerable bearing on research in medieval wind instruments. In general, there were few documents written during this time that pertain specifically to wind instruments. (Treatises on instruments did not begin to appear until after 1500). The principal writers on music in the medieval age were the monks in the monasteries and cathedrals, and they were primarily interested in Church musical practices. Those few scholars who did comment provide a very dim view on instruments, perhaps due to their association with secular entertainment. For example, John Cotton remarks in his *De Musica* (late eleventh or early twelfth century): "Wind instruments sound indiscretely, like the laughter or groaning of men, the barking of dogs or the roaring of lions." Hence, for information relative to instruments we must look to secular sources such as works of art, and poetic and literary references. Among these sources there is much uncertainty and ambiguity in wind instrument nomenclature up to about 1300.

Evidence concerning wind instrument usage in the early Middle Ages is very slight. In England, the little information available, however, tends to show that the Roman spirit was far from dead. Though the Empire had ceased, the numerous army garrisons located throughout Europe must have left traces of instruments later copied by military forces. The continuing Roman influence is to be seen in such bits of evidence as the extant art miniatures of the eighth century which picture the Roman lituus and tuba. In addition, there is mention of the short conical horn called the *bugle* in English ballads and also depicted in artworks. These bugles, which were named after a wild oxen formerly found in England, were made of twisted horn fitted with a copper bell. They were used primarily for blowing signals or calls for the hunt, the banquet hall, and the night watch. Interestingly, long after the Continent had adopted the newer *clarion* (a long cylindrical trumpet of the fourteenth century) England still favored the short conical bugle, a preference that continued into modern times.

The second principal wind instrument of the early Middle Ages is called the *cornett* in England, *zink* in Germany, and *cornetto* in Italy. It is unrelated to the modern day cornet except for the cupped mouthpiece (found after 1300), and evidently it was an English invention, since the earliest illustrations are all of English derivation. The motivating idea behind its invention was probably the desire to increase the range of lip-reed instruments beyond the lower harmonic series, which at most were two or three tones on short horns and on tubes of greater length (Roman cornu and tuba) about nine harmonic tones. The earliest illustration of a cornett dates from an eleventh-century Anglo-Saxon Psalter. Its characteristics include a curved tube made of horn, which extends about twelve inches, and six finger holes placed in succession along the upper side of the instrument. The player evidently blew into some form of mouthpiece-like cavity.

In moving ahead to the end of the twelfth century, specifically to the time of the Crusades, we find several important items of information: (1) evidence of the continuation of the Roman instruments and practices, and (2) the appearance of new forms of wind and other instruments, which were to play a big role in the evolution of ensemble and military music in Europe. From the chronicles we learn that the English king, Richard the Lionhearted (reigned 1189–1199), employed a band of musicians who played the lituus, tuba, and buccina. Instruments in the opposing Saracen band included the shawm (*surnay*), trumpet (*nafir*), horn (*buq*), reedpipe (*zamr*), drum (*tabl*), kettledrum (*nagarah*), cymbals (*suney*), and bells (*jaljil*). The mingling of East and West in the Crusades brought forth the eventual European adoption of many Eastern instruments, namely the *shawm*, which is the successor of the aulos; the *kettledrum*, later called the timpani and used in the baroque orchestra; and the *trumpet*, or *buzine*, which evolved into two forms: (1) a wide-bored, low-pitched brass instrument, and (2) the *clarion*, a shorter, more cylindrical instrument, which became the modern trumpet.

Although the exact date of the introduction of the organ into the Church is not known, the instrument was in common use in England by the eighth century. The organ erected in the Cathedral at Winchester, England, in the tenth century had 400 pipes and 26 bellows, which were pumped by hand by 70 men, and was played by 2 organists at 2 keyboard-like panels. Each keyboard was fitted with 20 slides, which were pulled and pushed by the performers. An illustration of the slide mechanism is to be seen in the preceding example. A stationary organ such as this was called a *positive* organ. In addition, we also find depicted in works of art the *portative* model, which was suspended around the player's neck while the left hand worked the bellows and the right hand played the one-octave rank of pipes.

Summary

The early Middle Ages was a time of the founding of the Christian Church and its liturgy. The doctrine and social organization laid down by the patristic fathers somehow brought cohesion into a distraught and confused world. Consequently, the age produced a style of art and music that represented the ideals of a mystical philosophy. The somber, ordered movement of the chant and the asceticism of Romanesque architecture were artistic equivalents of the words of St. Augustine. From the work of the devout scholars appeared faint signs of an advancing art: (1) an ordered corpus of chant that served the medieval communities of worship; (2) the invention of organum as the first substantial indication of the creative spirit; and (3) the formulation of basic principles of music theory and notation. On the other side of medieval existence, the minstrels, quite removed from the dignity and sanctity of the monastic life, fostered the invention and perpetuation of native folk expression.

PRINCIPAL CONTRIBUTIONS IN THE HUMANITIES:
THE ROMANESQUE ERA (250–1150)

MUSIC

Adoption of music by Early Christian fathers; largely attributed to
  St. Augustine (354–430)
Cultivation of music in monasteries begins sixth century
Chant codified by Pope Gregory (540–604)
Ancient modes reclassified by Odo of Cluny, c. 900
Secular music begins to emerge, *jongleurs* in France c. 900
Introduction of Arabic instruments into Europe, 900

PHILOSOPHY

St. Ambrose (340–397), *On the Holy Spirit*
St. Jerome (340–420), translated the vulgate
St. Augustine (354–430), *Confessions, City of God*
Boethius (480–524), *The Consolations of Philosophy*
Peter Abelard (1079–1142), *Sic et Non*
Otto of Freising (1111–1158), *Two Cities*
John of Salisbury (1115–1180), *Polycratics*

ART

Romanesque begins to emerge, c. 500
Hagia Sophia begun in Constantinople 527, completed 565
Zenith of Romanesque, 1000–1100
St. Denis started c. 1140, beginning of Gothic style
Chartres Cathedral begun c. 1194
Norman architecture (offshoot of Romanesque) introduced in England,
  c. 950
Notre Dame Cathedral begun 1163

LITERATURE

History of the Franks (594), Gregory of Tours
Moralia (c. 590), St. Gregory the Great
Beowulf (c. 700)
Ecclesiastical History of the English Nation (731), Bede
Chanson de Roland (c. 1130)
Metalogicon, on the seven liberal arts (c. 1170), John of Salisbury
Aucassin et Nicolette (c. 1200)
The Nibelungenlied (written c. 1200, based on fifth-century events)

HISTORICAL EVENTS

 325 Council of Nicaea
 374 St. Ambrose consecrated as Bishop of Milan
 413 St. Augustine formulates Church doctrine
 455 Rome sacked
 476 End of the Roman Empire
 529 Benedictine Order founded
 590–604 Gregory I Pope of Rome
 650 Rise of monasteries, to 1100
1054 Final separation of Eastern and Western Church
1066 Norman invasion of England
1095 First Crusade
1100 Cathedrals as centers of learning
1150 Rise of universities, Oxford (1167), University of Paris (1170)
1189 Richard Couer de Lion, King of England

4

THE GOTHIC ERA
(1150–1400)

GOTHIC LIFE AND IDEAS

The Cathedral was the sum of revelation. In it
all the arts combined, speech, music, living drama
of the mysteries and the mute drama of sculpture . . . Man there renewed the sense of unity
of his being and regained equilibrium and harmony.

Emile Mâle, *The Gothic Image*

Overview of the Period The late Middle Ages represents, on the one hand,
the culmination of the medieval world and, on the other, the beginnings
of the rebirth of learning known as the Renaissance. The "Towering
Gothic" is, to be sure, a fitting title for an era that transcended the previous epoch and reached toward heaven in its art and ideas. Indeed, the
religious zeal that had motivated art and ideas since the Romanesque
period now reached its climax.

The awe-inspiring cathedrals—Chartres, Notre Dame of Paris, Mont-
Saint-Michel, and others begun at the turn of the twelfth century—stand
as a living testament of, not only a style of architecture, but an expression
of a prevailing world view. Although most readily observed in the magnificent cathedrals, the feeling of the times is clearly ingrained in musical
art as well. The distinctive musical language of the age, a truly international one, at least for the first hundred years of the Gothic period, was
shaped by musicians who successfully synthesized the experiences peculiar
to their day. Certainly, these creative experiences were born of divine
inspiration—an impulse that gave rise to a rich polyphonic style, as well
as to the spiritual wonders of Gothic architecture with its soaring spires
and mystical unity of God and man.

Although both Romanesque and Gothic Europe possessed profound religious faith, the Gothic period expressed its religious devotion in a different way and with a greater intensity, which was felt in all human endeavors. Essentially, the religious expression of the Romanesque was mystical whereas the Gothic was more dynamic and humanized. For a moment let us examine the social and cultural forces which molded this spiritual fervor of the age.

Ile-de-France, the medieval term for the area around Paris reserved for the personal domain of the king, is the region out of which arose the cultural leadership of France and the Gothic style. French architecture, philosophical ideas, and choral polyphony originated from *Ile-de-France,* particularly the University of Paris, and were copied by other regions of Europe. The reason for this esteemed position is to be found mainly in the strong monarchy of Philip Augustus (reigned 1180–1223) who organized and administered the leading civil authority in Europe. Under his rule arose the eminent University of Paris, with its distinguished faculty (Peter Lombard, Albertus Magnus, and Thomas Aquinas) who set the intellectual tone of the period. In short, it was inevitable that the scholarly and artistic atmosphere that produced Chartres, Notre Dame, and the *Summa* of Aquinas, was also to give us the great corpus of choral polyphony produced by Léonin, Pérotin, Pierre de la Croix, and their contemporaries.

Social Movements and the Strengthening Intellectual Temper   Society, the primal source and nurturer of artistic creation, took on a new profile in the late Middle Ages, from the fixed feudal and religious order of the Romanesque to one marked by fluidity of human movement and increased secularism. These characteristics are noted specifically in the flux of country folk to the rising towns, the establishment of overland trade routes and maritime commerce (given impetus by the Crusades, 1095–1200), and the rise of the kingship in France and England. Quite clearly, with the appearance of the wealthy middle class and strong national monarchies, feudalism and the parochial view of life were now declining. Also, with the passing of the Gothic years the cleavage between church and state increased, a movement undoubtedly accelerated by the growing religious skepticism and the new intellectuality.

A high concentration of scholarly productivity within a given epoch is generally shared by all areas of human activity devoted to art and ideas. The Gothic era, like the Great Age of Greece, exemplifies this point of view; the two epochs differ, of course, intellectually in degree and in purpose. The central point, however, is this—if the Athenian age represented the epitome of reason in the secular realm, the Gothic represents a soaring of intellectuality in things sacred. For example, the rational approach to theology in the thirteenth century was also the principle behind the work of the designers of the massive geometric monuments and of the polyphony sung in these magnificent cathedrals.

Several questions may be raised that will perhaps ultimately lead to an understanding of the musical spirit, if not the style and technique of the Gothic world: What is this intellectual attitude? Who were its proponents? Where was it focused? And how was it applied in the arts? The decline of the parochial view was undoubtedly hastened by the new learning symbolized by the development of the universities. The trend away from the cathedral and monastic schools, which began as early as the twelfth century (Oxford University founded 1167), gathered momentum by the thirteenth, beginning with the formal opening of the University of Paris (1200) and followed by Cambridge University (1209). The new learning of the thirteenth century is not identified by the adoption of a new curricula, although professional studies in theology and medicine were introduced at this time. Actually, the university studies were, for the most part, about the same as those of the older cathedral schools, namely the seven liberal arts divided into the quadrivium of mathematics, geometry, astronomy, and music, and the trivium of dialectic, rhetoric, and grammar. The new learning, in summation, can be defined as the growing intellectual and scholarly atmosphere generated by the new universities. Although the scholarly environment was still limited in terms of disciplines, it helped to provide a necessary climate for the eventual rebirth of learning.

The key elements behind the successful establishment of any center of learning—faculty excellence, financial support, intellectual camaraderie, and freedom to pursue truth—were apparently present at the University of Paris, the main community of scholars in the thirteenth century. Its beginnings go back to before 1200, when peripatetic students and instructors gathered informally as the *universitas* (guild or corporation). The geographic location, extensive economic activity of the area, and, most important, a strong civil patronage under the French monarchy, contributed to the rise of this important institution.

It was here that many outstanding music theorists exchanged ideas, and leading figures in philosophy taught the *scholastic method,* that is, the attempt to buttress religious faith through the application of reason. The roots of scholasticism extend back to Abelard who, it may be recalled from our previous readings, experienced considerable criticism by the Church for his method of inquiry (*sic et non*), which exposed discrepancies between the scriptures and the views held by the Church fathers. Abelard's spirit of critical inquiry championed by his later (fourteenth century) counterparts at Oxford and University of Paris (John Wycliffe, Duns Scotus, and William of Ockham) typify the new intellectuality which though devoted to the sacred realm, fostered an examination and evaluation of existing ideals. The resulting pursuit of a way of life, quite away from the spiritual, became known as the humanistic movement of the fourteenth century.

Aquinas' Synthesis   In the main, however, the thirteenth-century scholastics headed by Aquinas, the leading figure in Christian philosophy of the Middle Ages, were dedicated to the strengthening of the theological foundations, a task completed by Aquinas in his *Summa Theologica*—a synthesis of Aristotelianism with Christian ideals. Indeed, the *Summa,* combined with the zealous overt expression of faith in the dynamic Gothic cathedrals, represents the medieval apogee of Christian faith, for ironically, the gradual reversal of the pendulum is to be seen in the increasing tension within the Church leading to the Schism in 1378. By employing Abelard's scholastic method, Aquinas fitted together step by step the final statement of Latin Christian doctrine. The 631 doctrinal questions were placed in order beginning with the main proposition, and like the process of building a Gothic cathedral, each proposition was divided into subpropositions and answered by a citation of authority. Moreover, an unequaled mastery of dialectic directed all premises, like the giant Gothic spires and vaults, to God the supreme authority. Truly, God is to be known through the power of the mind; reason and faith were thus complimentary.

GOTHIC ARTISTIC IDEALS

Architects of Stone and Tone   Out of the epoch which saw the transition from castle to commune and from the dark shadows of the Romanesque to the beautiful towering Gothic, emerged a style of music that may be called "Gothic" because of its affinity to the labyrinthlike structures that gave it birth. Foremost among the artistic ideals shared by both music and architecture we note particularly the massing of elements above a broad, solid foundation resulting in a strong, vertical feeling and a tranquil, intellectualized mood, as opposed to the more somber, dark, and austere style of the Romanesque. Architecturally, Gothic builders achieved their ideals through the use of large, light-admitting stained-glass windows and, above all, by employing a series of pointed arches supported by flying buttresses—a technique that impels the eye to move from the massive base upwards to the highest pinnacle.

Musically, esthetic ideals were much the same. A juxtaposition of several freely flowing melodic lines over a solemn sustained Gregorian chant achieved a spiritual and intellectual expression equivalent to that of the reverence and majesty of the cathedral. Furthermore, the foundation of the cathedral, with its structural and symbolic power emanating from the design of the cross, was matched by the *cantus firmus*, a preexisting Gregorian chant placed at the base of the choral polyphony. And yet the comparison extends further. Just as Gothic architecture was thrust upward through successive placement of elements, musical art was based on a corresponding method of writing counterpoint. That is, melodies were placed successively on one another, frequently resulting in a strange, dissonant style. However, the heterogeneity of elements in both music and art, perceived as a whole, produces a unity and integration of design.

The Gothic cathedral, generally situated at the center of the medieval town, its tall spires dwarfing the surrounding community and its massive interior constantly the scene of civil and ecclesiastical activity, was unquestionably the central focus of all town life. Religious plays were given there, traveling clergy presented sermons beside its massive stone and stained-glass walls, which, on the inside, were decorated with religious artwork that informed the illiterate and enhanced the beauty of the edifice. The more than fifty cathedrals constructed in the century after 1160 follow

Amiens Cathedral, structural cross-section. Drawing from *A History of Architecture on the Comparative Method* by Banister Fletcher, the Athlone Press, London.

Chartres Cathedral. Left tower 377 feet high. Façade completed 1260

Figures from the west portals, Chartres Cathedral. 20'6'' high. Archives Photographiques, Paris

the Gothic style emanating from Ile-de-France. Oddly enough, following the great age, "Gothic" was employed derisively—that is, in contempt of medievalism—by artists and critics up until the nineteenth century. The main features of the Gothic include: a verticality of effect achieved by the use of a pointed arch, inner spaciousness achieved by huge supporting vaults, a pronounced upward thrust achieved by a series of arches and flying buttresses that counterbalanced the lateral thrust of the arch. In addition, the walls, in contrast to Romanesque, are thin and lightweight and nonsupporting. Stained-glass windows, which gradually take the place of walls, occupy large sections of free space. As in every facet of Gothic art and ideas, there is a dynamic balance at work: a downward and outward thrust of the vaults, an upward thrust of the floor piers, and a diagonal and inward thrust of the flying buttress. Thus, if one element of balance or keystone were withdrawn, the entire structure would collapse.

Gothic sculpture, as opposed to Romanesque, was a part of the organic whole, adding to the vertical effect through long, slender figures occupying pillars or niches as intrinsic features of the structure. The humanistic qualities of Gothic sculpture are perhaps the most striking characteristics that differentiate Gothic and Romanesque sculpture. Here, an over-all, poised serenity prevails, coupled with facial expressions and other physical features that are more natural than those possessed by the grotesque and ethereal Romanesque figures.

MUSIC OF THE THIRTEENTH CENTURY: ARS ANTIQUA

Continuation of the Notre Dame Leadership As we have already noted, the music of the thirteenth century is referred to as the *ars antiqua*. Interestingly, the practice of affixing labels to musical periods is found throughout much of Western music history. Its beginnings are traced to the fourteenth-century musicians, who looked back upon the previous century in much the same way that modern-day composers regard the nineteenth century. In short, it was the period of an older style, or *ars antiqua* (Latin-ancient art). The music of the *ars antiqua*, which is equally as distinctive as the Gothic edifices in which it was performed, issued forth from Paris—the font of all artistic and intellectual creation in the thirteenth century. Here, the work of the first Notre Dame composer, Léonin, who lived in the latter part of the twelfth century, was carried on into the thirteenth by Pérotin and his contemporaries.

Possessing the title of "Magister" in historical records, Pérotin stands out as the most important composer of the *ars antiqua*. The list of names of actual composers and noted theorists, however, still continues to be small at this stage of music history. In addition to Pérotin, the names commonly associated with the *ars antiqua* include Franco of Cologne (theorist) and Pierre de la Croix (composer). Considering the international scope of the music of this age, it seems feasible that numerous other musicians contributed to the development and dissemination of Gothic polyphony; unfortunately, thus far they have remained unknown.

The sacred polyphony that came from these dedicated musicians was truly of an international character, for, as far away as Scotland, Spain, and England, the French manuscripts were copied, performed, and imitated. Although there are some signs of an indigenous musical art in England (and in fact an active reciprocity between England and France), the large

Time-Line: Gothic
Music (Ars Antiqua)

1200	Perotin at Notre Dame until c. 1238
1240–1260	*Sumer is Icumen In* (England)
1250	Conductus and organum supplanted by the motet
1260	Franco's *Ars Cantus Mensurabilis*
1275	Tower bands started in Italy

collections of Gothic music found in these various countries all share the distinctive earmarks of French polyphony. Thus, the classic Gothic age or the *ars antiqua*, like the Great Age of Greece and eighteenth-century classicism, was one of universal musical style and practice. The basic style: Gregorian chant arranged into old and new molds or forms (organum, conductus, and motet). The common practice: the employment of these forms in the liturgy or in the various sacred ceremonies and activities of the Church.

Musical Styles and Forms of the *Ars Antiqua*

The date 1163 is a landmark in Gothic music and art: it was the year when the cornerstone of the Notre Dame Cathedral was laid in Paris. Although the details of Pérotin's life are somewhat obscure, it seems likely that he was connected with this newly begun cathedral as a boy chorister, beginning about 1180. Then, in later years he rose to the level of magister, as composer and choirmaster at the famed cathedral, a position he probably held until about the second or third decade of the thirteenth century. Before turning our attention to the techniques and musical styles of Pérotin and his contemporaries, it would be well to mention the chief musical forms of the period.

The earlier gigantic collection of organa, Léonin's *Magnus Liber Organi,* served as a guide and a monument of inspiration for Pérotin. For we find that a large portion of his creative work consists of the same genre—organa in not only two parts (*organum duplum*), but also *organa triplum* and *quadruplum.* Moreover, Pérotin and his colleagues at Notre Dame made arrangements of many of Léonin's compositions. In addition to organum settings of the various parts of the mass, the members of the Notre Dame group also created two new forms of composition, the *conductus* and the *motet.*

Organum   The chief type of composition to about 1250 was organum in three and sometimes four parts sung by select choirmen. Pérotin is important first of all for his work in setting the standard of three-part organa that prevailed throughout the *ars antiqua,* and, secondly, for the use of more definite rhythmic patterns in his polyphony. His organa, of course, like Léonin's, was sung in the liturgy, taking the place of the older monophonic (one part) singing of choir and cantor, which had been in vogue prior to the twelfth century. During Pérotin's time, several select choristers were designated to each voice part of the organa: tenor (lowest part), duplum, and triplum, the highest part of three-part organum. And judging from the appearance of the long, taxing tenor part with many sustained notes, an organ probably duplicated the tenor part in performance.

The style elements in Pérotin's organa include a greater use of definite rhythmic patterns (as opposed to Léonin's long, sweeping, and generally less rhythmic melodic lines), a division of musical material into sections or rows called *ordines* (again, in contradistinction to Léonin's more continuous, unwinding style), and repeated sections of identical material in the tenor part (the formal beginnings of the *basso ostinato* technique, a favorite device in the Baroque period). And, most important, we note a trend away from the older, organal style to the *discant style,* where the parts move together rhythmically in note-to-note fashion.

Later on, toward the end of the thirteenth century, it became increasingly popular to superimpose parts above a section of organum that was in discant style. These sections were called *clausulae* (Latin, meaning *ending*), since the ending portion of the organum was more frequently used for superimposing the additional voice parts. Moreover, many of these "clausulae" sections were separated from their context and performed as independent compositions. Other, more subtle techniques of composition used by Pérotin and his fellow composers include: *sequence* (the repetition of a melodic figure on a higher degree or step of the scale), some use of *canon* (exact imitation of one voice part by another), and *stimmtausch* (a form of imitation involving the exchange of short passages between two or more voice parts). The following example is illustrative of the Notre Dame style.

Notre Dame Organum, thirteenth century

Conductus Another group of polyphonic vocal forms of the thirteenth century are the *conducti,* Latin songs in which all the melodies are invented and all voice parts (usually two) move in regular rhythm. The Latin text of the conductus was either of a religious, political, or satirical nature. In some of these conducti we find long, melismatic textless endings, referred to as *conductus cum caudae* (conductus with tails), which many scholars believe were performed on instruments. The conductus originated in the liturgical practices of the twelfth century, evidently sung during the entrance of the clergy into the church.

English Trends

Britain, a country prominent by its absence in musical development thus far (except for its role in the dissemination of the Gregorian chant in the Romanesque era), finally makes its appearance. The British counterpart of the French conductus is the two-part polyphonic form called *gymel* (Latin, meaning *twin song*) and, most important, is composed of the new harmonic intervals, the thirds and sixths, hitherto unemployed in formal music composition. Many historians believe the British Isles to be the birthplace of these new consonant intervals. For, oddly enough, there are thirteenth-century English compositions (gymel and hymns) that show this propensity at the same time as the French are using the more archaic harmonizations in fifths, fourths, and octaves.

The English penchant for these consonants and a discant-styled counterpoint (same rhythm for all parts) is evidenced in one very well-known late thirteenth-century work entitled *Sumer Is Icumen In.* This polyphonic vocal piece is in the form of a round, but is, more accurately, a double infinite canon in which two musical themes are simultaneously imitated by the various voice parts. One canon is in the upper four parts and the other in the bottom two (called *pes* in the score). The word "infinite" means that the themes are repeated over and over as in a typical round like *Row, Row, Row Your Boat.*

Sumer Is Icumen In

The melody of the top canon is of a dancelike, secular character, the lower consists of a repeated dronelike figure. Curiously, both secular and sacred words are written in the score, indicating perhaps that the music could be performed in both secular and sacred surroundings. The English composition (actually given the title of *rota* in the manuscript, meaning *round*) is worthy of considerable merit not only musically but historically, since it is the oldest known canon and the oldest known six-part composition. Perhaps it is of greater significance that it clearly shows another early English penchant—the use of the newer major scale (generally associated with secular music in the Middle Ages) rather than the modal scale employed extensively in sacred music on the Continent at this time. We should bear in mind that both the Continent and England undoubtedly made use of the major scale; however, the essential point is that some scholars believe that England was the first country to use it extensively.

The Motet   About 1250 the conductus and organum types were supplanted by the new polyphonic form called the *motet*. The motet, which was in fact the most important form of the *ars antiqua*, reigned supreme throughout the thirteenth century and continued to be highly favored among composers until the death of Johann Sebastian Bach in 1750.

Earlier it was stated that the first organum of the Romanesque period (about A.D. 850) probably originated out of existing material, that is, by the addition of a melody above a Gregorian chant—and, moreover, not out of esthetic reasons but perhaps out of necessity. It is possible that the development of the motet was influenced in the same way, since the Church undoubtedly frowned on the invention of new forms that did not fit into liturgical practice. Hence, in this case the musicians selected a portion of existing organum, specifically a section in discant style (where two or more melodies move simultaneously in the same rhythm) and then added new words (*mots*, in French) to the part immediately above the tenor. This part, which was called the *duplum* in organum, is now given the name of *motetus*, hence the derivation of the motet form. Thus, originally the motet was not an independent composition but an integral part of the liturgy, consisting of words superimposed onto a segment of existing organum.

A short time after this new innovation appeared (probably as early as 1200), complete sections in discant style, fitted with new words, became severed from the organum proper and emerged as independent motet forms; they were, however, still used liturgically. These generally followed a particular structural pattern, which might be referred to as the "classical liturgical motet" of the *ars antiqua*. Normally, this type of motet had three voice parts (tenor, motetus, and triplum), the tenor part based on a Gregorian chant and two different Latin texts in the two upper parts, which generally paraphrased the Latin text in the tenor. Occasionally the melody of the upper part was taken from secular sources, since a definite lyrical or lilting melodic style is frequently noted in the triplum.

Although there were many different types of motets composed in the *ars antiqua,* about mid-century there began to appear a second principal category, obviously designed for a sophisticated, secular society. Perhaps the most outstanding feature of these motets is the employment of *polytextualism,* that is, different texts and even different languages (French and Latin) used simultaneously in the various voice parts. Also, the French secular musicians adapted the motet form to their carefree, romantic life by merely replacing the sacred Latin words by vernacular love lyrics. Also they frequently performed the motet with instruments (vielles and recorders) instead of voices.

Needless to say, the over-all effect of the Gothic motet seems incongruous to modern ears accustomed to the blending of elements into a closely knit ensemble of tones and words. However, we should bear in mind that the fundamental esthetic ideal at work here is the successive piling of elements—a practice quite uncommon in Western music. For example, the late medieval composer did not place voice parts and texts together in a homogeneous fashion, but rather in a juxtaposed manner. Moreover, where we find polytextuality and a seemingly incongruous admixture of sacred and secular elements, the intended meaning is perhaps to be drawn less from the over-all sonority than from the symbolical relationship of elements.

An examination of these relationships would go beyond the scope of these pages. However, let it suffice to state that symbolism in various forms—such as the popular trinity motif connected not only textually but in meter and interval relationships as well, the paraphrasing of one textual part by another in a different voice part, and the bold juxtaposition of secular and sacred elements (God and man) similar to Gothic iconography —may have been the central focus of musical meaning.

Of further importance is the type of listening audience that is mirrored in Gothic music. The simultaneous use of several different texts and different languages (Latin and French), and other esoteric devices such as parody, indicates a learned body of listeners.

Lastly, in these later motets we will also find a trend toward virtuosity in the upper parts, as indicated by the presence of many faster moving notes. It has often been said that the perfection of a technique in a particular art, be it sculptural, architectural, or musical, generally leads to excessive elaboration and ornamentation. This was certainly true of the Great Age of Greece, which deteriorated into the Hellenistic style; of this period of the Gothic, which saw its motets and cathedral style gradually becoming more flamboyant; and of the Baroque period which became eventually rococo. The highly developed motet of the late thirteenth century, with its new rhythmic innovations of considerable complexity, is generally associated with the work of Pierre de la Croix, during the last decades of the century.

Franconian Notation *Ars Cantus Mensurabilis* (*The Art of Measured Music*), written by Franco of Cologne about 1260, spelled the downfall of the old ligature method of notation. Briefly, the new system removed much of the uncertainty of the former by indicating pitches with more clearly defined symbols, and by differentiating binary (duple) and ternary (triple) division of notes by means of dots and vertical dashes, which later evolved into bar lines. Now the shape of the note rather than its position in a series of ligatures determined the time value to be given to a particular symbol. This system remained in practice for about a century—until replaced by Philippe de Vitry's mensural notation in 1320. The note signs of the Franconian system were four in number: (1) ▜ (double long) = ◦ (2) ▜ (long) = ♩ (3) ■ (breve, the standard beat pulse) = ♩ (4) ◆ (semibreve) = ♪

Example of Franconian Notation and Modern Equivalent

MUSIC OF THE FOURTEENTH CENTURY: ARS NOVA

Ars Nova   Ars nova, or new art, refers to the new musical innovations that came into being between 1300 and 1400 in the countries of France and Italy. Perhaps one of the first things that meets the reader's eye in glancing through historical writings on fourteenth-century music is the preponderance of musicians' names and musical treatises. In contrast to the anonymity that prevailed in previous epochs, many names now appear: Philippe de Vitry, Johannes de Grocheo, Johannes de Muris, Jacobus of Liége, Guillaume de Machaut, Francesco Landini, Jacopo da Bologna, Ghirardello da Firenze, and others. Thus, it is a century of rebirth of intellectual writings on music—what it should and should not be, and what rules should be adhered to in composing music. Of considerable importance is that we now have commentaries on contemporary musical happenings.

Among these writings are two significant works that perhaps most definitely point up the main issues and trends in the *ars nova*: *Ars Nova* by Philippe de Vitry (c. 1320), and *Speculum Musicae (Mirror of Music)* (c. 1330) by Jacobus of Liége. In the former de Vitry champions the new art, and in the latter a plea is made for the continuation of the ancient style of the *ars antiqua*. We will see that both win out; however, what is more significant is that now, for the first time in the Christian world, the carefree, lilting world of the dance and romance finds formal expression and a larger, more receptive and perceptive cultural elite as its audience.

A brief preliminary comparison of the ideals of the *ars antiqua* and the *ars nova* will bring the innovations of the latter into clearer focus. The *ars antiqua* relegated music to the sacred realm, surrounded by an atmosphere of musical concepts that had developed over a period of several centuries. These include *tempus perfectum* (triple meter), strict usage of the ancient modes, a general preoccupation with the scientific study of music, and the employment of sacred forms (organum, conductus, and motet).

The *ars nova*, in contrast, became characterized by a negation of many of the principles that dominated the tonal art of the thirteenth century: a new rhythmic freedom by the acceptance of *tempus imperfectum* (duple meter) along with the continued use of tempus perfectum, the rejection of the cantus firmus idea in Italy, and the increasing popularity of the secular, curved, and lilting melodic figures that now competed with the somber Gregorian chant.

Toward the Secular Point of View   Though the sacred polyphonic style of music became increasingly refined during the Gothic epoch, secular music took a giant step in fourteenth-century Italy. The Italian love sonnets of Petrarch and their musical counterparts, the *ballate* of Landini, were produced at a time when the gap between Church and State was widening, the vernacular was being chosen over Latin for literary expression (the *Sonnets* of Petrarch, the *Decameron* of Boccaccio, and the *Canterbury Tales* of Chaucer), and the study of ancient Greek and Roman classics was being revived in Italy. These dramatic changes—perhaps best described as the trend toward secularization—were precipitated by, and concomitant with, a number of social and intellectual movements. Possibly the most significant of these was, first of all, the dynamic split in the philosophical thought of the fourteenth century by the Nominalists and, secondly, the rise of humanism.

The momentous change in philosophy—the separation of reason and faith—was largely the work of the principal Nominalist[1] of the *trecento*, William of Ockham. The ground had been broken earlier by the most outstanding philosopher at the beginning of the fourteenth century, John Duns Scotus, who taught at the leading centers of learning, Paris and Oxford. He believed that the mysteries of faith could not be explained by reason. Ockham, also of the universities of Paris and Oxford (he was educated at Oxford under Duns Scotus), cut the ties that had integrated the *Summa* of Aquinas. In brief, he abandoned the medieval method of scholasticism, which attempted to prove the truths of Christianity through dialectic and logic. He argued, furthermore, that the Pope had no temporal power and that the Church could only be accepted on faith alone and not on reasoning.

[1] Nominalists held that "no higher levels or abstract entities exist, only concrete things can be named."

The Center of Humanism   Italy, the area in which the trend toward secularism first took root, became the center for *humanism*—the term given for the revival of the study of ancient Greek and Roman classics. Begun at first among a few scholars, chiefly Petrarch, the father of humanism, the movement spread and became one of the most important influences in the later Renaissance. Petrarch deserted medieval learning and led the way back to the classics, which were subsequently given an important position in the new university curriculum of the Renaissance. Theology was gradually replaced by the new studies of Latin grammar, literature, poetry, and history—the studies that came to be known as the *Humanities*.

Florence, because of its economic prosperity, political situation (Italy consisted of a number of independent city-states), and its somewhat apathetic attitude toward the Church, became the mecca of humanism. It produced many wealthy patrons of the arts; among the most famous was the Medici family, beginning with Cosimo de' Medici (1389–1464), a financier and politician who set the pattern for European culture in the Renaissance.

The Italian Ars Nova: Landini   Among the chief centers of Italian music we note Modena, Padua, Bologna, and the most active of all—Florence. Out of this city came the leading Italian *ars nova* composer, Francesco Landini (1325–1397). He lost his eyesight as a child through smallpox, and despite this handicap became very proficient in music theory and composition and as an organist. A cursory examination of his total creative output shows the great inroads that secular musical expression had made in Italy during the fourteenth century. Landini's extant works include 91 two-part and 49 three-part *ballate,* one *caccia,* and twelve *madrigals.* The *ballata* (plural *ballate*), is a polyphonic vocal composition for two or three voice parts, and is laid out in the form ABBAA. The madrigal, likewise a polyphonic vocal composition for two or three voices, generally employed a pastoral or amatory text; its formal scheme was AAB or AAAB. The *caccia,* meaning a hunt or chase, was a very popular fourteenth-century Italian composition consisting of two vocal parts in canonic form and usually based on a text dealing with hunting or fishing. A third part, an accompaniment, was played on an instrument.

From a fourteenth-century Italian Madrigal

The distinctive musical styles and techniques of Landini, as would be expected, are indicative of the new humanistic movement—full of color, rhythmic vitality, and individual expression. Above all, we note a tendency to place emphasis on sonority achieved through rich harmonies abounding with full triads, and a general avoidance of the harsh seconds and sevenths that were so prevalent in the *ars antiqua*. A particular favorite device is his use of the melodic progression, 7, 6, 8, at the cadence, which modern scholars have labeled the *Landini cadence*. (See Glossary).

In general, the Italian masters did not show the strong interest in the purely intellectual or abstruse devices employed by their French *ars nova* neighbors. Instead they strove for an emotional expression set in short forms with particular emphasis on the singing, lyrical melodic line.

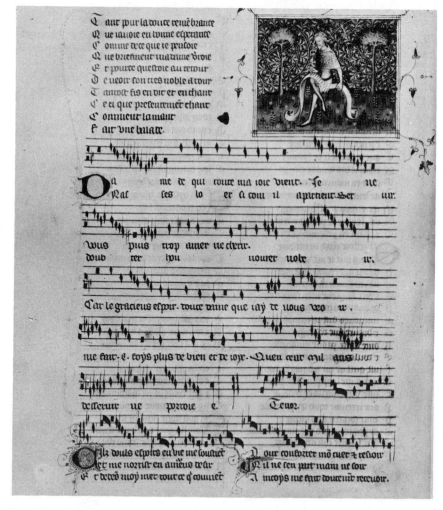

French Ars Nova Notation. From a ballade by Machaut. Bibliothèque Nationale, Paris

The French Ars Nova   Guillaume de Machaut (pron. *ma-show*), the outstanding French composer of the fourteenth century, was born in the northern French province of Champagne about the year 1300. Although educated as a cleric (and in fact he took holy orders at an early age), he served for approximately twenty years as a secretary to John of Luxembourg, King of Bohemia. Later he entered upon a life as musician in various royal French courts, including the service of the Duchess of Normandy and King Charles V. Following his appointment as canon at Rheims Cathedral, he continued in this position until his death in 1377.

The works of Machaut, which, incidentally, have been preserved in perfect form, include a mass for four voices (*Messe de Notre Dame*), 23 motets, 42 ballades, 21 rondeaux, 33 chanson balladées, and 19 lais. This listing shows not only a strong interest in sacred composition but a greater productivity in the secular forms. The 23 motets, for the most part, adhere to the *ars antiqua* style: three or four voice parts, a liturgical tenor sung or performed on an instrument, and different texts in the upper voices. A very distinctive feature in Machaut's motets is the use of the *isorhythmic* device; that is, a rhythmic pattern (called *talea*) and a melody are repeated many times in the tenor part. The French propensity for subtle and abstruse techniques is also shown in his utilization of a very intricate rhythmic structure and *hocket* (Latin, meaning *hiccup*, in which two voice parts alternate several notes with rests). Clearly absent now are the old modal rhythms.

The most outstanding achievement in sacred music of this age is represented in Machaut's *Messe de Notre Dame* (*Mass of Our Lady*), completed about 1364. It holds considerable historical significance since it is one of the first known complete settings of the Ordinary of the Mass. (Later, in the next century, the setting of the five divisions of the Ordinary: Kyrie, Gloria, Credo, Sanctus, and Agnus Dei, becomes a regular practice among the Burgundian composers). Prior to Machaut the medieval composers of polyphony, such as Léonin and Pérotin, favored the Proper of the Mass (see Glossary), setting numerous Alleluias and Graduals in polyphonic textures. This is not to say that composers did not write music for the Ordinary, but that as a general rule there was no attempt to compose a complete and unified mass setting such as we find in the Machaut *Messe de Notre Dame*. Here is heard a very quaint style of counterpoint based on four voice parts, which frequently move in parallel fashion (reminiscent still of the earliest organum, but which soon will be discarded until the twentieth century). Also appearing are frequent incomplete chords, isorhythm, ancient modes, and sharp dissonances. The voice parts correspond approximately to our soprano, alto, and tenor; as yet the bass range is not established. Truly, Machaut's sacred works, with their complex structures, soaring melodic lines, and lofty character exemplify the Gothic spirit of intellectual mysticism.

It is in Machaut's secular works that we find more of the true spirit of the *ars nova*. In many of his secular forms he abandoned the cantus firmus idea, as well as the principle of successive counterpoint, and intro-

duced a new style referred to as "melody with accompaniment." This
concept is a landmark in music history, since it indicates the general
beginnings of "vertical hearing," which gradually forms the basis of the
harmonic as opposed to the contrapuntal style. Toward the end of the
Renaissance the harmonic technique is firmly established.

Ballade, Guillaume de Machaut

Innovations in Notation: de Vitry   At the bottom of much of the technical
development in music of this age is the work of Philippe de Vitry. In
1320 he wrote his important treatise on music theory, the *Ars Nova,* in
which he expounded on the principles of binary rhythm and advanced the
techniques of musical notation. Composers thus now had at their disposal
a clear method for indicating duple and triple meter, and two new signs
for notes shorter than the semibreve (◆): the minim (♩) and the semi-
minim (♪). The central feature of the de Vitry method is the distinctive
way in which he designated duple and triple meters. For duple, a half
circle is written at the beginning of the music; triple meter is indicated
by a complete circle. There are many other interesting features of the
de Vitry system that the reader may wish to investigate in further study.

     Most of Machaut's music is written in the de Vitry method of nota-
tion. In contrast to the more squarelike figures of the *ars antiqua,* French
ars nova notation makes use of more streamlined diamond shapes. The
notes, which are frequently given stems as in modern notation, are black
except for occasional red notes, which are employed to indicate a *hemiola*
(a change in meter from triple to duple).

INSTRUMENTAL MUSIC OF THE LATE MIDDLE AGES

The Gothic Instruments

Before turning to Gothic instrumental practices, let us briefly outline the principal instruments of the age. Since these are still undeveloped in terms of homogeneous families, it will be expedient to present them according to the basic method of tone production.

Chordophones (1) *Vielle:* Sachs believes that the vielle was the principal instrument in the music life of the medieval world. It is a continuation of the Romanesque fiddle or vielle, normally built in the shape of a guitar, and equipped with five strings. (2) *Lyre:* A small harplike instrument held in the arms. (3) *Clavichord:* An oblong wooden box containing approximately fifteen strings running lengthwise, which when struck by metal *tangents,* produced a metallic effect. (4) *Harpsichord:* This crude predecessor of the baroque form was fitted with a number of strings, which were plucked by *plectrums.* (5) *Hurdy-gurdy:* A mechanical fiddle in which a revolving wheel rubbed the strings, also called *organistrum.* (6) *Lute:* A pear-shaped body fitted with a varied number of strings, which were plucked with the fingers. (7) *Rebec:* A shoulderless, long, thin, stringed instrument of Eastern origin. (8) *Psaltery:* A small, wing-shaped zither whose strings were plucked. (9) *Dulcimer:* A small zither whose strings were struck with small hammers.

Aerophones (1) *Recorder:* A small wooden pipe with six or seven finger holes, possesses a flutelike tone. (2) *Shawm* (called *piffero* in Italy): Also a wooden pipe with a double reed and finger holes, predecessor of modern oboe. (3) *Trumpet:* This instrument evolved into two forms in the late Middle Ages: (a) the *clarion,* consisting of a three-foot straight metal tubing, small bore, cup-mouthpiece and high pitch; in the fourteenth century it is called the trumpet and appears in folded form. (b) The *buzine,* introduced about 1200 or earlier by the Crusaders from the East; it is approximately six feet in length, straight, conical, low-pitched, and fitted with a mouthpiece. (4) *Sackbut* (or French, *saqueboute,* meaning *push-pull*): This evolved from the older *buzine* by adding a slide mechanism. The oldest drawings show the same structure as the modern trombone. (5) *Cornett* (old English spelling for cornet): A wooden instrument with finger holes and cup-mouthpiece, it evolved into a slender form in the fourteenth century from the more ancient, funnel-shaped horn style dating from Romanesque England. (6) *Bagpipes.* (7) *Organ:* This instrument appeared in two forms: (a) the *portative,* dating from the twelfth century, was held by a sling over the shoulder; the left hand worked the feeder bellows while the right pulled slides; beginning in the thirteenth century actual keys were introduced. (b) The second type of organ, the *positive,* or stationary, form, had its ancient (Romanesque age) slides replaced by levers in the thirteenth century, followed by modern black and white keys in the four-

Minnesinger Playing the Vielle, about 1300. From the Manesse Manuscript, Heidelberg University Library

teenth century. Organs were of a three-octave range and were the first instruments to become entirely chromatic. In the fourteenth century Machaut referred to the organ as the "king of instruments."

Membranophones (1) *Tambourine:* A small round frame fitted with a stretched skin top and bottom and jingles on the side. (2) *Tabor:* A small drum struck with sticks, similar to the modern snare-drum principle.

Idiophones (1) *Cymbals.* (2) *Bells:* Frequently hung in tuned series. (3) *Triangle:* A small metal bar bent into a triangular shape.

Gothic Performance Practices

Background   The instrumental ensemble continued to exist in a rather primitive state in the late Middle Ages. It did not as yet stand as a fully formed independent art form, for still unborn was the practice of writing ensemble music for specific types of instruments. The preparatory development prior to the emergence of the established ensemble began to take place near the end of the Gothic period, when instruments were grouped according to *haut* (loud) and *bas* (soft) qualities.

Not until 1500 do we find the appearance of ensemble music having clearly designated parts. Up to that time instruments either (1) reinforced or duplicated the voice parts in vocal music, (2) performed music by rote or note (for undesignated instruments), or (3) played adaptations of vocal music, a procedure that became increasingly popular by 1500. The principal activities in which the Gothic instrumentalists took part included such sacred presentations as liturgical drama, religious processions, and mystery plays; and, in the secular realm, minstrel entertainment and civic tower music ceremonies.

The Church's View   What was the Church's attitude concerning instrumental music in the Gothic age? The reader may recall that in general the early ecclesiastics looked upon liturgical instrumental performance with disfavor. However, a number of sources show that instruments were played in the church, perhaps not liturgically, with increasing popularity during the period 1200–1300. Ernst Meyer contends that the Church attempted to strengthen its position among the masses through the appeal of instrumental music.

After 1300 the officials apparently altered their views and again made vehement attacks on instruments, with the exception of the organ, which, of course, had been accepted earlier in the actual Church service. Despite these attacks it seems likely that even after 1300 one or two instruments, though not designated in music manuscript, continued the *ars antiqua* practice of supporting voice parts in liturgical performance. The absence of texts in many voice parts seems to further substantiate this point of view.

Although the ecclesiastics generally disapproved of their use in the service, instruments were an important part in peripheral activities of the Church such as religious processions, liturgical drama, and mystery plays. And what is even more interesting is that the performers included minstrels. According to Edmund Bowles, "the most splendid of all religious processions during the Middle Ages was held during the Corpus Christi festival which was instituted by Pope Urban IV in 1262 to be held on the first Thursday following Trinity Sunday." The central feature of this gigantic ceremony was a parade of clergy and laymen, who escorted the sacrament through the city after Mass.

Upon the issuance of a bull by Pope John XXII in 1316, the Corpus Christi festival was established as part of canon law and the practice spread quickly throughout Europe. In addition to a colorful array of personages, including clerics, priests, city fathers, singers, deacons, and the bishop, many minstrels took part, playing trumpets, vielles, guitars, and lutes. The Spanish festivals apparently favored stringed instruments, for frequently cited in the sources are guitars, vielles, and lutes. These instruments and others such as flutes and recorders often accompanied the vocalists in such forms as hymns, psalms, and motets evidently sung during the procession.

Instruments in Medieval Drama   The liturgical drama, which had begun as early as the tenth century with the addition of tropes to the Introits for Christmas and Easter, flourished in thirteenth-century France. Most of the liturgical dramas dealt with such subjects as the biblical "Story of Daniel," "The Plaint of Rachel," and the miracles of the Saints, which were generally referred to as *miracle plays,* such as the St. Nicholas miracle play. Although undesignated in the manuscripts, we know that instruments took part in these dramas. The literary and artistic sources refer to the use of the portative organ, vielle, bells, cymbals, trumpet, drums, recorder, and rebec, to name a few.

The faint beginnings of the modern opera are to be found in the so-called mystery plays, which were very popular in the fourteenth and fifteenth centuries. The "mystery" (corrupted form of the Latin *ministerium,* meaning *service*), which was an outgrowth of the liturgical drama, continued with dramatic representations based on biblical subjects such as the Creation and the Acts of the Apostles. Music was used only incidentally in these plays, for popular songs, processions, and fanfares.

During the fourteenth century, particularly in England, the mystery play underwent considerable secularization: laymen rather than clergy became the actors, Latin was replaced by the vernacular, and the play was staged in the public square. Other changes took place, such as the discarding of the serious atmosphere and purpose of the earlier representations; instead, satirical plays on contemporary life with interjections of comedy and dancing appeared. Minstrels often participated in these plays by providing instrumental music that appealed to the public. The record books of the various theater companies give some indication of the instruments employed by the minstrels, for we find pipes, flutes, drums, harps, and fifes frequently listed.

In all of these early instrumental performances—the religious processions, liturgical drama, and mystery—the instruments were grouped together heterogeneously. A mixture of chordophones, aerophones, idiophones, and membranophones abound in historical documents, art miniatures, poetic and literary references, and sculptural decorations dating from the early Middle Ages. The conscious selection of instruments based on tone quality, technical capabilities, blending characteristics, range, and acoustical needs was unknown until society developed an environment conducive to the growth of secular music. With the rise of monarchies and particularly the wealthy classes, beginning in the fourteenth century, instruments began to move toward the foreground in European life.

Emergence of the Wind Ensemble   It is difficult to comprehend that the orchestra that finally appeared in the Baroque period (1600–1750) evolved from the crude instrumental practices of the Middle Ages. Chief among these are the early *tower* ceremonies on the Continent, and the *minstrel* and *wait* activities in England. In all three, aerophones were highly favored; in fact, they were the first instruments to become organized as a homogeneous performing group. Later in the Renaissance certain forms of chordophones (specifically, viols[2]) were fully developed into an ensemble, and by 1500 became a very important part of English and European musical culture. By 1600 various aerophones, and chordophones merged to form the rudimentary beginnings of the orchestra.

The medieval groups of instrumentalists known as *tower musicians* on the Continent, and as *waits* and *minstrels* in England, constitute the most important beginnings of the wind ensemble. The first two date back to the early Middle Ages, when they were employed to stand guard on the city or courtyard walls and towers and to sound the alarm for fires and approaching enemies; the latter were the king's and noblemen's personal musicians. Existing records tend to show that the tower musicians on the Continent were the first to become organized into performing ensembles.

In Siena, Italy, about 1275, six musicians were employed by the city to play at ceremonies and state banquets in addition to their protectorate duties. The instruments played were generally of the trumpet and horn class, and usually included the shawm. Undoubtedly, carrying power and brilliance of effect were uppermost in the selection of these instruments. In 1479, the German equivalent to the tower bands, the *Stadtpfeifers* became established in Leipzig. These state musicians were given a uniform and a yearly wage, for which they played mainly at weddings, processions, and public ceremonies.

In England, the minstrels contributed significantly to the development of the ensemble by their practice of grouping instruments according to tonal quality—a pattern that becomes fairly consistent in the fourteenth and fifteenth centuries. The English waits, on the other hand, did not emerge as a dominant force in ensemble music until later in the Renaissance, when they appeared under the aegis of the municipality. Up to about 1400 they were primarily guardians in royal households. In subsequent pages we will examine their role in Renaissance instrumental music.

Gradually, beginning in the fourteenth century, there is a definite trend toward combining instruments according to loud and soft families, particularly in England among the minstrels. Perhaps the clearest description of the "loud" and "soft" instruments is to be found in the anonymous fourteenth-century poem *Les Echecs Amoureux:*

> When people wish to dance, or to stage a grand celebration, the loud (*haut*) instruments are played, for their great noise pleases the dancers better; they include trumpets, tabors, nakers, cymbals, bagpipes, shawms and cornetts. But when less noise is required one plays taborpipes, flutes and doucaines, which are soft and sweet, and other such soft (*bas*) instruments.[3]

[2] Predecessors of the modern, bowed, stringed instruments.
[3] Anthony Baines, *Woodwind Instruments and Their History* (New York: W. W. Norton and Company, Inc., 1957), p. 232.

In addition to the independent or itinerant minstrels who did much to spread secular music in English towns and hamlets, the dependent or established minstrels in the royal court also contributed to the growth of instrumental music, particularly wind instruments. An examination of the royal records dating from the beginning of the fourteenth century reveals a definite trend in this regard. For example, contained in the records of Edward III (reigned 1327–1377) are indications of the rising number of brass instruments that were becoming established in the royal court of this period: five trumpets, two clarions, five pipes, three waits (shawms), and a drum. Further evidence of the emerging wind band in England is provided by a report of a mummer parade for Prince Richard in 1377, which included over a hundred disguised horsemen, some equipped with trumpets, sackbuts, cornetts, and shawms.

During the reign of Edward IV (1461–1483) the court minstrel band was given its first real advancement, professionally and musically speaking. Aside from maintaining a band of trumpets, shawms, and pipes, Edward granted the minstrels a royal charter (1469) to protect their station from being usurped by artificers. It was the first attempt to clarify the functions and privileges of the king's band. Here, then, is the beginning of the organized wind band in the court.

Agincourt Carol; composed in commemoration of Henry V's victory over the French at Agincourt (1415)

The Repertory of English Instrumentalists   Although there is considerable data indicating the existence of group instrumental performance in England during the Middle Ages, the earliest actual music written for instruments (undesignated) originated in the thirteenth century. This music may be placed into two categories: polyphonic instrumental dance music called *estampies*, and *conducti caudae*. The estampie, which we mentioned as having originated in France near the end of the twelfth century, probably found its way into English secular life either through the dissemination of the minstrels or through the scholarly intercourse that prevailed between England and France during the Gothic age. The English musicologist Dom Anselm Hughes reports that several estampie dance pieces were found in the same English manuscript as the famed *Sumer Is Icumen In*, which dates from England in the late thirteenth century.

Another important source of music is the thirteenth-century vocal form known as the *conductus cum cauda*, which contains instrumental-like sections as preludes, interludes, or as finales in the conductus proper. Because of their textless and dancelike character, many writers believe they were played by instruments such as vielles, recorders, or shawms. Several examples of this type were found in a manuscript (dated about 1250) at St. Andrew's in Scotland. These dance tunes, like their counterparts the estampies, are mainly in two parts, and in all respects resemble the estampie pieces. Above all, we note the distinctive, lilting rhythmic figures and the gay secular feeling that is imbued in most of these English dance tunes.

In the fourteenth century the English minstrels' repertory included the estampie and undoubtedly the popular Italian dance forms, the *saltarello* and *trotto*, which are to be found in several English sources. According to the writings of the period the estampies and the Italian dance tunes were probably played most frequently by vielles and recorders.

The later court bands of the established English minstrels (after 1300) may have also played the *carol*, a gay, dancelike form that dates back to earlier times. As to the popularity of the carol as a secular form in the years when the English ensemble was being formed in the court, we need only cite several references. One of the earliest dates from about the time of Edward II (reigned 1307–1327), according to Ritson:[4]

Now gynnith the geste of nobles	Now begins the festival of nobles
At theo feste was trympying,	At the celebration was trumpeting,
Pipyng and ek taboryng	Piping and tabor-playing
Systolyng and ek harpyng	Sistol (guitar) and harp-playing
Kyyg pleyng and ek syngyng	King playing and singing
Carolyng and turmetyng	*Caroling* and tournamenting
Wrastlyng and ek flymyng,	Wrestling and running about,

From a slightly later date (1400) an interesting account of the minstrels' instrumental accompaniment in the carol is given in the romance of Sir Cleges. On Christmas eve "he recollects how he has spent all his estate on the great feasts that he held at Christmas time":[5]

[4] Joseph Ritson, *Ancient Songs and Ballads* (London: Reeves and Turner, 3d ed., 1877), p. 1. (Translation by Dr. Joseph Jenks.)

[5] Richard Greene, *A Selection of English Carols* (Oxford: The Clarendon Press, 1962), p. 28. (Translation by Dr. Joseph Jenks.)

Sore syzthyng, he hard a sovne
  of dyvers mynstrelse:
	Sadly sighing, he heard a sound
	  of diverse minstrels:

Of Trompus, pypus, and
  clareaneris,
Of harpis, luttis and getarnys,
  a sitole and sawtre
	Of trumpets, pipes and clarions,
	Of harps, lutes, and getarns, a
	  sistole and psaltery

Many carellys and gret
  davnsyng;
On euery syde he harde syng-
  yng, in euery place trewly.
	Many carols and great dancing;
	On every side he heard singing,
	  in every place truly.

Except for a few isolated examples, the music of the carols prior to 1400 is not extant. The largest collection of carol music is from the fifteenth century. The singular character of most of these pieces—a lilting secular rhythm—must have been present in previous carols due to the dance origins of this form, which go back to the medieval French *carole,* a secular round dance. Greene states that the dance carol was known in England after the Norman invasion, if not before. By around 1550 the nonreligious carol was replaced by the sacred Christmas carol. Let it suffice to state that the bulk of the fifteenth-century carols are identified by a pronounced dancelike movement, a two-part polyphony, and definite metrical feeling. Though these fifteenth-century carols bear what Bukofzer calls "the mark of composed art," they show the popular appeal of its melody and uncomplicated harmony, and moreover "repeated notes, simple and often angular melodic lines, and harmonic simplicity . . . still remind one that the carol was once a dance."[6]

Summary

The Gothic age was a great age for arts and ideas. The intellectual power that had placed God at the center of all man's activities in the Romanesque now humanized religion and art. Human reason and the spiritual, considered complementary by the Scholastics, worked together to build towering monuments of stone, sound, and words. Musical art, like architecture, strove heavenward for perfection, resulting in many significant achievements: (1) an expansion of sacred musical forms (motet and a complete setting of the Ordinary of the Mass), (2) an advancement in the techniques of composition (isorhythm and hocket), and (3) an improved system of notation that now permitted the designation of exact note lengths and notes of smaller value.

[6] Manfred Bukofzer, "Popular and Secular Music in England," *The New Oxford History of Music,* Vol. 3 (London: Oxford University Press, 1960), p. 122.

With the eclipse of the Gothic in the fourteenth century, there appeared a definite trend toward the things of this world. Thus, greater recognition was given to popular or native art among the elite, particularly in Italy, where the famous Medici family began to emerge as the leading cultural patron in Europe, and in England, where the royal court fostered the rise of organized minstrel music. This unprecedented surge in secular art produced numerous new musical forms, such as the madrigal, caccia, saltarello, and ballade. The minstrel activities provided two very important contributions to the foundations of English music: first, the spirit of native English music characterized by a joyful secular gaeity and, second, the rudimentary beginnings of the instrumental ensemble.

REPRESENTATIVE WORKS IN THE
HUMANITIES: GOTHIC ERA (1150-1400)

MUSIC

(thirteenth century, the *ars antiqua*)
Music activity continues to be dominated by the Notre Dame group.
New forms: *motet, rota* (round), *polyphonic conductus.*
Ars Cantus Mensurabilis (*Art of Measured Music*) by Franco of Cologne.

(fourteenth century, the Ars Nova)
Era of great advancement in secular music, centered in Italy and France.
New Italian secular music forms: *caccia, ballata, madrigal.*
New French secular music forms: *ballade, virelais, rondeau.*
Acceptance of duple meter.
First polyphonic setting of the mass by Machaut (*Messe de Notre Dame*)

PHILOSOPHY

Thomas Aquinas (1225-1274), *Summa Theologica* (the epitome of medieval scholasticism)
Roger Bacon (1214-1294), *Opus maius* (Major Opus)
John Duns Scotus (1265-1308), *Opus Oxoniense* (*Oxford Opus*)
William of Ockham (1280-1349), *Commentary on the Books of Sentences*
John Wycliffe (1320-1384), *Trialogus,* also Bible translation

LITERATURE

Vincent of Beauvais (fl. 1250), *Speculum maius* (an encyclopedia of medieval learning)
Dante Alighieri (1265-1321), *Divina Commedia*
Francesco Petrarch (1304-1374), *Sonnets*
Boccaccio (1313-1375), *Decameron*
Geoffrey Chaucer, (1345-1400), *Canterbury Tales*

ART

Noted Gothic structures:
> Chartres rebuilt 1224
> Notre Dame begun 1163, completed 1235
> Amiens begun 1220, completed 1280
> Rheims begun 1211, continued to 1427
> Mont-Saint-Michel completed 1250

Niccola Pisano revived the classical inspiration in sculpture, Pisa, c. 1260.
Giotto (c. 1267–1337) founded the Renaissance style of painting.
Florence as center of art, beginning about 1340.

HISTORICAL EVENTS

1200   University of Paris formally chartered
1209   St. Francis of Assisi (1182–1226) founded the Franciscan order
1209   Cambridge University founded
1215   Magna Carta signed
1231   Inquisition begins, Gregory IX
1273   Hapsburg family founded by Rudolph
1295   First modern parliament in England
1300   Feudalism declines; absolute monarchies rise
1320   Term *ars nova* applied to new art by Philippe de Vitry
1324   Papal Bull by John XXII decried the musical excesses in liturgy
1337   Outbreak of 100 Years War
1349   Black Death
1376   Wycliffe's translation of the Bible
1377   Death of Machaut, France's leading composer of ars nova
1378   Beginning of Papal Schism
1397   Death of Landini, Italy's leading composer of ars nova

5

THE RENAISSANCE

(1400–1600)

BACKGROUND

The Renaissance is the name of a many-sided
but yet united movement, in which the love of
the things of the intellect and the imagination
for their own sake . . . make themselves felt.
            Walter Pater, *The Renaissance*

The Nature of the Renaissance

Although generally thought of as embracing the fifteenth and sixteenth
centuries, the boundaries of the Renaissance, as with any period, are not
clearly defined. However, there can be little doubt that the fifteenth century was the time of a gigantic intellectual and artistic awakening. Men
of this epoch witnessed such an intense stirring of ideas and artistic
inspiration that they regarded their age as a renascence, a time of rebirth
and revival, an awakening of man to the world of ideas, beauty, imagination, discovery, and experimentation.

This intellectual renewal was felt in all aspects of human existence:
art, music, politics, religion, literature, science, and geographical exploration. The spirit of the Renaissance spread northward from Florence the
city of its birth, and gradually permeated the important centers of Europe.
Thus, the movement reached its full expression in the various countries
at different times, moreover, the artistic achievements were different for
each country. For example, Italy produced her greatest works in the
plastic arts, the Low Countries excelled in choral music and painting, and
England contributed most significantly in drama and instrumental music.

A knowledge of the intellectual and artistic undercurrents, and
particularly the common artistic gestures, qualities, and attitudes analogous

to all of the arts, will obviously lead to a deeper understanding of Renaissance music. Hence, the essential preliminary questions with which we are concerned are: What effect did the new wave of intellectual thought and artistic consciousness have upon musical creativity? And secondly, what is the stylistic relationship of music to the other fine arts? Since a complex interaction took place in the arts and society, space permits only a brief summary of the principal shaping forces of the period and the ensuing stylistic directions in art in general and music in particular.

Humanism The humanistic movement that had begun as early as Petrarch and Boccaccio in the fourteenth century was one of the dominant forces that brought forth profound changes in European thought and culture during the Renaissance. The first humanists were scholars who championed the revival of ancient Greek and Roman classics. In the Renaissance the term humanism took on a much broader meaning, referring generally to a multifaceted attitude that emphasized a love of this life, its sights, sounds, and sensations, as opposed to the asceticism of medieval man. Also characteristic of the humanistic view is a great and unbounded interest in art, letters and scholarship, classical ideals and studies, and a recognition of the worth and dignity of man and his capacity to achieve self realization through the power of the intellect.

Hence, the typical man of the Renaissance elite was a many-sided man with varied intellectual and cultural interests, such as philosophy, music, painting, sculpture, and particularly literature. To the humanist, language and literary skills were of upmost importance. His veneration of the Latin classics and his polished and refined use of the language stand out as the major characteristics of the Renaissance learned man. Interestingly, the composers of this age, especially those of the sixteenth century, are equally adept in musical and literary matters.

In the fine arts, humanism became manifested in a new esthetic arising from man's awareness of the world and his increased powers of aural and visual perception. Patterns, colors, shapes, lines, gestures, sounds, and subject matter derived from or associated with a wider range of human experience are now present in the arts. For example, we may speak of certain *humanistic traits* (as opposed to the more ascetic, other-worldly traits of the medieval period) such as a concern for (1) richness of visual and tonal color (illustrated in the Netherlanders' new oil techniques and in their rich, sonorous masses and motets); (2) the glorification of the human figure (sculptures and paintings by Michelangelo and Leonardo da Vinci); (3) sensual perception (the paintings of Giorgione and Titian); (4) lifelike poses and expressions (the works of Raphael and Michelangelo); (5) human tragedy and comedy (the plays of Shakespeare); and (6) the rhythmic pulse of the dance (Elizabethan dance pieces for keyboard and ensemble). In essence, humanism inspired the creative mind to seek out new artistic means for expressing an enriched gamut of feelings and emotions now brought to the artist's conscious level.

Humanism was not a popular movement among the masses but was confined to artists, scholars, and interested patrons. It was fostered chiefly by the elite class and humanistic popes. Humanism brought the world of art and ideas to a higher plane; moreover, the movement encouraged the habit of regarding intellectual and artistic activities as valuable social ventures to be highly prized and sought after. Clearly, it removed the fine arts from their former cloistered setting and brought them out into the light of day for esthetic contemplation by society.

Other Undercurrents: Reformation and Counter Reformation   Paradoxically, although the secular way of life (worldly affairs, money, banking, and trade) thrived in the Renaissance, the sacred expression predominated in European fine arts. In England, however, the secular mode became well established in the latter part of the sixteenth century. Two underlying factors seem to account for the continuation of the sacred theme in music and painting. First, the Church's extensive history as the chief patron of the arts—a position that was gradually usurped by wealthy private patronage at this time—and, secondly, the Church's attempt to buttress itself against the encroachments of Luther's Reformation.

The Protestant Reformation begun by Martin Luther in 1517 was preceded by numerous reform movements, which the Church dismissed as heresies (the Waldensians under Peter Waldo in France during the twelfth century, the Lollards under John Wycliffe in fourteenth-century England, and the Hussites under John Huss in Bohemia in the fifteenth century). When Luther posted the ninety-five theses (1517) attacking the sale of papal indulgences, the time was ripe for a reform movement, since Luther had the backing of many German princes and militant peasants. With the subsequent formulation of the Augsburg Confession in 1530, the Lutheran Church was established in most of the German states.

A central tenet of the new faith was the direct relationship of man and God without an intermediary church or priest. Hence, the hierarchical system of the Catholic Church and its elaborate external rites and ceremonies were replaced by a simpler version of Christian faith that emphasized the morality of Gospel love. Luther introduced into the Lutheran service numerous musical innovations which will be touched upon in subsequent pages.

Following the surge of German Protestantism and other movements, such as England's break with Rome in 1534, the Catholic Church sought to strengthen its position by unifying its practices and reaffirming traditional beliefs and principles. The Council of Trent, which met sporadically from 1545 to 1563, had a noticeable effect on the arts. In its attempt to purify religious arts, this body of Catholic reformers criticized some artists for various flagrancies, such as the excessive display of the nude figure and the use of too many worldly elements in religious paintings. Some composers were censured for mixing secular themes in the mass and for their employment of elaborate counterpoint, which obscured the words. The over-all effect of the Counter Reformation upon sacred music was, however, of significant scope. Under the leadership of Palestrina (1525–1594), the polyphony of the Catholic Church reached its ultimate state of refinement, principally in the countries of Italy and Spain.

Invention of Printing   The progress of humanism was greatly accelerated by the invention of printing. The Gutenberg invention of movable type (1454) opened up new vistas for education—it freed learning from its dependence upon scribes, who laboriously reproduced manuscripts at great expense, and also rapidly increased the circulation of knowledge that was once confined to a few church scholars.

Advancement was also made in music printing in the second half of the fifteenth century, notably in Rome and Venice where liturgical books (missals) were printed. These were prepared in a two-step operation called the "double impression method" whereby the staff and notes were printed separately. The standard practice followed for most liturgical music during the Renaissance was to print the staff lines in red and the notes in black. In 1501 Ottaviano dei Petrucci of Venice published the first book of printed part music using metal type and multiple impressions. This significant contribution, entitled *Harmonice Musices Odhecaton,* consists of ninety-six secular pieces (chansons) of three and four parts.

Italy—The Starting Point of the Renaissance   Intellectual fermentation and social and economic change worked together in bringing about the Renaissance, which first took hold in Italy. The intellectual progress stemmed, as we have already noted, from the rise of humanism among scholars, writers, and artists, who shook off the limited and outmoded concepts of the medieval period. Italy began to assume economic leadership in the Middle Ages as a result of her establishment of sea routes in the Eastern Mediterranean and land routes to the Low Countries in the north. Venice, Genoa, and Florence rose to commercial prominence, the latter becoming a center of money lending, banking, and textile manufacturing at the dawn of the Renaissance.

Other factors contributed to Italy's dominance: her commercial supremacy arising from a system of modern banking as opposed to the medieval barter system, and particularly the Italian city states' disdain for the feudal order and church control so firmly entrenched in the northern countries. However, in the late Renaissance (sixteenth century), due to geographical discovery the commercial center shifted to the Atlantic seaboard, where new trade routes were created by Spain and England. With the exception of choral polyphony, which was the invention of the Netherlands' composers, Renaissance art and ideas moved northward in this period of economic expansion. But the cultural center was still located in Italy, specifically in Florence during the early Renaissance and Rome in the late or High Renaissance.

Origins of Renaissance Art   The primal stage of Renaissance art dates back to the late medieval period—the dawn of the Renaissance—and most notably to Niccola Pisano, Italian sculptor of the thirteenth century, and to Giotto, an Italian painter of the early fourteenth century. Pisano (c. 1225– c. 1284) is usually cited for his distinctive use in sculpture of the classic or Greco-Roman tradition, which stressed monumentality, calm serenity, and lifelike features. His break from the then-current Byzantine and

Giotto di Bondone, *Flight into Egypt*. Fresco Arena Chapel, Padua. Alinari, Art Reference Bureau

Romanesque decorative sculpture to a Greco-Roman conception (free-standing figures, not integrated with the architectural background), marks Pisano as a forerunner of the Renaissance.

Giotto (1267–1337), who is generally regarded as the founder of the Renaissance style of painting, departed from the medieval tradition of symbolical treatment of subject matter and instead created works based on direct observation of the world. In addition to painting figures possessing human features (smiling faces, uplifted eyes, postures that bespeak feeling and fullness of body), Giotto replaced flatness and hollow space with bulk and depth. In the works of Giotto and Pisano are the traits that foreshadow the coming of the artistic credo of the Italian Renaissance: a lifelike quality in painted and sculptured figures in contrast to the more rigid and ethereal forms of the medieval period, a personal characterization as opposed to the impersonal expression of the preceding era, and the use of monumental form as opposed to the decorative mode typical of the Middle Ages.

Early Italian and Flemish Art

During the early Renaissance (fifteenth century) the leading artistic centers were Italy and Flanders; both instituted independent and concurrent movements in art. Italian art of the fifteenth century represents the initiatory period of the Renaissance, a time when the foundations for drawing and painting for all of the Renaissance and even subsequent periods were laid. Italian artists experimented with new principles of anatomy, perspective, space, and composition. In addition to casting off the supernatural figure style, they discarded the medieval prejudice toward nudity and created figures with exact anatomical structure and a living and breathing quality embodied in facial and muscular features. Among the leaders of this period are Masaccio (*The Expulsion of Adam and Eve*), Donatello (*David*), and Botticelli (*The Birth of Venus*).

Flemish Art Of equal prominence in music and art were the Low Countries (present-day Holland and Belgium). The group of artists who were active in this region are commonly called the Netherlands or Flemish School. Hubert and Jan van Eyck, generally referred to as the founders of the Netherlands School, established a style of painting that remained dominant until the end of the fifteenth century. The Flemish masters gave careful attention to fine details and texture (microscopic convention) and to precise description of objects presented in space (telescopic convention). The over-all effect is one of clarity and precision, resulting partly from the demanding medium (transparent oils) but more directly from the artists' attempt to produce an exact duplication of what the eye sees in nature. Examples of fifteenth-century Flemish art include *The Ghent Altarpiece, The Arnolfini Marriage,* and *The Madonna with Chancellor Rolin* by Jan van Eyck.

MUSIC IN THE EARLY RENAISSANCE (1400–1450)

Sacred polyphony, the chief mode of musical expression in the Renaissance, had its beginnings, not in southern Europe where humanism had its strongest hold, but in the northern region, where musical practices were firmly rooted in a tradition dating back to the early Middle

Sandro Botticelli, *Birth of Venus.* Tempera on canvas, 6'7" x 9'2". Uffizi, Florence

Ages. This tradition, the foundation of the Renaissance style, is essentially that of the majestic, reverent, and dignified melodic style derived from Gregorian chant. Other ingredients, of course, make up what is called the "Renaissance musical language," such as distinctive contrapuntal and harmonic techniques and treatment of musical form. These aspects of the Renaissance style or language were mastered by the fifteenth-century Netherlands composers and perfected by Netherlands-trained musicians in the sixteenth century. The latter, who had migrated throughout Europe by 1550, brought the sacred polyphonic style to its final peak of refinement and grandeur in the High Renaissance.

English Influence: The New Sonority Perhaps the most fundamental difference between medieval and Renaissance music is in the over-all sound or sonority. Medieval music has a more austere, dark-hued sound in contrast to the richer, brighter, more sonorous quality of the Renaissance. Specifically, the esthetic effect of medieval sonority, that is, its dark-hued quality, is attributed to the types of intervals used between the various melodic lines or parts. Generally, as we have seen, the perfect intervals—the octave, fifth, and fourth—were used, resulting in a quaint, archaic form of harmony. The more modern sounding third and sixth, the imperfect intervals (having less simple ratios), were not generally employed until the early Renaissance. The movement toward a richer sonority, based on a harmony of imperfect intervals, began in early fifteenth-century England and was subsequently taken up by the Netherlands composers. The leader in establishing the new harmonic sonority of the early Renaissance is the English composer John Dunstable (d. 1453). In addition to using the imperfect intervals, he arranged the tones of the triad in a new fashion—with the third of the chord ("E," for example, in the C E G chord) as the lowest tone in the bass. In modern theory practice this is referred to as the *first-inversion chord.* Dunstable frequently wrote harmonic passages in which a series of first-inversion chords were used. This type of harmonic writing was called *discant* in England and *fauxbourdon* on the Continent. The effect is one of richness and fullness of sound, as illustrated in this next example.

Lau - da - mus te.   Be - ne - di - ci - mus te.

× = First inversion

Example of the New Sonority, England late fourteenth century

Dunstable, who was mainly active on the Continent as musician to John, Duke of Bedford (Henry V's brother and Regent of France 1422–1435), apparently introduced British sonority to the Netherlands composers. Most of his work, and that of several other English composers, are found in Continental manuscripts of the period. Most of Dunstable's work consists of sacred pieces in three parts such as settings of hymns, antiphons, and motets. The historical importance of Dunstable is threefold; he was instrumental in (1) fostering the trend toward vertical thinking in musical creativity (homophonic texture), (2) establishing the complete triad (1 3 5), and (3) introducing the first-inversion chord into the harmonic vocabulary.

The Burgundians: Dufay   Taking the great heritage of Catholic Church music in general and the English concepts of sonority in particular, the first Netherlands composers (referred to more frequently as the Burgundians) assimilated these and other techniques and developed a musical style that became standard throughout Europe. The essential outlines of this style include: a preeminence of counterpoint written in four to six parts; purity and beauty of undecorated melodic line; slow, graceful, and dignified rhythmic movement; meticulous care in setting of Latin texts in sacred polyphony (as well as vernacular in secular polyphony); and the use of imitation as the basic principle of structural unification.

The first stage of the Renaissance style was completed in the first half of the fifteenth century by Burgundian musicians. These composers and musicians were so named because of their affiliation from 1419–1467

Jan van Eyck, *The Annunciation.* 1428. Panel (transferred to canvas), 36½ × 14⅜″. Washington, National Gallery of Art. Andrew Mellon Collection.

El Greco, *Burial of Count Orgaz.* 1586. Oil on canvas, 16′ × 11′10″. San Tomé, Toledo. Mas: Ampliaciones y Reproducciones.

Two panels from Ghent Altarpiece by Hubert and Jan Van Eyck. Panel 11'3" x 14'5".
Completed 1432. St. Bavo, Ghent. A.C.L.—Art Reference Bureau

with the court of Philip the Good, Duke of Burgundy. The dominions of
the Duchy of Burgundy comprised most of present-day Holland, Belgium,
northeast France, Luxembourg, and Lorraine. Not only was the court of
Philip the Good the most lavish and resplendent of all northern Europe,
but it was also the chief center of the arts. It was inevitable that such a
cosmopolitan court, whose outstanding musicians were drawn from
various regions, would develop a style of music that became universally
known and practiced in the leading courts of Europe. The spread of this
musical language during the course of the Renaissance was achieved through
artistic interchange often as a result of royal marriages, which by 1550
disseminated Burgundian culture and the Renaissance style throughout
Europe.

Among the Burgundian artistic coterie were the eminent painters
Jan van Eyck, and his successor Rogier van der Weyden and the leading composers Guillaume Dufay (pron. Du-fa-ee) and Gilles Binchois
(pron. Ban-shwa). Dufay, the master musician of the Burgundian school,
began his musical training as a chorister in the Cambrai Cathedral in

1409. During the early part of his career (from about 1420–1426) he was employed as a musician in the wealthy Italian court of the Malatesta family. His membership in the papal choir at Rome (1428–1437) led to numerous positions in the clerical realm, including canonries at the cathedrals of Tournai, Bruges, and Cambrai. At Cambrai Dufay resided on a more or less permanent basis from about 1440, supervising the cathedral's musical activities and contributing many sacred works to the choral repertory.

Frequent sojourns to Italy must have enabled Dufay to become familiar with Italian musical style, and more importantly to experience the artistic climate, which emphasized the classic ideals of balance, clarity, simplicity, and exactness of structure. The Italian experiences combined with his native northern background perhaps account for Dufay's unique historical position: on the one hand he continued the strong current of traditionalism and on the other he demonstrated the spirit of experimentation and innovation so characteristic of the early Renaissance artist. His creative output (predominantly sacred, with thirty-five mass movements and eight complete masses) and choice of forms (mass, motet, chanson) show a strong Gothic affinity, but his content has a modernistic flavor. In essence, Dufay began to instill a new blood into old forms.

Aside from the more obvious Gothic tendencies mentioned above, Dufay's traditional manner is further mirrored in his penchant for the cantus firmus principle (the use of a borrowed melody upon which a composition is constructed), the Landini cadence, and perfect chords at cadences. The more forward side of his creative nature is to be found in his complete assimilation of the English discant style, and the melodic use of the interval of a third—both of which give a brighter hue to the essentially somber mood of the mass and motet. Another interesting feature Dufay introduced is the stronger harmonic feeling at the cadences, where we perceive a more definite progression of the chords V to I.

There are other aspects of the basic Renaissance style which gradually evolved from Dufay and his followers: a homogeneous blend of all voice parts, rather than the heterogeneous mixture of voices and instruments characteristic of the medieval period; an increased range resulting from the addition of the bass part; group or choral performance rather than the soloistic (one voice to a part) rendition common to the Middle Ages; a highly specialized treatment of the mass form; and the universal employment of the compositional technique called *imitation*. The last two points need to be discussed further.

Dufay and his successors turned enthusiastically to writing settings of the mass, with the result that a larger quantity of music in this form was created than ever before. This increased interest in mass composition probably stemmed from a greater demand for the complete setting of it, since the Church now used the new form of the mass as a regular part of the service. The establishment of the complete Ordinary of the Mass as an accepted musical form is attributed to Dufay and his Burgundian colleagues. Prior to their time only parts of the mass were generally set to music, the noted exception being the famous *Messe de Notre Dame* by Machaut in the late fourteenth century.

Singers and Instrumentalists Performing in High Mass. Engraving 20″ x 12″ from *Encomium musices*, c. 1590. Courtesy, Music Library, Yale University

Furthermore, in the hands of the Burgundians all parts of the mass were occasionally unified through the repetition of short melodic figures (called *head motives*) in each of the five movements or sections. Later, Dufay also employed the same cantus firmus for all movements. A very striking feature that shows the inroads humanism had made by this time is the secular cantus firmus, that is, a popular tune of the day, appearing in the mass entitled *Se La Face Ay Pale* written by Dufay about 1460.

The Chief Vocal Forms of the Renaissance

The three principal vocal music forms up to mid-sixteenth century—the mass, motet, and chanson—are closely related: polyphonic in texture, written for voices, and of four to six parts. Distinct differences do exist, however. The mass is of considerable length, divided into five sections or movements of the Ordinary, uses a Latin sacred text and is usually of a dignified, majestic mood. The motet is shorter, in one continuous movement, draws upon a wide range of subject matter taken from the Bible and written in Latin. The Flemish or Netherlands chanson, that of Dufay, Binchois, and their successors Jan van Ockeghem and Josquin des Prez, is based on a French secular text (usually pastoral or amatory),

Filippo Brunelleschi. Façade, Pazzi Chapel, Cloister of Church of Santa Croce, Florence. Alinari, Art Reference Bureau.

and has the same polyphonic texture of the mass, including its continuous musical flow; however, there is some tendency toward a more rhythmic, pulsatile style. The sixteenth-century chanson is represented mainly by the French composers, Claudin de Sermisy and Clément Jannequin, and is highly rhythmic, pulsatile, in duple meter, usually in a light, almost homophonic texture, and has clear-cut phrases and section endings.

The Rise of a New Esthetic in Art and Music Another fundamental characteristic of Renaissance music is the extensive employment of the technique of imitation, which began to appear during the Burgundian era. Imitation refers to the use of the same or similar melodic ideas (usually short fragments) in different voice parts successively. The technique which dates from the early Middle Ages, became increasingly prevalent during the late fifteenth century. By 1500 it was an identifying feature of practically all polyphony.

The rapid rise of imitation at this time may have been influenced by the changing concepts that were affecting all art—namely the spread of the humanistic attitude and its reaffirmation of classic ideals in art. The movement that gave fuel to the spread of these ideals was *Neoplatonism,* centered in Florence. The restoration of Platonic doctrines as a result of the establishment of the Platonic Academy in Florence (1462) by Cosimo de' Medici, led to a concept of beauty in the arts that was markedly different from the medieval period.

Marsilio Ficino (1433–1499) who was commissioned by Cosimo de' Medici to translate the works of Plato, introduced a theory of art, largely drawn from Plato and his interpreters, which had a marked influence on late fifteenth- and early sixteenth-century artists. The principal tenet, which unquestionably strengthened the direction of art and music, was that "beauty can exist only when there is a harmony of parts, where no discordant element intrudes upon the balance and symmetry of the whole." Furthermore, "beauty is attained through relationships and correspondences between elements of the work."[1]

In art, this new esthetic came to be realized in a balanced and symmetrical arrangement of subject matter into geometrical formations such as the triangle, rectangle, quadrangle, and the most perfect of all geometrical forms, the circle. Moreover, a harmonious blending of colors was achieved by echoing or imitating colors from one part of the painting to another. In architecture, the esthetic was realized in uniform structures with balanced elements, simple undecorated lines, and regular placement of columns, doors, and windows. In general, the calm effect of the horizontal, rather than the restless vertical line of the Gothic, prevailed. Needless to say, the works of the Italian masters in painting, sculpture, and architecture—Michelangelo, Leonardo, Raphael, and Brunelleschi—exemplify this theory of art.

In music, the governing esthetic ideal emphasizing proportion, harmony, and relationship of parts is best seen at work in the Netherlanders' technique of imitation, purity of melodic line and harmony, and in the trend toward a perfect blend of all voices in choral performance. In conclusion, it might be said that the Burgundians initiated the ideal in musical art and that it was brought to fruition by composers in the High Renaissance.

MUSIC IN THE HIGH RENAISSANCE 1450–1600

Overview Renaissance music reached maturity during the period 1450–1600—extending from the time of the Flemish composer Josquin des Prez to the leading figure of Elizabethan England, William Byrd. At this point the Renaissance musical language, its techniques, forms, and performance

[1] Beckman C. Cannon, Alvin H. Johnson, and William G. Waite, *The Art of Music* (New York: Thomas Y. Crowell Company, 1960), pp. 148–149.

Time-Line: Late Renaissance Music

1501	Music Printing, Petrucci
1502	des Prez: *Missa L'Homme Arme*
1517	Luther introduces new musical practices in German Churches
1525	Palestrina born
1534	Beginning of Golden Age of English music
1540	William Byrd born
1550	Modern violin emerges
1560	Palestrina: *Pope Marcellus Mass* (c. 1555–1560)
1560	Carlo Gesualdo born (1560–1613) Madrigals in mannerist vein
1585	Giovanni Gabrieli, first organist, St. Mark's, Venice
1594	Death of Palestrina
1597	Gabrieli: *Sonata pian' e forte*
1599	Holborne: *Pavans & Galliards*

practices, attained a state of completion and mastery. However, the period was far from static. As in any period, new styles and forms began to emerge and to vie with the old. The new lines of development are particularly noticeable in the latter stages of the period, when definite murmurs of the baroque appear.

If one were to describe the state of the mainstream of music in the High Renaissance, the term "enriched" would perhaps be most appropriate. It was essentially the traditional musical language of the Burgundians enriched by the intermingling of both sacred and secular elements and geographical styles; predominantly the mystical, reserved expression of the north (Netherlands) and the clarity and warmth of the south (Italy), brought to perfection by such leading composers as Josquin des Prez, Orlando di Lasso, Giovanni Palestrina, and William Byrd.

The musical greatness of the High Renaissance is attributed partly to the unusual technical facility of the composers and, to a larger extent, to a new expressive quality arising from a fusion of words and music on a deeper, more emotional plane. Whereas formerly the composer was expressive in terms of his inner (religious) feelings, the High Renaissance composer was more profoundly affected by the climate of the outer world, with its vast array of new colors, sounds, and ideas. Moreover, the skilled Renaissance composer combined his humanistic literary talents and highly developed and refined musical techniques to produce tone paintings of both his inner and outer world.

The two principal classes of musical forms for these basic expressions were the sacred (mass and motet) and secular (chanson). The madrigal and many other new types of musical forms, including instrumental, arose after 1530, marking a definite tendency to pull away from the classical sacred style of the High Renaissance. This brief prelude to the Baroque period is called the *Mannerist Movement*, and marks the close of the Renaissance.

Artistic Climate of the High Renaissance   The sixteenth century represents an excellent example of stylistic unity in the fine arts. Not only do we find a close parallel between the main currents in art and music, that is, similar qualities and features, but also a similarity in the way the Renaissance style in art and music is transformed from classical serenity and beauty to the disturbed expression of the Mannerist Movement, culminating in the grand and ornate style of the Baroque.

Italy, the originating point of the Renaissance, was also the emanating source of inspiration for the High Renaissance. Leonardo, Bramante, Machiavelli, Castiglione, Raphael, and Michelangelo, the giants of the Italian Renaissance, completed their work in the last part of the fifteenth and early sixteenth centuries. By 1530 all of these leading figures were deceased with the exception of Michelangelo, who lived well into the Mannerist period. Thus, the Italian High Renaissance covered roughly eighty years, from about 1450 to the year 1530, the approximate starting date of Mannerism in art. The time span of High Renaissance music is about the same; however, it extends much later, to about the death of

Palestrina in 1594. Interestingly, Mannerism begins to appear in some forms of music (madrigals) about the same time as art, toward the mid-century mark.

In the fields of music and art there is no abrupt change from early to late Renaissance, since from the beginning of the great revival there had been a continuous movement toward the lofty and grand classical style finally attained in the High Renaissance. Certain basic differences, however, do exist. For example, in the sixteenth century the problems that had occupied fifteenth-century artists, such as representation, perspective, space and anatomy, were no longer stressed as the most important aspects of art. Now these techniques were completely mastered, and considered a natural part of every artist's creative ability.

The change from what we generally refer to as the early Renaissance to High Renaissance seems to have occurred in the latter part of the fifteenth century when the cultural capital shifted from Florence to Rome. The plans for building a huge St. Peter's cathedral inaugurated by Nicholas V, and the completion of a new chapel at the Vatican (1481), motivated an interest in large monumental works of art which were needed to decorate the new edifices. Consequently, artistic style shifted from the realism characteristic of the fifteenth century to idealism reminiscent in many respects of ancient Greece. For example, in place of realistic works on a small plane (landscapes and portraits), we find themes of cosmic importance (Biblical and historical subject matter), a massive display of wall paintings and sculptures, and refined, idealized figures in which anatomical features are presented with scientific accuracy. Typical examples include Michelangelo's *Sistine Ceiling* paintings depicting the Old Testament and Raphael's giant frescoes of ancient scenes such as *The School of Athens* and *Parnassus*. In contrast to the more flamboyant splendor of the Italians, the northern artists such as Bosch, Dürer, and Brueghel continued for the most part the symbolical, mystical, and somber expression characteristic of the Gothic.

Stylistically, High Renaissance art and music have much in common, for ingrained in both are the ever-present esthetic principles of ancient Greece: idealism, beauty and perfection of form, dignity and solemnity, simplicity and moderation, and control. These are the qualities that seem to characterize the great choral works of the period—those of Josquin, di Lasso, and Palestrina.

Italy, specifically Rome, then, was the cultural center of the period—an artistic mecca that attracted the leaders in art and music. This fact accounts for the assimilation of musical styles in the masterworks of the period. For in these we find an esthetic balance of northern and southern elements resulting from the constant musical and cultural interchange that took place in Rome and other leading Italian cultural centers such as Florence and Venice. Why was Italy the mecca for the arts? Two reasons seem uppermost: first, the significant intellectual and artistic heritage dating back to the fourteenth century and, secondly, the establishment by wealthy patrons of a climate conducive to the growth of the arts. Given such nurturing, it was logical that art would succeed in such fertile Italian soil.

Raphael, *The School of Athens.* Fresco, 26′ x 18′. Alinari, Art Reference Bureau

Another supporting factor for Italian dominance in the arts: the powerful move by the Catholic clergy to establish Rome as the cultural and religious center of the world. Consequently, the vast wealth of the popes was used to rebuild and transform Rome on a monumental scale, beginning with Pope Julius II, who in 1503 commissioned Bramante to create elaborate plans for St. Peter's Basilica, which was begun in 1506 but not actually completed until the Baroque period. For this and the large Sistine Chapel at the Vatican (finished earlier, in 1481), the ambitious patron of the arts, Julius II, summoned prominent artists such as Michelangelo and Raphael to create the mammoth frescoes that the vast edifices required.

The Mannerist Movement   It is difficult to precisely define Mannerism, since it seems to be more of a state of transition than a style; that is, it is an era in which there is no one central movement or common artistic denominator. It is a brief period (about 1530–1600), marked by a reaction against the classicism of the High Renaissance; clearly it is a time when, as Sypher states, "the Renaissance harmony, clarity, and unity are disturbed."[2]

An important treatise, which undoubtedly deeply affected artists and musicians at the time of the approaching eclipse of the Italian High Renaissance, was Valla's translation of Aristotle's *Poetics*. The substance of Aristotle's treatise is that art imitates nature; moreover, it does not copy natural objects, such as scenery, but action and emotional states, such as anger and remorse.

Mannerism began to appear in art about 1530, in a shift in taste from the calm reserve and dignity of the Renaissance proper to the extravagant, bizarre, capricious, and experimental. Paintings of the new generation abound with much movement, gesticulation, tension, and action, coupled with a cluttered, unbalanced, restless appearance. The clear-cut lines of classical High Renaissance are now dissolved. An early indication of the impending movement appeared in Michelangelo's *Last Judgment*, completed in the Sistine Chapel about 1541. Instead of the peace, physical beauty, and harmonious order of his earlier works we find chaos and despair. The Italian artists Parmigianino and Michelangelo, the Venetians Titian and Tintoretto, and the Spaniard El Greco are considered among the main figures of the Mannerist Movement in art.

The Mannerist expression began to come to the fore in music shortly after 1530, when the first Italian madrigals were published. The picturesque tone paintings by Luca Marenzio, for example, in which various actions and emotions in the text are imitated, mark a definite break with the classical style in the masses and the motets of the High Renaissance. The trend toward a text-dominated style, the musical representation of various emotional states, and the creation of large, massive, and restless tonal palettes by Venetian composers, constitute the chief musical currents in the Mannerist period and eventually converge as the main foundations of the Baroque musical style.

THE RISE OF REGIONAL DIALECTS (SCHOOLS)

The writer of a general history of musical style must, unfortunately, bypass many important names and events associated with the various periods. This must be the case here if the aim is to provide information that will enable the reader to identify and differentiate the mainstreams of musical style. Hence, as we now turn to the music of the High Renaissance, a very brilliant and rich period, our attention will be focused only on the leaders of the main "schools" of composers prominent during the time 1450–1600.

The mainstream of musical creativity—sacred polyphony—is basically the same for all schools of the High Renaissance: Flemish, Roman, English,

---

[2] Wylie Sypher, *Four Stages of Renaissance Style* (New York: Doubleday and Company, Inc., 1955), p. 118.

Spanish, and Venetian; the exception, of course, is the music of Germany, which is based largely on the ideas of Martin Luther and his followers. Even though no drastic difference exists in the musical language employed by the various schools, each region or school is significant. Each contributed something uniquely different to the development of musical art—either in musical form, new techniques and devices in musical composition, or new performance media. Moreover, each school exemplifies a particular musical dialect that was influenced by prevailing social, intellectual, or artistic conditions in that geographical region. Concerning the second stream of music—the secular—we find that for the most part both sacred and secular polyphony are much alike, stylistically speaking, until after 1500. Then, strong nationalistic secular expressions begin to appear, chiefly in the music of Italy and England.

Some of the representative composers of the main schools of the High Renaissance are as follows:

Flemish:	Josquin des Prez (1450–1521), Orlando di Lasso (1532–1594)
Roman:	Giovanni Palestrina (1525–1594)
Spanish:	Cristóbal de Morales (1500–1553), Tomás Victoria (1548–1611)
German:	Johann Walther (1496–1570), Michael Praetorius (1571–1621)
English:	Thomas Tallis (1505–1585), Christopher Tye (1500–1572), Thomas Morley (1557–1603), William Byrd (1543–1623)
Venetian:	Adrian Willaert (1490–1562), Giovanni Gabrieli (1557–1612)

The Flemish School: Josquin des Prez Of the noted northern (Flemish) composers living in the age when the High Renaissance blossomed forth, Josquin undoubtedly ranks at the top of the list. Not only is he highly regarded by present-day music scholars and knowledgeable listeners, but he was also greatly esteemed by his own contemporaries, who referred to him as "the best of the composers of our time." His musical importance may be summed up in this way: first, his work represents the culmination of the Renaissance musical language and, secondly, his style served as a model for the entire sixteenth-century generation of sacred composers.

A Frenchman, Josquin was born about 1450 in Hainaut. He is said to have received his early music education as a choirboy in the church at St. Quentin; afterward he studied under Ockeghem, the great contrapuntist of the Flemish school of composers, active 1450–1550 in the region of France and the Netherlands.

As was the custom, Josquin and his northern contemporaries carried on an active musical interchange with Italy as a result of their extensive employment in wealthy Italian courts. However, it was Josquin's own distinctive fusion of Italian and Flemish subtleties, combined with an unusual mastery of technique, that has retained his name with the all-time masters of musical art. Josquin's assimilation of the southern musical spirit probably originated as early as 1459, when he began his musical career as a singer at the Milan cathedral (remaining there until 1472). His Italian sojourn also included a post as musician to Galeazzo Sforza from 1474 to 1479. And in Rome, from 1486 to 1494, he served as a singer in the papal chapel. In 1500 he finally returned to his native soil, where he was principally active in the service of the French King Louis XII.

Stylistically, Josquin's work represents the peak of the extensive development of the Netherlands mode of expression and, at the same time, the beginnings of the modern, humanistic concept of musical creativity, in which the composer attempts to mirror musically the emotional connotation of the text. In many ways his historical position is similar to Beethoven's. Josquin gathered together with consummate skill all the techniques of musical composition that had been gradually unfolding since Dufay, particularly the complex contrapuntal devices of his mentor, Ockeghem. The end result is a pleasing mixture of the Gothic penchant for complexity of form, contrapuntal imitation, and the humanistic concern for feelingful expression.

The motet, which served as the vehicle for Josquin's most significant achievements, constituted a large segment of the composer's creative output; he wrote over a hundred of them. The question arises as to why the motet was so heavily favored by Josquin and his Flemish contemporaries. Probably because of the greater compositional freedom and flexibility the form offered, as opposed to the strict form of the mass with its set number of movements, standard text, and established musical conventions. The motet, therefore, offered a wider range of creative invention musically and textually since the texts were drawn from the Bible, which provided a new and enlarged source of subject matter.

Motet, Ave Maria by Josquin des Prez

The stress now placed on text selection points up the growing trend in the method of musical creativity: that of employing a literary subject (in Latin and usually from the Bible) as the initial starting point in composing music. Gradually this concept developed to a point where the text in late sixteenth-century madrigals practically dominated the music, leading eventually, by 1600, to the birth of opera.

Josquin's method of text setting became standard in the sixteenth century. Briefly, it consisted of giving each phrase of the text its own short melody or motive, which is imitated in succession by the various voice parts. At the end of each phrase of text there is a musical cadence; however, to avoid a "closed" feeling, Josquin overlaps or dovetails the ending cadence with the start of the new phrase. The resulting effect is one of continuous musical movement, so characteristic of sixteenth-century polyphony.

In the contrapuntal style of Josquin's masses and motets, we generally find four or five parts woven together into a fully blended sonority; however, each part is completely independent melodically and rhythmically. The all-pervading technique of imitation unifies the entire composition and adds to the continuous, nonsectional effect. Harmonically, Josquin shows a strong leaning toward a modern conception of chord progressions in his use of dominant-tonic movement and a bass line that moves more and more by dynamic intervals of fourths and fifths instead of by the step movement common during the Middle Ages.

Josquin's treatment of the mass is also characteristic of the sixteenth century. Like his contemporaries, and unlike most composers since the golden age of sixteenth-century polyphony, Josquin did not demonstrate a strong leaning toward melodic invention. Instead, we find composers of this time borrowing themes from both sacred and secular sources. Most of Josquin's masses (a total of twenty), employ a secular rather than a sacred melody as a cantus firmus. An example of this type of mass is the *Missa L'Homme armé* (*The Armed Man*), printed in 1502. Another typical procedure of the age is referred to as the "parody technique," in which a complete section or passage of music from another mass, motet, or chanson serves as the principal musical material.

The humanistic tendencies are in full evidence in Josquin's masses. For example, we note that worldly or popular tunes like *Ma Maîtresse* (*My Mistress*) and *L'Homme armé* are subtly woven into the musical fabric of these sacred works. Scholars have given various reasons for this practice of borrowing and parodying. Perhaps the custom was precipitated by an overreliance on the age-old cantus firmus principle, thus negating true creative spontaneity. Or perhaps the custom stemmed from a desire to create a more lifelike humanistic musical expression, which could be achieved through the use of lilting secular themes.

The practice of borrowing themes in musical composition has, since the time of Josquin, been widely followed, notably in the theme and variation form that evolved among the English keyboard composers in the late Renaissance and extensively used in the Baroque and classical periods. Of course, what marks a distinctive creative work is the way in which the composer treats the given melody, either harmonically, rhythmically, or contrapuntally. In this regard, Josquin excelled in his contrapuntal manipulation of the borrowed theme and in his setting of tone combinations that enhance the emotional connotation of the text. Of his numerous works in the choral idiom (twenty masses, one hundred motets, and over seventy chansons), perhaps the most famous are the *Missa Hercules*, *Missa L'Homme armé*, the motet *Ave Maria*, and the chanson *Faulte d'argent* (*Lack of Money*).

The Roman School: Palestrina   Josquin's monumental synthesis of the musical trends of the fifteenth century paved the way for further artistic enrichment of the Renaissance musical language. In the sixteenth century, various regional groups or schools of composers that had assimilated the now-stabilized Netherlands style either (1) further perfected and refined it (the Roman School); (2) transformed it into other idioms for chamber instruments and new sacred settings for the Anglican Church (the English School); or (3) expanded it through the addition of massive instrumental and choral forces (the Venetian School).

Giovanni Pierluigi da Palestrina, the composer who is frequently regarded as the consummate perfectionist of the Netherlands style, was born in 1525, four years after the death of Josquin. Many social changes occurred at this time that threatened the solidarity of the Catholic Church such as the sacking of Rome (1527) by German troops, the start of Luther's Reformation in Germany (1517), and the numerous religious disturbances in England leading to the eventual break with Rome (1534).

As a consequence of these and other troubles, the Catholic Church established a Council at Trent, which met on an irregular basis from 1545 to 1563 to plan measures for strengthening the Church. This action—the Counter Reformation—was undertaken to cleanse internal corruption and malpractices, and to stem external disturbances. Concerning the liturgy, the council objected to, among other things, the large number of sequences that had come into use since the tenth century (all but four were excluded by the council), the multiplicity of performers vocal and instrumental, the use of secular melodies in the Mass, and the complicated polyphony that obscured the words. The council recommended the restoration of traditional practices and ideals: a return to purity and simplicity of musical expression.

The Italian Palestrina, deeply affected by his religious convictions and the happenings at the Council of Trent, devoted his talents to the movement and became the leading musical representative of the Counter Reformation. His sacred works and those of his followers in the Roman School became accepted by the Church as models of liturgical music. Palestrina's sincere dedication to the Church is mirrored in the large quantity of compositions in the sacred vein, including one hundred and two masses and over four hundred motets.

The qualities that seem to stand out in Palestrina's work include definite Gothic traits such as a serenity of mood, a feeling of formality, solemnity, mysticism, and a detached impersonal expression. These are mixed with the Italian Renaissance interest in clarity, beauty of line, simplicity, majesty, harmony of elements, monumental form, and perfection. The complete mastery of the Netherlands tradition is evident in his work; however, his is an idealistic, sublime interpretation in which all musical elements—counterpoint, melody, harmony, and rhythm—seem to have been subjected to an unusual degree of refinement.

Pope Marcellus Mass, Giovanni da Palestrina

To illustrate: in his melodic structures we note a purity of style, in which the secular elements of his contemporaries are excluded. Instead, he retains almost completely the Gregorian chant as the melodic basis. Again, contrary to his colleagues in the High Renaissance, he avoids chromaticism and does not permit rough edges (unusual skips) to appear in the graceful melodic lines. All tones move smoothly, flowingly, in a conjunct manner.

The ancient Church modes were still used during the time of Palestrina, although the trend is definitely toward the establishment of two basic modes: the Lydian, F to F (with flatted B), and the Aeolian, A to A. Shortly (by the Baroque period) these become known respectively as the major scale (Lydian transposed to each of the scale degrees, giving twelve major scales) and the minor scale (Aeolian pattern transposed to each of the scale degrees, giving twelve minor scales).

Contrapuntally constructed, each of the four or five voice parts in the mass and motet are independent, yet they blend perfectly into one homogeneous sonority. Moreover, the voices perform *a cappella* fashion, that is, without instrumental accompaniment. Imitation, of course, prevails throughout, serving to unify the work.

Harmonically, the principal chords are the triad (placed in a wide variety of positions for unusual sonority effects), and the first inversion chord. The essence of the Palestrina style seems to be in the meticulous and flawless treatment of dissonance. On each beat (usually measured in half notes) only notes belonging to the harmony could be used. Dissonant notes (not in the chord or harmony) were to be used only on the last half of the beat.

All dissonant notes were to be approached and quitted by step motion. The most common devices used for inculcating a slight dissonant flavor were the *passing note* (a dissonant note appearing on the last half of the beat between two notes a third apart) and the *suspension,* in which a tone is held over into a chord with which it is foreign or dissonant and resolved down by step, becoming a part of the underlying chord or harmony.

(a) Passing note   (b) Suspension

Treatment of Dissonance, Age of Palestrina

The German School: The Protestant Chorale   When Martin Luther posted his famous ninety-five theses in 1517, a style trend was soon set in motion that was to be felt in the next two hundred years of German music, reaching its apex in the music of J. S. Bach. The essential spirit of the style is derived from the simplicity and strength of the Protestant hymn or chorale which served as the foundation of the Lutheran liturgy.

In his plans for reform, Luther, himself a skilled musician, wished to modify portions of the Catholic liturgy to conform with his doctrines and evangelical teachings. These emphasized the placement of the congregation in an active role in the church service. For churches located in large German cities (where traditional music was well established), he advocated the retention of the Latin Mass; however, a number of alterations were suggested. Among these were the omission of the Credo and the Agnus Dei from the Ordinary; substitution of a German chorale (hymn tune) for certain portions of the mass in place of the traditional Catholic plainsong or chant; and the substitution of German chorale texts for Latin (Luther wrote many of these texts including the well-known *Ein' feste Burg ist unser Gott* [*A Mighty Fortress Is Our God*]).

Divergent levels of education and varied musical training and background of rural congregations led Luther to make further modifications. Therefore, in these smaller churches German prose texts and chorales could be substituted for any of the Latin portions of the Mass, and simple tunes or songs could be interjected at any point in the Lutheran service.

Undoubtedly the most distinctive musical innovation to come out of the German Reformation was the congregational hymn, called *choral* in

German (meaning *Church song*) and *chorale* in English. Requiring many such chorales, musicians of the new Lutheran churches devised the needed music through (1) original creative work, (2) borrowing of tunes from Catholic sources such as plainsong, (3) adaptations of well-known love songs (such as Isaac's *Innsbruck ich muss dich lassen*), and (4) adaptations of German medieval folk and religious songs.

Markedly different from plainsong, these chorales are characterized by (1) strophic construction (same melody for different lines of text), (2) strong metric character, (3) clear-cut phrases as opposed to the long-breathed lines of chant, (4) text in German rather than Latin, and (5) slow steady pulsation derived from strong harmonic progressions. These characteristics gradually came into clearer focus in the chorales of the late sixteenth century.

German Chorale by Johann Walther, 1524

Among the many famous musicians who contributed in the massive task of building a repertoire for the newly founded Lutheran Church were Johann Walther (1496–1570) and, at the turn of the century, Michael Praetorius (1571–1621), and Johann Hermann Schein (1586–1630).

English School: The Rise of Independent Instrumental Music   The waits and minstrels, the chief English instrumental musicians of the Middle Ages, continued to be active in the Renaissance. A third group, the King's Musick, contributed considerably to wind music in the late sixteenth and early seventeenth centuries. The minstrels were, from their beginning in the medieval period, talented musicians either independent or established in a court or household of the nobility. Until about 1400, the waits, as we have seen, were primarily watchmen with some musical ability in wind-instrument playing. After 1400, their occupation gradually changed from royal guardians to professional musicians possessing considerable skill in reed- and brass-instrument performance.

Their performances included plays, masques, weddings, holiday celebrations, and town festivities honoring visiting royalty. The earliest public

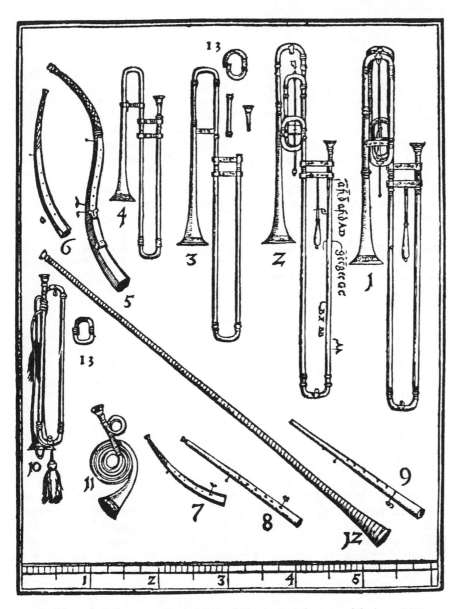

Sackbuts and Cornetts. From Michael Praetorius' *Syntagma Musicum*, 1618
(Sackbuts Nos. 1–4; Cornetts Nos. 5–9)

concert in England is traced to Norwich in 1553, when it was proclaimed that the waits were to perform at the Guild Hall every Sunday and holiday of the summer months.

The cornett and the sackbut of the medieval period were retained as the instruments of the waits and King's Musick. However, new additions were made to each of these instrument families, resulting in the complete consort or wind ensemble. The added instruments were the treble, descant, and tenor cornett and the tenor and bass sackbut. Later, in the seventeenth century, other types of sackbut were added to the ensemble.

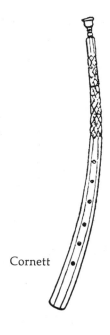

Cornett

Viol

The instrumentation of the waits' ensemble was not standardized, since historical documents show a variety of wind instruments: shawm (oboe), curtal (bassoon), sackbut, cornett, and recorder. Either a complete consort, in which all instruments were of the same family, or a broken consort of unlike instruments was used, depending on the availability of instruments. A few isolated pieces of wind music in manuscript form are dated prior to 1600, notably a work by Robert Parsons (c. 1570) and Anthony Holborne's *Pavans, Galliards . . .* of 1599. These, and the numerous historical citations relating extensive instrumental activity, indicate the existence of organized wind ensemble performance in the sixteenth century.

Music of the Royal Court: Chamber Music   English music reached a high level in the royal court of the sixteenth century. The level of refinement achieved by the composers of the royal court is to be partially explained by the changing social and cultural forces that ushered in the artistic climate of the English High Renaissance. The waits and minstrels, of course, contributed to the dissemination of music to the masses, but basic to the tremendous upsurge in the secular instrumental activities of these groups was the social and cultural change that began as early as the thirteenth century and reached its climax in the sixteenth.

With the rapid rise of trade and industry came forth the new literate merchant classes and their secular interests, which took hold in the newly arisen towns. "The homes of the new half-town-half-country gentry all over England," writes Meyer, "became the centres of art and culture. . . . With the new standards of comfort and taste there arose a vivid musical culture. The production of instrumental music in particular increased with great speed."[3]

Not only was municipal music affected by these sweeping changes, but also the music of royalty (the King's Musick). This large body of royal musicians, imported mainly from Italy, first came into prominence under Henry VIII (reigned 1509–1547), who set a precedent by maintaining a band of over sixty performers. Out of this rich musical culture arose the art of chamber music, which reached its zenith during the reign of Elizabeth (1558–1603). Bowed instruments called *viols* were initially the instruments used for chamber music; however, beginning at the turn of the sixteenth century, some chamber music was also written for wind instruments. Bowed instruments were in a state of flux in the Middle Ages, but by about 1500 two fundamental families appeared: *viole* (*viola,* sing.) *da braccio* (braccio = arm, thus arm-viols) and *viole da gamba* (gamba = leg, thus leg-viols).

The viola da gamba family of bowed instruments, which were held vertically on or between the legs, included in descending order: treble, tenor, bass, and double bass. These viols had sloping shoulders, six to seven strings, flat backs, and a delicate soft tone quality. They were ex-

[3] Ernst Meyer, *English Chamber Music* (London: Laurence and Wishart, 1946), p. 66.

tremely popular in sixteenth-century England, where they were referred to simply as "viols." Let us examine briefly the growth of music written for these highly sophisticated chamber instruments.

Even though the court of Henry VIII became permeated with the growing spirit of the English Reformation following his split with Rome in 1534, the sacred polyphonic style, particularly the Netherlands School of Josquin, was emulated in the choral compositions written by the royal composers. This strong interest in polyphony also carried over into the instrumental field, where hundreds of arrangements were made of choral works for viols. These pieces were actually motets shorn of their texts and scored for four or five viols, each playing a separate part.

Ultimately, however, several composers, notably Taverner (1495–1545) and Tallis (1505–1585), broke away from the motet arrangements and produced original instrumental compositions for viols called *in nomines*, which were based on a sacred cantus firmus in essentially the same style as the vocal motets. Nonetheless, they were the first definite examples of composed instrumental chamber music.

In the second half of the sixteenth century, the style of the *in nomine* changed considerably. Idiomatic writing became established; that is, composers used figures characteristic of viol playing such as runs, skipping movements in the melody line, slurs, and repeated note patterns. Representative of this trend is Christopher Tye (1500–1572), who may be rightly called the first great composer of chamber music. He wrote nineteen *in nomines* for ensembles of four to six viols.

The next phase of English chamber music, which occurred in Elizabeth's reign, was introduced by a new form for viols or for a keyboard instrument called the *fantasia,* or *fancy.* The chief composers of this form were William Byrd (fourteen fantasias) and Orlando Gibbons (twenty-seven fantasias). The name *fantasia* was of Italian origin, used by Willaert in his instrumental ensemble compositions dated Venice, 1559. The English treatment of the fantasia, however, was definitely original.

English fantasias first appeared in the last decade of the sixteenth century as an outgrowth of the *in nomine's* general polyphonic structure. However, in place of the continuous and more sedate style of the *in nomine,* composers like Byrd, Gibbons, and Thomas Morley introduced clear-cut sections set off by definite cadences. Also, lilting, angular themes were taken from popular vocal music of the day and from the popular dance forms (allemande, courante, sarabande, and gigue), which were sweeping the English countryside. The fantasia form continued through the seventeenth century to the time of Henry Purcell, the last significant composer in this idiom.

The Arrival of Chamber Wind Music   Some chamber music for wind instruments also began to appear during the reign of Elizabeth. A few pieces from a slightly earlier date are available; however, in the main, wind music did not develop until the end of the sixteenth century. This is not only true of England but also of Italy, where we shall see, momentarily, significant contributions in brass music. Indicative of the trend in England

Soprano
Recorder

Lute

Bass
Recorder

is Anthony Holborne's *Pavans, Galliards* . . . of 1599, consisting of sixty-five short pieces, mainly stylized dance pieces for viols, violins, or wind instruments. Each bears an unusual descriptive title, such as "The Tears of the Muses" and "The Fruit of Love."

As the complete title of Holborne's work indicates, the pieces are playable by wind instruments, and since consorts of wind instruments were common at this time, it seems likely that they were played by a combination of cornetts and sackbuts, probably two sackbuts and three cornetts. Although Holborne's music is only designated as "playable" by wind instruments, it is nonetheless an important work. In embodying all of the new features, as opposed to the predominantly sacred style of previous wind music, his contribution represents the turning point in wind instrumental composition. From here it was merely a matter of adding instrumental names to the written parts—the next step which was completed by John Adson (1611), who announced the golden era of English brass music.

In devoting his creative talents to the popular dance forms in his *Pavans, Galliards* . . . , Holborne mirrored the common practice of his age. Apart from creating stylized and artistic compositions based on popular tunes and forms, Holborne, like many others, continued the dance rhythms and melodies of the people. Without a doubt the ancient secular art of the minstrels now became widely disseminated through the dance movement, which truly marked an important social change, for, as Meyer writes: "During the last twenty years of that century (sixteenth) the popularity of dance music broke all previous bounds. Practically the whole of Europe was held, as never before or since, in the spell of a rage for dancing."[4]

On the artistic plane, the court of Henry VIII and particularly that of Elizabeth gave impetus to the new creative spirit by providing the atmosphere in which the gay country dances and tunes of England (represented by the dump, jig, and hornpipe) and those of the Continent (pavane, allemande, courante, and galliard) could develop as artistic forms of musical composition.

The impact of these dances upon composing in the instrumental media was indeed great, for now the sacred style—its continuous, unending melodies based on the quiet mood of the Gregorian chant, nonpulsatile rhythms, and thick contrapuntal texture—could not be easily adapted to the new molds, which called for a more objective type of melody and a homophonic texture. The humanization of musical art created a wider potential of expression for the newly formed string and brass ensembles, as well as for all other instrumental media that followed this artistic upheaval, particularly music written for the harpsichord and clavichord.

English Keyboard Music   Another great English contribution to the heritage of Renaissance music is the extensive literature composed for the two very popular kinds of keyboard stringed instruments in use at this time: the

---

[4] *English Chamber Music*, p. 97.

plucked type (*harpsichord, spinet,* or *virginal*) and the struck type (*clavichord*). In the former type the key mechanism plucked the string by means of a quill set in a "jack" (see illustration). The harpsichord was built in a wing shape (like the grand piano), with strings extending from front to back, and, in the upright form, stringed from left to right. The English harpsichord is known as *cembalo* in Italian and *clavecin* in French. The virginal or spinet was a smaller, oblong model of the harpsichord, which was lightweight and portable.

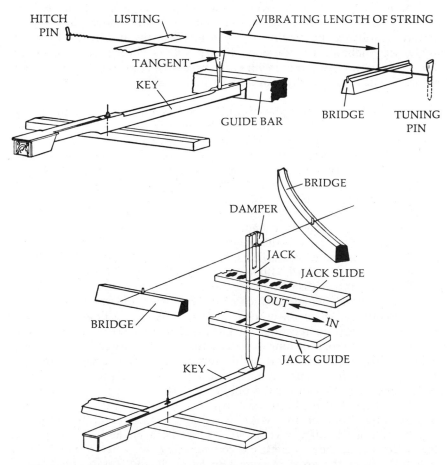

Clavichord (top) and Harpsichord. Courtesy, Boston Museum of Fine Arts

In the clavichord, the strings were strung from right to left and were struck by a brass tangent set in the end of each key. The tone of the instrument is very light and delicate in contrast to the louder harpsichord. From these two instruments evolved the modern piano (invented by Cristofori in 1709), in which the strings are struck by hard felt hammers.

The late sixteenth century witnessed an extraordinary surge of creativity in works for the harpsichord or virginal. Chief among the virginalists were William Byrd, Giles Farnaby, and Thomas Morley. Much of their music is represented in the largest collection of English keyboard music, the *Fitzwilliam Virginal Book*, compiled around 1620, which contains almost three hundred pieces written in the late sixteenth and early seventeenth centuries. Included in the immense collection are fantasias, dances, preludes, and numerous sets of variations.

The theme-and-variations form was widely used by William Byrd, the leading composer of the age. His works in this genre do not follow the polyphonic vocal style of writing but are mainly homophonic, and instead of utilizing the continuous form of the mass and motet, they are highly sectionalized. The variation begins with a simple tune, generally of a secular nature, and then, with each successive appearance, it is altered or varied harmonically, rhythmically, or melodically.

The English Madrigal   Composers of England's Golden Age also produced a considerable quantity of music in the new secular polyphonic vocal form, the madrigal, invented by the Italians earlier in the sixteenth century. It was mentioned before that a great influx of Italian culture had begun under Henry VIII, who imported a large number of musicians for his King's Musick. It does not seem strange then that the madrigal, which was first published in Italy in 1533, gradually worked its way into English life. By the time of the first English madrigal publication, *Musica Transalpina*, in 1588, the new form had completely permeated English society.

Actually, England was the only country to fully transform the madrigal into its own native style. The distinct English character of the many madrigals by Morley, Byrd, Gibbons, and Weelkes results from the clarity and rhythm of the English language and the down-to-earth subject matter drawn from the sights and sounds of the English countryside. Moreover, no other country, in quantity or in quality, equaled the English achievements in madrigal composition. In Elizabethan days the madrigals were sung by a small group of four to six amateur singers seated about a table, each with his or her part. This highly sophisticated and subtle expression of madrigal art, like chamber music for viols, was designed for intimate social gatherings and not for the public concert.

Even though copied after the Italian form, at least in general structural features (four or five voice parts and contrapuntal texture), the English madrigals' distinctive freshness, exuberance and jovial quality clearly denote an independent, indigenous art. Also, whereas the Italians used texts from the great masters like Petrarch and Tasso, the English texts were drawn from the works of popular literary figures of the day. Pastoral subject matter complete with sound effects prevails in many English madrigals, as in John Bennet's *Thyrsis, Sleepest Thou?*, which contains colloquial words such as "hold up," "cuckoo," and "hollo." Some forty publications appeared in England between 1588 and 1627, including works by the leading madrigal composers William Byrd (1543–1623), Thomas Morley (1557–1603), Thomas Weelkes (1575–1623), and John Wilbye (1574–1638).

Madrigal, "About the May Pole,"
by Thomas Morley

In that very brief moment of English history, the creative spirit in music, which had remained dormant since the beginning of the fifteenth century, suddenly blossomed forth, and with it a true English expression that had been concealed in native folk tunes and dances. That great outpouring of musical art, which was primarily in the secular vein, had been hastened by England's development as an independent nation free from the ties of the Catholic Church. Consequently, the traditional sacred polyphonic style had given way to the dancelike, tuneful melodies that had become thoroughly assimilated in the Elizabethan age. In other parts of Europe, however, the traditional musical language of the Renaissance continued strong, notably in Venice, where the climax of Renaissance musical art turned toward the Baroque.

The Venetian School: Mannerism   In the latter part of the sixteenth century, the final phase of the unfolding Renaissance musical language took place in the wealthy city of Venice. Whereas the Roman School refined the language in the spirit of classicism, and the English transformed it into Protestant idioms and chamber music transcriptions, the Venetians increased its sonority through powerful sounding bodies of instruments and voices. At the core of the Venetian expression, however, was the stately, reverent, ever-present spirit of the Gregorian-chant melodic style, woven through thick, massive polyphonic textures.

The Venetians, moreover, interjected into the Netherlands style a restless, shifting, compulsive movement in which the classically balanced lines of the Renaissance musical language are frequently truncated by antiphonal exchanges between various instruments and voices and by sudden bursts of loud and soft. This disturbed balance is prominent not only in the music of Venetian composers such as Giovanni Gabrieli, but also in the work of their contemporaries in other arts and parts of the world: in the poetry of John Donne, the plays of Shakespeare, the paintings of Tintoretto and El Greco, and the madrigals of Gesualdo. These artists are representatives of the Mannerist Movement of the sixteenth century; musically the movement is most pronounced in Italy in the last decades of the century.

Mannerism was born of confusion and crisis, a time of many eruptions in the political, social, and religious life of northern and southern Europe beginning about 1520. As we have already seen, the earlier religious schisms, the Reformation in Germany, the split between Henry VIII and Rome, the Counter Reformation and the Inquisition, the sacking of Rome and the scientific findings of Kepler and Galileo after the turn of the century, shook the ordered Renaissance world. These happenings are perhaps most vividly and collectively mirrored in the artistic taste that arose in Venice, a city-state that was at its peak culturally and economically in the late sixteenth century. It was here, in contrast to the strong traditionalism of Rome, that progressive developments appeared in art and music. Both of these areas of creativity exhibited similar qualities and features, which gradually fused to become the Baroque.

Among the qualities found in the new artistic taste of the Venetians are (1) *an emphasis on spacious designs.* For example, Palladio's buildings, the

Tintoretto, *Transporting the Body of St. Mark*. Alinari, Art Reference Bureau

large monumental dimensions of Tintoretto's paintings, Giovanni Gabrieli's expansive new musical forms (*canzona* and *ricercar*), and the massive performances by large choral and instrumental ensembles at St. Mark's Cathedral in Venice; (2) *a disturbed sense of proportion and perspective*. For example, the unnatural, elongated human forms in El Greco's paintings, the irregular, almost asymmetrical architectural designs of Palladio, and the tossing back and forth of unequal sound masses in Gabrieli's works; (3) *an intensification of emotional expression*. For example, the ghostly light and nightmarish atmosphere in many Tintoretto paintings, as well as slashing, zigzag lines and hidden inward angles, as in Tintoretto's *Transporting the Body of St. Mark* and the use of sudden changes in dynamics and shifting of sounds from one musical ensemble to another, as in Gabrieli's compositions; and (4) *a reconciliation of opposites*[5] especially evident in contrasting textures, as in the placement of smooth and rough materials in architecture, clothed next to unclothed figures in painting, and the juxtaposition of small and large ensembles in musical performance.

The lineage of Venetian composers extends from Adrian Willaert, a Netherlander who was appointed choirmaster at the magnificent St. Mark's Cathedral in 1527, to the leading figure and culminator of the school, Giovanni Gabrieli, who held the position of first organist at St. Mark's from 1586 to his death in 1612. All of the Venetian composers assimilated the basic Netherlands language; more importantly, they found new ways of performing it, new forms in which the language could be placed, and new musical techniques for greater musical expression.

Concerning the first contribution, the expansion of performance resources, the Venetians were influenced to a marked degree by the immense structure of St. Mark's, which featured the domed Greek-cross plan. (The Gothic, in contrast, generally used the Latin-cross plan, with its centralized choir loft at the end of a long nave.) Willaert was the first to experiment with various divided choral ensembles placed at different points in the church. It was Gabrieli, however, who brought the Venetian style to its peak in the closing years of the century. The performance of the Netherlands styled polyphony (masses and motets) was provided by *chori spezzati*, that is, broken or separate choruses, which were placed in various positions of the church and sounded forth in alternating and full (*tutti*) fashion. In addition, wind instruments were also deployed at different points in the giant structure, either in conjunction with choral groups or separately in their performance of the older forms (mass and motet) and the new *ricercar* and *canzona* (See Glossary).

The unusual placement of the performing groups within St. Mark's led to several acoustically derived musical techniques, which became trademarks of the Venetian style, such as *antiphony* (the exchange of a musical phrase between one instrumental or choral group and another), the *concertato principle* (the pitting of one soloist or group against another

---

[5] William Fleming, *Arts and Ideas*, rev. ed. (New York: Holt, Rinehart and Winston, Inc., 1963).

St. Mark's Cathedral, Venice. Alinari, Art Reference Bureau

in a kind of musical duel), and the extensive use of *contrast*. This technique is found in alternating passages of loud and soft, small and large groups, low- and high-pitched voices or instruments, full scoring and thin, organ and full choir, and chordal texture mixed with polyphonic texture.

The Venetians made a definite advancement in the field of instrumental music. They were the first to introduce concerted instruments and voices in cathedral music. Out of this practice came the independent brass ensemble, principally under Giovanni Gabrieli. Thus, while the English contributed a secular style of brass music, the Venetians introduced a style closely allied to the Netherlands sacred tradition. The principal brass instruments used by Gabrieli and his fellow composers were the same as those in England: the cornett (called *cornetto* in Italy), the sackbut (called *trombone* in Italy), and quite frequently the organ which was included in the instrumentation, as well as the viol.

Among Gabrieli's many works, published mainly under the heading of *Symphoniae Sacrae* in 1597 and 1615, are the *In Ecclesiis*, a nonliturgical motet scored for double choir and a six-part instrumental group of three cornetts, violin and two trombones; *Canzon quarti toni a 15* for two choirs of cornetts and four trombones, and one choir of violin and four trombones; and *Sonata pian'e forte*, for two four-part instrumental ensembles including a cornett and three trombones in the first and a violin and three trombones in the second.

Summary

The history of music in the Renaissance is divided into two epochs, the early Renaissance of the fifteenth century and the High Renaissance, extending from the late fifteenth century to the beginning of the seventeenth. During the first epoch the basic musical style of the period, sacred choral polyphony, was formulated by the Netherlands composers; the second epoch witnessed its dissemination and perfection.

With the coming of music printing, new instruments, university music study, and especially an unprecedented patronage by the Catholic Church and wealthy private citizens, music became recognized as an art form and rose to a high peak of refinement.

Two main musical currents are discernible in the Renaissance, the most important of which is the sacred Netherlands style. The second, the secular style, became prominent in the third decade of the sixteenth century, following on the heels of many social and political upheavals, notably the Protestant Reformation, the Counter Reformation, and particularly the English break with Rome in 1534. And with this new world view came forth the great moment in English music, when chamber, keyboard, and madrigal art was produced in both quantity and quality.

At the close of the sixteenth century the Mannerist Movement in music reached its greatest height—and at the same time announced the approaching Baroque. The Venetian musicians, led by the Gabrielis, added breadth and power to the Netherlands style, bringing to a climax a development that had spanned several centuries.

REPRESENTATIVE WORKS IN THE HUMANITIES:
THE RENAISSANCE (1400–1600)

MUSIC

Major trends: Of prime importance is the rise of the Renaissance musical language (choral polyphony) in the Netherlands in the fifteenth century and its dissemination and perfection in the sixteenth century. Independent instrumental music comes to the fore in the late sixteenth century, as well as strong nationalistic tendencies in musical art. The invention of music printing, the growth of court music, the wealthy patronage of the arts, and the granting of degrees in music (Cambridge, 1463), contribute to transform music from its medieval utilitarian position to a high art form.

PHILOSOPHY

No new philosophy appears; however, the Neoplatonic movement has a strong effect on artistic theory and creativity. Neoplatonism was begun by Cosimo de' Medici, who established the Florentine Academy (1462) and commissioned the translation of Plato's works into Latin (completed by Ficino in 1482).

LITERATURE

1470	*Morte d'Arthur*, Sir Thomas Malory
1511	*The Praise of Folly*, Desiderius Erasmus
1514	*The Prince*, Niccolò Machiavelli
1516	*Utopia*, Sir Thomas More
1528	*The Courtier*, Baldassare Castiglione
1532	*Gargantua*, François Rabelais
1580	*Essays*, Michel Montaigne
1588	*Doctor Faustus*, Christopher Marlowe
1590	*The Faerie Queen*, Edmund Spenser
1594	*Romeo and Juliet*, William Shakespeare
1601	*Hamlet*, William Shakespeare

ART

1425	Sculpture for Baptistry in Florence begun by Ghiberti
1430	*David*, Donatello
1432	*Ghent Altarpiece*, Jan and Hubert van Eyck
1478	*La Primavera*, Sandro Botticelli
1495	*Temptation of St. Anthony*, Hieronymus Bosch
1498	*Last Supper*, Leonardo da Vinci
1504	*David*, Michelangelo
1506	St. Peter's begun at Rome
1508	Sistine Chapel ceiling begun by Michelangelo
1511	*School of Athens*, Raphael
1514	*St. Jerome in His Study*, Albrecht Dürer
1538	*Venus of Urbino*, Titian
1560	*Wedding Dance*, Pieter Brueghel
1576	*Ascension of Christ*, Tintoretto
1586	*Burial of Count Orgaz*, El Greco
1610	*View of Toledo*, El Greco

HISTORICAL EVENTS

1378	Beginning of Papal Schism
1386	Heidelberg University founded
1405	Duchy of Burgundy (until 1477)
1431	Jeanne d'Arc executed
1434	Medici family cultural leaders in Italy, to end of century
1453	End of One Hundred Years' War
1453	Constantinople falls to Turks

1454   Gutenberg invents printing (movable metal type)
1460   First Doctor of Music degree awarded, Oxford
1463   First Bachelor of Music degree awarded, Cambridge
1492   First voyage of Columbus
1501   First music printed
1509–1547   Henry VIII King of England
1517   Luther posts ninety-five theses
1519–1521   Magellan circumnavigates the globe
1534   England breaks from Roman Catholic Church
1545–1563   Council of Trent
1558–1603   Elizabeth, Queen of England
1588   Defeat of the Spanish Armada

6

THE BAROQUE PERIOD
(1600–1750)

BACKGROUND: THE BAROQUE SPIRIT

> The Baroque overwhelmed heresy by splendor,
> it did not argue, but proclaimed; it brought
> conviction to the doubter by the very scale of
> its grandeurs . . .
>   Wylie Sypher, *Four Stages of Renaissance Style*

Artistic taste seems to follow a cyclical pattern in the history of Western musical art. If the Renaissance represented a renewal of ancient Greek ideals of balance and restraint, the Baroque signifies a swing of the stylistic pendulum in the opposite direction—to freedom and spontaneity of expression or, simply stated, from the classic to the romantic. The Baroque, however, cannot be adequately defined in such simple terms, for its music, like its art and literature, is complex; it is also, in its own distinctive way, dramatic and powerful.

These traits began to gather force among the Mannerists of the late sixteenth century: Tintoretto, Titian, El Greco, Gesualdo, and Gabrieli. However, the actual beginning of the Baroque is usually dated 1600, and its ending 1750, the death date of J. S. Bach. In the course of 150 years were written some of the world's greatest monuments of music, many of which are a part of the permanent repertory in today's concert halls. They cover a variety of forms and styles, ranging from the musically simple but intensely dramatic early Baroque opera to the superhuman strength of J. S. Bach. Diverse as they may seem these works are, in varying degrees, bound together stylistically by an artistic ideal that seems to pervade all secular and sacred modes of expression.

In determining this ideal, our preliminary discussion will, again, draw upon analogies in the visual arts. This is done for several reasons.

The common artistic traits of a period are more clearly understood by the general reader when related to all of the arts and especially the visual arts, where a graphic representation of the style trait is frequently more meaningful than a discussion in abstract terms. Uppermost is the fact that the visual arts made the most forceful pronouncement of the new expression beginning in the late sixteenth century. In essence, they set the scene for the gigantic Baroque drama that unfolded in all of the arts. Musical art, too, with the subsequent rise of dramatic vocal music and the powerful organ and orchestral forms, also contributed a style analogous to that so exuberantly proclaimed by the architects, painters, and sculptors. Our preliminary study will begin with a brief discussion of the wellsprings of the Baroque style—the social and intellectual context of the period and the major creations in the visual arts that gave impetus to the movement—and conclude with a summary of the characteristics of the Baroque expression.

The Complex Nature of the Baroque To begin with, the word *baroque* is, apparently, derived from the Portuguese *barroco,* meaning an irregularly shaped pearl. The term was applied in a deprecatory manner to Baroque art by eighteenth- and nineteenth-century critics. To them the art of this period was bizzare, grotesque, and overly ornate. The modern world has, of course, reversed this judgment, for highly valued today are the artworks of Bernini, Rubens, Caravaggio, Vermeer, and Rembrandt, and the music of Corelli, Vivaldi, Scarlatti, Bach, Handel and many others who have been discovered in the great twentieth-century revival of the Baroque.

Occasionally we may identify the creative outlook of the age by the use of such artistic categories as "classicism," which reflected the rationalistic and idealistic way of life of the Greeks, and "mysticism," the other-worldly interests of medieval man. However, in the case of the Baroque period, the identification of the dominant attitude becomes a difficult task, since the era is very complex intellectually, socially, and politically, which consequently leads to a proliferation of musical styles and practices. To illustrate, Protestantism and Catholicism were both strong and important as emanating sources of views and practices concerning sacred music. Although sacred music did not dominate musical creativity as it did for most of the Renaissance, the Catholic tradition of polyphony continued undiminished, particularly in Rome, where Church composers, imbued with the Baroque spirit, created massive and elaborate choral works in the Venetian manner. However, the most striking innovations in sacred music occurred among the German composers such as Schütz, Buxtehude and J. S. Bach, who contributed significant choral and organ music for the Lutheran Church.

Secular music made significant strides during the Baroque, largely due to the shifting social structure that is now identified by widespread absolutism and the rising bourgeois. The effect of absolutism upon the arts was particularly significant in France, where all the arts were given unparalleled royal patronage and where a wide variety of secular music (opera, ballet, and chamber music) flourished. With a newly acquired

Caravaggio, *The Lute Player*. Gallerie del Piemonte, Turin, Bettmann Archive

economic status, the middle class also shared in the expanding European culture. No longer was music solely the interest of the elite. Increasingly it became a public affair, as attested by the opening of public opera houses in Italy in the seventeenth century. And for the first time public taste played an important part in the shaping of musical style. This occurred in the field of opera, which underwent a gradual transformation from an esoteric art form (early 1600s) to a public-dominated expression at the end of the seventeenth century.

The period also witnessed two significant intellectual movements, generally referred to as *Rationalism* and the *Enlightenment.* The former term is applied to the rise of scientific thought in the seventeenth century and the latter to the application of reason to social, political, and religious matters in the eighteenth century. Outside of a pronounced vein of rationalism (that is, classical restraint and formalism) in French fine arts, these movements exerted little influence on the arts until the rococo emerged in the early 1700s. For the most part, however, the rationalistic expression is alien to the Baroque preference for drama and passion. Not until the late eighteenth century (the classical period proper) did music really become imbued with the rationalistic spirit.

The Beginnings of the Baroque Expression   It is very difficult to date the beginnings of any period or movement; hence we must seek an unusual clustering of artistic signs that seem to foreshadow an impending change. These signs seem to have been most strongly manifested in sacred art in the latter part of the sixteenth century, at the time when the religious upheavals and internal turmoils threatening the Catholic Church became resolved. Having stemmed the tide of Protestantism and regained an inner balance, the Catholic Church moved forth in a self-confident, triumphant mood. A prime factor behind the settled state of affairs within the Church, and the dynamic rise of the baroque style in general, was, as we have seen, the Council of Trent, whose deliberations earlier in the sixteenth century led to the formulation of ecclesiastical policy that had a dramatic effect upon the arts. A vigorous reaffirmation of traditional views and practices, and a heightened importance of the arts in worship, were some of the results of the Counter Reformation.

The new outlook concerning the role of the arts in worship was one of the strongest forces in the shaping of the Baroque style. Essentially, it was the idea of reaching the spirit of the worshiper through dramatic sense impressions. The construction of the Church Il Gesù (the mother church of the new Jesuit Order founded by Ignatius Loyola), in Rome, 1575, marked the change in policy regarding sacred art. The architecture and vestments of this, and many other churches that sprang up in many parts of Europe, became splendorous, extravagant, and ornate displays. All the arts (music, architecture, sculpture, painting, and theater), the various structural elements (twisting spirals, circles, and columns) and materials (plaster, granite, and marble) were multiplied and fused together. The eye of the worshiper was met with the rich ornate swelling and swirling movements of elements that moved upward in a mystical

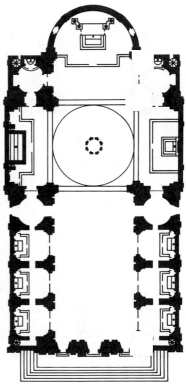

Giacomo Vignola and Giacomo della Porta. Il Gesù, Rome. *c.* 1575–1584; (left) façade, 105′ high, 115′ wide; (right) plan. Italian State Tourist Office

atmosphere. Several other important landmarks in the rise of the Baroque include the Carracci's ceiling fresco in the Farnese Palace in Rome 1604; *The Calling of St. Matthew,* painted by Caravaggio in 1593; *The Descent from the Cross,* painted by Rubens in 1614; and the completion of the façade of the colossal St. Peter's in Rome, 1612.

The all encompassing Baroque spirit was also felt in the new secular musical form—opera, invented by the Italians and represented in its earliest form by *Euridice* by Peri (1600), and *Orfeo* by Monteverdi (1607). Although initially not as grandiose and elaborate as early religious art, Baroque opera gradually became a stylistic counterpart to the "colossal Baroque," which was so dynamically and triumphantly expressed in the visual arts, originating chiefly in Rome. The Catholic musicians were

St. Peter's Basilica and the Vatican, Rome, Colonnades by Gianlorenzo Bernini, 1656–1663. From Vatican Photo Archives

also affected by the new esthetic, notably Orazio Benevoli, who created huge polychoric works (that is, employing four or more separate choral groups) that were performed in the spacious St. Peter's in the 1640s. Located at different points in the vast edifice, the multichoral bodies sounded forth in a gigantic stereo effect. Baroque theatricalism and pathos were also present in another new sacred music form called the *oratorio*, which was a religious musical drama. Early in the Baroque period oratorios were fully staged in Italian churches, and in the late Baroque they were performed without scenery and costuming in the concert hall.

Characteristics of the Baroque Expression Upon first examination of the arts and music of this period, one notes a strong resemblance to the High Renaissance—a massiveness and grandeur that seem to echo the world of Raphael, Michelangelo, Leonardo Da Vinci and Palestrina. Examples of Baroque art that emulate these qualities include: St. Peter's in Rome; the luxurious palace and gardens at Versailles; the painting *Disembarkation of Queen Maria de' Medici* by Rubens; and the poem *Paradise Lost* by John Milton. Baroque music mirrors these qualities in many ways, principally in spectacular operatic stagings, in oratorios, and in gigantic organ toccatas and fugues.

A closer examination of the Baroque style in all of the arts discloses the presence of the Mannerist influence: a dynamic movement, an inner tension and swelling, the contrasting of light, dark, and shadow—in short, the *dramatic* or *emotional* element. This is to be found in the tragic Baroque operas (*Orfeo*, for example), in the thunderous, cascading movement of the organ toccatas and fantasias, in the musical duels between soloists and full orchestra in the concertos, in the surging, ever driving bass in most instrumental music of the period, and in the deeply moving texts of the oratorios. Above all, a source for generating emotion and feeling in Baroque music is the dynamic opposition of musical elements, whether it be large group against small, high against low, soft against loud, or theme against countertheme, as in the great fugues by Bach.

One need not look far to find the dramatic element in the other arts of the Baroque: in the play of light and shadow in such realistic works as Caravaggio's *The Calling of St. Matthew*, Rubens' *The Lion Hunt*, and Bernini's sculpture *The Ecstasy of St. Teresa*; in the juxtaposition of many swirling, upward-moving architectural and sculptural elements inside many Baroque churches, such as the Il Gesù in Rome and the huge Benedictine church at Zweifalten, Germany; in the shadowy, mysterious atmosphere of Rembrandt's *The Night Watch*; and in his more deeply moving personality studies such as *The Supper at Emmaus*, which dramatize faith, pity, and suffering.

In our general summary of the basic characteristics of the Baroque we should also add two more qualities: the *extravagant* mode of expression—a rich, lavish display—and the *decorative*—the use of intricate, detailed design. In the late Baroque, when the power and strength of the great movement became expended, these latter qualities were highly developed in the Rococo (about 1715–1770). The extravagant element is demonstrated everywhere in the arts: in the aristocratic and lavish paintings of Rubens, in many of Milton's works, in the sumptuous staging of opera, in mammoth architectural spectacles such as the Palace of Versailles, and in the resplendent gathering of gigantic musical forces for such performances as the Royal Fireworks and Water Music Festivals in England under Handel. Decoration and elaboration are readily found in the interiors of many baroque churches, in the courtly, aristocratic paintings of Rubens, and in the frescoes by the Carracci. Musically, the decorative element appears in the ornate melodic lines of the solo song (aria) in opera and most notably in the melodic lines of French lute and harpsichord music. Here the decorative principle takes the form of various types of trills, grace notes, and turns (see Glossary).

Broad Aspects of Musical Style   It is not possible to approach the musical language of the Baroque in the same general manner as was followed for the Renaissance. Except for the rapid growth of secular music in the late sixteenth century, Renaissance musical style tended toward a oneness of expression—sacred polyphony—which emanated from the great Netherlands and Italian composers. The Baroque, on the other hand, is much more complex, due to the variety of musical idioms (operatic, orchestral, keyboard, chamber, and so on) and larger number of composers. Thus the reader will need to begin with a consideration of the broad aspects of style in order to gain the necessary perspective of the Baroque and to differentiate it from the preceding period of the Renaissance. Further listening experience involving selected works will lead to a comprehension of specific idioms and composers' styles.

Baroque musical style differs from that of the Renaissance in several respects. Generally speaking, the Baroque is to be identified by the following characteristics: (1) a wider variety of forms (concerto, opera, oratorio, cantata), compared to the predominantly vocal forms (mass, motet, chanson) of the Renaissance; (2) a simpler texture instead of the thick polyphonic texture of the preceding era; (3) a kinetic, on-going rhythmic motion based on a regular metrical movement ($\frac{2}{4}$, $\frac{3}{4}$, and so on), instead of the more flexible and nonmetrical patterns of much Renaissance choral music; (4) a continuous bass part usually standing out in high relief from the total musical effect, as opposed to the fusion of bass part in Renaissance polyphony; and (5) use of major and minor keys and scales in place of the modal system.

In summary, the Baroque movement, which originated in Italy, was the tangible fulfillment of an artistic trend stemming from the Venetian artists and composers of the Mannerist period. The inherent power, exuberance, and triumphant mood seem to have been nurtured by the restabilized Catholic Church in the late sixteenth century. The Baroque artists' and musicians' expressive language generally involves the statement of an idea in a spacious form, with power, force, extravagance, and elaboration of detail. Although there are exceptions, we will usually find these to be present in most literature, music, painting, sculpture, and architecture of the Baroque. In the following pages we will see how these qualities evolved in the development of Baroque music.

It will be convenient to divide the music of the period into two segments: early Baroque (1600–1685), and late Baroque (1685–1750). The first part is principally identified by an extensive concentration in dramatic vocal music and the latter by the creation of the modern orchestra and its forms, as well as new chamber music forms and the keyboard sonata. There is, of course, no clear line of demarcation between the end of the Baroque and the beginning of the next major period, the Classical Age (1750–1800). The mid-eighteenth century, the time of Bach's death (1750), which marks the close of the Baroque, is an era of many crosscurrents in music, chief of which is the classical style emerging from the Rococo period (1715–1770). The Rococo, which is sometimes treated as an extension of the Baroque, will be covered under the rise of the Classical Age in the next chapter.

EARLY BAROQUE MUSIC (1600–1685)

The Rise of Dramatic Vocal Music

The New Sound Ideal: Monody In the closing years of the sixteenth century, the strong literary trend that had been gathering momentum in music since the early Renaissance, finally burst forth. The leaders of this movement were a circle of Renaissance humanists—poets, musicians, and scholars—known as the Florentine Camerata. This elite group of intellectuals, which met regularly at Count Bardi's home in Florence beginning about 1580, discussed theories of music, Greek drama, and formulated a new esthetic ideal that greatly affected the course of Baroque music.

The new type of musical expression devised by the Camerata is called *monody*, from the Greek *monodia*, to sing alone. Its principles were first presented by Vincenzo Galilei (father of the renowned astronomer) in *Discourses on Ancient Music and Good Singing*, written about 1580. Briefly summarized, these principles are as follows:

1. Music is to be subordinate to the words of the text.
2. Elaborate polyphony cannot express clearly the emotions of the text.
3. A single vocal melody and chordal accompaniment is advocated instead of complex polyphony.
4. The vocal melody should be in the style of a speechlike recitation, that is, the musical rhythm should imitate the rhythm of speech, and the melody line should imitate the natural inflections of the speaking voice.
5. The singer should perform the melody with much expression and dramatic feeling.

The opening of the seventeenth century, then, saw the coming of a new dramatic style of music, quite opposed to the thick contrapuntal textures of the Renaissance. For a time the art of counterpoint was set aside in favor of vertically arranged tones (homophonic texture), which could provide the expressive accompaniment necessary for the vocal soloist's declamation of a dramatic text. Later, toward the end of the seventeenth century, counterpoint was restored and remained as the mainstay of Baroque musical art.

To return to the beginnings of monody, we note that the Florentines favored an instrumental accompaniment that could provide a harmonic background for the soloist. Thus, instruments that could produce chords, such as the lute, harpsichord, and organ became the preferred types. The name given to this accompaniment was *basso continuo* (or continuous bass, so called because of its constant presence throughout the music). Moreover, by the beginning of the seventeenth century, it became standard practice to include a cello or viola da gamba as well. The music for the basso continuo usually consisted of a single melody in the bass clef with a series of numbers (6, $\frac{6}{5}$) below it. These indicated the various types of chords to be played above the given bass part.

Time-Line: Early Baroque Music

1600	Florentine Camerata, birth of opera. *Euridice* by Peri
	Beginnings of oratorio
1607	Monteverdi: opera, *Orfeo*
1637	Public opera theatres begin in Venice
1640s	Polychoric style at St. Peter's by Benevoli
1642	Monteverdi: opera, *Coronation of Poppea*
1664	Schütz: *Christmas Oratorio*
1680	Neapolitan opera dominant, A. Scarlatti
1689	Purcell: opera, *Dido and Aeneas*

Thus, the harpsichord player was expected to "fill in" or to improvise over the bass melody. The other member of the basso continuo, the cello or viola da gamba, doubled the bass melody. The basso continuo idea was employed extensively throughout the Baroque, first used as the only accompaniment for the early operas and then later becoming the heart of every Baroque instrumental ensemble. Toward the end of the Baroque (c. 1740) when the symphony began to replace the concerto form, the basso continuo gradually disappeared from musical practice.

The Dramatic Vocal Music Forms   Among the members of the Florentine Camerata were several composers who applied the monodic principles to musical composition. From their experiments and those of their contemporaries, emerged the dramatic vocal genres of the Baroque: opera, solo monody, oratorio, and cantata. A brief description of these forms will be followed by an overview of opera—the dominant musical expression of the early Baroque.

Opera   Baroque opera may be defined as an elaborate theatrical presentation, that is, involving costumes and scenery, in which the entire text (called *libretto*) is set to music. Usually it is based upon a secular plot, which may be in the form of a tragedy (*opera seria*) or comedy (*opera buffa*). Intrinsic features that gradually evolved in the early Baroque include the use of sung declamatory passages (called *recitative* and modeled after dramatic speech) and complete solo songs called *arias*, which are constructed on purely musical grounds, having distinct form, phrasing, and melodic contour. The instrumental accompaniment gradually developed from the simple basso continuo used for the first operas to, by the eighteenth century, a full orchestral group.

Solo Monodies   This general classification refers to all types of vocal solo music, such as solo madrigal, arias, and canzonets, which were printed by the hundreds beginning early in the seventeenth century. These solo songs, which may be regarded as a type of vocal chamber music because of their intimate expression and lack of staging, first appeared in Giulio Caccini's collection of music *Nuove Musiche* (*New Music*), printed in 1602. An excellent example of solo monody is Caccini's solo madrigal, *Dovrò dunque morire?* (*Must I Die Then?*), from his *Nuove Musiche*.

Oratorio   Although the oratorio is similar in some respects to the opera in its basic structure (chorus, soloists, and instrumental accompaniment), it differs in its use of religious subject matter (usually drawn from the Bible) and of a narrator who relates the unfolding story, and in its concert method of performance, that is, without stage scenery and costumes. This is the type of oratorio that is most often performed today. In general, the oratorio of the early Baroque period differs from the late in that the former type was performed in church as a religious drama with full staging and scenery, while the latter type (Handel), although continuing the sacred theme, was presented in a secular setting and without stage equipment and costumes.

The beginnings of oratorio go back to 1600, to Emilio Cavalieri's *La Rappresentazione di Anima e di Corpo* (The Story of Soul and Body). The trend toward the late Baroque type of oratorio was initiated largely by Giacomo Carissimi (1605-1674), who aside from abolishing the stage presentation, established the chorus and narrator as integral parts of this highly dramatic vocal form. Carissimi, moreover, is considered to be the leading Italian master of the seventeenth-century oratorio. His most famous work is *Jeptha*, composed about 1650. In Germany, the greatest composer of oratorios was Heinrich Schütz (1585-1672), whose master-pieces include *The Seven Last Words* (c. 1645) and the *Christmas Oratorio* (1664).

Cantata   This vocal form, which first appeared as a *camera* (chamber) *cantata* for one or two voices and basso continuo, gradually developed into a substantial form by the late seventeenth century. Although the chamber cantata is much shorter than the opera, it is similar by nature of its secular and dramatic content—like a small scene extracted from an opera. Because of its sophisticated and more subtle intellectual char-acter, and lack of theatricality (no costumes or staging), the chamber cantata was the chief interest of the discriminating elite rather than the masses in the public theater. The leading composer of cantatas during the early Baroque was Alessandro Scarlatti (1659-1725), who composed approximately six hundred works in this form. The secular or chamber cantata was the most frequent type to be found in seventeenth-century Italy; however, in the late Baroque, the *cantata da chiesa* (church cantata) is particularly common because of the work of J. S. Bach in Germany.

Seventeenth-Century Opera: Background   By far the most important musical happening of the seventeenth century was the creation of opera. Little did the men of the Camerata realize that from their exclusive intellectual realm would arise a musical form that would become the dominant idiom of major European composers for a century and a half. It is inter-esting to note, too, that opera is the oldest of the large musical forms. The second-ranking form, the concerto, began about seventy years after opera (c. 1670) and the symphony came into being early in the next century (c. 1730).

Perhaps the most striking feature about opera of the seventeenth century is its quantity rather than quality. Several factors may account for this rather dismal picture, which is, however, brightened by the ap-pearance of several musical geniuses who will merit close attention. First, we must understand that the early Baroque was a time of musical inno-vation, that is, new forms—opera, cantata, oratorio, and so on—were created. Also, an entirely new concept of musical creation, monody, came into being. It was, in short, an experimental age, whereas the late Baroque, we will find, is an epoch of musical maturity—when styles and practices tended toward standardization and perfection.

Secondly, we must understand the inherent nature of opera and how this form differs from others. The major instrumental forms (sym-phony, concerto, string quartet, and so on) represent the private, more personal realm of creativity and are subject only to the composer's own esthetic principles. Opera, on the other hand—due to its theatrical structure, subject matter, dual relationship of librettist and composer, and, above all, expense in staging—is a more self-conscious art form. It is thus more openly subject to the varied and changing tastes of its audience. And this fact seems, in part, to account for the less than ideal state of opera in the seventeenth century.

Baroque opera began as a high art form, that is, as the creation of idealistic-minded intellectuals. However, with the subsequent opening of public opera houses (in Venice, the leading center of opera, in 1637) it became increasingly an economic venture that reflected the interests and tastes of the masses. In the classical period of the eighteenth century the opera was revitalized by Gluck, and it reached its greatest heights in the hands of Mozart.

Our third point is the problem of text vs music—a problem that is clearly illustrated in the operas of the early Baroque. In their attempt to emulate principles of classical drama, the first opera composers, such as Peri and Caccini (1600), placed the text in a dominant position. Music was actually an accessory, a mere framework, and was used in a subordinate fashion to intensify the meaning of the text. The composers, however, became dissatisfied with this arrangement and by about 1630, in Rome, began to introduce devices that placed increased emphasis on music per se. The aria, a pure song, was used to break up tedious stretches of recitative (speechlike passages of singing). And by the end of the seventeenth century the purely musical aspects completely dominated, to the point that the libretto was regarded as an accessory, and the principal item of interest of those in the audience was the aria.

What compounded the problem now (late 1600s) was that emotional expression, the essence of musical art, was lost in the tremendous public interest in vocal virtuosity, which practically obliterated opera as an art form in the late seventeenth and early eighteenth centuries. However, the problem of balance between text and music was successfully treated by several Baroque opera composers, namely Monteverdi and so some extent Alessandro Scarlatti, who is to be remembered for his advancement of the musical portion of opera. Again, esthetic balance seems to have been achieved by Gluck and Mozart in the classical era and by Weber, Verdi, Puccini, and Wagner in the nineteenth century.

A fourth problem that has direct bearing on understanding opera of the Baroque, and for that matter of all periods, is that of subject matter. Opera must draw from human experience for its sustenance; therefore, the subject matter generally reflects the life about it—the customs, habits, events, and language. Again, unlike the abstract aspects of the symphony and concerto, these intrinsic features have meaning only in terms of our understanding of the age. The witticisms, expressions of passion, comedy, and tragedy do not have the same meaning today. The operatic work, therefore, must be listened to against the backdrop of the period itself. Moreover, like all operas, those of the seventeenth century illustrate yet another basic problem—the conflict of reality with unreality.

For example, due to the medium, the story must be telescoped, resulting in distortion of time. Also, there is the unnatural convention of accompanying action, even in the most dire moments, by singing and the frequent extension or prolongation of the dramatic climax for purely musical reasons.

One may wonder how the opera form ever developed with all of these complexities. And yet it is precisely because of its richness and complexity that many are attracted to it. On the one hand there is the double nature of the poetic text with its euphonic, sensual qualities of the sound of words and the appeal to the intellect through symbols, and, on the other, the double nature of the music, with its intensity of expression and an internal logic and order unparalleled by any of the other arts. It is this duality of expression of *tone* and *word* that continually challenged seventeenth-century opera composers.

The Development of Italian Opera *Euridice,* by Jacopo Peri, composed in 1600, is generally regarded as the first opera. An earlier opera, *Dafne,* written by Jacopo Peri and Ottavio Rinuccini in 1597, is unfortunately lost. Peri's *Euridice,* which was not yet called an opera but a "pastoral fable," consisted of a prologue and ten scenes and was complete with costumes and sumptuous scenery.

The plot, which is based upon the Greek myth of Orpheus, begins with a scene in a meadow where a joyful wedding dance is being held to celebrate the marriage of Orpheus and Euridice. Orpheus learns from Daphne that Euridice has been bitten by a snake and is dead. Wishing to have his bride restored, Orpheus attempts to follow her to the lower regions of the earth, where he pleads with Pluto to release her. In contrast to the tragic ending of the Greek myth, in which Orpheus looks back and loses his Euridice forever, the opera ends with the couple happily joined together again in the meadow.

Although very sparsely constructed musically, it contains all the fundamental features of opera: solo songs, choral passages, and instrumental accompaniment of several instruments (harpsichord, large tenor lute, and bass viol), which provided the basso continuo. For the most part the work consists of continuous recitative, occasionally interrupted by a few moments of song, and accompanied throughout by the ever-present basso continuo. In summary, the opera was more of a literary than musical work, the melody line adhering closely to the rhythm and inflection of the spoken word.

With Claudio Monteverdi (1567–1643), unquestionably the leading composer of the early seventeenth century, the inherent dramatic and expressive power of the opera form is realized for the first time. Although not a Florentine, (working mainly at Mantua and Venice), Monteverdi continued the same general style of the Florentines; however, his work is decidedly advanced in dramatic characterization, in emotional expression, and in musical construction. His first opera, *Orfeo* (1607), which is considered the first operatic masterpiece, utilizes the same plot as Peri's *Euridice;* however, what immediately separates the two works is Monteverdi's genius.

This is particularly evident in the scene when Orfeo, having learned of his wife's death, expresses his profound grief and his determination to enter the terrible underworld and rescue Euridice. In this scene, in which Orfeo sings the recitative "Tu se' morta" (Thou art perished), strange, dissonant chords and an angular melodic line (in declamatory style) with chromatics, dramatically convey his intense sorrow and remorse. In contrast to Peri's opera, Monteverdi employs a large orchestra of thirty-six players, including two harpsichords, two contrabass viols, ten viole da braccio, harp, two small violini, two large lutes, two organs, three viole da gamba, four trombones, a portable organ, two cornetti, a little flute, a high trumpet, and three muted trumpets. In addition to an introductory, overturelike piece called a *toccata,* the instrumentalists played *ritornelli* (recurring sections of the same thematic material) and provided expressive and colorful accompaniments. This large instrumentation was, however, the exception in seventeenth-century opera, since for the most part only the basso continuo, occasionally augmented by several stringed instruments, prevailed.

Recitative from *Orfeo* by Claudio Monteverdi

Monteverdi's last great work, and according to many the most significant opera of the seventeenth century, *L'Incoronazione di Poppea* (*The Coronation of Poppea*) was composed at the end of his long career as maestro di cappella at St. Mark's in Venice, in 1642. Although it does not have the elaborate choral and orchestral forces, this work ranks with his earlier *Orfeo* in its power and vividness of expression. Instead of using a plot based on a mythological subject, however, Monteverdi, as did his contemporaries at this time, now turned to historical subjects. In *Poppea,* the plot centers around the mistress of Nero, Poppea, and her successful attempt to depose Nero's wife, the Empress Octavia.

Monteverdi's dramatic and musical achievements, specifically, his power to present characters as real people and his ability to mirror their inmost feelings musically, ranks him with the best of opera composers. Perhaps it is this single quality above all else—truth in the expression of emotion—that brings continual praise to the operas of Monteverdi, Puccini, Wagner, and others. This characteristic of greatness is the result of blending musical genius with a strong sense of the dramatic. Reliance on musicianship alone to the neglect of the dramatic is not the answer. Unfortunately, as we have already mentioned, this idea became increasingly manifest during the course of the seventeenth century.

In order to understand this plight we must examine the trend in musical thinking preceding and following the giant of the age, Monteverdi. Italian musicians have always had a leaning toward the lyrical, the beauty of unadorned and uncomplicated melodic line, and clarity and simplicity of form. These traits, which extend deep into Italian musical history, may account for the strong trend in the mid-seventeenth century away from the pre-eminence of drama to a more lyric concept of opera. This movement was given impetus in Rome, earlier in the century, when long stretches of recitative were interrupted by the introduction of arias.

Thus, the purely musical element began to come to the fore in the opera: the aria increasingly became the main musical item, and sensuously beautiful melodies became the ideal, rather than drama and passion. This trend coincides with the rise of public opera theaters. The taste of the masses became dominant, and with increasing rapidity opera became characterized by its use of elaborate and extravagant scenery, lavish stage machinery (shipwrecks, storms, and so on), a great number of characters, and stereotyped dramatic situations involving mistaken identity, female and male impersonations, and burlesque episodes. Musically the opera degenerated into a succession of arias that were frequently borrowed from other operas and based on popular tunes. The vocal soloists dominated the opera, particularly the *castrati* (male soprano singers), who could perform unusual feats of singing.

Although these tendencies were continued by the next group of Italian opera composers at Naples (the Neapolitan School) beginning in the late seventeenth century, the decadent Venetian influence was largely broken by the leader of the Neapolitans, Alessandro Scarlatti. Scarlatti's influence extended into the eighteenth century, as evidenced in the numerous operatic works of Handel, the leading exponent of the Neapolitan tradition. Scarlatti weakened the Venetian hold through his musical rather than dramatic ability. He established what came to be known as "Neapolitan opera," generally characterized by a distinct division of text and music, historical rather than mythological subject matter, and heavy emphasis placed on the aria and vocal virtuosity.

In the older, pre-Neapolitan operas, composers strove for dramatic continuity, that is, recitative was followed by aria in a continuous fashion in an attempt to mirror the flow of the dramatic action. With the advent of Neapolitan opera, the dramatic and purely musical elements were placed in separate compartments. To illustrate, the story was related in the recitative portion and then, immediately following, an aria was sung in which the character would comment and reflect upon the previous action as set forth in the recitative.

The central feature of the Neapolitan opera was the aria, usually in ABA form, in which the singer was expected to improvise on the last repetition of the first section (A). That is, the singer would introduce various types of ornaments such as grace notes, trills, scales, arpeggios (see Glossary) and even virtuosic cadenzas on the final cadence. Interestingly, the cadenza eventually became a standard part of the classical concerto.

Among the many other interesting developments attributed to the Neapolitans is the division of recitative into two distinct types: *recitativo secco* ("dry recitative"), a rapidly moving dialogue usually accompanied by harpsichord only; and *recitativo accompagnato* (accompanied recitative), a more dramatic discourse with orchestral accompaniment. The Neapolitans also preceded the opening act of the opera by an overture (then called *sinfonia*) made up of three parts, fast-slow-fast. Its driving, forceful rhythm, clarity of phrase structure, and homophonic texture became the dominant characteristics of the classical symphony, which began to emerge about 1740. Some of the best examples of Neapolitan opera include *Tigrane, Mitradate,* and *Griselda,* which are to be found among the more than a hundred operas composed by Alessandro Scarlatti. Although oftentimes caught in the press of public popularity, which forced him to lose sight of high artistic ideals, many of Scarlatti's works display a richness of musical invention, particularly in the aria and its accompaniments. It is interesting to note, moreover, the gathering germinating forces of the classical spirit in Scarlatti's work: clarity, conciseness, balanced melodic phrases, and homophonic texture. In many respects we will find that the Neapolitan opera, and the overture especially, is the ground from which many traits of the classical style emerged later in the eighteenth century.

The Spread of Opera: France and England   As early as 1645 the French began to import Italian opera. However, they did not adopt the new form until late in the century, probably due to their preoccupation with their own cultural creations: the classical tragedy (Corneille and Racine) and the ballet, which had begun in France in the fifteenth century. The central figure in French opera, and indeed the supreme leader of seventeenth-century French music, is Jean-Baptiste Lully. Of a humble Italian background (born as Lulli in Florence, 1632), Lully traveled to Paris as a young boy and became employed as a kitchen scullion. At the age of fourteen he joined the king's famed *les vingt-quatre violons du roi* (the twenty-four violins of the king). An exceptional violinist and a personal favorite of the young Louis XIV, Lully became director of all royal musical activities, including chamber and orchestral music, and, in 1672, the director of the new French opera established in the royal palace. In this post, which he held until his death in 1687, Lully composed sixteen works in the opera form, or what the French called *tragédie lyrique,* including *Thésée* (1675), *Phaëton* (1683), and *Armide* (1686).

French opera differs from Italian opera in many respects, most important of which, perhaps, is the style of recitative, which in French opera was modeled after the refined speech of professional French actors. This type of recitative, referred to as "rhetorical recitative" by some writers, follows precisely the accent, length, and inflection of French syllables. This highly stylized and refined treatment of the text has a definite "classical" ring, so characteristic of French theater of this period. It is interesting to note that this vein of classicism (which antedates what is generally thought of as the classical period in the arts, 1750–1800) dates back to the early seventeenth century, when the French literary movement, with its emphasis on elegance, correctness of expression, and refinement, began to take shape.

Another powerful influence upon French culture, including musical art, was the founding of the Académie Française in 1634. Consisting of noted literary figures who ruled on practically all literary and artistic matters, this select body of connoisseurs greatly affected artistic directions in France from the seventeenth to the nineteenth century. The Académie favored moderation, conciseness, restraint, exquisiteness, and the importance of rule over individual taste—definite classicistic tendencies, which underlie the French opera and keyboard music of this period.

The strong French interest in the dance is also important in relation to the opera and to other musical forms which appeared in the Baroque and later periods. Lully, who composed a large number of ballets (*ballet de cour*), included the ballet as an integral part in opera. Actually, ballet, the chief cultural contribution of seventeenth-century France, was the source of a number of dance forms which were later to have an important role in instrumental music. These include the *gavotte, bourrée, rigaudon,* and *minuet,* which are frequently found in the Baroque suite, played by solo harpsichord or orchestra. The minuet was eventually adopted as the third movement in the classical symphony.

Curiously, the opera furor did not affect England until the eighteenth century, when the Neapolitan-styled operas of the German-born Handel became the rage. Unfortunately, England's musical contribution in the seventeenth century—compared to her great achievements in the preceding century—were very sparse. Aside from considerable chamber music (fantasias and ensemble sonatas or trio sonatas), little was done in dramatic vocal music, at least nothing that would compare with the Italian furor. The *masque,* a popular type of English court entertainment in the sixteenth and seventeenth centuries, was more of a spectacle than a drama. Elaborately staged and modeled after the French ballet de cour, it consisted of a succession of dances ranging from crude comic to the macabre, and danced by both professionals and members of the elite audience. The latter participants were called *masquers* (hence the name of this form), and usually wore exotic disguises. These dances were accompanied by voices and instruments and separated by spoken dialogue, recitative and solo songs. The most famous English writer of masques was Ben Jonson (*The Vision of Delight,* 1617). Noted composers of masque music include William Lawes (1602–1645), Matthew Locke (1630–1677), and Henry Purcell (1659–1695). The latter composed the only true English opera of the seventeenth century, *Dido and Aeneas* (1689), of which the final aria, "When I am Laid in Earth," is widely celebrated. Purcell also wrote incidental music for various dramas, and a considerable amount of chamber music, for which he is most famous.

Instrumental Music of the Seventeenth Century

The Status of Instrumental Music Opera and other forms of dramatic vocal music overshadowed instrumental music in the early Baroque. The developments that did occur in the instrumental idiom are to be found chiefly in music for solo instruments: organ music in Italy and Germany, and lute and harpsichord music in France. However, chamber music, and here we are referring to ensemble music for two or more instruments, did not dwindle during the early Baroque. The development here, although less than in solo instrumental music, was one of formal clarification. That is, the many names of various forms (such as sonata, canzona, ricercar), which were used at the beginning of the century to represent practically any musical design and combination of instruments, began to be thinned out into several fairly defined ensemble forms by 1650.

Two such forms, the *sonata da chiesa* (church sonata) and *sonata da camera* (chamber sonata) were cultivated by the Italians beginning in the last half of the century. Since these represent the achievements of Arcangelo Corelli, who announced the arrival of the great age of Italian instrumental music at the end of the seventeenth century, they will be discussed in subsequent pages, under the late Baroque.

Music for the Organ: Italy and Germany The greatest period of organ music extends from the sixteenth-century Venetian masters at St. Mark's (Merulo and the Gabrielis) to the German musical genius, Johann Sebastian Bach, the culminator of the Baroque. The principal qualities of the Baroque —power, drama, boundlessness, ornateness, and breadth of expression— are perhaps most completely represented in the music for organ. To grasp this we must realize that the organ was a virtuoso instrument even as early as the Venetians, who used it to play all of the parts of a polyphonic composition. In a sense it was the most perfect of instruments, since it could, by itself, produce (1) the complete fabric of music, both contrapuntal and harmonic; (2) the complete musical range; (3) technical passages; and (4) dramatic shadings in volume and tone color. Thus the organ became the instrument of the virtuoso and a medium for brilliant technique and profound emotional expression. Occasionally technique outweighs the expressive in this period; however, in many of the works of the leaders—Frescobaldi, Buxtehude, Pachelbel, and Bach—the two aspects are aesthetically balanced.

The Venetians first realized many of the potentialities of the instrument and created some of the principal organ forms (ricercar, canzona, and toccata). However, the idiom was greatly advanced by the leading Italian organ composer and virtuoso of the early Baroque, Girolamo Frescobaldi (1583–1643), at St. Peter's in Rome during the first half of the century. His work represents the musical equivalent of the dynamic and boundless spirit that burgeoned forth in early Baroque art. His organ works seem to be musical representations of the mystical architectural dramas found in such churches as the Il Gesù and St. Ignazio in Rome. Contained in his Herculean toccatas is a driving, ever-reaching restlessness punctuated by strange dissonances and bold syncopations. And yet at other times, in typical Baroque fashion, there is a strange religious calm that enhances the power and sweep of these architectural monuments of tone.

Frescobaldi's stature rests chiefly on his extraordinary gift for treating musical ideas through such means as the theme and variation principle, and through such contrapuntal devices as diminution, augmentation, and imitation. The favored forms include the *toccata, partita, ricercar,* and *canzona.* The *toccata* is usually a brilliant display piece, consisting of fast-moving scale and arpeggio figures. Its form is free (no set pattern), largely due to its rhapsodic nature that is given to sudden changes in mood and rhythmic restlessness. The *partita,* in the early seventeenth century, referred to a series of variations. Later in the century German composers began to use it in the sense of the suite. The terms *ricercar, fantasia,* and *canzona* were, unfortunately, applied rather indiscriminately to polyphonic instrumental compositions early in the seventeenth century. However, according to Grout, "the ricercar and fantasia were built on a theme or themes of sustained legato character. The tendency was to develop the themes in such pieces in continuous imitative counterpoint. The canzona had a livelier, more markedly rhythmic melodic material and composers tended to emphasize division of the material into sections."[1] Many of Frescobaldi's canzonas still show the inherent spirit of the Renaissance chanson from which the form was derived, namely the opening rhythmic motive ♩♩♩ and the chordal style.

In the north the great tradition of organ music was continued mainly by Buxtehude (1637–1707), organist at Lübeck, Germany (where the young Bach had traveled many miles to hear the great master), and Johann Pachelbel (1653–1706), the principal figure in the crystallization of the *fugue.* The fugue, the most musically interesting and challenging form used by Baroque organ composers, evolved from the ricercar. Already in the seventeenth century, German composers were beginning to use the name *fuga* for pieces in the ricercar style.

The basic features of the fugue may be sketched briefly. It is a polyphonic composition in which one theme (called a subject) is first stated alone in one voice part in the tonic key and answered (imitated) in another key (dominant or subdominant) by a second part. Then other parts sound the subject or its answer in succession. When the various parts have stated either the subject or the answer, the first section (or *exposition*) is completed. Several other expositions may follow before the fugue's close. This type of fugue was perfected by J. S. Bach in the late Baroque.

[1] Donald J. Grout, *A History of Western Music,* (New York: W. W. Norton and Company, Inc., 1960), p. 299.

Fugue by Johann Pachelbel (1653–1706). From *Anthology of Music for Analysis* by
Albert Cohen and John D. White. Copyright © 1965 by Meredith Corporation.
Reprinted by permission of Appleton-Century-Crofts.

French Lute and Keyboard Music In addition to the spectacular and elaborate opera and ballet, the French also concentrated on the miniature—music for the lute and harpsichord. In many respects these exquisite pieces heralded the approaching rococo period, which was to arise in France in the early eighteenth century. The lute of the sixteenth and seventeenth centuries had a pear-shaped body, a fretted fingerboard and eleven strings, five pairs of which were tuned in octaves or unison. It had a deep, rich tone, owing to its bass range and double stringing. Since the strings were paired rather than single (as on the modern guitar), the player had to pluck each string of the pair with extreme accuracy.

Idiomatic considerations, that is, the natural capabilities and limitations of instruments, have played a major part in the evolution of music written for specific types of instruments such as the lute, organ, and violin. For example, the organ became the preferred instrument for polyphonic textured music because of its keyboard structure and pedals, which permitted the playing of several different parts simultaneously. Also, the new violin, which was widely adopted by the Italians in the seventeenth century, was given two fundamental types of melodic material: (1) sustained, legato patterns suited to the violin's bowing technique and (2) characteristic fast-skipping movements easily performed by the violinist. The same is true of the lute. Its structure lends itself to a dominantly chord-structured music with a natural rhythmic pulse—in short, to the music of the dance. The dance origins of lute music extend back to the sixteenth century, when pairs of dances, notably the pavan-galliard combination were favored. These first lute pieces were very simple, consisting of a tune with chordal accompaniment. Later, lute music became more intricate; in addition to dance music, transcriptions of chansons were played.

In seventeenth-century France, the lute was the instrument of the virtuoso, represented chiefly by Denis Gaultier (1597–1672). His major contributions to the lute repertoire are in a collection entitled *La Rhétorique des dieux* (*The Rhetoric of the Gods*), composed by Gaultier in the 1650s. This music consists of a series of popular dances (pavan, courante, and so forth) each provided with a descriptive title such as *La Coquette virtuosa*, and composed in a highly stylized and refined manner. The dances are grouped into sets according to key (for example, five allemandes, eleven courantes, four sarabandes, and so on, all in C major, constitute a set).

Gradually, the harpsichord (called *clavecin* in French) attained considerable importance during the late seventeenth century and eventually surpassed the lute in popularity—probably because of the harpsichord's simpler, more modern notation and melodic and harmonic agility.

Interestingly, many of the melodic and harmonic patterns characteristic of lute music were absorbed into the new French harpsichord expression. The same type of stylized dance music, and even the characteristic lute technique (broken chords and ornamentation), were emulated by the leading French harpsichordist-composer of the period, Jacques Chambonnières (c. 1602–1672). A contemporary of Gaultier, and musician to Louis XIII and XIV, Chambonnières was the most brilliant harpsichord artist produced by seventeenth-century France. His work is contained in a collection called *Pièces de Clavessin*.

The French preferred the word *ordre* for these loosely organized series of harpsichord pieces. They represent an important phase in the development of the *suite,* which began as early as the paired dances played by the Renaissance lutenists. The suite form was completed by the Germans around 1700. The latter musicians (particularly Froberger) organized the dances into a definite unified musical whole, consisting usually of four dances: allemande, courante, sarabande, and gigue; quite frequently an optional group (minuet, bourrée, gavotte) was added.

MUSIC OF THE LATE BAROQUE
(1685–1750)

The Supremacy of Italian Instrumental Music: Corelli

Following a period of heterogeneous activity in the early part of the Baroque, Italian ensemble and orchestral music burst forth in full grandeur in the late seventeenth century. The Italian composers, notably Corelli and Vivaldi, brought the development to its highest peak during the last quarter of the seventeenth century and early part of the eighteenth, an era that may rightfully be called the golden age of Italian instrumental music.

While a vast number of concertos were written for the trumpet and other wind instruments, the dominant instruments of this great hour in music were the stringed instruments, the modern violin, viola, cello, and double bass. Many of the new stringed instruments that had now superseded the older Renaissance viols were made in the early Baroque by the Amati family, the first leading violin craftsmen; the art of violin-making reached its climax with Antonio Stradivari (1644–1737) in the early years of the eighteenth century. A large body of works in which the stringed instruments were an integral part, such as church and chamber sonatas, solo sonatas, and concertos, were composed by the Italians and imitated throughout Europe.

The center for this amazing instrumental creativity was in the Italian city of Bologna, where during the last quarter of the century more sonatas and other instrumental music were composed than in any other city in Europe. Bologna has always had a strong musical culture; however, instrumental music was given impetus in 1657, when Maurizio Cazzati was appointed musical director of Bologna's Church of San Petronio. The huge edifice of San Petronio became the scene of widespread usage of ensemble music as a means for enriching the religious service. It became customary to perform a sonata or concerto during the various parts of the service, usually just before the Mass. Bologna's musical life was further enhanced by the abundant support of the wealthy class and especially by the founding in 1666 of the Accademia Filarmonica, a music academy that later became world famous.

It was this musically rich environment that Arcangelo Corelli (1653–1713) entered at the age of thirteen, to begin his first study of the violin.

Paolo Veronese, *Marriage at Cana*. Detail. Oil on canvas, 21'10" x 32'5". Louvre, Paris
Alinari, Art Reference Bureau

Four years later he enrolled in the famed Accademia Filarmonica, where
he studied violin and theoretical subjects in music. From 1685 until his
death in 1713, Corelli was active in Rome, where he wrote a large number
of sonatas and concertos under the patronage of Cardinal Pietro Ottoboni,
an enthusiastic follower of the arts.

Forms and Styles   As can be seen from the following list of Corelli's
instrumental works, his chief musical forms are the *trio sonata, solo sonata*
and *concerto grosso*. The trio sonata is so-named because of its three designated parts of two violins and continuo (*continuo* implying both a keyboard[2] instrument and a low-pitched stringed instrument such as the
cello). The solo sonata, which is for violin and continuo, was less common at this time; however, during the next period, the classical, it became
a major musical form. The concerto grosso, composed for a number of
instruments, marks the beginning of orchestral music.

[2] The organ was the customary keyboard form for the church sonata, whereas
the harpsichord was used for the chamber sonata.

Opus (Op.) 1	12 trio sonatas (da chiesa) published 1681
Op. 2	11 trio sonatas (camera) and a chaconne published 1685
Op. 3	12 trio sonatas (da chiesa) published 1689
Op. 4	12 trio sonatas (camera) published 1695
Op. 5	12 solo sonatas published 1700
Op. 6	12 concerti grossi published 1714

It will be noted above that Corelli differentiated his trio sonatas by the terms "sonata da chiesa" (church sonata) and "sonata da camera" (chamber sonata). Although Corelli was by no means consistent in his treatment of these forms, certain prevailing characteristics may be noted. The sonata da chiesa was intended for church performance, as generally evidenced by its more serious tone and solemn adagio opening. It usually utilized polyphonic texture, and was divided into four separate movements having the tempos slow, fast, slow, and fast. The sonata da camera, which was designed for domestic performance due to its lighter mood, frequently consisted of a series of short movements based on the conventional dances of the period, such as the sarabande, allemande, gavott, and gigue.

Stile concertato, the Baroque style in which one instrument or body is pitted against another in a kind of musical duel, is perhaps most clearly demonstrated in the new form—the *concerto grosso* (meaning *grand concerto*) —which was introduced by the Bolognese composers at the end of the seventeenth century. Corelli's concerti exemplify an experimental stage of development, since some have three, four, or more movements. The three-movement concerto eventually became established by Corelli's successor, Antonio Vivaldi. However, the basic idea of the concerto grosso— the contrasting of two bodies of instruments, the *concertino* (solo group of several players) and the *ripieno* (the accompanying full group) is found in Corelli's concerti. Although his works are constructed on this concertino-ripieno dualism, they do not differentiate the two bodies into clear-cut groups having separate thematic material. This phase of the Baroque concerto was brought to fruition by Torelli (1658–1709) and particularly Vivaldi (1675–1741).

Sonata da Chiesa in E Minor by Arcangelo Corelli

Corelli's Sonata da Chiesa in E Minor   This sonata (Op. 3, no. 7), published in 1689, has in its first movement the characteristic majestic and reverent qualities common to many church sonatas. Only twenty measures in length, the opening movement is based on a melodic idea that after its abrupt upward step of a sixth, slowly drifts downward in conjunct motion. Alternately, the various string instruments (two violins and cello), supported by the organ, imitate this theme in close succession. Above are the first few measures of this sonata. Note the *figured bass* in the continuo. It may be recalled from earlier reading that these numbers constituted a kind of musical shorthand, and indicated the harmony or chords to be filled in by the keyboard player.

Vivaldi

The life of the second leading figure of this period, Antonio Vivaldi (1675–1741), stands in contrast to that of Corelli, the musician of high Roman society. Educated in music and for the priesthood, Vivaldi, due to ill health, eventually turned completely to the music profession. His principal work was done in connection with the Conservatory of the Pietà in Venice, a conventlike institution for orphaned girls. For almost forty years (1704–1740) Vivaldi held the musical directorship of the conservatory, a post that included conducting, composing, and teaching. A flourishing program of music studies and concerts was carried on as an important part of the institution's educational curriculum. For the orchestra, which numbered about thirty to forty players, Vivaldi composed a great quantity of music, particularly in the concerto form, which was performed at the school's public concerts and festivals. Clearly, his main contribution was the perfection of the Baroque concerto in which form he composed over four hundred works.

His concertos follow the three-movement plan of fast, slow, fast. The bulk of these are, however, solo concertos in which one instrument (normally a stringed instrument) is juxtaposed against the full orchestra. The concerti grossi, which constitute a smaller segment of his creative output, employ the concertino-ripieno division of the orchestra, but in contrast to Corelli's concerti, each of the two groups is assigned contrasting thematic material. Following the style of Corelli and other Bolognese composers, Vivaldi's themes gradually unfold in long, ever-moving, and ever-changing patterns. The Vivaldi orchestra is greatly expanded over the string-dominated group of Corelli. The strings are, of course, uppermost; however, other instruments are frequently called for, such as flutes, oboes, horns, and trumpets, providing a greatly enriched orchestral sound. Of the many concertos by Vivaldi, *The Four Seasons* (1725)—depicting musically fall, winter, spring, and summer—is perhaps the most famous. Interestingly, this is one of the first orchestral works to employ the *programmatic principle*—that is, basing the composition upon something outside of music—a concept common to the romantic era of the nineteenth century.

The Concerto Grosso in A minor (Op. 3, no. 8) provides a typical example of Vivaldi's treatment of this Baroque form. It has the usual three movements of fast, slow, fast, and makes use of the concertino-ripieno grouping in the first and last movements. The concertino group in this instance consists of two violins, which compete, musically speaking, with the accompanying full group. A significant feature of many Vivaldi concerti is the *ritornello*, a recurring theme played by the ripieno. Alternating with the ripieno theme are *episodes*, for example, sections in which the concertino plays contrasting material. These structural principles are illustrated in the following diagram of the opening of the first movement of Vivaldi's Concerto Grosso in A minor.

RIPIENO   *CONCERTINO*   *RIPIENO*   *CONCERTINO*   *RIPIENO* . . . .
Ritornello I   Episode   Rit. II   Episode   Rit. III
(main theme)

The Rise of the Keyboard Sonata: Kuhnau

At the close of the seventeenth century, the sonata idea of the Italians was transferred to the harpsichord by Johann Kuhnau (1660–1722), J. S. Bach's predecessor at St. Thomas' Church in Leipzig. Solo music for harpsichord, of course, dates back to the early Baroque and to such composers as Chambonnières in France (ordres or suites) and the German Froberger, who was instrumental in crystallizing the suite form into the somewhat standard plan of allemande, sarabande, courante, and gigue. However, the suite form, with its emphasis on such French Baroque characteristics as stylized dance movements, thin texture, highly ornamented melodic line, and light mood, did not entirely satisfy the more serious German musical temper that was coming more strongly to the fore at the close of the seventeenth century. The separation of French and German keyboard styles appeared with the work of Johann Kuhnau, whose sonatas frequently show the German propensity for a heavier texture, counterpoint and fugue, and a more serious mood.

Kuhnau's principal contributions include *Frische Klavierfrüchte (Fresh Clavier Fruits)*, composed in 1696, consisting of a series of "sonatas" of four or five movements, each designated allegro, adagio, presto, and so on, and *Biblische Historien (Biblical Stories)*, dated 1700 made up of six keyboard sonatas, each of which is based on a biblical event such as "David and Goliath," "Jacob's Wedding," and the "Suffering and Healing of Hezekiah." The more dramatic and serious mood, which is to become so characteristic of much German music in the centuries following, is demonstrated in the "Hezekiah" section of the Biblical sonatas.

From the Biblical "Sonatas" of Johann Kuhnau

Scarlatti

The beginning of modern piano keyboard technique is to be traced to the Italian composer Domenico Scarlatti (1685–1757), son of the famous opera composer Alessandro Scarlatti. Unquestionably, Scarlatti ranks among the leading keyboard composers of music history: Bach, Beethoven, Mozart, Schumann, Chopin, and Brahms. Although an innovator of idiomatic techniques (crossing of hands, arpeggios, scale figures, repeated notes, and so on), which influenced generations of successors, Scarlatti's greatness lies in the especially distinctive style he consistently injected into the more than five hundred sonatas he composed for the harpsichord.

The formal pattern of these sonatas is quite simple: one short movement divided into two sections (A B), each set off by a definite cadence. These sonatas have a strong impelling movement and a clarity of texture (homophonic), in which emphasis is placed upon a scintillating, sparkling melodic line and supporting chords beneath. A few sonatas are written in a pensive, reflective mood; most are, however, lively and joyful. In many respects these sonatas foreshadow the growing classicistic trend, a trend particularly evident in their clarity or texture, clear-cut melodies divided into definite phrases, bright, outgoing mood, and over-all polish and refinement.

Sonata in D by Domenico Scarlatti

THE CULMINATION OF THE
BAROQUE: BACH AND HANDEL

Bach

Life Sketch   The music of the Baroque came to a grand climax with the contributions of Johann Sebastian Bach and George Frideric Handel. Both composers were born in the same year (1685) and died but a few years apart (Bach in 1750, Handel in 1759). Though both composers created in the eloquent and ornate musical language of the age, each is identified by a distinctive underlying artistic creed. For example, Handel, an extrovert and an international figure, was largely motivated by the public's demand for the colorful and extravagant Baroque opera and oratorio, which became so popular in England during the eighteenth century. Bach, on the other hand, a scholarly introvert who was motivated by deep religious feelings, dedicated his life to serving the Lutheran Church through his music. Both contributed significantly to music; however, the Baroque was most clearly epitomized in the work of J. S. Bach, who synthesized and summarized the principal styles and trends of the period in his own distinctive way. With the emergence of these two leading figures, the musical supremacy of Italy, which originated in the early Baroque was gradually usurped by a long line of German and Austrian composers. This heritage began with the Baroque musicians Schütz, J. S. Bach, and Handel, and eventually included C. P. Bach, Stamitz, Haydn, Mozart, Beethoven, Schumann, Brahms, Wagner, and Bruckner, ending with Mahler who died 1911, over one hundred and fifty years after Bach.

Perhaps more words have been written about Bach than any other composer. Moreover, above the music of all the Baroque composers, his seems to have found the greatest admiration among present-day musicians and devotees of serious music. Since this is not a comprehensive history of music, it is not the intent to explore the reasons for this esteemed position, nor to systematically catalog and analyze the works that make up the monumental Bach legacy. At most all that can be attempted is a cursory glance at some of his musical achievements and a brief sketch of his life experiences that had a direct bearing on his musical style. Perhaps in this way we can at least "open the door" for the listener to a world of musical greatness.

In terms of sheer quantity alone, the creative output of Bach is staggering—well over a thousand works, covering all the major forms of the Baroque (except opera), both sacred and secular, vocal and instrumental. These range in scope from the brief chorales to the expansive and complex B minor Mass. In large measure, the choice of vocal or instrumental idioms and the actual genres were determined by the resources and requirements that existed in the various music positions Bach held during the fifty years of his creative life.

Some writers, notably Hans David and Arthur Mendel (*The Bach Reader*), have pointed out that perhaps Bach's greatness can be attributed to the rich musical ancestry from which he stemmed. Born in Eisenach

Johann Sebastian Bach. Picture Collection, New York Public Library

Germany, in 1685, J. S. Bach represented the culmination of many generations of musicians who had lived in Germany since the sixteenth century. The lineage began with Veit Bach (c. 1580–1619) and ended with Johann Christian, the last of Johann Sebastian Bach's musician sons, who died in 1782. One child of the large family (eleven of Bach's twenty children survived) lived into the nineteenth century (Regina Suzanna, 1742–1809). Moreover, there is, apparently, one direct descendant of J. S. Bach still living in Eisenach today (Paul Bach, born 1878).

Following the death of both parents before his tenth birthday, young Sebastian came under the care of his older brother, Johann Christoph Bach, an organist who had studied with the renowned Pachelbel. The musical environment of his brother's household, and particularly his instruction in harpsichord and organ, provided a suitable foundation for the budding musician, who was eventually to become the outstanding organist and composer of the eighteenth century.

In his fifteenth year, J. S. Bach won a scholarship to St. Michael's School in Lüneberg. Here the maturing youth encountered a cosmopolitan atmosphere and received excellent academic instruction, which included Latin, Greek, religion, rhetoric, logic, and, of course, music. The scholarship, which covered tuition, room and board, stipulated that Bach participate in the school's choir, which performed at the principal church services of the institution, funerals, weddings, and civic processionals. Bach's musical horizons were further expanded by his listening to the playing of the noted organist Georg Böhm at St. John's Church in Lüneberg and to the French-style chamber and keyboard music at the nearby French court at Celle. It was during his Lüneberg experience that Bach began composing his earliest works, the organ preludes and variations.

Arnstadt Shortly after his graduation from St. Michael's School, Bach obtained his first important musical position, as church organist and choir director at Arnstadt, where he remained from 1703 to 1707. The first of his more than 200 church cantatas were composed here (notably *Denn du wirst meine Seele* (Suffer not Thou my soul), as well as several organ fugues and preludes. It was during this period that Bach traveled on foot to Lübeck, about 200 miles distant, to hear the renowned organist Dietrich Buxtehude. He remained over the allotted time, and on return was reprimanded by his superiors. And thus began a series of skirmishes with church authorities; such disagreements plagued Bach the rest of his life. Moreover, his newly composed organ compositions (showing heavy traces of Buxtehude's influence) were criticized for their dazzling cadenzas, dissonant harmonic progressions, and chromaticisms. The church fathers were evidently pleased to learn that the young genius had decided to accept the organ post at St. Blasius' Church in Mühlhausen, where Bach remained only a short time (1707–1708). During this period he married a distant cousin, Maria Barbara Bach, and began to compose in earnest. He completed, among other sacred works, the famous chorale prelude *Ein' feste Burg ist unser Gott (A Mighty Fortress Is Our God)*, which was composed for the Reformation Festival in 1708.

Weimar   At Weimar during the years 1708–1717, Bach was employed in the court of Duke Wilhelm Ernst, as chapel organist and chamber musician. This proved to be a pleasant position in many ways. Not only was his income doubled over his previous post, but, more importantly, the strong Lutheran environment was conducive to Bach's deeply religious musical conceptions. Duke Wilhelm, a man of firm religious convictions, had a particular interest in organ music. And thus it was here that Bach composed most of his great organ compositions, such as the Toccata and Fugue in D minor, the "Little" Fugue in G minor, and the gigantic Passacaglia in C minor. It was also at Weimar that Bach's second son was born —Carl Philipp Emanuel, the most famous musician of the Bach offspring.

Cöthen   For some strange and unknown reason, Bach chose the position as *Kapellmeister* (court musical director) at the castle at Cöthen under Prince Leopold. The Cöthen directorship afforded no opportunity for Bach to further his church music career, since Prince Leopold, a devout Calvinist, showed little interest in elaborate church music. Hence, between the years 1717–1723, Bach devoted his efforts to composing secular music, specifically chamber music and solo works, including such well-known examples as the two- and three-part inventions (for clavier), the three sonatas and three partitas for unaccompanied violin, the six suites for unaccompanied cello (the violin and cello pieces were written for the key players in Bach's chamber orchestra), the six trio sonatas, the English and French Suites for clavier, six concertos (the famed Brandenburg Concertos) and the first part of the collection of clavier preludes and fugues entitled *The Well-Tempered Clavier.*

Shortly after the death of his first wife, Maria Barbara (1720), Bach married Anna Magdalena, who bore him seven children. This marriage also produced several sons of exceptional musical talent: Johann Christoph Friedrich and notably Johann Christian, who, with his older brother Carl Philipp, contributed to the rise of the classic style in the mid-eighteenth century.

Oddly enough, Bach's employment at Cöthen was evidently terminated as a result of a change in the artistic life of the palace. The prince's wife, who was apparently resentful of Leopold's extensive preoccupation with music, instigated a general decline of musical activity in the palace. Thus, it was during this time of enforced inactivity that Bach composed the first part of the *Well-Tempered Clavier* (1722). Ironically, soon after Bach accepted the new position at Leipzig, the prince's wife died.

Leipzig   Bach was thirty-eight when he accepted the highly prestigious position as cantor (musical director) at St. Thomas' Church in Leipzig. His predecessor was Johann Kuhnau, who had adapted the sonata idea to the harpsichord. In the staunch Protestant city of about 30,000, Bach was in charge of music at two large Lutheran churches (St. Thomas' and St. Nicholas') which required much of his time and creative energy. On an alternating basis, the new cantor provided the music for the main Sunday church service at each church. The service, extending from seven to eleven o'clock A.M., usually required a cantata, a motet, several chorales, and the Kyrie and Gloria of the Lutheran Missa Brevis (short mass). In addition to furnishing all of this music for each Sunday service, he had to provide choral music for numerous special programs such as at Christmas and Easter, Passion music for Good Friday (he wrote three large works of this type), and funerals. For a time, Bach helped supervise the children living in the school at St. Thomas' and also taught Latin and the Catechism.

The Leipzig cantorship was, to say the least, much more complicated than his relatively peaceful position at Cöthen. His output at Leipzig was amazingly great, especially in view of the many duties that consumed his time. Instead of chamber music, Bach was concentrating on sacred idioms; thus, most of his greatest choral works were created at this point in his life. These choral works include over two hundred cantatas (among them the famous *Christ lag in Todesbanden* of 1724), the B minor mass, and the three extant *Passions* (*St. John, St. Matthew,* and *St. Mark*).

Bach's tenure at Leipzig was fraught with tension as a result of constant friction between himself and church officials. The final phase of this long series of conflicts was attained when Johann August Ernesti became rector. Ernesti was completely unsympathetic to Bach's needs and to church music in general. Thus, working conditions became increasingly intolerable, reaching a climax in 1738, when Bach completely turned away from sacred choral music and devoted his genius to highly personal and abstract instrumental creations, including the last part of *The Well-Tempered Clavier, A Musical Offering* (dedicated to Frederick the Great) the Goldberg Variations, and *The Art of the Fugue,* which was left uncompleted at the time of Bach's death in 1750. Ironically, both Bach and Handel had eye disorders that were treated by the same oculist, Sir John Taylor. The operations were unsuccessful and both composers spent their last days in darkness.

Prelude and Fugue No. 1 in C Major   Perhaps the best known work by J. S. Bach is the *Das Wohltemperierte Clavier* (*The Well-Tempered Clavier*), consisting of a series of forty-eight preludes and fugues. In using the general keyboard classification of "clavier," Bach undoubtedly intended that the works be played on either the clavichord or harpsichord. The title of the collection refers to a "well-tuned" instrument. However, some writers believe that the title alludes to the modern "tempered" system of tuning, in which each of the twelve semitones within the octave are tuned equally, thus permitting use of all the major and minor keys. Although Bach did not "invent" equal or tempered tuning, his *Well-Tempered Clavier* marks the establishment of the complete major and minor key system early in the eighteenth century.

The Prelude and Fugue No. 1 from the first part of *The Well-Tempered Clavier* is representative of the technique and style employed by Bach in this collection. The prelude, a short introductory piece in a free improvisatory style, is based on a melody presented in the form of a broken chord pattern (notes of the chord sounded in succession instead of simultaneously). This pattern is woven through various related keys and various dissonant chord combinations, which provide a steady rise and fall in tension, gradually reaching its dissonantal peak in the closing measures.

Prelude No. 1, *Well-Tempered Clavier* by J. S. Bach

The fugues of *The Well-Tempered Clavier*, as with others in the large body of contrapuntal works by Bach, do not follow a set pattern. As a general rule they are between fifty and seventy-five measures in length and are built around a brief melodic idea (called the subject), which is imitated in succession by the various voice parts (usually four). The accompanying fugue for the Prelude No. 1 is based on a clearly marked subject of two measures' length. Like many of the Bach subjects, it has a lilting rhythmic vitality and a distinctive beginning of long note values. The subject gradually gains increased motion through a series of quick-moving notes of smaller duration:

Subject from Fugue No. 1, *Well-Tempered Clavier*

The subject of this particular fugue (No. 1 in C major) is first presented in the alto part (in the tonic key of C), and the answer[3] is stated by the soprano part in measure two. As the fugue unfolds, the various parts sound either the subject or answer in succession. (Note the appearance of the subject and answer in the following example). Quite frequently,

[3] The *answer* is the subject imitated at a different pitch level, usually in a key a fifth higher (the dominant) or fourth higher (the subdominant key).

as in this example, Bach's fugues end in a climactic fashion, punctuated by a long sustained tone, called a *pedal tone,* held by the bass part during the last few measures. Above the pedal tone the upper parts clash in strong dissonant fashion as they seek their final goal—the closing cadence.

Opening, Fugue No. 1, in C Major, *Well-Tempered Clavier*

Cantata: Ein' feste Burg ist unser Gott   The reader may recall, from the readings in the early Baroque, that the first cantatas dated from the early seventeenth century and were chiefly secular-styled compositions performed by a solo voice and continuo in small, intimate surroundings. During the late seventeenth century, the sacred cantata rose to prominence in Germany and reached its apex in the work of J. S. Bach, who composed about two hundred and sixty-five during his Leipzig period (1723–1750). These vocal forms were employed as an integral part in the Lutheran liturgy and generally were referred to as *Hauptstücke* (principal works), which were performed prior to the sermon at the Sunday service. Interestingly, Bach also composed twenty-four secular cantatas, which were written for special occasions, such as civic and university ceremonies, birthdays, weddings, and the like.

There is no set pattern to the sacred cantatas of Bach. However, many of these works are identified by (1) a number of sections or movements such as arias (solo vocal passages), recitatives (sung declamatory passages, in a speechlike style), duets and choruses; (2) a continuous narrative text of a religious nature; and (3) instrumental accompaniment. Many of the Bach cantatas are of small proportions, that is, for a vocal solo or duet with only a continuo accompaniment. However, for special events such as Christmas, Easter, and Ascension Sunday, he composed many larger works requiring full choir, soloists, and orchestra. Moreover, the particular Sunday of the Church year called for a particular type of text, which also accounts for the wide variety of expressions found in these works.

One distinguishing feature quite commonly observed in these works is the employment of a chorale tune that serves as a musical foundation for the entire composition. This melody is generally woven through all the divisions of the cantata, serving to unify its complex contrapuntal texture. Usually it is restated in full force in the four-part harmonization that brings the cantata to a close with a feeling of power and majesty. Sometimes the theme is developed in the various movements of the cantata through fugal treatment or through the theme and variations technique, as in the famous cantata *Ein' feste Burg ist unser Gott.* This cantata, appearing as No. 80 in the series of cantatas published by the Bach-Gesellschaft, was written for the bicentennial celebration of the Augsburg Confession. It represents the festive type of cantata, as indicated by its large structure and performing body: it consists of an eight-movement plan, with vocal soloists, chorus, and an orchestra of three trumpets, timpani, three oboes, two oboes d'amore, two oboes da caccia, organ, and a string section of violins, violas, cellos, and basses. It should be borne in mind, however, that the orchestra used by Bach at Leipzig was generally under twenty players. Bach arranged this cantata into the following form:

1. Full choir and orchestra; the choral melody is developed in fugal style
2. Aria for bass and soprano (accompanied by oboe, violins, violas, and continuo)
3. Bass recitative
4. Soprano aria
5. Chorus (orchestra and choir)
6. Tenor recitative
7. Alto and tenor duet
8. Chorale

Brandenburg Concerto No. 2 in F Major Bach composed a set of six concerti grossi, which were dedicated to the Margrave of Brandenburg in 1721. As with many of his other compositions, such as the cantatas and the *Well-Tempered Clavier,* Bach provides each concerto with its own distinctive musical character, either as to instrumentation, form, or treatment of the solo instrumental group. With the exception of Concerto

No. 1, he follows the concerto grosso form as developed by Vivaldi, that is, the three-movement plan of fast, slow, fast and the division of the orchestra into concertino (solo group) and ripieno (the accompanying group or the main instrumental body). However, these groups are not always separated into distinct bodies but are frequently mixed together in a contrapuntal web of sound. An interesting feature is to be noted regarding the use of the harpsichord in the Concerto No. 5. Here Bach relieved the instrument of its perfunctory duty of supplying the harmonic foundation and gave it extended sololike passages. The technique and skill demanded of the harpsichordist and of the other instrumentalists, in this and other concertos (notably the second, with its difficult trumpet part), clearly stamp these works as virtuosic.

The second Brandenburg Concerto is particularly noteworthy for its unusual concertino group, which is composed of wind instruments: the high-pitched trumpet, or clarino, recorder, oboe, and violin. The ripieno group consists of the customary strings and continuo. Following the pattern typical of many Baroque concertos, the work begins with a statement of the principal theme by the full orchestra. In the first solo entrance of the concertino, only one instrument is presented; then, in successive entrances, two concertino instruments are paired. Later, all four concertino instruments are pitted against the ripieno.

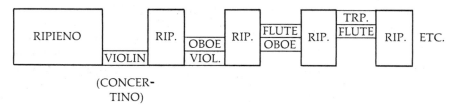

(CONCER-
TINO)

Structural Plan, opening of Second Brandenburg Concerto in F Major

The second movement, marked "Andante" and scored for only flute, oboe, violin, cello, and continuo, is based on a fugal development of the main theme. In the last movement (Allegro Assai), the full instrumentation

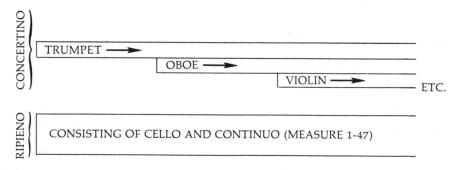

Structural Plan, opening of Last Movement, Brandenburg Concerto in F

of ripieno and concertino reappears. The principal theme (having the same driving force of the theme of the first movement) is given a fugal treatment by the instruments of the concertino, while the ripieno serves to form a kind of backdrop for the imitative dialogue in the concertino section.

The B Minor Mass   The culmination of Bach's work in the choral idiom was reached with his setting of the Ordinary of the Mass, completed about 1747 or 1749. Bach's interest in the mass form stemmed from the Lutheran practice of using the Kyrie and the Gloria in the worship service. This abbreviated form of the mass was performed at the principal Sunday service and on festival days. In 1733 Bach sent the Kyrie and Gloria of the B minor Mass to Frederick Augustus (the Catholic king of Poland) in an attempt to gain a court title, which was awarded three years later. The other movements of the gigantic work, the Credo, Sanctus, and the Agnus Dei, date from various periods of the composer's life. Each of the five parts of the Ordinary is divided into separate movements. For example, the Gloria and Credo have eight separate divisions or movements. In addition to a five-part chorus, the work requires vocal solos, duets, and an orchestra of trumpets, flutes, oboes, bassoon, timpani, strings, and organ. Understandably, the mass is too extensive for either the Catholic or the Lutheran Church, and thus, like Beethoven's *Missa Solemnis* and Mozart's *Requiem Mass,* it is normally heard in a concert setting.

Chorale Melody, *Christ lag in Todesbanden*
Original attributed to Luther *(top)*
Version used by J. S. Bach in Cantata No. 4

Handel

The life and work of the figure who personified the magniloquent aspects of the Baroque, stands in strong relief to his contemporary, J. S. Bach. In many respects both the music and career of Handel represent the summation of the more objective manifestations of the Baroque spirit, whereas Bach, on the other hand, represented the culmination of the more subjective artistic traits of that era of opulence and grandeur. Handel's dramatic and colorful flair appealed to the masses, and, in contrast to Bach, his popularity remained undiminished for a long while after his death. Bach's subtle artistry did not speak directly to the masses; consequently, lacking theatrical appeal, Bach's influence worked at a different pace and on a different level. It was only gradually, particularly after the revival of his works by Mendelssohn early in the nineteenth century, that his greatness was acknowledged by practically every musician, composer, and devotee of musical art. Handel, on the other hand, reaching out as he did to the masses, played an important role in the development of English musical culture during the first half of the eighteenth century.

Handel's early music education, consisting of the customary subjects of counterpoint, organ, and harpsichord, was acquired under Friedrich Wilhelm Zachow in Handel's native town of Halle in Saxony. After one year at the University of Halle, he went to Hamburg and performed in an opera orchestra as a second violinist. This close contact with Italian-styled opera, which was sweeping all of Europe by the opening of the eighteenth century, influenced Handel's esthetic outlook at an early age, for we note that at nineteen he wrote his first work, the opera *Almira* (1705). And even at this date he showed a penchant for the Baroque "grand manner," which was to win for him the following of many opera lovers. In Italy, from 1706 to 1710, through his associations with the leading contemporary Italian composers (Corelli, Alessandro and Domenico Scarlatti), Handel thoroughly assimilated the Italian style of opera established by Alessandro Scarlatti and the orchestral technique developed by Corelli. The opera *Rodrigo* (Florence, 1708) and especially *Agrippina* (Venice, 1709) marked his arrival as an opera composer.

With his name established in the operatic field on the Continent, Handel moved to London, where in 1710 he completed the widely celebrated *Rinaldo*. Shortly after, he and several members of English society formed an opera company called The Royal Academy of Music. This venture provided Handel with an opportunity to compose more than thirty operas. However, the company began to lose money and by 1728 the English taste shifted its focus from Italian to English opera, as attested by the acclaim of the middle class for John Gay's *The Beggar's Opera*, which parodied the Italian operatic style of Handel and his contemporaries. The desire of the English for works in their native language, and particularly the satirical writings of the music critics Addison and Steele (in the *Spectator*), contributed to the demise of the musical expression that had brought so much fame to Handel.

When the Academy failed, Handel devoted his talents to composing oratorios, which are, in effect, Handelian operas minus staging, costuming, and acting. Although produced in public theaters, these twenty-six works were based on religious subject matter generally drawn from Biblical passages. These include the oratorios *Israel in Egypt, Samson, Esther, Joseph, Joshua,* and *The Messiah.* Handel's creative output in the orchestral field was considerably less than in the vocal. Noteworthy are the twelve concerti grossi, Opus 6 (1740), three sets of six organ concerti (Opp. 4, 7), the *Water Music Suite* (c. 1717) consisting of twenty-five pieces, mostly popular airs and dances and scored for large orchestra; and the *Royal Fireworks Music* (1749) in five movements: Overture, Siciliana, Allegro, and Minuet I, II, scored for a large wind band.

Summary

In looking back over the Baroque three major movements seem to stand out above all else: the rise of opera, the establishment of the orchestra and its concerto forms, and the great period of Lutheran music brought to fruition by J. S. Bach. Essentially, the Baroque was an expression of two cultures: the Italian with its color and vivacity, and the German with its more serious, logical undertone. Both cultures were successively fused in the music of J. S. Bach the towering giant of the Baroque.

THE BAROQUE SUITE

DANCE	NATIONAL ORIGIN	METER	TEMPO
ALLEMANDE	Germany	$\frac{4}{4}$	moderately fast
COURANTE	France	$\frac{6}{4}$	moderate
or: *CORRENTE*	Italy	$\frac{3}{4}$	lively, fast
SARABANDE	Spain	$\frac{3}{2}, \frac{3}{4}$	slow, stately
GIGUE	England	$\frac{4}{4}, \frac{6}{8}, \frac{3}{4}$	fast, gay

Note: Other dances were frequently inserted after the sarabande such as the minuet, bourrée and gavotte. The suite form is observed in much music of the Baroque, notably in the harpsichord suites of J. S. Bach (*English Suites, French Suites*), in his six cello suites, violin suites; in the sonata da camera compositions of Arcangelo Corelli and harpsichord suites of G. F. Handel.

REPRESENTATIVE WORKS IN THE HUMANITIES:
THE BAROQUE (1600–1750)

MUSIC

Main trends: During the early Baroque (1600–1685), musical activity is centered in Italy. Creativity in the new Italian dramatic vocal forms of opera, cantata, and oratorio predominates. In the late Baroque (1685–1750), Italy and Germany are the leaders in music. In addition to opera, an intensive growth of instrumental music occurs: the orchestra and its new forms (concerto, concerto grosso) are established by the Italian composers (Corelli, Vivaldi), and new chamber ensemble forms appear. The Baroque comes to a close with the work of J. S. Bach, who synthesizes the main styles and trends of the period.

PHILOSOPHY

Rationalism is the name commonly given to the prevailing philosophical attitude of the seventeenth century—the age that saw the birth of modern science, represented chiefly by Galileo, Newton, and Kepler. Rationalism refers to the application of reason in the understanding of the physical world. The spirit of rationalism was greatly fostered by René Descartes (1596–1650), a scientist and philosopher who held that only natural data, not the supernatural, collected by scientific method of observation and experience, could be tested by reason. The rationalist mentality, with its concern for the measurable rather than the immeasurable (sense impressions), ruled the realm of ideas in the seventeenth and eighteenth centuries. Paradoxically, it did not come to the surface in the arts until the eighteenth century (called the Age of the Enlightenment), when the power of reason was applied to all human affairs, politics, government, and religion. Subsequently, the intellectual spirit was assimilated by the fine arts. The passion and drama of the Baroque subsided in favor of the restrained classical temper which first appeared in literature and some visual arts in the rococo (early eighteenth century) and then in painting and music in the classical era (late eighteenth century).

LITERATURE

1604 *Othello,* Shakespeare
1605 *Don Quixote,* Miguel de Cervantes
1636 *Le Cid,* Pierre Corneille
1637 *Discourse on Method,* René Descartes
1651 *Leviathan,* Thomas Hobbes
1663 *Paradise Lost,* John Milton
1664 *Tartuffe,* Molière
1669 *Diary,* Samuel Pepys
1677 *Phedre,* Jean Baptiste Racine

1678 *Pilgrim's Progress,* John Bunyan
1711 *Essay on Criticism,* Alexander Pope
1712 *Rape of the Lock,* Alexander Pope
1726 *Gulliver's Travels,* Jonathan Swift

ART

1575 Façade, Church of Il Gesù, Rome (early Baroque)
1593 *The Calling of St. Matthew,* Caravaggio
1604 Ceiling in the Farnese Palace, Rome, Carracci
1607 St. Peter's façade designed by Carlo Maderno
1610 *View of Toledo,* El Greco
1612 Louvre begun, completed 1690
1614 *Descent from the Cross,* Peter Paul Rubens
1624 *The Laughing Cavalier,* Franz Hals
1625 *The Disembarkation of Queen Maria de' Medici at Marseilles,* Rubens
1642 *Sortie of Captain Banning Cocq's Company,* Rembrandt van Rijn "Night Watch"
1646 *Ecstasy of St. Teresa,* Giovanni Bernini
1656 The great colonnades of St. Peter's (completed 1663), Giovanni Lorenzo Bernini
1675 St. Paul's Cathedral (London) begun by Christopher Wren, completed 1710
1684 Versailles Palace completed for Louis XIV
1718 *Embarkation for Cythera,* Jean Watteau (early rococo art)
1740 Church at Zwiefalten Germany designed by Johann Fischer, completed 1765 (German Baroque)

HISTORICAL EVENTS

1602 Galileo Galilei discovers law of gravitation
1603 James I crowned King of England (reigned to 1625)
1607 Founding of Jamestown colony
1609 *Astronomia Nova* (laws of planetary motion), Kepler
1618 Beginning of Thirty Years' War
1620 Pilgrims land at Cape Cod
1630 Boston founded
1632 Heliocentric theory of Galileo
1636 Harvard College chartered
1643 Louis XIV King of France (reigned to 1715)
1687 *Principia,* Isaac Newton
1701 Yale College founded
1715 Louis XV crowned King of France (reigned to 1774)

7

THE CLASSICAL ERA
(1750–1800)

*THE SOCIAL AND INTELLECTUAL
CLIMATE*

Then beauty of style, harmony, grace and good
rhythm depend on simplicity—I mean the true
simplicity of a rightly and nobly ordered mind
and character.

Plato, *The Republic*

Introductory Statement Following the climax of the Baroque in the first
half of the eighteenth century, musical style again altered its path. The
change was essentially from the grandeur, ornateness, and massiveness
common to much Baroque music and art to the classic style, characterized
by its clarity, balance, simplicity, and refinement. These characteristics
gradually came to the foreground after 1740 in Germany and Austria—
the center of classicism in music—and were most fully exemplified in the
music of the leading classicists, Franz Joseph Haydn (1732–1809), Wolfgang Amadeus Mozart (1756–1791), and in the early works of Ludwig van
Beethoven (1770–1827). As with all periods, the boundaries of the classical period (sometimes called the neoclassical era) are arbitrary. The
classicistic movement was foreshadowed in the music of the preclassicists:
Bach's famous son, Carl Philipp Emanuel (1714–1788), and his German
contemporaries (Monn, 1717–1750, Wagenseil, 1715–1777, and Stamitz,
1717–1757).

The ending date of the period is also arbitrary; however, the death
of Haydn in 1809 may be thought of as the concluding point. Beethoven's
earliest works (his First and Second Symphonies, for example) are gener-

ally regarded as classical in style. His Third Symphony (1803) marks his departure into the romantic style of the nineteenth century.

The classical period is chiefly one of unprecedented creativity in the instrumental idiom. The bulk of the music was composed in the new forms of symphony, piano sonata, and string quartet, as well as in the established concerto form. Sacred music continued, but was greatly diminished over the Baroque era. Opera maintained its popularity in Italy. In Germany, opera was replaced to a large extent by interest in the new symphonic idea. Among the principal composers, the genius Mozart, who created in all of the forms of the period, stands as the musical giant of the age in terms of both quantity and quality of music. Of the other leading figures, Haydn is best known for his perfection of the symphonic form (he composed approximately one hundred and four works in this genre), and Beethoven for his earliest symphonies, piano sonatas, and string quartets, which are in the "classic" style. His "romantic" phase (from 1803) will be taken up in the next chapter, under nineteenth-century romanticism.

The Crosscurrents in Eighteenth-Century Music   Musically speaking, the eighteenth century was far from being the quiet, reserved age we somehow associate with the rise of classicism. Despite the dominant rational tone that permeated arts and letters of the eighteenth century, there were several distinctive stylistic currents in music: (1) the Baroque was still strong until about 1750; (2) the rococo, or *style galant,* was the dominant expression in France during the reign of Louis XV (1715–1774); (3) the *empfind-samer Stil* (sensitive style) emerged in Germany about 1740; and (4) the period concluded with classicism as the prevailing mode in the last half of the century.

To make matters more interesting, the classic era proper occasionally witnessed strong traces of emotionalism as a result of the *Sturm und Drang* (Storm and Stress) movement in German literature in the 1760s and 1770s. By the time of Beethoven's third symphony (1803), this latent romanticism finally had broken open in full force in Germany and other European countries. Thus, contrary to many popular music appreciation texts, the eighteenth century is not to be viewed simply as the time of the expiration of the Baroque followed by the appearance of the classic era. This point needs to be stressed, since the listener will then be able to reconcile (1) the "classic" sounding works of C. P. E. Bach, written ten years before his father's death; (2) the continuation of the French Baroque keyboard style, which takes on excessive ornamentation and is called the *style galant* in the French rococo era; and (3) the seemingly non-classical bursts of emotionalism in the late works of Haydn and Mozart toward the end of the eighteenth century.

Social and Intellectual Movements Underscoring the Classic Temper   The question arises at this point: Why did Germany and Austria become the center of the classical movement in music? Although space limits the discussion of this important question, several contributing factors may be briefly touched upon. One dominant factor behind the flourishing musical culture in eighteenth-century Germany was the presence of an active patronage of the arts by both private and public interests. It may be recalled that, prior to the Baroque, the arts were supported chiefly by either the Church or the private benefactor—the princely court or wealthy family such as the Medici in the Renaissance. In the Baroque, beginning with the rise of public opera theaters in Italy, music increasingly became the concern of the middle class as well as the elite. And in the classical period, the composer found a large, receptive audience in both the private and public areas of music.

Wealthy patrons commissioned the writing of symphonies, sonatas, and chamber music for specific events, concerts, and festivities. And, on the other hand, the middle class clamored for both instruments (such as the popular harpsichord) and music suitable "for the connoisseur and dilettante"—words that frequently appear on the cover pages of printed keyboard sonatas of this age. Family music-making was also in vogue in Germany, where string-quartet playing became a favorite pastime of many cultured families. Perhaps the strongest impetus to public patronage of the arts was provided by the series of concerts offered to the public such as the *Concerts spirituels* in Paris in 1725 and *Liebhaberkonzerte* in Berlin in 1770. Also for the first time, the publication of music took on considerable economic importance for the composer. One of the largest publishers in the music world today, Breitkopf and Härtel, was established at this time (mid-eighteenth century). Among the first major compositions printed by this firm were works by C. P. E. Bach and Leopold Mozart, father of the leading classicist.

Germany at this time was not yet a national state. It consisted of numerous principalities such as Saxony, Prussia, and Bavaria. Moreover, each principality had its own highly developed court orchestra, opera, and chamber ensemble. Prominent among these cultural centers was the royal court at Potsdam in Prussia, where Frederick the Great developed a flourishing musical culture and where C. P. E. Bach established himself as a leading German composer. Another important center was Mannheim, where in the 1740s, one of the finest orchestras came into existence under the leadership of Johann Stamitz. From this orchestra emerged the orchestral techniques that were eventually to become the trademarks of every classical symphony. Vienna, the capitol of German musical classicism, was the spiritual home of the greats of the period—Haydn, Mozart, Beethoven, and numerous other composers whose works are now being uncovered through musical research.

Intellectual Trends—The Age of Reason   Although movements in the history of arts and ideas have no fixed beginning and ending, there is, nonetheless, a change in the intellectual and artistic atmosphere from epoch to epoch. This point, of course, has been made several times in these pages; however, it is perhaps most graphically illustrated when we compare the difference in the creative outlook between Baroque and classic period composers. The approach of Baroque musicians to musical creativity emphasized large, complex, and highly ornamented musical designs (Bach's fugues, toccatas, concerti, cantatas, for example); whereas the approach of the classicists emphasized less expansive and more restrained, refined, and unadorned musical ideas set in the neatly balanced forms of the symphony and sonata.

What is it that causes the shift in esthetic beliefs from one age to another? A multiplicity of interwoven factors could be discussed if space permitted. This much we can state with both brevity and assurance: musical art does not exist or develop independently of external forces in society. On the contrary, for, on the basis of our study thus far, we have observed that music, like all of the arts, tends to reflect or express the spirit (or *Zeitgeist*) of an epoch. Or, in the words of Wylie Sypher, "a style [in the arts] is more than the technique that goes into the making of the style, for a style expresses the whole consciousness of an age."[1]

The consciousness or dominant attitude of eighteenth-century classicism was the "rule of reason," which was applied to all matters—political, social, religious, scientific, and artistic. This era, which witnessed the proliferation of rational thought in all facets of intellectual life, is referred to as the Age of the Enlightenment. Reason became a religion; it stood as "the highest authority, as the universal arbiter in all matters." The roots of this world view stemmed from the seventeenth century, the time when rationalism was born in the field of science. Its champions in the Age of Reason included: Voltaire, who probed intellectually, and with a biting satirical pen, the social problems and ills of the Enlightenment (*Candide*, 1759); Pope, who mirrored the scientific temper of the day in a highly logical, measured, and restrained poetic style (*Rape of the Lock*, 1712); Locke, who interpreted the meaning of knowledge in the rationalist frame of reference of the Newtonian world: knowledge is to be identified with conceptions of size, figures, motion—those things that can be measured which are the "primary qualities" of our existence, as opposed to the "secondary qualities" such as colors, sounds, taste, and odor (*Essay Concerning Human Understanding*, 1690); Rameau, who applied rational thought to music and formulated the theory behind the modern major and minor key system (*Treatise on Harmony*, 1722); and Rousseau, who investigated the "law of Nature" and applied it to various areas of knowledge including education and government. His *Confessions* (1781) also exerted a strong influence on the beginnings of the romantic movement at the turn of the eighteenth century.

In the realm of the arts, the rationalistic pulse of the age was expressed in a renewed interest in certain qualities generally referred to as "classicistic." The meaning of classicism in the arts will concern us next.

---

[1] Wylie Sypher, *Rococo to Cubism* (New York: Vintage Books, 1963), p. xx.

THE PRECLASSICAL ERA: THE EMERGENCE
OF CLASSICISM FROM THE ROCOCO

The Rococo Before dealing directly with the classical period, some mention must be given to the rococo period and its relationship to the gradual rise of musical classicism. For the setting of the rococo we turn to France of the early eighteenth century (the reign of Louis XV, 1715–1774), and to the prevailing esthetic ideals of the painters, writers, and composers.

The classicistic vein, we found, was firmly entrenched in the arts of France during the seventeenth century: in the paintings of Poussin and Le Nain, in the operas of Lully, and in the plays of Corneille and Racine. It was the French artists' intent to avoid excessive display of physical action, to preserve dignity and decorum, and to create in a highly refined style. The French arts truly reflected the highly cultivated society of Louis XIV—a society in which the French language was purified and made clear, conversation made a fine art, and wit esteemed above all else.

This trend subsided shortly after the death of Louis XIV (1715). With the ascension of Louis XV to the throne, there was a change from large to small, from the formal to the intimate and playful. Friedlander *(From David to Delacroix)* refers to the movement as being away from the rational—to the sentimental, a movement to make sentiment the criterion for artistic judgment. Instead of *raison* and *bon sens, charme* and *esprit* were the catchwords of the literary salons around 1720. In the words of Friedlander, "this artistic mentality did not wish to live in the rarified atmosphere of reason and morality, but at the same time had no desire to descend into the depths of emotion. It attempted rather to capture the attractive surface of reality." Extreme refinement, vapidness of expression, and taste for the sensuously superficial and the elegant prevailed in almost all of the arts.

The leading representative in painting was Jean Watteau (1684–1721), whose art covered the walls of the new locale of French society— the fashionable Parisian *hôtels* with their intimate, playful surroundings. In this make-believe world Watteau painted such works as *Embarkation for Cythera,* and *The Champs Elysées,* in which ethereal, feminine, wispy forms and infinite fantasylike space replace Baroque power, drama, massiveness, and rhetoric.

These same characteristics are found in rococo music, led by François Couperin, "Le Grand" (1668–1733), who was the court composer to Louis XV. The name given to music written during the rococo era is *style galant,* which, like the paintings of Watteau, Boucher, and Fragonard is characterized by its emphasis on excessive decoration in the melodic line, pleasantness (almost neutral in feeling), grace, and elegance of expression. It is music written for the casual entertainment of the aristocracy—as atmosphere. And thus, surface treatment, manifested in

Time-Line: Classicism

1720's	Symphony (sinfonia) emerges, Sammartini, Italy
1740's	C. P. E. Bach "Sensitive style," northern Germany
1732	Haydn born
1756	Mozart born
1761	Haydn begins employ with Esterházy family
1762	Haydn: Symphony No. 7 Mozart (6 yrs.) begins European tour
1765	Mozart (age 9) Symphony No. 1
1770	Beethoven born
1787	Mozart: opera, *Don Giovanni*
1788	Mozart summer of 1788, last 3 symphonies No. 39, 40, 41
1791	Death of Mozart
1792	Beethoven begins professional music career, Vienna
1809	Death of Haydn

numerous types of trills, grace notes, and turns (see the following
example), replaces the more serious and profound treatment of musical
ideas so common among the Baroque composers.

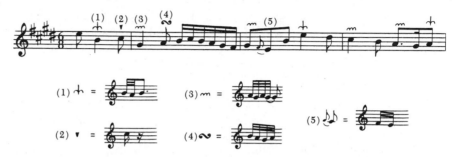

Example of "Style Galant" from François Couperin's *Pieces de Clavecin*

Fanciful titles such as *La Galante* and *La Voluptueuse*, among others,
were commonly provided these dainty, homophonic pieces, which were
normally written in the preferred form of the rococo, the suite (or *ordre*)
for harpsichord. These ordres are much like the Baroque suite in that
they are made up of a series of dance movements; however, they frequently contain many more dances than the usual Baroque suite of
the allemande-sarabande-courante-gigue plan. Interestingly, one highly
favored dance found in the ordre—the minuet—was eventually adopted
by the German classicists and became an integral part of the symphony
and piano sonata.

Further illustration of the rococo, and indeed its central focus, is
to be found in French interior decoration—in the numerous Parisian
hôtels, where the walls, panels, doorways, and ceilings are richly over-
laden with scrolls and a shell design (or *rocaille*, the origin of the word
rococo). The same type of esthetic ideals are to be found in English
literature at this time. Alexander Pope, the leading English literary
figure and counterpart to Watteau and Couperin, frequently clothed his
poetry in ornamental motifs and glittering surface decorations. His play
on atmosphere, surface decoration, and the world of make-believe
identifies him with the rococo. However, Pope also shows a considerable
leaning toward the classical; the pertinent traits of this side of his
creative nature will be mentioned later, under the classical period.

In concluding our discussion of the rococo, it might be said that
"this style did not need bold creative architects, powerful dramatists, and
robust musicians; it addressed itself to the decorator"[2] who worked
with small forms, avoided the philosophical probing of emotion, and
communicated to the elite of society.

[2] Paul Henry Lang, *Music in Western Civilization* (New York: W. W. Norton
and Company, Inc., 1941), p. 534.

Antoine Watteau, *Music Party. c.* 1719. Oil on canvas, 25½ x 36¼'. Wallace Collection, London

The Empfindsamer Stil (Sensitive Style) in Germany The *style galant,* as would be expected in this era of French cultural dominance, is also to be found in the work of the leading young German composers living in the early eighteenth century. Ironically, the older style of the senior composers, represented by J. S. Bach, was considered outmoded, too contrapuntal, and too complex for the "modern" German composers and listeners of the rococo age. Their taste was definitely for the less involved homophonic texture and simplicity of structure. However, despite the strong permeation of French *style galant* in many regions, a new esthetic ideal began to come to the fore about 1740 in northern Germany —the *empfindsamer Stil,* or *sensitive style,* in the music of C. P. E. Bach, the popular composer of the post-Bach era who set the stage, for the classic period.

The rococo lightness and intimacy are still felt in this new German music; however, the new style is imbued with an element quite foreign to the rococo mentality—human emotion. If the general temper of the classic age—that is, the concern for form, balance, restraint, and refinement —was born in the private aristocratic surroundings of the French court, the forms, the spirit, and inner content or musical language of classicism

François Boucher, *Toilet of Venus.* 1746. Oil on canvas, 42⅝ x 33½''. Metropolitan Museum of Art, New York
Bequest of William K. Vanderbilt, 1920

Rococo Interior, Salon, Hofburg Palace, Vienna. Austrian State Tourist Office, New York

are to be largely attributed to Sammartini in Italy and C. P. E. Bach and his German contemporaries in Mannheim, Berlin, and Vienna. The chief forms of classicism are the symphony and sonata; its spirit: a balance between the joyful and the serious or reflective; its content: distinctive, clear-cut themes, easily recalled, with marked rhythmic patterns. The final synthesis of these basic elements was completed by Haydn and Mozart.

Before outlining C. P. E. Bach's preclassical contributions, a brief description of the symphony and sonata must be given at this point because the subsequent discussion centers around these important forms.

The Keyboard Sonata Following the achievements of Scarlatti, who established many of the fundamental keyboard techniques and classical clarity of melody and texture, the keyboard sonata gradually acquired its rudimentary pattern of several movements, notably in the music of C. P. E. Bach. The keyboard sonata of the classic era proper—that of Haydn and Mozart—is usually in three movements, each having a different tempo and theme. Quite frequently the first and last movements are based on a particular structural plan called the *sonata form*. Thus, the word *sonata* may refer to a particular genre, or it may refer to a specific way of organizing the musical ideas within a movement. The earmarks of this sonata form include two contrasting themes, one in the tonic key and the second in the dominant. The opening statement of these two themes, sounded in succession, is called the *exposition section*. This is generally followed by a *development section*, in which one or both themes are elaborated upon (that is, presented in a new harmonic setting, or in a minor key as opposed to a major, or perhaps given a contrapuntal treatment, using imitation and other devices). The third and last section of the sonata form is called the *recapitulation section*, and in it the exposition section is repeated in its entirety or in shortened form.

EXPOSITION	DEVELOPMENT	RECAPITULATION
(usually two themes are stated, the first in the tonic key, second in the dominant)	(theme or themes are elaborated, broken up, combined, given new keys, etc.)	(repetition of exposition)

The Classical Symphony   The symphony follows the same plan as the keyboard sonata described above, except, of course, that it is played by an orchestra rather than the harpsichord or the *piano*, which, incidentally, became a favorite instrument in the classical era. Moreover, the string quartet is generally based on the same plan as the keyboard sonata and symphony, except that it is performed by four string instruments: cello, viola, and two violins. (The popular trio sonata of the Baroque is now replaced by the string quartet form).

THE CLASSICAL SYMPHONY
(common characteristics)

First Movement
   Tempo and character: usually fast (allegro) and lively; usually duple meter
   Form: frequently in sonata form
Second Movement
   Tempo and character: usually slow (andante) and lyrical
   Form: sonata form, song form (A B A), theme and variations, or rondo
Third Movement
   Tempo and character: stately minuet dance style (early classicism), much quicker in late period; triple meter
   Form: A B A
Fourth Movement
   Tempo and character: fast and gay, duple meter common
   Form: frequently in sonata form, sometimes in rondo form

C. P. E. Bach and his Contemporaries   To return to C. P. E. Bach, his main contribution to the keyboard sonata consists of his (1) delineation of themes in the exposition section of the sonata form; (2) rudimentary use of the development section (later established by Haydn in the 1780s) and (3) which is most important, the employment of *empfindsamer Stil* (sensitive style).

Unlike the style of composition of the powerful and profound Baroque, the sensitive style of C. P. E. Bach is characterized by its subtle nuances and shading in dynamics and dissonance. Particularly evident are the impetuous shifts in tempo and mood, simplicity of melodic movement, and light homophonic texture.

Quite naturally there is a mingling of the *style galant* in these works. However, the French style, primarily graceful and elegant, is subordinated to the Germanic urge for strong evocations of sentiment and nostalgia.

Analogous to the musical *Empfindsamkeit* are the similar trends in literature and painting, which were likewise witnessing a "wave of sensibility" beginning about the fourth decade; for example, *Clarissa* by the English writer Richardson (1748), the vogue of so-called cottage art in England, Sterne's *Sentimental Journey* written in Germany (1768), and the lachrymose paintings of Greuze in France.

Several other musical streams, more clearly classically oriented, were contemporary with C. P. E. Bach's *Empfindsamkeit*. Whereas C. P. E. Bach was inclined toward romantic moodiness, these other contemporaries, stressing the bright and joyful, provided the main spearhead of what was to finally burst forth as the classical period in music.

Beginning about 1745, the Mannheim group, led by the highly creative Johann Stamitz, gave form and substance to the chief instrumental type of the classical period, the *symphony*. This form had its nascent beginnings about two decades earlier among the Italian opera composers, particularly Giovanni Sammartini (c. 1698–1775) who composed approximately seventy-seven extant symphonies *(sinfonias)*.[3] In these works, the earliest of which date from the late 1720s, are to be found the essence of classicism, a radiant optimism expressed in lyrical, singing melodic lines and buoyant rhythmic energy.

Building on this Italian foundation, Stamitz pushed closer to the finished symphony form by using a contrasting second theme in the sonata form and also, from 1745, regularly employed four movements: fast, slow, minuet, fast.

In addition, the characteristic orchestral techniques associated with the classical symphony were developed: great dynamic contrasts from the very soft (*pp*) to the loudest (*ff*); the principle of crescendo; rocketlike themes that suddenly explode in a fast-ascending pattern; and violin

---

[3] These sinfonias were composed for operas (as introductory pieces, or *overtures*), as well as for the concert setting. Dr. Bathia Churgin and Newell Jenkins have catalogued 77 symphonies by Sammartini.

tremolos (rapid reiteration of a note by up-and-down movements of the bow). Most noteworthy is the full instrumentation of his orchestra in 1756 (see listing below); however, this full complement of instruments is the exception, since the classicists Haydn and Mozart normally wrote for an orchestra of twenty-five to thirty-five players.

flutes (2)
oboes (2)
bassoons (2)
horns (2)
trumpets (2)
timpani
violins I and II (20)
violas (4)
cellos and basses (8)

Other preclassicists were active at this time, including Monn (1717–1750) and Wagenseil (1715–1777), both from Vienna and both important for their assimilation of the humorous, light-hearted style of Viennese street songs we will find so strongly ingrained in the melodic style of Haydn and, to some extent, Mozart.

Here, then, we have the roots of classicism in music, resulting from a fusion of several styles: the refinement and elegance of the French, the bright lyricism of the Italians, and the formal synthesis of the Germans and Austrians.

THE CLASSICAL TEMPER IN THE ARTS

Derivation and Representation of the Classical Spirit in the Arts The classicistic movement in the arts came to fruition in the latter half of the eighteenth century, after the rococo had spent its energy. Classicism as a style period may be defined as a time when the esthetic concepts of ancient Greece and Rome were renewed in the fields of painting, architecture, sculpture, music, and literature. Influenced by the discoveries of ancient Herculaneum and Pompeii (1763), the writings of Wincklemann (*History of the Art of Antiquity*, 1764), and the "reassertion of the authority of reason" by the German philosopher Kant, artists, composers and writers turned to the ancient civilizations for inspiration and direction. They did not actually imitate the Greek achievements but rather attempted to capture the essence or distinctive qualities found in their fine arts. These qualities include clarity, balance, logical order, simplicity, refinement, control, and restraint; quite opposed to the grandiose and rhetorical style of the Baroque and the purely decorative and ethereal make-believe world of the rococo.

The classical period did not, of course, suddenly come to fruition in the middle of the century. The establishment of classicism in music was relatively late in the period (Haydn and Mozart about 1770), and in

Antonio Canova, *Pauline Bonaparte as Venus*. Marble sculpture, 1808. Alinari, Art Reference Bureau

painting very late in the century (David in the 1780s). Literature was the first of the arts to thoroughly assimilate the rational temper. This seems only natural, since language is the basic means of communication in all fields. The classical literary style began to be perfected as early as the age of Louis XIV, whose court cultivated a pure, correct, and logical diction. Louis' Académie—the selected group of artists and writers who governed French literary and artistic taste—attempted to establish a highly refined type of French as the norm or standard for good writing.

By 1700, under the influence of science, the growth of a reading public, and particularly the French Académie, English writers underwent a change in literary style: from the majestic, emotional, ornate style of the Baroque (Milton) to order, simplicity, lucidity, and precision (Pope). Moreover, if the general tone of the literature or journalism of the English masses was one of clarity, brevity, or directness, that of the elite was perfection and absolute refinement of expression. To the literary classicists like Pope, Collins, and Gray, "polish," not "fire," became the artistic credo.[4] Pope's work in particular represents the epitome of classicism, for we find in his poetry an emphasis on correctness of style, restraint,

[4] Preserved Smith, *The Enlightenment* (New York: The Crowell-Collier Publishing Company, 1962).

balanced phrases, clarity of structure, a bright, witty effect, and a polished "gentleman's" English. Most emphatically, personal idiosyncracy is subordinated to the universal norm—that of the refined language of society. Perhaps the creed of classicism is best summarized in a passage from Pope's *Essay on Criticism* (1711):

> Tis more to guide, than spur the muse's steed;
> Restrain his fury, than provoke his speed;
> The winged courser, like a gen'rous horse
> Shows most true mettle when you check his course.

Jacques Louis David (1748–1825) is the leader of the classic or neo-classic movement in French painting. One of his most famous paintings is the *Oath of the Horatii* (1784). In following the trend of glorifying the distinctive traits of the ancient Greek and Roman civilizations, such as virtue, self-control, dignity and manly strength, David chose as his subject a Roman father pledging his three sons to take up arms against the enemies of Rome. Stylistically, the painting is closely related to the works of the literary classicists: (1) clarity and simplicity of structure are present (lines are sharply drawn and uncluttered); (2) balance is stressed—the focal point is the swords, which are balanced on the left by the father and three sons and on the right by the weeping wife—moreover, the three columns provide a "balanced" background; (3) strength and solidity of form is represented by angular lines, body posture, and muscular features; (4) restraint of emotion—that is, rational control over the emotions—seems to prevail; and (5) refinement is stressed in the "ideal" human figures with their perfect physical proportions.

Classicism in English painting, though not oriented toward ancient subject matter, is represented by the portrait paintings of Gainsborough and Reynolds, in which polish, elegance, emotional control, and clarity of line predominate.

We will find these same traits in the works of Haydn and Mozart and in the early works of Beethoven. For example, the classic composer generally stresses *simplicity* in his melodic lines; that is, the rhythmic pattern is relatively simple, not cluttered with excessive ornamentation as was common in the *style galant*. *Clarity* is demonstrated in the composer's use of transparent orchestral textures, in which the various instruments are easily identified (instead of combining instruments into the greatly mixed timbres so common in the nineteenth century). *Control* is exhibited in the composer's holding in check the amount and use of dissonance, according to a strict rule of the period. *Refinement* is to be noted in the polished or finished touch given the melodic line—there is present the feeling that every note is in its proper, logical position, and that the melody is following a carefully prearranged path to its final cadence. *Balance* is found in the arrangement of the melodies (usually in two phrases), in the constant return to the main key center (the tonic), and most importantly in the use of the large symmetrical plan of the sonata form: exposition (A), development (B), and recapitulation (A). To this list of

Jacques Louis David, *Oath of the Horatii.* 1784. Oil on canvas, 10'10" x 14'. The Toledo Museum of Art Gift of Edward Drummond Libbey, 1950

basic characteristics we might add universality of expression, meaning that the main composers all wrote in the same accepted musical forms (symphony, piano sonata) and adhered for the most part to a common musical language (melodic and harmonic style). Moreover, like the literary classicism of Pope and others, musical classicism usually embodies a "bright," "witty" manner, as demonstrated in the lively tempos (in opening and closing movements), the scintillating rhythmic patterns, and use of the joyful-sounding major key.

Summary

Concomitant with the culmination of the Baroque musical style in the early part of the eighteenth century, the rococo movement centered in France brought forth the *style galant*—the musical equivalent of the delicate, decorative, and intimate designs found in French paintings and interiors. Its casual surface display belies, however, a highly rational mentality whose roots extend back to the seventeenth century. Musically its rational character (found in complicated trills, restraint of feeling, and required precision in execution), was a prelude to the classical period, which emerged about mid-century. Working in the constant shadow of the *style galant*, several German composers, under the influence of Italian clarity and the musical form of the operatic *sinfonia*, adapted the new expressive *empfindsamer Stil* to the new sonata and symphony. This early phase of classicism was completed by C. P. E. Bach, J. C. Bach, Johann Stamitz, and Georg Wagenseil. The next discussion will trace the final phase of the movement in the music of Haydn and Mozart.

HAYDN AND THE DEVELOPMENT
OF THE CLASSICAL SYMPHONY

Life Sketch In outlining some of the major aspects of Haydn's life, one automatically tends to draw comparisons with Haydn's compatriot of the classic age, Mozart. The two composers are poles apart in terms of family background, early childhood, music education, and personality. However, both used the same classic musical language—the neat phrases, clear-cut rhythms, cadences, and the same forms. However, the distinctive personal traits—the bold, happy, outgoing side of Haydn's nature and the highly refined, more sensitive nature of Mozart—are perceptible in their respective music.

Franz Joseph Haydn was born in 1732, at Rohrau, a little village in the eastern part of Austria, near the Hungarian border. In contrast to the auspicious beginnings of his contemporary, Mozart, who grew up in a culturally rich environment, Joseph Haydn was born of a modest family background. And in contrast to Mozart's protected and carefully nurtured youth, Haydn almost from the very beginning had to rely on his own resourcefulness. At the age of six he was sent to live with his uncle, Johann Mathias Franck, a school principal and musician in Hainberg. Again, in contrast to Mozart, Haydn's musical education was fragmentary and, for the most part, self-acquired. The young Haydn obtained, apparently, only general musical instruction (some training in clavier, violin, and singing) from his uncle, who was burdened with many responsibilities in the village school. Curiously, Haydn never became an outstanding performer on any instrument; even in his late youth he was only moderately proficient on his favorite instrument, the violin. Mozart, on the other hand, was an artist-pianist of international repute. However, even though Haydn lacked the precocity of Mozart, he must have acquired (mainly on his own) considerable skill in harpsichord and violin, for we note that during his early adult years in Vienna he taught harpsichord, played the violin in chamber ensembles, and later regularly conducted orchestral performances from the harpsichord.

At the age of eight the young Haydn entered the *kantorei* (school for boy choristers) at St. Stephen's Cathedral in Vienna, remaining here until his voice changed completely at the age of seventeen. Aside from extensive choral singing experience, little formal music education was offered; such instruction would have, undoubtedly, given the world a glimpse of Haydn's budding genius well before his late twenties (in contrast to Mozart, who had created his first nine symphonies by the age of twelve).

Following his dismissal from St. Stephen's, the teen-aged youth took up residence in Vienna and began to eke out his own existence by playing in Viennese street serenades and by giving private instruction in harpsichord. It was also at this time that Haydn made an intensive study of the sonatas and symphonies of C. P. E. Bach and received his first real formal instruction in counterpoint from Nicola Porpora. Gradually, the struggling musician began to make a name for himself. Through his teaching and chamber music performances in wealthy Viennese circles, Haydn's musicianship was recognized by the elite patrons of the arts. In 1759 he accepted the post of music director and chamber composer to Count von Morzin in Vienna. During his short stay, to 1760, Haydn acquired a foretaste of the work he would follow the remainder of his life: he conducted an orchestra of twenty-five, wrote several string quartets, and composed his first symphony (1759).

For almost the next thirty years (1761–1790), Haydn was in the service of the Esterházys, one of the wealthiest Hungarian noble families. The castle of Esterháza, located about eighty miles from Vienna and modeled after the court at Versailles, was a sumptuous edifice that had two theaters (one for opera and one for marionettes) and two large concert halls. Haydn, as the absolute personification of the eighteenth century royal court composer and musician, was assigned a number of duties: conductor of an orchestra of twenty-five players, coach and conductor for all operatic productions, and composer. His weekly schedule was a busy one for in addition to rehearsing the orchestra, he conducted two opera performances and two full orchestral concerts, and still found time to carry out a very fruitful schedule of composing. During his lifetime he amassed over a hundred symphonies, eighty-three string quartets, fifty-two keyboard sonatas, twenty-three operas, four oratorios, concertos, and over a hundred and fifty works (mostly in string-trio form) for the prince's favorite instrument, the baryton (like the viola da gamba, with the addition of twelve resonating strings beneath the fingerboard).

Between the years 1791 and 1795, Haydn devoted his efforts to a series of London appearances. Under the aegis of the impresario Johann Salomon, Haydn conducted orchestral concerts and wrote his last twelve symphonies (Nos. 93–104) referred to as his "London" Symphonies. He was widely acclaimed by Londoners who bestowed many honors on the renowned Haydn—culminating in an honorary doctor's degree conferred at Oxford in July, 1791 (for which occasion Haydn dedicated his Symphony No. 92, the "Oxford" Symphony). Following his London sojourns he resumed his position with the Esterházy family and wrote his last major compositions: two oratorios, *The Creation* and *The Seasons,* his last string quartets (Op. 76, Op. 77), and a magnificent concerto for keyed trumpet and orchestra (1796).

The Esterházy castle at Eisenstadt. The Bettmann Archive

Some Characteristics of Style: Examples from Early, Middle, and Late Periods   Haydn's creative genius touched many musical idioms: symphony, opera, string quartet, piano sonata, concerto, oratorio, and even the mass. However, the achievements that won him international fame in his day, and a permanent position in our own time, lay in the symphony—the form that sustained his interest for practically a lifetime. Confronted with his enormous creativity in the symphonic medium (104 symphonies), the modern listener, anxious to sample some of Haydn's greatness, may be somewhat bewildered by the range and scope of Haydn's gigantic symphonic treasure. Therefore, our focus at this introductory level will be upon a general view of his style periods and selected examples from each.

Haydn's creative life is usually divided into three phases: the first (rococo, 1759–1770), the second (emerging classic period, 1770–1782), and the third (age of maturity, 1782–1803). The early-period symphonies (Nos. 1 to early 40s) exemplify Haydn's strong interest in the rococo style. Not only do some of these works bear descriptive French titles ("Le Matin," "Le Midi," "Le Soir") typical of the French rococo, but the *style galant* is shown in his preference for the divertimentolike structures (light, entertaining chamber pieces, similar to the French ordres), lightness of texture, and an over-all playful, delicate effect quite unlike the mature Haydn of the later classical style.

The themes of these early symphonies are written in the Baroque manner: long and spun out (Haydn had not yet hit upon the regular, close-clipped phrases and shortened melodic style of classicism). Moreover, the development technique associated with the final phase of classicism is not yet present; instead, rococo repetition prevails. In the center of the small orchestra of about twenty-five is the harpsichord, whose soft, delicate plucking sounds tend to give a courtly aristocratic atmosphere to this music—ironically so, since we will find that, in his later work, Haydn, perhaps more than any other composer of his day, most fully demonstrated the Enlightenment's ideals. For we find him at the later date turning away from the aristocratic *style galant* and seeking his musical ideas in the world about him, in nature, Viennese street songs, folk dances, hymns, and Gregorian chant.

A typical work from Haydn's *rococo* period is the Symphony No. 7 in C major, subtitled "Le Midi," composed in the early days of his Esterházy employment (1761). The instrumentation is as follows:

oboes (2)	violins I
bassoon (1)	violins II
horns (2)	violas
flutes (2)	cellos and basses
	basso continuo (harpsichord)

In these early symphonies the alternating passages of concertino instruments and ripieno resemble the Baroque concerto style. But the presence of the Minuetto as one of the movements foreshadows the coming of what is to be a standard feature of the classical symphony.

Although Haydn is incorrectly called the "father of the string quartet," he did more than any other composer to draw the elements together into a standardized form. Most of Haydn's earliest quartets (listed as Op. 1 and Op. 2) are typical of the composer's pleasant and elegant rococo phase. Consisting of light, entertaining pieces loosely strung together, these are generally called "Divertimenti" rather than quartets, and were written in Haydn's pre-Esterházy days, probably 1755–1756.

However, beginning with the six quartets (Op. 3) composed between 1755–1766, the standard string quartet form comes definitely to the fore. We note the usual four-movement plan (Fast—Slow—Minuet—Fast) and the rudimentary outlines of the sonata form in the first movement. The fifth quartet in this series (subtitled the "Serenade" because of the song-like melody in the second movement) was probably composed early in the Esterházy period. Its first movement has a clearly marked sonata form as follows:

EXPOSITION (measures 1—90)	DEVELOPMENT (measures 91—138)
first theme (measures 1—16)	
second theme (measures 17—23)	RECAPITULATION (measures 138—224)

Concerning the second period (1770–1782), Haydn, beginning with the symphonies numbered in the 40s, abandoned the ephemeral *style galant* for the philosophy of the *empfindsamer Stil:* the idea of C. P. E. Bach that "music should not only entertain and delight but have a deeper meaning." Consequently, many of the symphonies of this period are imbued with a greater feeling of emotion achieved through use of minor keys, wider melodic skips, and sudden changes or fluctuations in tempo and dynamics. Uppermost are the classicistic traits: the establishment of the outer framework or mold of the four-movement idea of the symphony, including the development section in the first movement; down-to-earth humor in the final movement; and, above all, chiseled-out themes with clear-cut phrases, sharply defined contours, and striking rhythmic patterns. With the final passing of the *style galant,* the harpsichord is no longer an essential instrument in the orchestra, for the light, delicate sounds of the instrument are not attuned to the classicistic creed of clarity, strength, and economy of means. Moreover, the function of the harpsichord—to lend harmonic support to the ensemble—is now taken over by the horns, which are frequently given sustained chords.

Themes from Haydn's Second Creative Period.

Haydn's drive toward the classical traits of clarity, strength, balance and refinement, became fully realized about 1780—marking the start of his last period of writing. The chief characteristic of this final phase of his symphonic style was his intensive application of the development principle, that is, the working out or elaboration of musical ideas in the section immediately following the exposition portion of the first movement. The thorough treatment of the development section was heralded by Haydn in 1781, in his "Russian" String Quartets, which he himself declared as being written in "quite a new and special way." This portion of the first movement in his string quartets and symphonies had been, up to now, merely a brief episode or digression before going on to the concluding recapitulation section. Haydn's essential contribution to music was simply this: he made the development section an area of intense dramatic action and the main center of interest of the classical sonata form—indeed, as the testing ground of the composer's musicianship.

Haydn's interest in the development principle, tightness of form, and dual themes of the first movement is well established by the time of the so-called "Paris" Symphonies, which were commissioned for Paris concerts of 1785–1786. These symphonies are as follows:

Symphony No. 82 in C major ("L'Ours"—"The Bear")
Symphony No. 83 in G minor ("La Poule"—"The Hen")
Symphony No. 84 in E flat major
Symphony No. 85 in B flat major ("La Reine"—"The Queen")
Symphony No. 86 in D major
Symphony No. 87 in A major

Some writers have set off the "London" Symphonies, numbered 93–104, as the summit of Haydn's creative work. However, it is perhaps more meaningful to the general reader (and more accurate, musicologically speaking) to regard this phase as the logical continuation of his classic style, begun in the 1780s. Indeed, the "London" Symphonies, aside from stronger traces of romanticism, do not differ drastically from the "Paris" Symphonies. These final statements of the symphonist show Haydn as the supreme master of the idiom and its techniques, which took a lifetime to develop.

A representative work from the final period is the Symphony No. 104 in D major. This composition follows the customary plan of four movements: Allegro (with a slow introduction), Andante, Minuetto, and Allegro Spirituoso. Although the classicistic clarity of texture predominates, there is a "thicker" and heavier orchestral sound (foreshadowing romanticism), due to increased use of brass and woodwinds on a more independent basis. Up to now these sections were entirely subordinate to the strings. The sonata form is used in the first and last movements, and the symphony is greatly expanded over earlier works. Of considerable importance is his use of the Austrian *Ländler*, a heavy-footed folk dance that is frequently incorporated in the minuet movements of his later symphonies. Definitely, the minuet is now devoid of the traces of the polite *style galant* of the French court. Interestingly, Haydn's successor, Beethoven, further alters the minuet—seemingly in defiant contempt for the aristocratic connotations of the minuet—by turning it into a rollicking, dynamic movement called a *scherzo* (Italian, meaning a musical joke or jest).

Trumpet Concerto in E♭ (1796) by Joseph Haydn, First Page of Conductor's Score.

Franz Joseph Haydn. (1732–1809). Picture Collection, New York Public Library

Summary Haydn was the musical representative of the Enlightenment. In his work we can trace the demise of the aristocratically nurtured art of the rococo and the rise of a more democratic expression that drew its power from the world at large, that is, from the songs, dances, and religious expressions of Viennese life. In this respect Haydn exemplifies musically the dominant slogan of the age—"return to nature," championed by Rousseau and others of the late eighteenth century. Haydn has been incorrectly called the "father of the string quartet and symphony." Although he did not "invent" these forms, he was instrumental in establishing their "classical" structure and content, including the four-movement plan, the development technique, the bright, humorous quality of the outer movements, and the classical orchestra of woodwinds, brass in pairs, strings, and timpani.

Haydn's work was emulated by many, notably the young Mozart, who, by the age of thirty, completed the equivalent of Haydn's lifetime endeavor.

MOZART: EPITOME OF CLASSICISM

Life Sketch: Early Period (1756–1773)   Much has been written about the musical genius of the eighteenth century, Wolfgang Amadeus Mozart. Of the many studies, Einstein's *Mozart: His Character, His Work,* affords the deepest penetration into the musical style of Mozart. Turner's *Mozart: The Man and His Works* covers the composer's life as it is mirrored in his extensive correspondence to family and friends from early childhood to his last, poverty-stricken years in Vienna. Much of what follows is drawn principally from these two sources. In view of the scope and immensity of Mozart's achievements, an overview of his musical style periods and a summary of the prominent characteristics of his art would perhaps be most helpful to the reader.

In many respects Mozart stands in the same light as J. S. Bach—both represented the musical apex of the epoch, and both summarized the main trends and styles of the period in highest musical terms. Rather than uproot previous modes of creativity, the two composers refined and perfected the inner content of the established forms of the period. Interestingly, Beethoven, another member of the esteemed society of musical excellence and Mozart's heir, was a revolutionist who, after a short "classical" phase, ushered in a new romantic expression. His early work will be discussed following this appraisal of Mozart.

Mozart's creative life may be divided into three periods: the so-called "wunderkind" years (1756–1773) of amazing musical precocity; the middle period (1773–1781), the era of his emerging distinctive personal style; and the late period (1781–1791), the time of his most significant compositions and, ironically, a time of serious financial problems and professional frustration.

Wunderkind Years (1756–1773)   Born into a musically rich and economically secure family in Salzburg in 1756, Mozart, under his father's guidance, became by the age of six a clavier virtuoso and by twelve a budding composer. This astounding early record was due in large measure to the nurturing of the boy's musical genius by his father, Leopold, a well-known composer, conductor, and teacher in Salzburg. After discovering the three-year-old Wolfgang "picking out" thirds at the keyboard, Father Mozart began teaching him some pieces on the clavier. The extraordinary talents of the youth were soon made known to the world in a number of journeys, during which Leopold had his son (and occasionally his daughter) play before nobility in Europe and England.

These tours began in 1762, when the six-year-old Mozart and his talented sister Maria Anna spent most of the year in Munich and Vienna. Later (1763–1766), a tour covering more than three years encompassed Paris, London, and various German and Dutch cities. It was during this time, specifically in London in 1764, that Mozart was introduced to the music of Johann Christian Bach (the second leading musical son of Johann Sebastian Bach), which had a profound effect on the development of Mozart's early instrumental style. The last series of noted trips was taken to Italy between 1769 and 1773.

The first compositions (of a total of more than six-hundred completed in his lifetime) were written in Mozart's sixth year, including four minuets (K. 1, 2, 4, 5)[5] and two allegros (K. 3, 9a). An ingratiating andante in B flat, (K. 9b), composed in the following year, shows the boy to be very adept with chromatic harmony and also capable of expressing poignant feelings characteristic of the mature composer.

The phenomenal achievements of the youth are well known, including his polylingual ability, unusual performing skills, which placed him before leading rulers and courts of Europe, and his grasp of the symphonic techniques. He completed his first symphony by age nine, and, amazingly, eight more symphonies and his first opera, *La Finta semplice,* by his twelfth birthday.

Andante in B♮ K. 9b (incomplete) Composed by Mozart at the Age of Seven, 1763. *Mozart: The Man and His Works* by W. J. Turner, copyright 1938, Alfred A. Knopf, Inc. Reprinted by Permission.

[5] The "K." followed by a number refers to the catalogue designation made by L. von Köchel, who first codified the vast collection of Mozart's compositions.

An Unfinished Portrait of Mozart painted in 1782–1783, soon after his marriage, by Joseph Lange, his brother-in-law. New York Public Library

Stylistically, the early instrumental music of Mozart seems to be a combination of several musical currents or strains, principally the *style galant* and a bright, energetic, scintillating style called *opera buffa*, which was characteristic of the Italian comic opera of this time and which was the principal mode of the Italian *sinfonia* composers, chiefly Giovanni Sammartini.

The young genius Mozart probably assimilated the opera buffa style during his year's stay in London, beginning in April of 1764. Here the boy undoubtedly heard the symphonies of the native English composers, William Boyce and Thomas Arne. However, it was Johann Christian Bach who exerted the strongest influence on the lad.

Strangely, the classic mode we noted evolving earlier among the Italian opera composers and the Mannheimers, quickly spread through Europe. By the time Mozart visited London in 1764, the classic spirit had already been imported, largely through the work of Johann Christian Bach, official composer for the King's Theater in Haymarket. J. C. Bach's smooth, scintillating "classic" expression was acquired through his extensive association with Italian musical culture prior to his royal appointment in London.

Karl Geiringer, the noted musicologist, has written that Johann Christian

> had the pleasure of arranging for the appearance at Buckingham House of that unique youthful prodigy, Wolfgang Amadeus Mozart, age 8. . . . John [Johann] Bach was fascinated by Wolfgang, they became great friends and liked doing stunts together before an enraptured audience. He would for instance, have Wolfgang on his lap while they played the harpsichord together, alternating after every bar; or they would compose a fugue, Bach starting Mozart completing it. For the child genius this association with John Bach was of the greatest artistic significance, and his compositions clearly show the tremendous influence the mature composer exercised on him.[6]

Middle Years (1773–1782)   A decided change occurred in Mozart's music about 1773, from the Italian buffa to a style more expressive and personal. The new style arising from this transformation is noticeable in both his chamber works and symphonies. It possesses the more serious overtones so characteristic of the German and Austrian temperament.

Six of Mozart's quartets (K. 168–173), all written in the late summer of 1773, were created under the magic spell of the musical crossroads of Europe—Vienna. And, more importantly, they show the influence of the famed musician from Esterháza, Franz Joseph Haydn, whose newly composed quartets (Opp. 17 and 20, 1771 and 1772) greatly excited the youth from Salzburg. In essence, it was a "new" Haydn who inspired him, for, as Einstein writes: "Haydn, approaching his fortieth birthday,

[6] Karl Geiringer, *The Bach Family* (New York: Oxford University Press, 1959), pp. 411–412.

was tired of the galant style; he felt the necessity of deepening his work, of infusing it with greater seriousness, greater intimacy."[7]

Thus, feeling and passion replace *galanterie* in the Mozart gems of that eventful summer of 1773, but perhaps what most impresses the listener is their greater use of polyphonic textures, imitation, and fugue. The change is also noticeable in three important symphonies completed at this time: Symphony in C, K. 162 (1773), Symphony in G minor, K. 183 (1773), and Symphony in A, K. 201 (1774). In these, the sweetness of Italian buffa is replaced by rhythmic agitation, extreme contrasts of dynamics, sharp accents and a finer development of the thematic material.

Late Period (1781–1791)   Following the Mannheim and Paris tours taken with his mother from 1777 to 1779, Mozart settled in Vienna, where he remained, except for several brief periods of travel, for the rest of his short life. The latter years were fraught with disappointment and struggle. He continually sought important musical positions (such as the *Kapellmeister* position with King Frederick II of Prussia), but these attempts were completely in vain. In order to make ends meet financially he taught clavier and composition to wealthy patrons of the arts.

These activities were necessary even though he won many triumphs in concertizing and in his opera performances (four of his greatest operas were composed during this period). Perhaps much of Mozart's trouble stemmed from his lack of ability to manage his personal matters; moreover, his wife Constanze (whom he married during the Vienna years) was equally inept as a family manager. Further complication arose from Mozart's lack of diplomacy and an arrogant mannerism that prevented him from attaining the positions that he desired.

Incredible as it may seem, Mozart created more than two hundred of his most significant works in this period of hardship; a partial listing follows:

> Symphony No. 35 in D ("Haffner") (1782)
> Symphony No. 36 in C ("Linz") (1783)
> Symphony No. 38 in D ("Prague") (1786)
> Symphony No. 39 in E flat (1788)
> Symphony No. 40 in G minor (1788)
> Symphony No. 41 in C ("Jupiter") (1788)
> *Marriage of Figaro,* opera (1786)
> *Don Giovanni,* opera (1787)
> *Cosi fan tutti,* opera (1790)
> *The Magic Flute,* opera (1791)
> *Eine kleine Nachtmusik,* serenade (1787)
> Sonata and Fantasy in C minor for Piano (1784, 1785)
> Sonata in C major for Piano K. 545 (1788)
> Set of six "Haydn" String Quartets (1782–1785)
>   (dedicated to Joseph Haydn)
> 17 piano concerti (1782–1791)
> *Requiem* (1791)

[7] Alfred Einstein, *Mozart, His Character, His Work* (New York: Oxford University Press, 1962), p. 176.

Summary   Mozart explored every musical idiom of his day—attaining brilliant success in every form that he touched. The essence of his musical style, the indefinable quality or "tone" we immediately detect as Mozartian, was already present in his earliest works. His relationship with Haydn—beginning indirectly through his hearing of the Haydn quartets in the summer of 1773—was a deciding factor in the shaping of Mozart's mature style which was subsequently exhibited in the quartets and symphonies. On the other hand, Haydn was influenced by the genius of Mozart, as can be observed in the more lyric melodic style, greater refinement, fullness of sonority, and compactness of form in Haydn's later works. Both Haydn and Mozart built their symphonic style on the foundations furnished by the Italian *sinfonia* composers and the German musicians at Mannheim and Vienna.

Mozart's contributions to opera are numerous: he was the first to successfully use the symphony orchestra to enhance the vocal elements in opera. Although he did not reject the Neapolitan style (as did his contemporary Gluck), he perfected the materials and concepts such as the opera seria and opera buffa forms, the aria, and the recitative; and, more importantly, he, like Monteverdi a century earlier, gave his operas real characters, possessing feelings and emotions. Again, like Monteverdi, he found a balance between the dramatic and the musical.

PROMINENT CHARACTERISTICS OF MOZART'S MUSICAL STYLE

PREFERRED FORMS	Symphony (41)*	Piano sonata & fantasia (24)	Piano concerto (25)	String quartet (24)	Opera (22)
MELODY	1. Lyrical style (vocal oriented) 2. Smooth flowing line, divided into phrases 3. Clear melodic goals 4. "Mannheim sigh" at cadence (melody comes to rest from strong, accented dissonant note) 5. Diatonic; late period quite chromatic 6. Ornamentation common (trills and turns, mainly)				
HARMONY	1. Major and minor keys 2. Triadic harmony (three-note chords) 3. Dissonance carefully controlled 4. "Alberti bass" (broken chord figures repeated in bass)				
TEXTURE	1. Homophony predominates in early works 2. Polyphony common in late period				
RHYTHM	1. Regular, metrical rhythmic movement 2. Frequent interjection of rests and momentary pauses 3. Simple and constant rhythmic patterns 4. Tempo generally remains constant to end of movement or section				

ORCHESTRAL
TECHNIQUE

1. Clarity of orchestral texture (all instruments in orchestra easily differentiated)
2. In later works orchestra consists of four groups: strings, woodwinds, brass, and percussion
3. String group predominates
4. Size of orchestra in later period about 40 players

OPERATIC
TECHNIQUE

1. Established a balance between dramatic and musical
2. Restored excellence in musical portions of opera such as overture and aria, which is now devoid of spectacular vocal feats and improvisation common to Baroque opera
3. Skillful musical characterization
4. Used same forms and concepts of Neapolitan opera: aria, recitative (both secco and orchestrally accompanied), choruses, and overture
5. Made symphony orchestra an integral part of opera

* This is the traditional number; recent research has disclosed 50 symphonies.

BEETHOVEN: EARLY COMPOSITIONS

Life Sketch   The turning point from eighteenth-century classicism to the romanticism of the nineteenth century is generally cited in the music of Ludwig van Beethoven. Born in 1770, at a time when musical classicism was in full force in the music of Mozart and Haydn, and indeed when the classical spirit was fully manifested in all of the arts, it was inevitable that the first creative urges of Beethoven would be in the measured and controlled classicistic vein. Although some music historians have divided Beethoven's life into several periods, for our purposes a simple division of early and late, or classical and romantic, will suffice. The so-called classical phase extends from the time of his first works (notably the first two symphonies and string quartets [Op. 18]) up to 1803, the year when Beethoven completed his monumental Third Symphony (the "Eroica") and which marks the beginning of his romantic period. Our discussion at this juncture will pertain only to the highlights of his early life and work. His romantic style will be dealt with at the beginning of the next chapter, "The Romantic Age."

Beethoven was born in Bonn in 1770—the year that the fourteen-year-old Mozart was making his first sojourn to Italy and the year that Haydn completed his tenth year of employment in the Court of Esterházy. The story of Beethoven's rise to greatness despite tremendous physical and environmental handicaps is truly a phenomenon in music history. For example, Beethoven's family background was quite the opposite of Mozart's. His father was not a well-known, established musician as was young Wolfgang's (Father Beethoven was employed as a singer in the electoral court). Nor was there the careful guidance and cultural upbringing (Beethoven's father was, apparently, a coarse, unruly fellow with an intemperate liking for alcohol), nor was there the careful nurturing of musicianship. In fact, in many ways there is a close parallel between the early years of Haydn and those of Beethoven.

Actually, aside from some instruction in clavier and violin provided by his father, Beethoven was largely self-taught up to the age of eleven (1781), when he received lessons in composition from Christian Neefe, an organist and composer. Even Beethoven's formal education was terminated in his eleventh year. From about 1782 to 1792 he was employed as a musician (accompanist, organist, and violinist) in the Electoral Court. And outside of a few lessons with Haydn in Vienna in 1792, and a year of counterpoint with Johann Georg Albrechtsberger, Beethoven, like Haydn, acquired his performance and compositional skills through intensive personal effort.

In Vienna, in 1792, he entered the realm of professional music as a pianist, playing extensively in wealthy circles and making a name as a composer as well. Royalties from his music, fees for performances, and commissions from wealthy benefactors permitted Beethoven to live very comfortably as a professional musician; in fact, he was the first major composer to attain complete economic status.

In 1798 Beethoven discovered that he was beginning to lose his hearing. By 1802 the affliction had worsened considerably, to the extent that he was compelled to write, in most moving terms, an account of his incurable malady. This letter, known as the "Heiligenstadt testament," was addressed to his brothers and was to be read after Beethoven's death. This condition grew steadily worse, and by 1820 deafness was practically total—a time when Beethoven composed his last five great piano sonatas, the *Missa Solemnis*, the "Diabelli" Variations, and the last work, the Ninth Symphony, completed in 1824.

The music composed up to 1802–03—that is up to the Heiligenstadt document—follows the styles and formal outlines of Haydn and Mozart. The Symphony No. 1 in C major, for example, has the customary four-movement plan, sonata form in the opening and closing movements, "classic" sounding themes, and clarity of orchestral texture. However, there are some signs of Beethoven's own personal stamp: a heavy, boisterous quality in the fast movements, sudden crescendos, a lively third movement (formerly a sedate minuet, now a vigorous scherzo; Haydn, of course, also quickened the tempo of this movement in his latter period). And, above all, there is the ever-present emphasis on rhythmic drive and power, which although still somewhat tame, is so characteristic of almost all of his music.

The Second Symphony (in D major), although classically structured in themes and over-all design, possesses a greater feeling of breadth and scope. Beethoven seems to paint, orchestrally speaking, in long, sweeping strokes; moreover, this symphony has more of the dramatic flair and excitement that becomes so firmly ingrained in Beethoven's style, beginning with the Third Symphony, completed in 1803.

Oil portrait of Beethoven by Waldmüller, 1823

Summary   It seems that every epoch has its ebb and flow, when the common musical language of the era is fully explored and brought to perfection by a select few, and when a new mode of musical thought or style gradually emerges from the old expression to become the interest and challenge of the new generation of composers. In this regard, Beethoven may be considered the innovator, the stimulus, or the prime mover behind the rise of a new musical expression called *romanticism*—taken up next.

REPRESENTATIVE WORKS IN THE HUMANITIES:
THE CLASSICAL ERA (1750–1800)

MUSIC

Trends: Musical classicism begins to rise in Germany, beginning about 1740. This so-called preclassical phase is represented mainly by Bach's sons, Carl Philipp Emanuel and Johann Christian Bach, Johann Stamitz, and Georg Wagenseil. The classical era emerges in full force after 1760, with Haydn, Mozart, and the first compositions of Beethoven. Their work constitutes the final crystallization of the classical forms: the symphony and sonata, and the complete mastery of the "classic style" identified by its light-hearted spirit, clear homophonic texture, polished character, and logically ordered designs.

PHILOSOPHY AND ART

The eighteenth century is frequently called the "Age of Reason" and the "Age of the Enlightenment," the former because of the dominant position of the rational process and the latter because of the prevailing belief in the perfectability of man through his use of reason. The principal characteristic of this age is "the placement of reason as the highest authority, as the universal arbiter in all matters." The roots of this world view stemmed from the seventeenth century—the age when rationalism was born in the field of science. In the eighteenth century, the new religion of reason was applied to all moral, civic, religious, and artistic problems. Its champions were: Voltaire, Locke, Pope, Diderot, Condorcet, Rameau, and Rousseau. In the arts of literature, poetry, painting, sculpture, architecture, and music, the rationalistic pulse became expressed in a restoration of the "classical" principles of ancient Greek and Roman culture: clarity, symmetry of form, strength, control, restraint, and logical order.

LITERATURE

1711	*Essay on Criticism*, Alexander Pope
1712	*The Rape of the Lock*, Alexander Pope
1734	*The Essay on Man*, Alexander Pope
1751	*Elegy Written in a Country Churchyard*, Thomas Gray
1755	*Dictionary*, Samuel Johnson
1759	*Candide*, François Marie Arouet (Voltaire)
1760	*Ossian*, James Macpherson
1762	*The Social Contract*, Jean Jacques Rousseau
1764	*History of the Art of Ancient Times*, Johann Winckelmann
1766	*The Vicar of Wakefield*, Oliver Goldsmith
1771	*Encyclopedia Brittanica*, first edition
1776	*Sturm und Drang*, Friedrich Klinger
1781	*Critique of Pure Reason*, Immanuel Kant
1781	*Confessions*, Jean Jacques Rousseau

1786   First edition of Robert Burns' poetry
1788   *The History of the Decline and Fall of the Roman Empire*, Edward Gibbon
1788   *Egmont*, Goethe
1790   *Critique of Judgment*, Immanuel Kant
1794   *Progress of the Human Spirit*, Marquis de Condorcet

ART

1770   *The Blue Boy*, Thomas Gainsborough
1779   *Daedalus and Icarus*, Antonio Canova
1784   *Oath of the Horatii*, Jacques Louis David
1785   Virginia State Capitol designed by Thomas Jefferson
1787   *Lord Heathfield*, Joshua Reynolds
1788   *Paris and Helen*, Jacques Louis David
1789   *Brutus*, Jacques Louis David
1788   Brandenburg Gate built in Berlin
1798   *Sabine Women*, Jacques Louis David
1800   *Madame Recamier*, Jacques Louis David
1806   Arc de Triomphe built in Paris

HISTORICAL EVENTS

1751   *Experiments and Observations on Electricity*, Benjamin Franklin
1769   Watt's steam engine
1763   The ruins of Pompeii and Herculaneum discovered
1764   Spinning jenny, Hargreaves
1774   First Continental Congress, Philadelphia
1775-1783   American Revolution
1776   Declaration of Independence
1789-1794   French Revolution

8

THE ROMANTIC AGE
(1800–1900)

THE SETTING: A NEW SENSIBILITY (1800–1850)

> Music is the most romantic of all the arts—one
> might almost say, the only genuinely romantic
> one—for its sole subject is the infinite.
>   E. T. A. Hoffmann, 1776–1822

Introduction: The Coming of a New Era in Music By 1800, the whole of
Europe was caught up in the new artistic trend called *romanticism*. The
romantic tendency was very strong in almost all of the arts throughout
much of the eighteenth century, particularly in English and German literature. However, although there were many romantic tendencies in art
and music, these fields did not undergo a substantial change in style until
about the end of the century.

In music, the new era was proclaimed by Beethoven on April 7,
1805, the date of the first public performance of his Third Symphony.
This masterpiece, subtitled the "Eroica," is, in the words of Paul Henry
Lang, "one of the incomprehensible deeds in arts and letters, the greatest
single step made by an individual composer in the history of the symphony and in the history of music in general."[1] At its first public performance the "Eroica," like so many pioneering works, met with
unfavorable reaction. The halls of the Vienna Theater, which had echoed
the balanced, restrained phrases, and elegant style of classicism, now
resounded with power, fire, and demonic energy.

From reports we learn that the audience was shocked and astounded
by the hammer-stroke opening chords, the dynamic shifting and thrusting

[1] *Music in Western Civilization* (New York: W. W. Norton & Company, Inc.,
1941), p. 763.

of accents, and the breathtaking pace of the final movement. Critics referred to the composition as being "daring," "wild," "a fantasy," "of inordinate length," "of extreme difficulty," and "lacking unity." History has taught us that not only was the work misunderstood, but that it was the first major composition to "point the way" into the nineteenth century. Ironically, the path music was to follow is indicated in the very words of Beethoven's critics—a revolutionary new direction in which fantasy, imagination, freedom of form, daring invention, and virtuosity would become the chief elements of expression of practically every nineteenth-century composer.

The musicians of the first generation of romanticists, like their counterparts of the early Baroque, wanted to part ways with the old, to break tradition, and to experiment and find new ways for treating musical materials and forms. Occasionally, this romantic tendency is to be seen in certain moments in classicism, for example in Haydn's *Sturm und Drang* period, in the brooding melancholy of Mozart's Piano Fantasia in C minor in 1785, and in the highly charged finale of his last symphony, the "Jupiter," of 1788. However, the power of spontaneous emotion was finally unleashed by Beethoven.

The Romantic Mind   The youthful artistic attitude that favors experimentation, adventure, and unbridled, spontaneous inspiration, is an ever-present state of mind that cannot be confined to a single epoch. This, the romantic spirit, is a constant element in the artistic life of Western culture from one epoch to another, and present in varying degrees in all creative artists. Given the proper conditions, it can appear at any time; hence, due to social and intellectual changes and other factors, it may be present in stronger degrees at given moments in history. It would seem, too, that various social tensions give rise to peaks in romanticism, appearing as clearly marked style movements or epochs in the history of Western art and music, such as the Greek Hellenistic period, the Mannerist movement of the sixteenth century, and the Baroque and romantic eras.

Moreover, shorter, more incisive waves of romantic effusion are to be noted even in times when classicistic calm and balance generally prevail. For example, the "romantic" side of Leonardo da Vinci, according to Eric Newton, is to be seen "as an example of romanticism struggling to express itself in an unromantic age."[2] The same can be said of Haydn and his storm and stress phase of creativity. The appearance of romanticism is not always to be equated with underlying social change; however, this frequently seems to be the case. A good illustration is to be found in the very era of which we are currently speaking, a time of optimum tension in the arts and also a time of immense social change, of which many examples may be cited: the rise of the factory system, the emancipation of man stemming from the French Revolution, the beginnings of industrial capitalism, the development of modern transportation systems, the theory of evolution under Darwin, and the founding of modern psychology under James, Freud, and others.

[2] *The Romantic Rebellion* (New York: Schocken Books, 1964), p. 70.

Caspar David Friedrich, *Two Men Looking at the Moon*. 1819. Panel 13¾ x 17¼''. Staatliche Fotothek, Dresden

If Man became the central focus of the social revolution of the nine-teenth century, the arts of this era also show a preponderant concern for Man—his inner nature and his feelings and emotions, expressed in a highly personal style. This accounts for the romantic *spectrum,* that is, the vast number of individual styles (rather than one dominant mode character-istic of classicism) that prevailed in the arts of this period.

If the romantic by nature interprets reality through his infinite spectrum of inner feelings, then it would seem that only a description rather than a definition of romanticism is possible. This becomes readily apparent when we begin comparing the highly divergent styles of such composers as Chopin and Beethoven, and Schumann and Wagner. They are not united in terms of style but rather in what we may term the romantic frame of mind. In this connection, three primary modes of thought seem to direct or influence the various creative urges of the romantic: (1) a rebellion against the normative and the traditional in style and form, (2) a constant striving for originality with its accompany-ing invention and experimentation, and (3) an intense interest in ex-pressing personal feelings and emotions in the most poignant and dra-matic way. Other general characteristics of the romantic mind include an interest in nature ranging from peaceful, pastoral scenes to depiction of nature's violent and destructive forces; a longing for past ages (especially medieval culture); and a desire to know the mysteries of life and death.

The Classic and the Romantic Compared   Even in an age of intense passion there are continuing strains of the rational or classical mentality; that is, there are those who believe that the rules of composition are to be followed and that formal balance dictates content. To this group belong Mendelssohn and Brahms. The true romanticists, such as Schumann, Berlioz, and Wagner, differ from the classicists in their disregard for rules, canons, and traditions and in their subordination of formal considerations to freedom of expression. The element of conflict, so important to the romantic, is, however, also important to the classicist. He acknowledges the constant struggle between forces that threaten balance or equilibrium whether it be in the symphony, in which the conflict of themes or motives in the development section are ultimately resolved by the recapitulation section; in architecture, where lines instead of themes become the participants; or in painting, where forms or colors are brought into correct juxtaposition or balance. In short, as Eric Newton writes, the classic temperament delights in the equilibrium that results from the conflict of opposites.[3] The romantic, on the other hand, focuses his attention not on the balanced state of affairs, but on the struggle, the tension, and the pulling of forces. However, in his pursuit of the unusual and the bizarre, the romantic artist or musician must eventually grapple with one of the most difficult problems of his art: to seek order out of chaos, to make the irrational intelligible to the listener or viewer.[4]

Pre-romanticism: The Sources of the Movement   As with all periods, we must begin by looking for distinctive signs or landmarks that, taken together, provide a perspective or a kind of roadmap leading into the period. Without a doubt the most important of these is what Arnold Hauser calls the "dissolution of courtly art" and the development of "bourgeois subjectivism," the former referring to the style set by the French courts (refined, aristocratic, and rational), the latter to the taste of the middle class (sensualistic, natural, and spontaneous), which, during the course of the eighteenth century, gradually superceded the courtly art.[5]

Bourgeois subjectivism, then, constituted the cultural setting out of which the romantic movement emerged. The rapidly changing taste for the naturalistic and sentimental rather than the refined and elegant was felt in all of the arts of the eighteenth century: in the music of C. P. E. Bach (in his *empfindsamer*, or sensitive, style), in the French paintings of Greuze and Chardin, in the pastoral, picturesque writings of the English author Thomson, and in the novels of Richardson, to name but a few

[3] *The Romantic Rebellion*, p. 62.
[4] *The Romantic Rebellion*, p. 65.
[5] Arnold Hauser, *The Social History of Art* (New York: Vintage Books, 1951), vol. 3, p. 3.

representative examples. The writings of Voltaire—the choice of the typical reader of French bourgeoisie—clearly represent the middle-class point of view: antiauthority, anticlerical and antiaristocratic. Moreover, it was Rousseau, according to Bertram Russell, who gave form and direction to the already existing tendencies to "legitimize and encourage a display of feeling." In this regard, Rousseau's *Confessions* stands as an important testimony of the romantic mind. Rousseau, perhaps more than any other preromantic, gave the strongest voice in the revolt against the ethical and esthetic standards of the rococo. The cry was later echoed by Beethoven, who rebelled not only against the servant status of the court musicians of Haydn's and Mozart's time, but also against the overly comfortable, pleasant, and elegant qualities of the court expression. For Beethoven, born in the midst of bourgeois subjectivism, naturalism and emotionalism were the true inner urges, which were finally unleashed after a brief experience with the courtly style.

The Requirements of Romantic Music   Our preliminary examination discloses several other interesting aspects of the elusive phenomenon known as romanticism. One concerns the frame of mind of the listener, his preparation and mental orientation. For example, the very nature of the romantic's emotional approach to his art points up the futility of seeking an understanding of this music on purely rational grounds, that is, to approach it with the same set of expectations one would have in listening to a classical symphony. In classicism, the experienced listener is generally very conscious of the formalistic elements of music: the theme and its contour, its repetition, its variation, the balancing of A section by B, and the symmetry of form achieved by repetition of A after B (A B A). In romanticism, the composer focuses our attention on sound itself, and frequently sound for the sake of sound, for the haunting, moody connotations it evokes on the part of the listener. The formal elements are of course still there, but they are frequently subordinated to the expressive.

Perhaps the best way to describe it is to say that romanticism requires a complete personal involvement—a sinking of one's self into the work of art—and then only is it possible to fully appreciate the romantic's message to its fullest. For, as Marcel Brion writes, "one cannot reach the substance of romanticism by dialectical routes; only an immediate and total communion reveals that deep reality which reason alone will never uncover."[6]

Of course, real enjoyment of music of all periods requires complete absorption; but what the romantic wishes us to do, and demands, is a reliving of his creative experience, which addresses itself mainly to the senses and to the emotions. In other words, romantic music, especially that of the early stages of the movement, with its emphasis on the purely sensual elements of music (tone color, harmony, and rhythm) rather than the formal (musical design and structure) involves an emotional orienta-

[6] *Art of the Romantic Era* (New York: Frederick A. Praeger, Publishers, 1966), p. 13.

tion on the part of the listener. This is particularly true of the first-generation composers, such as Schumann, Schubert, and Chopin, who devoted their talents mainly to short, poetic "mood pieces," in which sheer sound captivates the listener. Tone painting with quaint chord progressions, dissonant tone combinations, and "blurring" of chords through the use of the pedal on the piano are more important to Schumann and Chopin than the use of the classicist's sonata form.

However, we will find that, as the romantic movement reaches its maturity in music (after about 1850), greater intellectual involvement is demanded on the part of the listener. For example, the music of the late romantics—Liszt, Brahms, Wagner, Bruckner, and Mahler—is written in larger, more intricate forms in which the conflict of musical and extra musical forces supplants the mood painting of early romanticism.

THE HEROIC PHASE: BEETHOVEN

Beethoven's Later Works: The Eclipse of Classicism   Early romanticism in music embraces the first four decades of the nineteenth century, from the time of Beethoven's later works to the art songs composed by Robert Schumann in 1840. Schumann, who died in 1856, was the last composer of the early generation of romanticists. His contemporaries include, in addition to Beethoven (1770–1827), Carl Maria von Weber (1786–1826), Franz Schubert (1797–1828), Frédéric Chopin (1810–1849), and Felix Mendelssohn-Bartholdy (1809–1847). Because of the vastness of the romantic era, our aim will be to cover only the leading figures who were closely aligned to the romantic movement centered in Germany and Austria. Moreover, rather than explore all of their music, we shall limit our discussion to biographical summaries, principles of style, and illustrative examples that most clearly embody the romantic spirit.

Although there were many individual styles during the romantic age, three tendencies or phases are to be noted: the *heroic*, under Beethoven; the *poetic*, represented by the young romantics Schubert, Schumann, and Chopin; and lastly, the *hyper-romantic*, led by Wagner, Bruckner, and Mahler.

As we have already noted, some music historians regard Beethoven as the first real romantic composer, while others think of him as the last member of the distinguished line of classicists, as the apex in the final statement of musical classicism. Both points of view must be acknowledged, since we find that even in his most progressive works there is a sense of form and balance, that is, a definite compulsion to restore order after turbulence.

Of one thing there is little doubt: Beethoven fully personified, in musical terms, the intellectual and esthetic spirit of the late eighteenth century. This is shown in his revolutionary attitude toward his art and profession, in his interest in nature as a source of inspiration and consolation, and in his desire to exalt the mysterious and demonic. Above all, with Beethoven musical creativity took on a highly individualistic character, in which each composition, although bearing traces of the composer's inimitable style, is treated as an entity in itself. In effect, each

John Constable, *Salisbury Cathedral from the Bishop's Garden.* Frick Collection, New York

work stands alone, possessing unique qualities that are an embodiment of the artist's inner feeling. These then, are the chief dimensions of Beethoven's esthetic creed that link him to the romantic movement. Furthermore, they are most vividly illustrated in his later works, especially in the Third, Sixth, Seventh, and Ninth Symphonies; the "Waldstein," "Appassionata," and "Hammerklavier" piano sonatas; the *Egmont Overture;* and the last six string quartets.

Third Symphony—the "Eroica"   Although only a short span of time separates the second and third symphonies (1802 to 1803), the brief period represents a giant step in the evolution of Beethoven's style. Concerned with the oppressive tendencies of the aristocratic classes, Beethoven originally dedicated the Third Symphony to Napoleon, whom Beethoven regarded as a liberator of the common man. However, upon learning that Napoleon declared himself Emperor in 1804, Beethoven exclaimed: "He is just like any other man, ready to tread the rights of man under his feet and serve nothing but his own ambition." Subsequently, the composer tore up the dedicatory page of the score and simply titled the work *Sinfonia Eroica* (heroic symphony).

    Historically, the "Eroica" appeared at a unique time and place, a knowledge of which may help us to understand the significance of the

"Eroica's" musical style. This symphony was created when classicism was at its apex and romanticism was bursting forth in Europe. Moreover, it emerged from a culture that had produced its greatest dramatists, Schiller and Goethe. Their works, like Beethoven's, disclose an underlying two-sided creative spirit that, on the one hand, exalts freedom of expression and, on the other, shows a devotion to inner logic and order. Moreover, there is a certain "heroic" quality evident in the works of Beethoven and his literary colleagues. This quality, which is identified by dramatic conflicts, great breadth, and climactic endings, is exemplified in all of the Beethoven symphonies, and in Schiller's historical dramas *The Robbers* (1781) and *Wallenstein* (1799), and in Goethe's *Faust* (Part One, 1808).

In many of Schiller's works, the heroic element is personified in the great-hearted champion of individual freedom who struggles and suffers in his striving for a great and noble cause. Understandably, the heroic theme—with its depiction of historical events, brave deeds and heroes, and weighty questions of life—requires, in the romantic frame of reference, a breadth of statement and a lofty, grandiloquent style. Beethoven, no less than Schiller and Goethe, could not be content with the sketchy fragments, aphoristic statements, and ephemeral moods so common to the next group of German romantics. But, rather, Beethoven and his contemporaries required power, dynamic opposition of elements, and sufficient time and space for the exposition and development of their heroic ideas.

Also, it is noteworthy that this early group of romanticists, Beethoven, Schiller, and Goethe, possessed another distinctive outlook toward their art that sets them apart from the next generation of romantics, and that is their continual regard for the rational, which still links them to the classical era. In the works of the three giants, we perceive a tempered romanticism in which, as Artz points out (*From Renaissance to Romanticism*), an outer and inner freedom prevails. Outer freedom stands for such things as revolt against oppression, antiquated rules, and intolerable social conditions. Inner freedom, however, represents not unbridled and uncontrolled emotion, but the willpower to restrain oneself.

In the Third Symphony of Beethoven we have a similar treatment of the heroic element in musical terms. The composer's title "heroic" is particularly fitting, since it is indeed a symphony of epic proportions and character. Generally it is fruitless to attempt to "read into" music of a purely abstract nature such as this symphony; however, a careful listening will bear out the relevance of the title. First, the composition is twice the length of a typical classical symphony. It has themes of a strong, forceful character and a power and sweep of movement that is quite unlike its predecessors. Perhaps the most important mark of the heroic is the principle of conflict and resolution, which Beethoven works out on a massive scale. Here, *conflict* is associated with the intensive development section, and *resolution* with the climactic ending, in which a feeling of balance and equilibrium is restored. It has been suggested that, in this symphony, Beethoven was attempting to express his own personal conflict between fate (fear of his affliction) and heroism (inner triumph). This view is given credence by the fact that it was composed at the time of his initial awareness of his hearing impairment.

Opening Theme from the "Eroica" Symphony by Beethoven

The romantic tendencies are quite striking in the "Eroica." In relation to Beethoven's previous symphonies, the composition is of increased size and has a greater range and depth of feeling. Adopting the broad definition, the word "feeling" refers here to various general states of emotion, such as joy, sorrow, anger, and grief, as well as to subtle, undefined nuances of emotion. Beethoven, through his artistic manipulation of tonal materials, created in the "Eroica" an intensity of feeling quite unknown to his classic predecessors.

For example, after the surging, joyful first movement, Beethoven presents a slow, mournful funeral march, which, despite its solemn, grave procession, builds (in a fuguelike section) to a great peak of exhilaration that overpowers the initial state of depression experienced at the beginning of the movement. A complete reversal of mood is provided in the spirited third movement (a scherzo in place of a staid minuet), and finally the symphony is climaxed with the terrific pace and relentless rhythmic charge of the fourth movement.

On a smaller plane of expression, Beethoven frequently startles us with such devices as the two sharp, stabbing chords in the opening measures, the sudden unexpected change in meter from triple to duple (near the close of the third movement), and the dramatic sounding of the eight hammerlike dissonant chords about midway in the first movement. The sudden dynamic shifts (from loud to soft and vice versa), unexpected rests, feverish tempi, shifts in meter, and deliberate use of bold dissonance, all show Beethoven's great zeal to push asunder the boundaries of classicism. A brief synopsis of the "Eroica" follows:

The jubilant first movement (in classical sonata form) opens with two hammerlike chords followed by the main theme in the cellos. This melody and the succession of other themes, which come and go with great rapidity, are not, however, complete melodies in the style of Haydn or Mozart, but fragments that eventually become wielded into a gigantic whole. The second movement, in the style of a funeral march, is based on a large rondo form, the main theme of which is first stated in the strings. An interesting feature is a fuguelike passage (*fugato*), which appears about midway in the movement. The third movement (Allegro Vivace), a very fast scherzo, begins with soft staccato notes in the strings, accompanied by a gradual buildup in momentum and power. The trio, or B section (the scherzo, like the minuet, has an A B A form) features three horns in a brilliant display. The breathtaking final movement, which opens with a fast flourish, is based on a theme-and-variations plan. The main theme, a simple folklike tune, is sounded first by strings in pizzicato style, followed by a series of nine variations and a short coda.

The Sixth Symphony—the "Pastoral"   The Fourth Symphony in D major was completed by Beethoven in 1806 and the Fifth, in C minor, was given its first performance along with the Sixth in 1808. The Sixth, in F major, although much more reserved than the preceding three symphonies, represents a landmark in the romantic movement. In this composition Beethoven inaugurated a new concept that was eventually to become the hallmark of later romanticism: that of adapting a program or story to the classic symphonic form. The "program" in the Sixth Symphony consists of Beethoven's impressions of nature.

Music written according to the romantic practice of basing a composition on an extramusical idea—that is, on something outside of the music, such as a poem, story, nature scene, historical event, or even a philosophical idea—is referred to as *programmatic music*. On the other hand, music that is devoid of such connotations—that is pure sound alone such as in the classical symphony or sonata—is called *absolute music*, and is characteristic of music written during the classical period.

Beethoven, we learn from his writings, had a true romantic love for nature. He wrote: "No one loves country life as I do. It is as if every tree and every bush could understand my mute inquiries and respond to them." And twelve years prior to his death, he proclaimed "Almighty God, in the woods I am blessed. Happy everyone in the woods. Every tree speaks through thee. O God! what glory in the woodland! On the heights is peace—peace to serve him." And in 1817, nine years after the "Pastoral" Symphony, he wrote to a friend in Baden, "When you wander through the mysterious forests of pine, remember that Beethoven often made poetry there—or, as they say, 'composed.'"

In typical romantic fashion, nature became a great source of inspiration to Beethoven. Its mysterious, ever-changing moods, its unpredictable, terrifying force and boundlessness, were idealized in musical terms. Just how much nature's moods and actions became objectified in Beethoven's music will, of course, remain unknown. However, certain definite signs of his intentions are most strongly manifested in his Sixth Symphony. For on the title page he wrote: *"Sinfonia pastorella* (pastoral symphony) or recollections of life in the country." Each of the five movements is provided with a title that gives the listener a clue as to its meaning:

> First movement: Pleasant, cheerful feelings aroused on arriving in
>   the country
> Second Movement: Scene by the brook
> Third movement: Happy gathering of villagers
> Fourth movement: Thunderstorm
> Fifth movement: Shepherd's song offering thanksgiving to the Al-
>   mighty after the storm

Of prime importance in relating Beethoven to the romantic movement is the question of how the composer achieved his idealized, abstract conception of nature through the use of musical symbols. In this work Beethoven paved the way for one aspect of the romantic musicians' creed, that is, the attempt to suggest and in some cases actually depict objects in reality. Music, of course, cannot accurately depict, but it can suggest or evoke certain images in the mind of the listener. Over the centuries, especially since the Renaissance, there has been a gradual expansion of the sources of musical imagery (military, religious, folk, nature, love). These are the wellsprings of musical art, serving directly or indirectly as a point of departure, an inspiration, or a kind of catalytic agent in the creative process. A simple folk dance rhythm, for example, becomes in Beethoven's Seventh Symphony an all-consuming esthetic principle around which the entire symphony is based. Thus musical imagery operates two ways: intrinsically, as inner inspiration for the composer, and extrinsically, for the listener, who may relate the image to something in his or her experience and identify it for what it is (folk song, folk dance, religious subject, military expression, and so forth). ·

Clearly, imagery derived from folk experiences and from nature served as inspiration for Beethoven in the writing of his Sixth Symphony. Some of the devices used to represent or suggest the mental pictures include a drone bass (in the opening movement), which is characteristic of folk dance music; its accompanying melody has a lilting vocal style typical of folk tunes. Also, it has been suggested that the melodic idea that follows has a birdlike quality analogous to the call of the American robin.

(a) Opening Theme, Symphony No. 6, Beethoven

The second movement's rippling undercurrent, consisting of triplets in the lower strings, is undoubtedly supposed to convey a pleasant, murmuring brook. The pastoral scene further unfolds with very real imitations of bird song. The flute trills in the manner of the nightingale, while the clarinet plays two downward notes of the cuckoo and the oboe supplies the high monotone of the quail. The third movement (Allegro) captures the festive setting of a country dance. Its triple meter, brusque leaping melodic line, and lively tempo clearly signify Beethoven's intent. The gaiety is soon interrupted by a dramatic storm complete with bursts of thunder (timpani) and whistling wind (high piccolos and strings).

(b) Principal Theme and Countertheme,
Opening of Second Movement, Symphony No. 6, Beethoven

Perhaps, however, what insures the Pastoral's continued presence in the concert hall is its essentially abstract nature. That is, the composer has suggested scenes to us but states that these are only reflections and not an attempt to depict nature in an exact way. Thus, verbal meanings have not been permitted to dominate the musical progression; the scene and peasant activities are only implied, allowing various interpretations.

The Ninth Symphony   As with many of Beethoven's works, the last symphony, in D minor (the "Choral"), required many years to germinate. The powerful work probably began to evolve as early as 1792, when the composer was taken with the idea of making a musical setting of Schiller's poem, "Ode to Joy." Beethoven's notebook sketches of 1814–1815 reveal the melodic germs that were to serve as the foundation for this gigantic musical edifice. In 1817 he set to work in earnest, eventually completing the symphony early in 1824. Its premiere performance, in Vienna on May 7, 1824, was enthusiastically received.

The Ninth rests on a different plane from all the previous symphonies. Whereas the mightiest of these—the Third in E flat and the Fifth in C minor—represent the ultimate in the conflict of titanic forces within the framework of the classical symphony, the Ninth completely sweeps away all the traces of the classical structure. And perhaps even more striking is its philosophical content—a concept that is to play an increasing role in the unfolding romantic movement. Let us briefly examine these two aspects—that is, the structural and the philosophical bases of the Ninth Symphony—and show their relationship to the romantic movement.

Structurally, the Ninth differs dramatically, not only from the symphonies of Haydn and Mozart, but from Beethoven's earlier works as well. There is the conventional symphonic plan of four movements, but these are quite unlike their classic predecessors. For example, there are extreme contrasts in tempo within the individual movement (particularly the fourth, which has nine successive changes in tempo). The movements are not arranged in the conventional classical pattern of fast (Allegro), slow (Andante), minuet (Moderato), and fast. In place of a slow, meditative second, Beethoven wrote a very fast, exhilarating movement marked "Molto Vivace." And in the third movement, instead of the classic minuet or a rollicking Beethoven scherzo, we hear a serene adagio.

As with earlier symphonies, Beethoven worked with motives rather than complete themes. These motivic figures are to be heard as unifying elements in all movements of the Ninth Symphony. Characteristically, these thematic germs are distinctive "leaping" figures of large intervals. To illustrate, the opening of the first movement is based on a downward leap of a fourth heard in the violins; the motive that follows is based on a three-note motto with a jarring up-and-down octave leap. Beethoven's earlier departure from classical thematic structure (notably in the "Eroica") is now carried to its fullest extent with these abstract motives, which generate and propel the musical flow in each movement.

Principal Theme, Symphony No. 9, Beethoven

The most unusual aspect of the symphony is the choral finale in the fourth movement. It is unusual because of its unprecedented use of a large chorus and vocal soloists and because of the philosophical message conveyed in a text based on Schiller's "Ode to Joy." There has been much debate about the fourth movement, specifically over its organic connection with the three preceding instrumental movements and its extremely difficult vocal solo parts, which go beyond normal voice range and technique.

Aside from these matters, there is little doubt that Beethoven wanted to communicate his personal philosophy of life in highest musical terms. Employing verses from Schiller's poem, he proclaimed joy as the power to unite men. Through tumultuous waves of orchestral and choral sonorities, and soaring, mystical choral parts in which the voices are treated like instruments, Beethoven seems to shout to the heavens in his joyful affirmation of the Divine Creator. Interspersed are two strange celestial interludes, whose reverent atmosphere is perhaps even more overpowering than the dynamic symphony's Herculean conclusion.

Part of Schiller's poem of 1785, from which Beethoven selected his text for the choral part, is as follows:

FROM "ODE TO JOY" BY FRIEDRICH SCHILLER[7]

"O Freunde, nicht diese Töne,
sondern lasst uns angenehmere
anstimmen, und freudenvollere."

Freude, schöner Götterfunken,
Tochter aus Elysium,
Wir betreten feuertrunken,

Himmlische, dein Heiligtum.
Deine Zauber binden wieder,
Was die Mode streng geteilt;

Alle Menschen werden Brüder,
Wo dein sanfter Flügel weilt.

Wem der grosse Wurf gelungen,

Eines Freundes Freund zu sein,
Wer ein holdes Weib errungen,
Mische seinen Jubel ein!
Ja—wer auch nur eine Seele

Sein nennt auf dem Erdenrund!
Und wer's nie gekonnt, der
stehle

"O friends, not these strains—
rather let us sing
more pleasing songs, and more
joyous."
Joy, thou gleaming spark divine,
Daughter of Elysium,
Drunk with ardor, we draw
near,
Goddess, to thy shrine.
Thy magic unites again
What custom sternly drew
apart;
All mankind become brothers
Beneath thy gentle hovering
wing.
He whose happy fortune grants
him
Friend to have and friend to be,
Who has won a noble woman,
Let him join in our rejoicing!
Yes—even were it one heart
only
Beating for him in the world!
But if he's never known this,
let him

[7] Reprinted by permission of Epic Records.

Weinend sich aus diesem Bund.	Weeping steal from our ranks.
Freude trinken alle Wesen	Joy is drawn by every creature
An den Brüsten der Natur;	From the breast of Nature;
Alle Guten, alle Bösen	All men good and all men evil
Folgen ihrer Rosenspur.	Walk upon her rose-strewn path.
Küsse gab sie uns und Reben	Kisses gave she and the ripe grape,
Einen Freund, geprüft im Tod;	A good friend, trusty to the last;
Wollust ward dem Wurm gegeben,	Even the worm can feel pleasure,
Und der Cherub steht vor Gott.	And the Seraph stands before God.
Froh, wie seine Sonnen fliegen	Glad as suns that He hurtles
Durch des Himmels prächt'gen Plan,	Through the vast spaces of heaven,
Wandelt, Brüder, eure Bahn,	Pursue your pathway, brothers;
Freudig, wie ein Held zum Seigen.	Be joyful as a hero in victory.
Seid umschlungen, Millionen!	Millions, be you embraced!
Diesen Küss der ganzen Welt!	For the universe, this kiss!
Brüder—überm Sternenzelt	Brothers—above the canopy of stars
Muss ein lieber Vater wohnen!	A loving Father surely dwells.
Ihr stürzt nieder, Millionen?	Millions, do you fall upon your knees?
Ahnest du den Schöpfer, Welt?	Do you sense the Creator, world?
Such' ihn überm Sternenzelt!	Seek Him above the canopy of stars!
Über Sternen muss er wohnen.	Surely He dwells above the stars.

Summary Beethoven passed through several stages in the evolution of his musical style. The first (1795–1802) is identified by its classical tendencies, such as clear textures and melodic outlines, balance, symmetry, and rational control. Representative examples from the first period include the first two symphonies, first three piano concertos, three string trios (Op. 1, 1795), six string quartets (Op. 18, 1798–1800), and the first seventeen of his thirty-two piano sonatas.

The second period (1803–1816), dating from the early stages of his affliction, represents a dramatic shift to the romantic style, with its greater emotion, unexpected changes in dynamics and tempo, an expanded and intensified development section, and emphasis upon drama and suspense. The main works of the period include the Third through the Eighth Symphonies, the "Waldstein" and "Appassionata" piano sonatas, Piano Concertos No. 4 in G and No. 5 in E flat (the "Emperor"), the *Egmont Overture*, and the "Rasumovsky" String Quartets (Op. 59).

In the third and final period (1817–1827), Beethoven's style became increasingly abstract, impersonal, and introspective. This "turning" inward of musical style was undoubtedly precipitated by Beethoven's deafness, which was virtually total by 1820, causing him to forgo normal social contacts and to withdraw into his own world. The works of the period, characterized by their intensive manipulation of thematic material, flexible form, and contrapuntal textures, include the *Missa Solemnis* (1822), the Ninth Symphony (1824), and the last string quartets. Thus, as with Bach, Beethoven turned to his most profound expression in his last years. And, again like Bach, these later works require repeated listening and considerable study for comprehension. Such an approach to Beethoven will reap a rich permanent harvest of listening enjoyment.

PROMINENT CHARACTERISTICS OF BEETHOVEN'S STYLE

PREFERRED FORMS	Symphony (9)	Piano sonata (32)	Piano concerto (5)	String quartet (16)	Opera (1)	Violin sonata (10)	Violin concerto (1)
MELODY	1. Themes constructed around motives, which serve as generating elements 2. Clear melodic goals, objective quality 3. Diatonic 4. Unornamented 5. Phrase-structured						
HARMONY	1. Major and minor keys 2. Triadic harmony, that is, common chords 3. Dissonance generally treated in manner of classicists, that is, resolved according to rule; however, more frequent use of startling dissonant effects (opening of First Symphony and in the first movement of the "Eroica").						
TEXTURE	1. Quasi contrapuntal texture in early works, last period highly contrapuntal.						
RHYTHM	1. Much emphasis on rhythm (essence of his style) 2. Regular, metrical rhythmic movement 3. Syncopation widely used (shifting of accents and sudden changes of meter from duple to triple or vice versa (as in the "Eroica").						
EXPRESSION	1. Considerable use of sudden contrasts in dynamics and tempo 2. Enlarged tempi range 3. Wide range of expression—from peace and serenity to robust humor and unprecedented strength and power						
ORCHESTRAL TECHNIQUE	1. Created wind-band section of orchestra, that is, wind instruments now frequently function as an independent body 2. Employed new instruments in symphony orchestra: trombone, English horn, piccolo, and various percussion (cymbals and bass drum) instruments 3. Expanded range and technique of instruments. 4. "Dark" orchestral color prevails due to emphasis on bass instruments						

Conductor's Score,
Opening Measures of the "Eroica"

FROM THE HEROIC TO THE
POETIC IDEAL

There is a pleasure in the pathless woods,
There is a rapture on the lonely shore,
There is society, where none intrudes,
By the deep Sea, and music in its roar:
I love not man the less but nature more,
From these our interviews, in which I steal
From all I may be, or have been before,
To mingle with the Universe, and feel
What I can ne'er express, yet cannot all conceal.

Byron

The marked change in the early decades of the nineteenth century, from the heroic to the poetic, stands out as the first major transformation of the romantic spirit. One of the main contributing factors behind this change was the dissolution of the boundaries that had separated the arts of the eighteenth century. Around 1800, poets, philosophers, painters, and musicians sought a new focus—a union of all the arts in which each reflected the spirit of the other. For example, lyric poetry strove for the mysterious, magical, and sensuous qualities of music. As Alfred Einstein relates, "Not only in Germany but also in England and France, the Romantic poets strove to create a new verbal music . . . . The more 'musical' a poem, the surer seemed its advance into new unexplored regions of feeling."[8]

Moreover, artists attached literary significance to their paintings, such as Delacroix's *The Death of Sardanapalus*, inspired by Byron's drama. The famous German painter Otto Runge compared the similarity between colors and tones. William Blake, the poet, musician, and painter, fully exemplified the trend toward a fusion of the arts. It is little wonder then that musicians attempted to capture the essence of the other arts—namely the *pictorial* and *literary* qualities. *Pictorial quality* refers to "picturelike" musical expressions, that is, musical pieces derived from or suggestive of scenes of nature or everyday happenings. Such expressions abound in Schumann's piano pieces, for example, *Kinderscenen (Scenes of Childhood)*, *Album für die Jugend (Album for the Young)*, *Carnaval*, *Waldscenen (Forest Scenes)*. *Literary quality* refers to musical expressions derived from or inspired by literature or poetry. This type is, of course, the essence of the art song *(lied)*, which flourished in the hands of Schubert and Schumann. Undoubtedly, the intense interest in fusing the arts tended to draw young

[8] Alfred Einstein, *Music in the Romantic Era* (New York: W. W. Norton & Company, Inc., 1947), p. 22.

composers away from the large-scale symphonic conception to the small-scale, poetic conception, but the significant achievements of Beethoven were also a contributing factor.

Many of the younger composers, working in the constant shadow of Beethoven's greatness, realized their inability to rise above the musical titan. Some continued to write in the same classical forms of symphony and sonata, but, the truly creative musicians, instilled with the romantic passion for experimentation and invention, turned in the opposite direction from Beethoven's dynamic, heroic style of romanticism, to miniature, intimate means of musical expression. The new esthetic values rested, not upon breadth and power, but upon subtle musical nuances and interplay of feelings and moods.

Where Beethoven introduced individuality to music creativity, these composers carried the romantic idea one step farther—they exalted the personality of the composer. And where the first great romantic dealt with the more objective states of emotion, such as joy, robust humor, sorrow, and the demonic, the young romantics delved further into the soul, revealing an infinite variety of moods and feelings expressing childhood reveries, amorous love, and picturesque scenes. Because their work stressed, for the most part, a lyrical, subjective expression in which fleeting mood pictures replaced the more powerful, large scale structures, we may characterize much of their music as *poetic*, in contrast to the *architectonic* style of Beethoven. We shall see later how architectonic ideals completely dominate the musical scene in the last half of the nineteenth century.

Inspired by the fresh, spontaneous poetic spirit, the new composers, like their fellow romantics in art and literature, breathed a new life into their art. These highly imaginative musicians aspired to communicate, not through the syntactical tonal relationships of the classicists, but rather through *feelings*. Their aim: to delight the listener, to stir him with sheer sensuous sounds, and to relate these sounds to literary and pictorial ideas. Such was the artistic bent of Schubert and Schumann.

The third composer to be discussed in the following pages, Frédéric Chopin, was least inclined toward the creation of pictorial or literary musical ideas. Instead, he devised still another kind of tonal art, one closely akin to the music of Schubert and Schumann. His piano nocturnes and preludes constitute a kind of wordless poetry, that is, abstract mood pictures or tone paintings in which the emphasis is on the communication of feelings and emotions, rather than on concrete thematic ideas.

Franz Schubert

Life Sketch   The circle of musicians who set the tone of romanticism during the early decades of the nineteenth century were all born about the same time: Schubert in 1797, Mendelssohn in 1809, and Chopin and Schumann in 1810. All but one, Chopin, were of Germanic heritage, and, although musical romanticism touched many countries, it was chiefly an

Austro-German movement from beginning to end. It is also interesting that each of the above illustrious figures made a distinctive contribution to the romantic movement: Schubert, the development of the German *lied;* Chopin, the style and character of early romantic piano music; Mendelssohn, orchestral "landscapes"; and Schumann, the psychologically based art song and piano piece.

Franz Schubert was unquestionably the master composer of nine-teenth-century *lieder.* He was born in a suburb of Vienna in 1797, at a time when Beethoven was just beginning to make his mark in the Viennese music world. The close proximity of the eminent Beethoven undoubtedly exerted a powerful influence on Schubert. For we shall see that the great song composer stands, stylistically speaking, at the point where classicism and romanticism converge, and that the two opposing tendencies are per-haps more clearly represented in him than in any other member of the first generation of romanticists.

In some respects Schubert resembles Chopin: both were caught up in the poetic spirit, which they adapted to music—Schubert to the song form and Chopin to the piano piece. However, the family background, personality, and musical achievements of the two composers rest on com-pletely different ground. Schubert's youth, for example, was quite unlike that of Chopin, who grew up in a comfortable home and in a highly cul-tured cosmopolitan atmosphere, in which refinement and social graces were naturally acquired. Actually, Schubert's early childhood seems to resemble Haydn's, whereas Chopin's bears a striking relationship to Mozart's. It is also noteworthy that the cultural background of these composers tends to be mirrored in their musical style: down-to-earth, folklike touches per-vade many of Schubert's lieder, and, quite expectedly, an over-all refined, delicate, and polished quality is ingrained in Chopin's piano compositions.

Father Schubert eked out an existence as a parish schoolteacher, a job that carried no salary but room and board and a pittance tuition from each pupil. Although Franz Schubert grew up in a less socially stimulating environment than his contemporary Chopin, he was given some music in-struction from his father and from the local parish organist, Michael Holzer. Family string-quartet playing also formed an important part in the music education of the young boy, who aspired to a musical career. However, the elder Schubert made it quite clear that Franz should follow his foot-steps in the field of teaching.

At the age of eleven (1808), young Schubert embarked on the same educational path as did Haydn almost seventy years earlier. A vacancy in the court chapel choir at the Imperial *Konvikt* (seminary) in Vienna led Schubert to try out for the position. Gifted with a splendid voice and an advanced knowledge of music, he won with little difficulty. Here, in addi-tion to regular academic subjects, he was permitted to receive special music instruction from the famous Italian Antonio Salieri, who also at one time had instructed Beethoven. Perhaps the most important musical events at the *Konvikt* occurred in connection with the small school orchestra, which played the standard "classic" repertoire and afforded Schubert an opportunity to perform as a violinist and to try his hand at conducting.

Eugène Delacroix, *Abduction of Rebecca*. 1846. Oil on Canvas, 39½ x 32¼". New York, The Metropolitan Museum of Art. Wolfe Fund, 1903.

Rembrandt, *Sortie of Captain Banning Cocq's Company of the Civic Guard.*
1642. Oil on canvas, 12'2" x 14'7". Amsterdam, Rijksmuseum.

In 1813, the sixteen-year-old Schubert left the *Konvikt* and subsequently enrolled at St. Anna Training College to prepare for teaching. Ironically, after one year at the college he became a teacher in his father's parish school, where he remained from 1814 to 1817. Odd as it may seem, the three-year stay was extremely fruitful from the standpoint of productivity. On top of his six hours' daily teaching of the three R's to elementary-age children, Schubert poured out an incredible amount of music, most of which constitutes a treasure of romanticism.

Beginning his surge of creativity in 1814 at the age of seventeen, he composed such noted examples as the Second Symphony in B flat, the Mass in F, and the famous art song, "Gretchen am Spinnrad" (Gretchen at the Spinning Wheel). Set to a text from Goethe's *Faust*, this composition announced the birth of the German romantic *lied*. 1815 was a most productive year: six operas, two masses, his third symphony (in D major), three sonatas, and one hundred and forty-four songs, including the well-known "Erlkönig," based on a poem by Goethe. In the following year (1816) he composed the fourth and fifth symphonies and over a hundred songs, including "Der Wanderer."

Outside of some summer teaching in 1818 and 1824 at the estate of Count John Esterházy in western Hungary, Schubert did not have regular employment the remainder of his short life. He led, for the most part, a kind of cultured-Bohemian life until his death in 1828. Fortunately the forlorn economic existence during these years was brightened by his association with a warm circle of intellectual friends who organized a "reading society" composed of writers, artists, and dilettantes such as the lawyer-poet Johann Mayrhofer, the singer Franz von Schobert (who offered Schubert considerable assistance in this difficult period), and the famous artist Moritz von Schwind, among others. The group held frequent gatherings called "Schubertiads," consisting of literary discussions, readings of the works of such poets as Tieck, Kleist, Heine, and Goethe, and musical performances by Schubert.

The members of Schubert's circle were not true Bohemians in the usual sense of the word. They were educated, cultured men who were rebelling against the decayed Viennese society and the sentimental taste of the bourgeoisie. The fact that these youthful romantics turned away from the bourgeoisie class needs to be underscored, since it marks a vital turning point in the romantic movement. To Schubert's group, and particularly to Schumann, the philistine taste of the middle class constituted a threat to musical culture. Thus, the new romantic's ideals, stressing intellectuality and culture, ran counter to the founders of romanticism, who in the *Sturm und Drang* era rejected the elite for the common man.

Constantly striving for financial stability, Schubert wrote a number of unsuccessful operas and made several attempts to procure a conducting position. It was not until 1821 that some of his music began to be published, and then only by private subscription. Perhaps it was due to Schubert's retiring personality and dislike for appearances in formal society that recognition of him as a great song composer did not extend much beyond private circles of intellectuals.

Unfortunately, he died at thirty-one—before he could experience the recognition that was heaped upon him later in the nineteenth century. It is doubtful if Schubert ever heard his two finest symphonic works. The Symphony No. 9 in C major, for example, was "discovered" by Robert Schumann in 1838, ten years after it was completed, and the world renowned Symphony in B minor, the "Unfinished" (1822), was not given its first performance until 1865.

Schubert's Romantic Nature: The Art Song   Earlier, it was stated that Schubert stood at a point where classicism and romanticism converged. When we glance over the total output of this prodigious artist, the two-sided creative nature becomes evident, at least in outward respects. On the one hand, we note his classic leaning in regard to choice of forms: he wrote nine symphonies, twenty-two piano sonatas, and fifteen string quartets. But on the other hand, many of the six hundred art songs and a vast number of small pieces for piano not only show the romantic concern for the miniature, but especially the melancholy, the dreamy, and the sentimental. This is particularly true of the eight *impromptus* and the six *moments musicaux,* which are actually brief "mood pieces" in which one mood is presented in concentrated form.

Although admired for their youthful freshness the early symphonies, unfortunately, suffer from an obvious mirroring of Mozart and Beethoven. The Symphony No. 8 in B minor, the "Unfinished," composed in 1822, provides by far the most rewarding music experience for the listener. To be sure there are classic traits, such as a clarity of melodic line and texture, and use of strict sonata form. But what strikes the listener, especially in the first movement, is the prevailing dark moodiness, the many dynamic changes, and the power of expression so characteristic of Beethoven.

Schubert's musical significance extends to many other forms such as the String Quartet in D minor, the Mass in G, and the "Trout" Quintet. However, his real romantic contributions, and for that matter his distinctive personal quality and originality, lie in the art-song form. In contrast to his symphonies and sonatas, he demonstrated complete mastery of the song form right from his very first creative attempts.

The art song (or *lied*) may be defined as a musical setting of a lyric poem for voice and piano. The form originated during the classic era, but, it was not fully developed and widely used until the nineteenth century. Its brevity, literary basis, and unrestricted form became an excellent vehicle for the romantic's spontaneous flow of feelings. The essential features of the form include a solo vocal part, an accompaniment (normally piano), a text drawn from a lyric poem and emphasis on one mood. Generally, there is no preconceived formal design, since the art song form is determined by the content of the poem. Some art songs follow the *strophic* form, in which each verse is sung to the same melody and accompaniment. Others, like most of the Schubert songs, are in *through-composed* form, in which the music changes with the meaning of the text, as in "Der Erlkönig." Schubert drew his texts most often from Goethe, adapting over seventy

"The Trout,"
Art Song by Franz Schubert (1817)

of his poems; other texts include works by Ossian, Klopstock, Heine, Mayrhofer, Schiller (over forty texts), and Shakespeare.

"Der Erlkönig," composed in Schubert's early youth, stands as a characteristic expression of the early romantic interest in strangeness and wonder. Based on Goethe's narrative, the work is a miniature drama centered around three figures, each of whose character is clearly portrayed in musical terms. The setting is a dark, dismal night. A father is madly galloping on horseback through a dark forest, holding a sick child in his arms. Suddenly, the terrified youngster sees the Erlking, spirit of death, approaching through the mist. The father tries to persuade the child to ignore the evil spirit, who then tries to coax the infant away. Enraged that he will not go with him, the Erlking grasps the arm of the child, who utters a cry of anguish. In a state of shock the father dashes homeward with the boy in his arms. Suddenly, abrupt silence discloses that death has triumphed.

In this medium, Schubert is undeniably the master. Strange, dissonant chords and bass tones depict the mystery and darkness of night. Different pitch levels assigned to each of the three figures delineates their character: high range, the child; middle, the Erlking; and bass, the father. And on a deeper level, successive, ascending key modulations enhance the child's increasing feeling of terror. The piano accompaniment has several important functions in Schubert's songs: to support the solo voice, to create and maintain the desired mood, and to provide "imagery" through characteristic rhythmic and melodic figures, such as the galloping effect provided by the triplet rhythm in "Der Erlkönig," the spinning wheel motion in "Gretchen am Spinnrad," and the swimming of fish in "Die Forelle" (The Trout).

Schubert's successor in the art-song field, Robert Schumann, carried these techniques to a deeper, psychological level some twelve years after Schubert died. However, before turning to the leading champion of romanticism we will briefly discuss the work of Frédéric Chopin, who successfully transplanted the poetic ideals of early romanticism to the piano idiom.

Frédéric Chopin

Life Sketch Chopin's most significant contribution to the romantic movement was his invention of the idiomatic piano style. This fact is attested to by a long list of imitators extending into the twentieth century. It is not in terms of the Beethovenian scope and depth that we value much of Chopin's music, but rather in his unique handling of the miniature forms. The disregard for this important phase of romanticism—that is, the miniature—resulted in considerable controversy earlier in this century over the esthetic value of his music. In equating greatness with size, some writers placed Chopin among the lesser-ranking composers, since his work was confined almost exclusively to short, miniature forms for the piano. In more recent years music critics and historians have recognized the "poetic" expressions of Chopin (especially his preludes, nocturnes, and ballads), to be an important phase of the romantic movement. The lesser side of Chopin—his purely technical or didactic pieces—no longer form the center of esthetic argument, because these examples are accepted for what they are. A similar situation exists with much of the music of two other romantics: Niccolò Paganini and Franz Liszt.

There is, of course, much to be taken into account in making value judgments in music. On the basis of the historical development of music and the criterion of social heritage (the acceptance and fostering of music examples from one generation to the next), it would appear that scope and breadth of thought are two important parts of the total criteria. But they must be taken into consideration along with other factors, such as originality, depth and truth of expression, and grasp of musical techniques. Moreover, such value judgments must be made against the intellectual and cultural spirit of the age; that is, we cannot weigh the esthetic value

Eugène Delacroix, *Frédéric Chopin*, 1838. Louvre, Paris. Courtesy of Bettmann Archive

of earlier music on modern scales. In summary, Chopin, needless to say, does not match the stature of Beethoven, Bach, or Mozart, but he does fulfill one major requirement—originality of thought as shown in his devising of the characteristic style of romantic piano music and, particularly, the harmonic idiom of romantic music in general.

The early background of Chopin reads much like that of Mozart. Nicholas Chopin, the father of Frédéric, attained to considerable distinction as a professor of French at the Warsaw Lyceum. Under the careful guidance and cultural nurturing of his parents, young Chopin formed the good manners and refinement characteristic of the Polish nobility. His lifelong relationship with the aristocracy began at the age of eight, when he played the solo part in a piano concerto presented for charity by the Polish elite.

In 1831 he moved to Paris, where he performed in wealthy circles and mingled with ambassadors, princes, and ministers. Here, his rise to fame was primarily in the fashionable world of the salon, beginning in the home of the Paris Rothschilds, who introduced him to the aristocratic world. In contrast to many musicians, who were still treated as servants, Chopin was acknowledged not only as a superb virtuoso but as a gentleman of distinction, a role he played exceedingly well, with carriage, manservant, and clothing from exclusive shops. In this fashionable social whirl he gave lessons to the families of the nobility and performed at private concerts (one in 1841 brought him 6000 francs).

After making several appearances before the general public (and after critical rebuffs), Chopin was convinced that his intimate playing style was unsuited for large public hall concerts. Thus, his last public appearance in Paris was made in 1835. Undoubtedly these events contributed to his increasing interest in publishing his earlier music and creating anew. His music began to be published in 1832, commencing with the sets of mazurkas (Opp. 6 and 7) and followed by numerous works in 1833 and 1834. Chopin's music was favorably received by critics in France and in Germany, where the budding music critic Robert Schumann heartily hailed Chopin in the *Neue Zeitschrift für Musik* (*New Music Journal*), which appeared in 1834.

Chopin's life shifted completely when, in 1836, Franz Liszt introduced him to the French novelist George Sand (Mme. Dudevant). This famous literary figure was indeed a personification of romantic fiction, as Herbert Hughes writes: "A voluptuary without vice, who could take delight in recording her erotic impressions; a woman in whom the qualities of compassion, of hypocrisy, of pure motherliness and of the vampire were grotesquely mixed."[9]

In the tempestuous romance that followed, a great amount of piano music was created, mostly during his visits to Mme. Sand's château at Nahant. She encouraged him to create and took care of the frail and sensitive artist during his frequent periods of illness.

[9] "Chopin," *Lives of the Great Composers* (New York: Penguin Books, 1947), p. 77.

During the last three years of his life very little serious creativity was undertaken, mainly due to the grave state of his health. Most of his time was taken up with his teaching; however, in 1847 he again performed in Paris (for the first time in five years), and in 1848 he made two visits to London, playing before the queen and other notables of English society. As with many of the early romantics, his life ended before his fortieth birthday.

Musical Style   As we have already mentioned, Chopin's musical contributions are entirely in the piano idiom; in fact it might be said that he created a new idiom, a kind of musical poetry set in the keyboard style. Of his more than two hundred piano compositions, there are only a few traditional forms, such as his three sonatas and two concertos. The rest are Chopinesque innovations such as *études, scherzos, ballades, preludes, nocturnes, mazurkas,* and *polonaises.*

These compositions are analogous to Schubert's songs: in addition to stressing one mood or feeling, they are generally short, intimate, homophonic, strongly lyrical, and of free form. That is, they do not follow any preconceived established pattern, but rather the form grows out of the musical content, in a free-folding, spontaneous fashion.

There seems to be more than a casual relationship between Chopin's piano style and the French rococo. This is evident chiefly in the compositions that display much technique and decoration, such as the waltzes and études. Here Chopin seems to use the tonal language less in an instrumental or functional manner and more in an incidental, decorative fashion. As with the rococo artists and musicians, the focus is on dazzling surface decoration, thus leaving little room for expressive elements. Frequently the listener is more impressed by the technical virtuosity that conveys the idea than the idea itself. Needless to say, virtuosity for its own sake comes dangerously close to obliterating true musical expression in this romantic age. This is particularly true in certain works of the famous virtuosic performer-composers, such as the violinist Paganini and the pianist Franz Liszt.

The occasional overshadowing of the virtuosic over the expressive side of music indicates the chief difference between the music of Schubert and Schumann on the one hand and Chopin on the other. Many of Schubert's and Schumann's compositions (especially the songs and piano pieces) have a simple, folklike quality, and are rooted quite frequently in German folklore. In contrast, Chopin's music is highly idealistic, and largely removed from the mainstream of life. However, he frequently uses native Polish elements, which he transforms into abstract designs, such as the basic rhythm of the mazurka. The études are chiefly didactic in nature, built as they are around one particular technical element, such as an arpeggio, a scale, or perhaps a chord figure. The most expressive, and therefore the most valuable pieces to the listener, are the nocturnes, ballades, and especially the twenty-four preludes, which demonstrate Chopin's true originality in mood painting.

In conclusion, Chopin's invention of a new piano idiom led him to the most important contribution to romantic music—that of its harmonic basis. The harmonic language of Chopin and that of succeeding romantics is identified by a thicker chord texture and a more colorful harmony resulting from use of many chromatics, numerous key modulations, and greater dissonant level.

Prelude No. 20 in C Minor,
Frédéric Chopin

Robert Schumann

Romantic Position   With the name of Robert Schumann (1810–1856), the third figure in the eminent group of early romanticists, we approach the climax of the poetic phase of the movement. In his early work we find many of the characteristics of young romanticism brought into full display in their many forms and colors. Everywhere in his music there is the feeling of experimentation, spontaneity of expression, and a constant reflection of inner emotions and desires. Revealed in his emotional outpourings is the full spectrum of romanticism: images of early childhood, sentimental declarations of love, and expressions of moodiness, despair, melancholy, and the tragic. Without a doubt Schumann is the most romantic of the romantics. And in his later works the freshness and spontaneity of his youth give way to a strange, hybrid form of classicism, which in its dark-toned heaviness seems to be a prelude to the grand climax of the movement, which occurred in the last half of the century.

"Eusebius" from *Carnaval* by Robert Schumann

"Florestan" from *Carnaval* by Robert Schumann

Chiarina" from *Carnaval* by Robert Schumann

Why is Schumann considered by many to be the most romantic of the romantics? Perhaps the answer is simply that he strove the farthest in fulfilling the romantic's ideals. His all-seeking romantic temper led him to experiment in all the forms, to champion against musical philistines (the uncultured and unenlightened) through his writings on music, and above all attempt to make his music a mirror of his inner and outer life. This point is particularly basic to grasping a full appreciation of his music. Life and music are perhaps more closely interrelated in Schumann than in any other romantic figure; hence his compositions seem to be more personally "inscribed" than those of his fellow composers. For example, after listening to his piano pieces and songs, we somehow seem to sense the warmth and compassion of Schumann the person, the human, rather than Schumann the technician or virtuoso. The personal presence, is, of course, an undefinable, intangible element, but it is nonetheless there. By employing the musical language of the period completely as a vehicle for conveying feelings and moods, which take the composer and the listener into the realm of the heart and into nocturnal shadows, Schumann seems to come close to fulfilling the romantic credo.

Robert Schumann. Picture Collection, New York Public Library

Our preliminary overview of Schumann shows him at the crest of the first wave of romanticism, as one who synthesized the early romantics' forms, ideals, and dreams. His creativity, covering the years 1830 to 1856, follows on the heels of Schubert (d. 1828) and is contemporary with Chopin (d. 1849), Liszt, and Berlioz.

As a composer his temperament was ideally suited to the romantic forms of art song and piano piece. He employed the song form of Schubert, giving it, however, a new psychological interpretation. His piano pieces are in the same miniature vein as Chopin's, but they are somewhat less idealistic and virtuosic and of a more personal introspective style. His attempts in the symphonic and sonata forms, undertaken later in his life, were less successful, and, again like Schubert, it is the youthful Schumann who speaks most directly, poignantly, and pleasingly to the modern listener.

Life Sketch   The three leading "poetic" musicians of early romanticism, Chopin, Schubert, and Schumann, have many characteristics in common. They were all born about the same time, they lived short lives, composed in the same poetic vein, and were of highly sensitive, temperamental dispositions, and all began creating their major works early in life: Schubert at seventeen and Schumann and Chopin at twenty. However, it is amazing that Schumann is the only one whose creative pattern is closely aligned to his life experiences. In the case of Schubert, for example, outside of isolated pieces that seem to have some bearing on external happenings, there is little of the life-art relationship that we

Clara Wieck Schumann. Picture Collection, New York Public Library

find in Schumann. There is even less evidence in Chopin, the most abstract and idealistic of the three composers. A brief overview of Schumann's life will bear out this striking characteristic of his art.

The leading romantic's life is easily divided into three periods: youth and university period (1810–1830), Leipzig years (1830–1844), and final period (1844–1856). The second is most important to us here, since this is the time of his most significant contributions—his chief piano compositions, his art songs, and his musical journalism.

Schumann was born into a middle-class family in Zwickau, Germany, in 1810. His father, a bookseller and printer, was apparently a man who had worked hard to establish his business and who took great pride in his cultural tastes. Naturally, as Schumann grew he was greatly influenced by his father's musical and artistic leanings. To say the least, the environment was highly conducive to the development of respect and appreciation for the fine arts and humanities.

Although not a musician, August Schumann was determined to provide the youngster with experiences that had been lacking in his own youth. Hence, piano instruction was provided the seven-year-old boy by the local musician, Johann Kuntszch. Furthermore, the early childhood acquaintance with his father's abundant supply of books, and especially the works of the German romantic poet Jean Paul (Richter), was undoubtedly a decisive factor in shaping Schumann's artistic nature. Later, as Schumann became a composer of songs, he frequently used the emotional poetry of Jean Paul in addition to works of Heine and Goethe.

Two years after the death of his father, the eighteen-year-old was sent to Leipzig University to seek a law degree. During the following two years of study his mind was definitely not upon jurisprudence, since we learn that the hours supposedly spent in law lectures were actually secret periods of piano practice and "poetic communions" with the works of Jean Paul and Heinrich Heine. Also, during his university days he met Leipzig's leading piano teacher, Friedrich Wieck, and undertook a serious study of piano with the renowned man. Little did Schumann realize the complicated relationship that would later develop between himself and Wieck's daughter, then nine years of age. Already at this early age, Clara showed the remarkable piano skill and virtuosity that would eventually establish her name in the leading concert halls of Europe.

Schumann's short period of university study ended in 1830, when he finally completely ended his legal explorations. With great idealistic aplomb, Schumann announced his decision in a letter written to his mother which in part reads as follows:

> . . . Now I am standing at the crossroads and am scared at the question which way to choose. My genius points towards art, which is, I am inclined to think, the right path . . . There certainly can be no greater misery than to look forward to a hopeless, shallow, miserable existence which one has prepared for oneself. But neither is it easy to enter upon a career diametrically opposed to one's whole education, and to do it requires patience, confidence and quick decision. I am still at the height of youth and imagination, with plenty of capabilities for cultivating and ennobling art, and have come to the conclusion that with patience and perserverance, and a good master, I should in six years be as good as any pianist, for pianoforte playing is mere mechanism and execution. . . . This battle against myself is now raging more fiercely than ever, my good mother. Sometimes I am daring and confident in my own strength and power, but sometimes I tremble to think of the long way I have traversed and of the endless road which lies before me.[10]

However, the irresoluteness of his decision did not hold up against his constant romantic inclination to want to try everything in music, which eventually included performance, composition, journalism, and conducting. His ambition for a performing career was aborted in 1832. In an attempt to obtain a "shortcut" to pianistic technique he contrived a mechanical device for the fourth finger that permanently crippled his right hand. Since a concert career was now impossible, he turned to his true "calling," composing, which he actually had already begun two years earlier with his first opus, the "Abegg" Variations for piano, published in 1831.

[10] Joan Chissell, *Schumann* (New York: Collier Books, 1962), pp. 33–34.

The following ten-year period of composing became a decade of intense piano creativity; indeed, it was a time in which he wrote his most significant works in this vein. These are chiefly character pieces with quaint titles, such as his Opus 1 ("Abegg" Variations), Opus 2 (*Papillons* [*Butterflies*]), and Opus 9 *(Carnaval)*.

Like Schubert, Schumann also enjoyed the companionship of intellectual friends—poets, writers, and musicians whose never-ending discussions in the famous Leipzig *Kaffeebaum* covered all the principal artistic problems and controversies of the day. Uppermost was their concern for the inroads made by the philistines in German culture, foremost of which was the public's demand for keyboard "acrobats" who played "from the fingers rather than the heart."

As a result of these artistic gatherings, Schumann and a group of friends (including Wieck, who became a director) formed a new music journal, the *Neue Zeitschrift für Musik*, which presented its first issue in April, 1834. Soon after, the editorship was given to Schumann, who for the next ten years contributed many imaginative and inspiring articles, which unquestionably did much to strengthen German musical culture.

In an attempt to counter the philistine movement, he created an imaginary society, the *Davidsbündler* (David's League), a band of progressive-minded artists (who were actually his close collaborators under strange pseudonyms). It is also in these series of Davidsbündler articles that we learn of Schumann's schizoid personality (first disclosed in his letter to his mother in 1832). In adopting the pseudonym of "Eusebius," Schumann expressed his introverted and dreamy nature, and, conversely, in "Florestan" the extroverted, forceful, and masterly side of his personality is revealed. And as we will see, this dualism was carried beyond his journalism into his piano works, *Carnaval* and the *Davidsbündler Dances*.

The year 1840, like 1830, was a turning point in the composer's life. After four years of struggling for Friedrich Wieck's permission to marry Clara, Schumann obtained a court order allowing the couple to carry out their long-awaited plans. The marriage gave Schumann a new lease on life; it opened up a whole new vein of creativity, which suddenly poured out in a grand effusion of songs. More than a hundred of his two hundred and fifty songs were composed in the great "song year" of 1840. Clara occupied an important position in relation to these and other works, for, as he related in true romantic fashion, she was frequently the inner stimulus for these works. Then, almost as quickly and unexpectedly as he entered upon song composing, he advanced into the larger, more complex forms of symphony and chamber music.

In 1844 there was also a turning point. After Clara's Russian concert tour in that year, Schumann had a breakdown in his health. He thus relinquished the editorship of the journal and departed for a restful sojourn in Dresden. Residing here from 1845 to 1850, he next moved to Düsseldorf, where he was musical director from 1850 to 1853. A series of very trying experiences as orchestral conductor in Düsseldorf, combined with increasing emotional disturbance, provoked a complete mental disintegration, which occurred in 1854. Two years later, Clara, with her close companion Brahms at her side, laid Schumann to rest in Bonn.

Characteristics of Style: Piano Music   Ranking among the greatest treasures of piano music are the many miniature pieces composed by the youthful romanticist Schumann. After reading over the events of his life it is understandable that the piano should occupy his first creative thoughts. Denied a pianist's career, he turned immediately to the keyboard idiom, completing approximately twenty-six works in the first creative period (1830–1840).

Stylistically, all of these pieces share a unique group of characteristics. They are relatively short, spontaneous "mood pictures" rather than large-scale dramatic dialogues characteristic of the classicists. Tightly knit in structure, their unity is achieved through the repetition of a rhythmic figure, an arpeggio or perhaps a series of octaves in the bass, as in "Nordisches Lied" (Northern Song). Above all, we note an improvisational quality, that is, as if they were composed on the spur of the moment or suddenly created in a burst of passionate inspiration. Like Schubert, Schumann did not gradually develop this unique language over a period of years, but spoke at once in his early years with sureness of his objective and artistry. His later works, the sonatas for piano and the symphonies, do not have the youthful spontaneity and imagination that have given his piano pieces a permanent position in the concert repertory.

In seeking the meaning of Schumann's quaint expressions in the piano idiom, it is necessary to change our focus from the customary external point of view—that is, the music itself—to include the internal—the composer—as well. The inner and outer world are more clearly interrelated in Schumann's music than in that of any other major composer. This unusual approach to musical composition is manifested in two basic ways: (1) in the musical characterization of his double personality, and (2) in the use of some extramusical idea, such as a name or place that serves to spark his creative imagination. Several excellent examples of this unusual approach to creativity are to be found in his piano music.

Carnaval (Op. 9), composed in 1834–1835 and perhaps Schumann's most famous piano composition, is made up of a series of twenty short pieces, each provided with a descriptive title such as "Chiarina," "Estrella," "Pierrot," "Florestan," and "Eusebius." The latter two, of course, represent Schumann's two-sided personality: Florestan, the outgoing, gregarious Schumann, and Eusebius, the dreamy and introspective artist. It is noteworthy that this dual nature is also exemplified in Schumann's *Davidsbündler Dances* for piano, and even in his orchestral works, in the form of sudden impulsive shifting from the moody Eusebius to the stormy Florestan. His use of various names in *Carnaval* serve as outside or external sources of inspiration. In actuality, they are a kind of musical characterization: Chiarina is Clara Wieck, Estrella is Ernestine von Fricken.

Chopin and the violin virtuoso Paganini are inimitably portrayed through certain musical traits generally associated with each artist.

Schumann's use of external ideas (extramusical ideas) for musical inspiration is best exemplified in the *Carnaval's* four-note pattern (A E♭ C B), which is woven through all twenty pieces. The motto is derived from the German town, *Asch*, the birthplace of Ernestine von Fricken, Schumann's first romantic interest. Translating "Asch" into notes, S is E♭ in German, and H is B♮. Schumann also used the extramusical principle in his first piano work, the "Abegg" Variations; the name Abegg is apparently derived from another early acquaintance, Meta Abegg. Other examples of the Schumannesque-technic include G A D E in *Armes Waisenkind* and B A C H in the six fugues (Op. 60) for organ.

Joan Chissell states that, just as the nineteenth-century romantic poets such as Heine and Eichendorff could crystalize a mood or emotion into several lines of poetry, Schumann likewise could express his own feelings in the short character pieces for piano.[11] In using the song form of Schubert he followed the same path—he set the poems of Heine, Eichendorff, and others into unusual psychological mood pictures. These cover a wide variety of moods or emotions, delicate and dreamy as in *"Mondnacht"* (Moon Night), passionate expression of love in the *Dichterliebe* (Poet's Love) Song Cycle, and the patriotic "Die beiden Grenadiere" (Two Grenadiers), or despair and sorrow as in, again, the *Dichterliebe*. Most of the Schumann songs closely follow the mood of the poem; thus, the *through-composed form* prevails for most of the two hundred and fifty songs. The piano part in his songs has a more important role than in the Schubert compositions; in fact, here the piano part is in many instances of greater importance than the vocal part, particularly in the postludes, when the pianist closes with a solo passage quite frequently more expressive than the vocal melody.

Orchestral Music   Many of the later works of Schumann are in such classical forms as the symphony, string quartet, and string quintet. As we have said, these do not have the spontaneity and the lyrical quality of his songs and piano pieces. In striving for an architectonic expression, similar to the classics, Schumann encountered considerable difficulty in extending his lyrical ideas over great lengths of musical canvas. Lacking the developmental power of Beethoven, he often strung together a series of ideas that did not have sustaining values. In short, the lyrical element, which is rightfully at home in the small forms, prevails.

Of the four symphonies, the first (the "Spring" Symphony) is most frequently performed. The fourth, the Symphony in D minor, is particularly significant from the standpoint of structure. Its continuous one-movement form is the predecessor of the programmatic *symphonic poem*, which becomes established shortly by Franz Liszt and is widely used throughout the remainder of the romantic era.

[11] *Schumann*, p. 121.

"Armes Waisenkind"
(The Poor Orphan Child) by Robert Schumann

MID-CENTURY ROMANTICS

Berlioz and Liszt:
The Programmatic Ideal

Introduction: The Increasing Role of Literary Ideas All in all, the romantic period was a time of considerable literary influence upon musical style. Following Schubert's and Schumann's fusion of poetry and music in the art song, composers, beginning about midway in the century, increasingly sought literary connections in music. These ranged from rather brief titles applied to movements or sections of orchestral pieces (as in Liszt's *Faust Symphony*, in which the titles of its three movements are drawn from the three main characters in Goethe's *Faust*), to more elaborate texts set to music, as in Berlioz's *Symphonie fantastique* (1830) and Liszt's *Les Préludes* (1848). Wagner's use of mammoth plots in his operas (music dramas), and Mahler's extended texts in his gigantic song cycles and symphonies, represent the epitome of the literary influence in late nineteenth-century music.

Of course, the practice of combining music and words is as old as music itself. But what is so significant in the nineteenth century is the tremendous emphasis placed upon literature (poetry and prose) as a source of ideas and inspiration. Moreover, what makes this aspect of romanticism so pronounced is the fact that the literary influence was considerably less in the preceding period. For we noted that the characteristic expression of the classical era was predominantly "pure music," that is, abstract instrumental music in the form of the symphony, sonata, or concerto.

It has become customary to refer to orchestral music based upon some literary or extramusical idea as *program music*. The characteristic treatment of the programmatic principle, mainly the achievement of the romantics in the last half of the century, was applied chiefly to the symphony, symphonic poem, and the symphonic song cycle. Beethoven, it may be recalled, is generally cited as the first romantic composer to employ the programmatic principle in the orchestral field, specifically in his Sixth, or "Pastoral," Symphony. Berlioz, however, was the first leading romantic to treat the programmatic idea in a more elaborate and realistic fashion.

Berlioz: Precursor of Late Romanticism Hector Berlioz, the composer who laid the foundations for the final burst of romanticism in the orchestral field, was a Frenchman, born in 1803. His first major work, the *Symphonie fantastique*, composed in 1830, stands as a milestone in the romantic movement. As with many significant works frequently appearing in advance of their rightful period, this powerful symphony seems out of place among the predominantly aphoristic expressions of Schubert, Chopin, and Schumann. But when we observe that the *Symphonie fantastique* followed Beethoven's Ninth by only six years, we come to the full realization that the Beethovenian spirit of dynamic, sweeping romanticism never expired, even in a time of feverish interest in the poetic vein of composing. Thus, Berlioz stands as a connecting link between Beethoven and late romanticism.

The presence of these contradictory streams of romanticism in the 1830s—that of the poetic and the powerful or profound—can be partially explained by their geographical origins and the shifting of the nerve center of romanticism. The poetic musicians Schubert and Schumann were German romantics, living and breathing the "poetic" atmosphere of Heine, Jean Paul, and Eichendorff. The composer of the *Symphonie fantastique,* on the other hand, created in a different atmosphere and locale. Berlioz's work stemmed from the age of revolution in French art—when French theater dramatically turned away from the classical "unities" to an intense, individualistic expression heralded by Victor Hugo's *Hernani.* This unusual drama was first presented in 1830, the same year as Berlioz's famous *Symphonie.* Thus the center of romanticism shifted to France, as attested to by the abundance of extraordinary achievements in the fine arts, including the writings of Hugo, the paintings of Delacroix, and the music of Berlioz and Liszt. The French dominance in music was only momentary, however; the German musicians soon again resumed their leadership, which they held to the end of the era.

It would be incredulous, of course, to call Berlioz the founder of the late romantic style, since the traits of late romanticism were present in a dormant state in much early romantic music. There is, however, considerable justification for referring to Berlioz as the first composer to consistently employ the underlying artistic creed that is woven through most late romantic music, namely, the extreme amplification of *imagination, mysticism,* and *human feeling.*

Berlioz was, indeed, the pacesetter for the movement. For shortly after the appearance of his monumental works (such as the *Symphonie fantastique* of 1830, *Harold in Italy* of 1834, and the *Damnation of Faust* of 1846, among others) there appeared in quick succession a series of similarly styled compositions: twelve of Liszt's symphonic poems (1848–1858) and his *Dante* and *Faust Symphonies,* and Wagner's elaborate music dramas, which began to emerge after 1850. These highly romantic works, although of differing form, are bound together, not only by their exaggeration and amplification of human feeling, but also by the more serious and intellectual tone of romanticism that they employ. In short, Berlioz and his immediate successors signalized the radical shift in esthetic ideals that had taken place by mid-century: from the small scale to the large, from light to heavy, from the intimate poetic expressions of the art songs and piano pieces to the epic symphonic and operatic structures.

Eugène Delacroix, *Dante and Virgil in Hell*. Louvre, Paris

Berlioz: Life Sketch Born in 1803, near Grenoble, France, Hector Berlioz
grew up in a strong cultural environment in which an interest in the
classics and music was cultivated as a natural way of life. His father, a
successful physician, fostered the youth's artistic bent by teaching him
what little he knew of music. At the same time, he hoped that young
Berlioz would follow a medical career (as disclosed in the attempt to encourage his study of anatomy by the reward of a new flute). However,
these efforts, which remind one of Schumann's similar creative path, were
in vain for the youth's interest in medicine was clearly subordinated to
music.

After a short period of college medical studies, the high-strung Berlioz was finally permitted to carry out his ambition, that of studying music at the famed Paris Conservatoire. During this period of study he competed several times for the Prix de Rome, finally winning it in 1830 with the composition *The Death of Sardanapalus*, inspired, apparently, by Byron's poem or perhaps by Delacroix's painting of 1829. The Prix de Rome carried with it three years of study, but Berlioz spent only part of the time in Rome, where he made some revisions in his first symphony and composed his second, *Harold in Italy* (1834).

Unfortunately, much of Berlioz's music was not warmly received in Paris. Hence, under economic pressure, he turned to journalism in 1835 and became a music critic for the *Journal des Debats*, remaining in this post for nearly thirty years. His work in this field, like Schumann's, constitutes an important body of writings in the history of musical criticism. However, his creative energy in music did not subside, for we note the following works from the years 1835–1855: the third and fourth symphonies (the *Symphonie funèbre et triomphale* of 1840 and *Romeo and Juliet* of 1839), his first opera, *Benvenuto Cellini* (1838), the mighty *Requiem Mass* (1837), and the *Damnation of Faust* (1846), based on Goethe's famous drama.

It is lamentable that Berlioz's works fared so poorly in Paris—beginning with his early unsuccessful attempts to acquire the coveted Prix de Rome, the failure of *Benvenuto Cellini* to win the opera public, and the production of the *Damnation of Faust*, which put the composer seriously in debt. In contrast, his foreign travels to Germany and England as a conductor, beginning in the 1840s, brought him fame. Ironically, acceptance in his own country was not achieved until late in his life, when, in 1856, he was elected a member of the famed French Académie.

The Berlioz musical profile is much the same as his personality: high-strung, compulsive, imaginative, grotesque, melancholy, eccentric, and intense. Berlioz, like Schumann, put his whole self into his music and thrived on the extramusical idea, which served as a kind of catalytic agent for his creative imagination. Schumann, we found, reflected his sensitive, introspective nature in his piano music and songs. Berlioz seems to have projected his compulsive and bombastic nature into his highly dramatic orchestral works. Viewed from the twentieth century, his significant contributions and characteristic romantic disposition place him in the same circle with his leading contemporary Frenchmen in the arts: Hugo, the master of the new French romantic drama, and Delacroix, the most outstanding French painter of the nineteenth century. This trio of artists is, moreover, bound by the same artistic philosophy: an interest in the strange and the macabre, depicted in the most vivid and realistic manner. Witness for example, Hugo's literary masterpieces *Les Miserables* and *Hernani*, and Delacroix's *Dante and Vergil in Hell*, *The Lion Hunt*, and the *Massacre at Scio*.

The *Symphonie fantastique*, referred to as an "instrumental drama" by its composer, was probably inspired by De Quincey's *Confessions of An*

English Opium-Eater, which appeared in France about this time. The "program" devised by Berlioz centers around a young artist who, under an overdose of opium, has a series of dreams, most of which are bizarre and grotesque. The dreams evolve about the artist's beloved, who is represented throughout the symphony by a recurring theme or *idée fixe* (fixed idea). The program or story of the five-movement symphony unfolds in the following manner:

The first movement, entitled "Reveries and Passions," depicts, through compulsive shifting rhythms and sensuous harmony, the artist's longing for the beloved. It begins in a serious, melancholy mood, apparently representing the artist's state of mind prior to his meeting of his beloved, then suddenly the tempo changes into allegro and we hear for the first time the idée fixe in the violins and flutes. The movement closes with organlike chords, suggesting perhaps a state of religious consolation, as mentioned by Berlioz in his accompanying program (see thematic chart).

The second movement has this caption: "A Ball: At a ball, in the midst of a noisy, brilliant fête, he finds the loved one again." Here, the young artist sees only glimpses of her as the party dances a rather fast and graceful waltz. The third movement, which has a pastoral setting, is entitled "In the Country." He hears two herders, who serenade each other with shepherd melodies, one played by the English horn and the other by the oboe. In the fourth movement, "March to the Gallows," he dreams that he has murdered his beloved and thus suffers the consequences under the guillotine.

The fifth and last movement, "Dream of a Witches' Sabbath," depicts a grotesque orgy in which sorcerers and monsters gather together for the artist's funeral. Orchestral shrieks and groans and high-pitched clarinet squawks nearly blot out the melody of the beloved, which is now, however, sounded as a bizarre dance tune mingled with the weird sounds of the *Dies Irae* (toll for the dead), played by the bells.

Summary Berlioz occupies a very important position in the romantic movement. In fact, it might be said that much of the music of the late nineteenth century rests upon his many innovations. Uppermost of these is the programmatic principle and his numerous contributions to orchestral technique. These are so numerous that all we can do here is mention a few, such as his use of orchestral sonority for its own sake, that is, for sheer coloristic effect; the introduction of many new instruments in the orchestra, such as the English horn, bass clarinet, contrabassoon, harp, and exotic percussion; and use of the new valved brass instruments. Berlioz, also greatly expanded the number of instruments in the orchestra and deployed them in a virtuosic manner, as if the total orchestra were a solo instrument capable of executing great feats of technique.

His most important contribution to musical form is the recurring theme idea (idée fixe), which permitted his successors to ·unify greatly extended compositions. As romantic composers increasingly turned away from the classical symphony form to a lyrical conception of composing, this structural device enabled them to coordinate and to tie together long strands of musical ideas. Notable examples are found in the works of Liszt and Wagner—Berlioz's leading romantic successors.

Principal Themes, *Symphonie Fantastique* by Hector Berlioz

Franz Liszt and the Symphonic Poem If we may judge music reviews and reports correctly, Franz Liszt was undoubtedly the leading pianist of the romantic era. As a performer he was a virtuoso and showman par excellence. As a true artist—a role he assumed when excessive virtuosity and theatricality did not dominate—he was the foremost champion of the piano music of the great masters. Unfortunately, the taste of the French salons (Liszt's habitat as an aspiring musician) leaned heavily toward philistinism, including the showy, bravura style of performance staged by such keyboard acrobats as Kalkbrenner and Thalberg. In this atmosphere Chopin, too, had found that "solid musical fare had to be served with decorative garnishes." Further indication of an empty, frivolous society, strongly reminiscent of the rococo, was the need to demonstrate pianistic supremacy via a public contest, such as was held between Liszt and Thalberg. It is little wonder then, that our present-day image of Liszt should be so strongly associated with "technique" rather than with creation. But beneath the façade is the lesser-known side of the musician, which came to the surface in his expressive performance of the masters and in his later life, when he supplanted the career of a virtuoso with that of a composer, conductor, and teacher. In this vein, he made three main contributions to the romantic movement: (1) the development of a new musical form called the *symphonic poem*, or *tone poem*, which was used extensively by his successors up to the early twentieth century; (2) the principle of *thematic transformation* (similar to Berlioz's idée fixe except that the recurring theme is presented in different guises); and (3) the expansion of piano technique.

Understandably, Liszt's stature as a composer is not that of a major figure. In fact, his total output, though highly diffuse, is negligible in the area of the larger forms, consisting of two symphonies, the *Faust* and the *Dante*, a dozen symphonic poems and two piano concertos. The remainder of his catalogue is chiefly that of miscellaneous vocal works and arrangements and a large body of didactic piano literature.

Uppermost among the major works of Liszt performed today are the *Faust Symphony* (three character studies of Faust, Gretchen and Mephistopheles), the Piano Sonata in B minor, and the symphonic poem *Les Préludes*.

The highly melodramatic symphonic poem, *Les Préludes*, composed in 1848, is the most popular of Liszt's orchestral works. It exemplifies a particular kind of program music that was widely emulated by subsequent romantic composers. Instead of basing his symphonies and symphonic poems on an elaborate story, Liszt merely gives us a musical characterization, as suggested by the themes or titles of the works. Thus, he is chiefly concerned with abstract sounds rather than with objective depiction of human action and events (as in Berlioz's *Symphonie fantastique*), or, as one writer commented, he gives us "tone paintings" rather than realistic tonal "pictures" or stories.

Liszt composed *Les Préludes* in 1848. Two years later he revised it with an appended program note derived from Lamartine's *Méditations poétiques*. In the original edition, the title of Liszt's symphonic poem is provided in quotation marks: "What is life but a series of preludes to that unknown song whose first solemn note is tolled by death?" The complete text of the poem is as follows:

> Is not our life but a series of preludes to that unknown song whose first solemn tone is tolled by death? Love is the enchanted dawn of every life, but are not the first joys of happiness disturbed by some tempest whose force destroys its glorious illusions? And where is the deeply wounded soul which upon experiencing such a tempest does not attempt to find peace and solace in the calm of pastoral

life? Yet, man cannot linger long in the existence of nature and seeks
out the dangerous post whenever the trumpet calls him to its ranks
in order to regain knowledge of himself and full control of his
energy.

Liszt's program deals with a theme favored by the late romantics:
man against fate. This type of weighty, philosophical probing of man's
nature—as opposed to the psychological revelations of Schumann and other
poetic romanticists—is characteristic of late nineteenth–century music. This
esthetic ideal is so prominent that we may call this phase of the movement
"profound romanticism." Vast tonal dialogues inspired by cosmic themes,
such as the destiny of man, death, and transfiguration, pervade much of
the music of the late nineteenth century, especially the works of Wagner,
Mahler, and Richard Strauss.

Les Préludes, as we have mentioned, is in the *symphonic poem* form,
Liszt's chief contribution to the romantic movement. The essential features
of the form are as follows: it is in the orchestral medium, of one continuous movement and has an underlying program, related to or suggestive
of a story, poem, philosophy, scene, and so on. *Les Préludes* is divided into
four sections, which correspond to the four basic ideas in the Lamartine
poem. It opens with a rather lengthy introduction, in which the all-
important, unifying, three-note germinal theme is announced softly in
the strings and forcefully in the brass:

(a) Germinal motive, beginning of *Les Préludes*

(b) Motive (bracketed), opening brass passage

Four preludes follow, each of which conform to the four varying moods
of the poem: (1) love, the greatest fulfillment of life, (2) the struggle for
an ideal, (3) the solitude of nature, and (4) the return to conflict.

Liszt employs his technique of thematic transformation throughout
all of *Les Préludes;* that is, the three-note germinal theme identified by its
upward inflection (skip of a fourth) is to be heard in varying guises in all
of the four sections. Sometimes it is in a different key or in a different
rhythmic setting, or is set in a different timbre or instrumental color,
but it is always recognizable as a constantly recurring idea in the vast tonal
structure. It should be pointed out in this connection that Wagner adopted
the same formal principle for his gigantic music dramas, calling it a
leitmotif, or *leading motive.*

Following Berlioz's general esthetic, Liszt scored *Les Préludes* and his
other orchestral works for a large orchestra of strings, woodwinds, brass,

and percussion, including the "new additions" made by Berlioz, such as the harp, English horn, bass clarinet, and contrabassoon. Outside of Liszt's virtuosic deployment of instruments (an idea carried over from his piano idiom), his striking romantic sound can be attributed chiefly to a lush, colorful harmony. Chromatic harmony (dissonant-sounding chords containing notes "outside" the prevailing key), largely the innovation of Chopin, was further developed by Liszt for conveying various romantic states of mind such as suspended, transitory moods, tension, longings, and unequalled dramatic climax. Wagner, whose work represents the final stage of this harmonic style, carried the idea of chromatic harmony to its complete exploitation at the end of the century. However, before turning to Wagner, let us briefly examine the musical style of Brahms, the "conservative" romanticist.

Brahms and the Classical Point of View

The leading conservative of the romantic movement, Johannes Brahms, was born in Hamburg in 1833. His life span (1833–1897) places him in the same era as Liszt and Wagner. The relationship ends there, however, since Brahms' esthetic principles were quite different from his two contemporaries. Whereas his fellow romantics were representative of the avant-garde, Brahms continued the classic tradition of the symphony and sonata as inherited from Haydn, Mozart, and Beethoven.

As a child, Brahms showed considerable promise in piano, but his few public appearances did not establish his name as a prodigy. Coming from a lower-middle-class home, Brahms had to earn his money by playing in cafés and taverns and by composing light, entertaining pieces under an assumed name. Still in his teens, he composed quantities of music (including a complete musical setting of Heine's *Buch der Lieder*), which did not satisfy his strict, self-imposed standards, and consequently these youthful works were relegated to the furnace. Such an intense desire for perfection, established in his early life, stands out as one of the most important formative factors in the evolution of Brahms' mature style—a style that is predominantly reserved, restrained, and somewhat austere.

In 1853, during a concert tour as an accompanist to the noted Hungarian violinist, Reményi, Brahms met the dashing celebrity, Liszt, who showed considerable interest in his compositions; the musical interest, however, was not reciprocated. Also on this same tour Brahms met Schumann, who praised the young musician in an article in his *Neue Zeitschrift für Musik*. Subsequently, a strong friendship developed between Brahms and the Schumanns, resulting in a further strengthening of Brahms' high artistic ideals. When Schumann died in 1856, Brahms comforted Clara in her time of sorrow. Ironically, the strong devotion he showed Clara for many years after the death of her husband never developed beyond the level of friendship. Generally depicted as a rather coarse, gruff-appearing man with a highly sensitive nature, Brahms lived an austere, lonely existence much of his life.

Brahms' first phase of creativity, which began in the 1850s, was primarily in the chamber idiom, and, like Beethoven, he was keenly challenged by this difficult idiom throughout his life, completing some twenty-four works over a forty-year period from 1854 to 1894. These include sonatas for violin, cello, and clarinet, piano trios, and various kinds of quartets and quintets, for strings alone and strings and piano in combination. In the period 1860–1870, his choral decade, Brahms turned out some of his finest choral music, notably the famous *Deutsches Requiem* (1868), *Alto Rhapsody*, and the scintillating *Liebeslieder Waltzes* for mixed voices and piano duet. The more than two hundred songs, like his chamber music, are distributed over a period of forty years. These are generally modeled after Schubert; however, the piano part plays a completely secondary role, which sets these songs apart from those of Schubert and Schumann. It is in the texts of the songs, which abound with amorous subject matter and sentimental moods, that we note the true romantic nature of the composer.

The orchestral idiom occupied much of Brahms' creative energy in the latter part of his life. Outstanding instrumental examples include the *Variations on a Theme by Haydn*, a violin concerto, two overtures, the *Tragic* and the *Academic Festival*, which was composed to commemorate his honorary doctorate from Breslau University in 1879. Brahms also wrote a virtuosic double concerto for violin and cello, and four magnificent symphonies. The first of which, the Symphony in C minor, dates from 1876 (when Brahms was forty-three) and the last in E minor, from 1885.

Symphony No. 1 in C minor (1876)
Symphony No. 2 in D major (1877)
Symphony No. 3 in F major (1883)
Symphony No. 4 in E minor (1885)

The Classic vs the Romantic Nature of Brahms Indications of Brahms' deep concern for the restoration of classic principles of balance and restraint are to be noted in both his creative work and in his protestations against the futuristic trends represented by Wagner and Liszt. The programmatic principle of Liszt and the elaborate music drama of Wagner were not akin to Brahms' creative outlook and temperament. Although Brahms held to the classic principles of Haydn, Mozart, and Beethoven, a definite romantic tone pervades most of his music. Let us examine this dualism in greater detail.

Romantics, we have found, favor color either in harmony, melody, or orchestration, or in all of these elements. For example, Schumann and especially Chopin stressed a colorful harmony, as shown by their use of chromatic chords (diminished sevenths, augmented chords, and the like). Berlioz contributed a colorful spectrum of instrumental sounds through a skillful orchestration technique and new instrumental additions to the orchestra. Brahms' romantic side is revealed chiefly in the underlying harmony and secondly in the melancholy, brooding mood that prevails in many works.

In Brahms' style there is a very strong relationship to Beethoven's. In his instrumental works, Brahms, like Beethoven, prefers to express general states of mood or emotion spread over large, spacious tonal areas. Also, the Beethoven principle of dynamic development, leading to a definite climax and resolution of tension is also common to Brahms, especially in the large forms. The romantic temperament is seen, too, in his use of minor keys, large-striding melodies spanning over an octave as in the opening of the Third Symphony, and an all-pervading, dark tone quality resulting from heavy emphasis on low-pitched instruments in the orchestral scoring.

As a classicist, Brahms was deeply concerned with matters of form, balance, and restraint. Notably absent is the nervous, compulsive shifting of mood and the grotesque and eccentric expressions so common to Berlioz's *Symphonie fantastique* and Liszt's *Faust Symphony.* Instead, restraint of movement and power, and an over-all calm seems to prevail. Other classic traits can be readily observed in his use of the sonata form (generally in the opening movements of his larger forms), where classical balance is represented in the exposition-development-recapitulation scheme. And, like Haydn and Beethoven, Brahms employs the conventional or classical instrumentation in his symphonies: woodwinds in pairs, the standard brasses, timpani, and the usual string group.

The progressive orchestral methods of Berlioz, Liszt, and Wagner, which were chiefly coloristic and virtuosic, did not interest Brahms, who followed traditional procedures of scoring. A decided Brahmsian trademark exists, however, in his technique of dividing themes up among various instruments, producing a "broken-work" type of orchestration (as opposed to assigning large segments of thematic material to single instruments or a group of instruments). Unlike many composers of the romantic movement who wrote in many idioms, Brahms' unique musical profile—a melancholy, reserved, almost austere personality—is stamped into practically everything he composed, be it art song, piano sonata, or symphony.

THE CLIMAX OF THE ROMANTIC MOVEMENT
(1850–1900)

Toward Exaggeration and Elaboration The period extending from the middle of the nineteenth century to the early years of the twentieth, and encompassing Wagner, Bruckner, and Mahler, marks the culmination of a great epoch in musical art. As with the earlier romantics, there is no clear-cut style system evident among these highly diversified composers. However, there is a particular esthetic concept, generally shared by all, that we may call *hyper-romanticism.* For, deeply ingrained in the musical thinking of these leading German romantics, is an extraordinary liking for *exaggeration.* This tendency takes many forms, such as the intense desire to amplify feelings and emotions, to seek an understanding of the profound mysteries of life, and to expand the limits of musical art, including its time scale (performing time), its subject matter, its harmonic founda-

Time-Line: Late Romanticism	
1851	Wagner: *Oper und Drama*
1859	Wagner: *Tristan und Isolde*
1867	*Die Meistersinger*
1868	Bruckner: Mass in F minor
1869	Brahms: *Liebeslieder Waltzes*
1874	Bruckner: Symphony No. 4 "Romantic"
1876	Brahms: Symphony No. 1
1882	Wagner: *Parsifal*
1883	Death of Wagner
1896	Bruckner: Symphony No. 9 and death of Bruckner
1897	Death of Brahms
1907	Mahler: *Symphony of 1000*
1909	Mahler: *Das Lied von der Erde*
1911	Death of Mahler

tions, and its performance medium, which now reaches gargantuan proportions. The late nineteenth century was, to be sure, an era of grandeur,
immensity, and superlative expression unequalled in previous periods of
music.

These traits of hyper-romanticism are most completely personified
in the music of Wagner, Bruckner, and Mahler, whose musical heritage
stems from the very heart of the romantic movement in music—Germany
and Austria. Although these three titans are markedly different in style,
they possess the intense drive to ascend to the highest mystical regions
and pronounce to the world their supreme statement of romanticism.
Thus, the late romantic composer frequently looks to the world beyond,
to the mystic regions of legend, mythology, and the supernatural for
inspiration. The early romantic, in contrast, turned to his own immediate
world and expressed his feelings and thoughts regarding less complicated
subjects, such as sentimental love, childhood reveries, or pastoral scenes,
or else he merely set down abstract musical ideas in miniature musical
forms. To be sure, the early romantic delved into nocturnal shadows, but
for the late romantic these shadows were darker and more mysterious.

The seeking of high mystical regions and the striving for the summit that we feel so strongly in the works of these late romantics seem
to be analogous to striving for the summit of some gigantic peak. This
idea is not perhaps as naïve as it may appear when we examine the great
struggle for an ideal in the life of Wagner, and particularly the nature of
his musical style. Wagner's melodies, and many of those of his two leading contemporaries Bruckner and Mahler, are generally long, sweeping,
and seemingly endless, stopping only briefly on tonal plateaus, which are
momentary resting points in what seems to be a great ascent. With the
long-awaited climax there is an overwhelming release of tension, as the
constant stream of dissonant harmony becomes resolved in tonic harmony,
and concerted sounds of cosmic magnitude and force bring the work to a
triumphant close. Hence we hit upon one of the essential points of difference between early and late romanticism: the center of gravity or main
point of interest is not the development section so prominent in Beethoven, nor the lyrical, moody melodic line of Schumann and Schubert, but
rather the *climax*. A series of dramatic situations or episodes, skillfully
designed in the manner of a Dostoevski novel and containing powerful
germinal motives, are woven together into a vast tonal drama that gradually gains in momentum and tension.

Being vitally concerned with dramatic effect, the ultimate in musical
forces is required. Orchestral bodies had to be expanded to more than
twice the size of the late classical orchestra, and new instruments created
(such as the haunting Wagner tubas). New instrumental combinations for
a richer, thicker sonority were devised, and the emphasis on drama, with
its required gradual buildup of tension, led to greatly extended musical
forms. The effect of all of these newly devised musical techniques is perhaps what Wagner was striving for: a suprapowerful musical force that
would transport and engulf the listener in vast tonal waves of volume,
orchestral color, and lush harmony.

Caspar David Friedrich, *Mountain Peaks.* Nationalgalerie, Berlin

The Cultural Setting: The Folk and Nationalistic Spirit in German Culture
Compositions by the three giants of late romanticism, Wagner, Bruckner, and Mahler, possess certain elements, in addition to the aforementioned subjective esthetic qualities, that bind these figures together. Broadly speaking, the elements are folk and nationalistic in character: in Wagner it is a strong feeling of nationalism rooted in German mythology; in Bruckner it is a penchant for melodic figures tinged with German and Austrian folk character (in the scherzos and in the earthy, pastoral horn calls); and in Mahler it is chiefly in his use of German folk poetry.

The presence of these stylistic elements in music is easily understood, for the nineteenth century was a time of unprecedented interest in German culture—an interest that extended to all of the arts, painting, literature, poetry, drama, and music. From the very beginning of the romantic movement, writers, artists, and musicians maintained a close connection with German folk poetry, legend, medieval heritage, landscape, and folk activities. In music, the first signs of the approaching German nationalism were announced in the opera form by E. T. A. Hoffmann, a celebrated literary figure and painter; his best known opera, *Undine* (1816), discloses characteristic romantic traits in its folklike melody and supernatural scenes. But the real founder of German romantic opera was Carl Maria von Weber whose famous operas, *Der Freischütz* (1821) and *Oberon* (1826), established the framework of German romantic opera, later culminated by Wagner. Abounding in Weber's works are forested German landscapes, the supernatural, and ancient folk tales.

One of the most important cultural developments to have a great impact on practically all of German music in the romantic era was the popular folk music movement, which began in Germany about 1770. Included among the earliest collections of folk music were J. A. P. Schulz' *Lieder im Volkston* (1782), J. A. Hiller's *Lieder für Kinder* (1769), and Herder's *. . . Ossian und die Lieder alter Völker* (1773). In turn, the poetry of Goethe and Heine, whose work was often inspired by these folk collections, served as the basis for the art songs of Schubert and Schumann, and were used as late as Brahms and Mahler. In particular, the stylistic roots of the last leading German romantic, Gustav Mahler, are to be found in the gigantic collection of German poems, folk songs, and carols (dated as early as the sixteenth century) collected under the title *Des Knaben Wunderhorn (The Youth's Magic Horn)*, by the poets von Arnim and Brentano and published 1806–1808.

Painters also rediscovered the Rhine, German village scenes, mountains, and Gothic castles captured in a dark-toned, nostalgic mood. Following the work of Koch (d. 1839), who was the first artist, according to Brion to "take an especial interest in mountains and to portray them with equal regard for their reality and their poetry,"[12] Carus (d. 1869) provided a metaphysical approach to painting nature. In his *Nine Letters on Landscape Painting*, he writes:

> A man contemplating the magnificent unity of a natural landscape becomes aware of his own smallness and, feeling that everything is a part of God, he loses himself in that infinity, giving up, in a sense, his individual existence. To be engulfed in this way is not to be destroyed; it is a gain: what normally one could only perceive with the spirit almost becomes plain to the physical eye.[13]

The movement in German art attained its highest point in the paintings of Caspar David Friedrich (d. 1840), the most important of all German romantic painters. In many of his works, such as *The Chalk Cliffs of Rugen* (1818), *Two Men Looking at the Moon* (1819), and *The Cross and*

[12] Marcel Brion, *Romantic Art* (New York: McGraw-Hill Book Company, Inc., 1960), p. 120.
[13] *Romantic Art*, pp. 99–100.

Cathedral in the Mountains (1811), we can sense many of the same qualities that are suggested in Wagner, Bruckner, and Mahler. These include a vastness of form, strength and massiveness, a reaching for infinity, and the subordination of man to the mysteries and power of nature and the supernatural.

From this rich background of Germanic culture, mysticism, and nationalistic leanings, emerged Wagner, Bruckner, and Mahler—Wagner, who drew his creative inspiration from German mythology; Bruckner, from the Austro-German vein of melody and Baroque mysticism; and Mahler, from German folk melody and poetry.

Richard Wagner

Of all the late nineteenth-century composers Wagner (1813–1883) must be placed at the summit of the romantic epoch. He greatly extended and enriched the romantic concepts of harmony, melody, orchestration, and form, and brought to complete fruition the romantic ideal of unification of the arts.

We have observed that the romantic styles throughout this period have been as numerous and highly divergent as the composers who created them. These musicians were, however, bound by their common interest in originating a new language, one that was governed less by rules or social custom and more by individual temperament and personality. Actually the language was not new. It was basically the traditional system of harmony and melody greatly enriched by extensive chromaticism and placed into new molds. It was "new" in the sense that tonal combinations were employed *freely* for their *psychological* rather than *rational* meaning, that is, for their power to express various emotional connotations. Whereas the earlier romantics used the new musical language to suggest various emotional states and to enhance the dramatic content of a text or story, Wagner carried the idea one step further; his objective was to completely transport the audience into the world of feelings, moods, and emotions via the medium of total theater, in which drama and music are one.

Life Sketch   It is hard to believe that Wagner, born in Leipzig in 1813, entered the world at the same time as the poetic romanticists Schumann and Chopin, who developed an entirely different musical esthetic. Perhaps our perspective of Wagner's life will become clearer when we note that he began to reach his stride after 1850, at a later age than his predecessors, who attained their creative peak earlier in life. Also, Wagner, who died in 1883, lived a much longer life than most romantics, completing most of his major works in his later years, in contrast to the youthful contributions of Schumann, Schubert, and Chopin.

Wagner's educational background and early music experiences do not disclose signs of extraordinary latent talent in musical and literary creativity. At the Kreuzschule in Dresden, young Wagner showed much interest in Greek and German poetry and tragedy but little enthusiasm for music. It is quite remarkable that the operatic giant of the romantic movement did not show a real interest in music until his late teens, when he finally plunged into an intense study of Beethoven's works. Several minor compositions, including a symphony and a piano sonata, were composed at this time. However, at the outset of his career his chief interest lay in conducting.

From 1833 to 1849, Wagner held numerous operatic conducting posts in Germany, the most important of which was at Dresden from 1843 to 1849. Also, his earliest operas were composed during this period: *Rienzi* (1842), *Der fliegende Holländer (The Flying Dutchman)* (1843), and *Tannhäuser* (1845). The last of this series of traditional-styled operas, *Lohengrin*, was completed in 1850. This opera foreshadowed his future music dramas in its more continuous flow of music (as opposed to the sectional style of traditional opera, with its recitative-aria sequence), its use of symbolism, and recurring theme idea, or *leitmotif*.

The turning point in Wagner's life came in 1849, when, as a result of his participation in the May Revolution of that year, he was forced to migrate to Switzerland, where he remained in exile for about ten years. Here, he wrote his theories on art, including the famous *Oper und Drama* (1851), an exhaustive study on esthetics that forms the philosophical groundwork for his invention, the *music drama*. This new form of opera became the framework for his gigantic tetralogy, *Der Ring des Nibelungen (The Ring of the Nibelungs)*. This collosal work, which was partially completed during his exile, consisted of *Das Rheingold (The Rhine Gold)*, *Die Walküre (The Valkyrie)*, *Siegfried*, and *Götterdämmerung (Twilight of the Gods)*. The entire work, which was finally completed in 1874, represents the sum expression of Wagner's theories and the capstone of his creative work. Three other music dramas were completed in the latter part of his career: *Tristan und Isolde* (1859), *Die Meistersinger von Nürnberg* (1867), and *Parsifal* (1882).

Of the many ideas presented in his comprehensive treatise *Oper und Drama*, those pertaining to the rationale for breaking with traditional opera and his phenomenal plan for assigning equal rights to "tone" and "word" are most pertinent here. Deploring the terrible state that opera had fallen into, Wagner cited two basic causes of the dilemma: first, the superficial librettos, which were addressed not to humanity but to "the cultured sensibilities of a select social group," and, secondly, the traditional structure of opera with its emphasis on the aria, which had been designed to show off the singer's technique rather than "display any truth of feeling." "In essence, music which should be the *means*, had been made the *end*, and drama had become the means."

A guiding factor in Wagner's creation of a new operatic ideal was provided by Beethoven. In his study of the Beethoven symphonies, a new logic founded not on reason but on inner feeling was revealed to

Wagner. He believed that the great orchestral genius had cultivated the expression of human feeling to a high degree, but the limits had been reached in the instrumental idiom. However, in his Ninth Symphony, Beethoven had demonstrated that it was possible to extend the boundaries by the addition of *voices.* Thus, where instrumental music previously provided only an incomplete representation of emotion, music could now become complete with the addition of the *word.* Hence, in the Wagnerian music drama the outer action is carried by the sung words, while the inner action (that which is beyond words, such as feelings and desires) is carried by the orchestra. Actually, the focal point of Wagner's music drama is not the melody but the orchestra, which functions at the subjective and even subliminal level of the listener, calling forth images of persons, places, feelings, and desires, each of which is associated with its own particular recurring theme or leitmotif.

Since the essence of drama is conveyed through feeling and not understanding, the new art form must be centered around the senses rather than the intellect. Consequently, the drama's action must transcend the world of reality. The customary historical subject matter of traditional opera, with its emphasis on everyday physical things, is therefore to be replaced by mythological subject matter. Moreover, to enhance the esthetic impact of the drama, all of the arts—painting, music, poetry, sculpture, and dance—were to be brought together on the stage. The aim: to transport the individual member of the audience "out of himself," and to make him completely responsive to the artistic expression of the various media presented on the stage. Emotion, then, becomes "the supreme and unique legislator." Thus romantic ideals attained their zenith with Wagner.

Wagner's Orchestral Contributions   Wagner's distinctive treatment of the orchestra and its instruments is one of the most significant contributions of the entire romantic movement, influencing practically every musician of his era. And when his music dramas are not readily accessible, concert audiences experience the Wagnerian "mystique" through his overtures, which are widely performed by symphony orchestras throughout the world. These overtures owe their lasting quality to their musical invention, richness of orchestral effect, and completeness of expression, for they are, as it were, miniature orchestral music dramas. Also regularly performed are the orchestral pieces extracted from the Wagner operas, including: "The Magic Fire Music," and the "Ride of the Valkyries" from *Die Walküre,* "Siegfried Idyll" from *Siegfried;* "Good Friday Spell" from *Parsifal,* and the "Funeral March" from *Götterdämmerung.*

It is obviously difficult to measure the impact that Wagner's orchestral techniques had upon his fellow romantic composers, Bruckner and Mahler, and upon the leading post-romantic composers of the twentieth century, such as Strauss and Sibelius. The influence is perhaps best described as a general philosophy of orchestral writing that permeated the musical atmosphere of the late nineteenth century and early twentieth. Its essential features include virtuoso treatment of the total complex of players (individually and as a group); unusual weight, strength, and breadth of orchestral sound; a rich sonority rooted in full brass; and extension of the orchestral range, both high and low, to its limits.

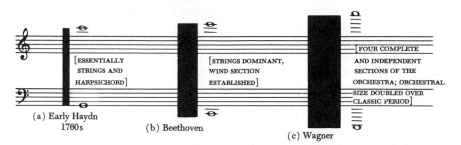

Comparative Orchestral Weight (number of instruments) and general range:
a. Early Haydn, 1760s b. Beethoven c. Wagner

Aside from its emphasis on massiveness of sound produced by a large orchestra, the Wagnerian style calls for individuality of all instrumental sections. For example, no longer do the strings hold the continual focus of musical ideas, for now not only does every section possess executant powers—that is, is capable of extended solos as a group—but each has a complete instrumentation and is assigned full chords, which provide a richness of sonority never heard before.

The English horn, bass clarinet and contrabassoon, which were of course used before by Berlioz, now are regular members of the woodwind section. For Wagner and all late German romantics, the brasses serve as the organic foundations of the grand orchestra, establishing the deep, resonant sonority so characteristic of their work. In *Die Götterdämmerung* Wagner employed a huge brass section, including four French hornlike instruments of his own invention called the "Wagner tubas," eight regular French horns, three trumpets, bass trumpet, three trombones, bass trombone, and tuba. The technical capabilities of the horn, trumpet, and tuba were greatly expanded at about this time, with the wide acceptance of the new modern valve system invented by Blühmel earlier (1818) in the century.

Summary   Wagner's unusual sonority—a "cosmic sonority," as one writer described it—is attributed to the complete instrumentation and harmony in each section of the orchestra, expanded orchestral range (deeper range through the addition of lower-pitched brass instruments and higher string range) and, above all, to the subdivision of the string section. That is, the violins, violas, cellos, and even basses are divided into several sections, each playing a separate part, as opposed to the classic method of giving each string section, violins, violas, etc., one or two parts played by all instruments in that section. Thus, the "splitting up" of each string section into several parts provides an ethereal quality especially effective with muted instruments, as in the opening of *Parsifal.*

Beneath the huge orchestral façade is the unique Wagnerian harmony (actually an extension of the Chopin-Liszt style), characterized by its constant movement of voice parts, thick, quasi-contrapuntal texture, and extensive chromaticism. In conclusion, in addition to creating a new form of opera, Wagner expanded the orchestra to its maximum and created new techniques of orchestration that greatly influenced his post-romantic successors. Also, he extended the traditional tonal system of major and minor keys and chords to its maximum limits, eventually giving rise to new harmonic systems under the impressionists (Debussy) and the expressionists (Schoenberg).

Anton Bruckner

Late Nineteenth-century Trends In the wake of Wagner's spectacular achievements in music drama, musical style reached a crossroads in the last two decades of the century. Two stylistic trends became apparent: one, the continuation and expansion of German romanticism by Bruckner and Mahler and, the other, the beginning of the impressionistic movement by Debussy in France.

Firmly steeped in the Viennese tradition, Anton Bruckner (1824–1896) and Gustav Mahler (1860–1911) provided a superlative finale to the century of romanticism. Committed to the romantic belief that instrumental music could express something deeper than words, a belief especially true of Bruckner, these Viennese romantics chose as their chief musical medium the symphony form of Beethoven. Thus, the creative focus of this final stage of romanticism shifted from the theater to the concert hall, and specifically to the symphony, which became increasingly mystical in character and titanic in proportion.

The Wagnerian influence is particularly striking in these late symphonies, especially in the strength and breadth of the orchestra, whose gigantic sounds seem to echo some primeval or cosmic origin. The Wagnerian spirit is also noted in the greatly increased time span of the symphony; a single Bruckner movement is sometimes as long as a complete classical symphony. Moreover, the orchestration of these late romantic composers, especially Bruckner, is truly Wagnerian—thick, richly colored, and founded upon heavy, dark, brass sonorities. However, the intrinsic features of the Bruckner and Mahler compositions are, as we shall observe, highly individual and original, bearing little relationship to Wagner.

Unquestionably, Anton Bruckner is one of the most fascinating (and enigmatic) symphonic composers of the romantic era. Often criticized for their great length and enormity of conception, Bruckner's works possess a particular haunting, pastoral quality quite different from any other romantic symphonist. Unfortunately, the Brucknerian character has only recently been revealed to concert audiences in this country, a lamentable situation that seems to stem from several causes. For one thing, much of the popular writing and opinion on Bruckner has tended to give a distorted view of the composer. Rather than revealing him for the true musician that he was—a master contrapuntist, organist, and original choral and symphony composer—many have emphasized the eccentricities of his personality and ridiculed his anti-twentieth-century mode of expression.

Naturally, Bruckner's art has encountered much difficulty in our fast-moving, materialistic age. The modern listener, in making his initial acquaintance with one of the most mystical of romantics will need a different "preparatory set," or mental attitude, than that which he would bring to a more abstract, late twentieth-century composition. With Bruckner there is no compromise, no reliance on programmatic elements, no substitution for complete involvement on the part of the listener. For true appreciation one must succumb to his quaint world of murmuring forests, pastoral valleys, and peaks that resound with medieval hymns of praise. In summary, the attempt to apply modern esthetic principles to his work, the feeling of anti-German romanticism (notably prior to and during the Second World War), and particularly the confusion arising from falsified scores, have hindered a full appreciation and understanding of Bruckner in our time. Fortunately, the past few decades have seen a gradual renaissance of his music, especially in Germany under the famed conductor and Bruckner interpreter, Eugen Jochum.

Life Sketch Hans Redlich's distinctive study[14] of Bruckner's life and music discloses a picture of a quiet, unpretentious, introverted, rustic, village musician intensely dedicated to the Catholic Church. However, these characteristics mask a composer whose creative expressions plumb the depths and soar to great heights of religious joy, calling to mind the sacred music of the Gothic and the Baroque. Some writers suggest that perhaps Bruckner was actually a "mystic" or a kind of rustic genius who, unlike Wagner, did not champion his own cause but rather worked in anonymity. Bruckner's religious devotion and inspiration is sensed in practically every page of his scores. His musical moods, ranging from pastoral-like simplicity and a strange celestial calm to mighty exhortations of joy and jubilation, afford a refreshing change in the romantic style at the peak of its movement.

The essence of this peculiar brand of romanticism seems to be an all-pervading tone of religiosity, which undoubtedly stemmed from Bruckner's long affiliation with the Catholic Church. Born in 1824, the composer spent his boyhood in a remote Austrian village where life had changed little in a century, and where the Church had remained strong as a dominant cultural influence. Representative of this religious heritage is the famous monastery of St. Florian's, renowned for its great library, choral music traditions, and beauty of its Baroque-styled architecture. Its

---

[14] *Bruckner and Mahler* (London: J. M. Dent and Sons, Ltd., 1963).

dramatic atmosphere, with its ornate designs, complexity, and grandeur, bear more than a casual relation to Bruckner's Baroquelike masses and symphonies.

Desirous of following a schoolmaster's profession like his father, young Bruckner became a student and chorister in the St. Florian monastery. It was here that he began his lifelong association with the Catholic Church and its musical heritage, and it was also here that he assimilated the germinating elements of his grand masses and symphonies. After St. Florian's, he held several schoolteaching posts and organ positions in various Austrian villages. In 1856, competing against many rivals, Bruckner won the organ position at the Cathedral of Linz, where he remained for twelve years. In the interim he traveled frequently to Vienna, where he studied counterpoint with the renowned Simon Sechter, teacher of theory and organ at the Vienna Conservatory.

It was during his Linz tenure that Bruckner wrote the bulk of his choral music, including three great masses: the Mass in D minor (1864), the Mass in E minor (1866), and the Mass in F minor (1868). The shifting of his creative outlook, from the choral to the symphonic idiom, was undoubtedly influenced by his hearing of Wagner's music, particularly a performance of *Tristan und Isolde* in Munich in 1865. It was then, as one writer jokingly stated, that Bruckner met his second deity, Richard Wagner, to whom the quiet admirer later dedicated his Third Symphony (1873).

As Bruckner grew in musical stature, he eventually settled in Vienna (1868), where he succeeded the deceased Simon Sechter as professor of theory and organ at the Vienna Conservatory. During his Vienna period Bruckner concentrated chiefly on the symphonic idiom, completing nine monumental works in this form. Two other symphonies, in F minor and D minor, were regarded by the composer as student works and outside of his canon of nine. All but the First Symphony were composed in the Vienna period, and all underwent considerable revision and modification.

Symphony No. 1 in C minor (1866)
Symphony No. 2 in C minor (1872)
Symphony No. 3 in D minor "Wagner" (1873)
Symphony No. 4 in E flat major "Romantic" (1874)
Symphony No. 5 in B flat major (1877)
Symphony No. 6 in A major (1881)
Symphony No. 7 in E major (1883)
Symphony No. 8 in C minor (1885)
Symphony No. 9 in D minor (1896)

The Bruckner Musical Profile   The problem of summarizing the characteristics of Bruckner's style is somewhat less than with many romantic composers. The reason is that Bruckner's music did not undergo a stylistic evolution, as with Beethoven nor a periodic fluctuation in choice of forms, as with Schumann. Although there is a noticeable difference between early and late symphonies, the Brucknerian "fingerprints," which are clearly engraved in the First Symphony, are imbued in all his other works.

His creativity, falling neatly into the choral idiom in his early period (prior to Vienna) and in the orchestral in the late, sprung from profound religious experiences. During his long association with the Catholic Church, Bruckner developed a predilection for certain liturgical elements that served as cornerstones for his masses and then later for his symphonies. These elements include a polyphonic texture (at times heavily homophonic in the symphonies), use of ecclesiastical modes, chorale themes (especially in finales of symphonies), the continuous melodic movement so characteristic of sacred medieval and Renaissance polyphony, and an all-pervading "religious" mood. The characteristic romantic obsession with pure sound as a mystical power of communication is perhaps most amply demonstrated in the music of Bruckner. Schumann and Chopin applied the concept to smaller piano forms, and Berlioz and Liszt, using it in conjunction with an accompanying program, applied it to the orchestral idiom. But Bruckner, perhaps, is more successful since he does not rely on a program that frequently detracts from the mystery of sheer sound. Having no definite connection or relation to verbal or literary meaning, the mysticism is that much more enhanced.

Bruckner's symphonies, with their solemnity of procession, vast sonority, and enormous power, seem to be giant paeans of religious faith and ecstasy, spiritual transformations from some great religious epoch of the past. They are, like his earlier masses, thick textured and imbued with various liturgical elements, such as plainsong, triads in root position giving an austere harmonic sound reminiscent of Palestrina, slow majestic chorale melodies and rhythms, and an organlike sound in the orchestration.

The symphonies are modeled after the four-movement plan of Beethoven: Allegro, Adagio, Scherzo, Allegro. However, in place of the tightly knit, logical Beethovenian structures, Bruckner emphasizes mood rather than themes, creating long, rambling movements that stretch the symphonic mold to its breaking point. For example, the length of the Seventh Symphony is about eighty minutes. Rooted in the Ninth Symphony of Beethoven, which begins with a vague, primordial stirring, Bruckner's creative esthetic stresses the subconscious level rather than objective classic procedures. To illustrate, instead of clear-cut thematic details, tonal complexes or masses, chiefly in harmonic form, seem to hover on the threshold of comprehension, as vague-sounding unities, emerging from time to time as themes in complete, concrete form. Such an esthetic tends, of course, to negate symphonic form and to stretch it to unusual proportions. Rather than following a logical plan of stating and developing themes in a nice, tight, compact form, Bruckner prefers to meander over immense areas, progressing in a terraced fashion from one plateau to another, each generally differentiated by a huge climax. The development technique is used, but it lies unobtrusively beneath the powerful waves of sound.

James Wyatt, Fonthill Abbey. 1796. No longer standing. From Robert J. Gemmett, "The Critical Reception of William Beckford's Fonthill," in *English Miscellany: A Symposium of History, Literature, and the Arts*, XIX (1968)

The allegro tempos are not "fast" allegros, since their ponderous orchestration and processional, majestic rhythms tend to restrain their forward propulsion. In this regard, Capell has pointed out the similarity of Bruckner to Wagner. Both, he states, command a majestically deliberate pace unknown to other composers.[15] Bruckner's scherzos (more so than any other movement) usually have the closest connection to our earth existence. Based on the Austrian dance called the *Ländler*, the scherzos have a boisterous, rustic effect resulting from a strong rhythmic figure. Generally, Bruckner adheres to rhythmic and metrical simplicity, preferring four-square meters and phrases and majestic rhythmic figures reminiscent of liturgical practice, particularly the quintuple figure ♩♩♩♩♩ which is a distinctive Bruckner trademark.

[15] Richard Capell, "Anton Bruckner," in *The Symphony*, edited by Ralph Hill (London: Penguin Books, 1954), p. 216.

Excerpt from Conductor's Score,
Symphony No. 9 by Anton Bruckner

Bruckner's themes, possessing strong masculine and heroic qualities, are quite unlike those of many earlier romantics, such as Schumann and Chopin. At times, however, there is a very sweet lyrical quality similar to Schubert. Most of the principal themes have a wide-leaping melodic movement, encompassing intervals of a fifth, seventh, or octave, and when sounded are like chiseled or sculptured blocks of tone. Bruckner's statement of these themes generally follows a particular pattern in the opening movements. After a vague or perhaps mysterious tremolo of the strings or woodwinds, the main theme, sounded by a horn seemingly from afar, dramatically "announces" the symphony, that is, provides the setting, atmosphere, or mood of the work. And then gradually there is a general stirring of the vast orchestra, indicating the presence of some mighty dormant force.

The Fourth Symphony, the "Romantic," which ranks with the Seventh in popularity, departs from the serious tone of the first three symphonies and radiates a joyful, pastoral quality. The Fourth as well as the Fifth and Sixth Symphonies are more optimistic, and generally suggestive of pastoral scenes similar to Beethoven's Sixth. In addition to evoking visions of spacious landscapes, Capell is impressed with their stirring horn calls, which suggest huntsmen in the far distance and peasant dances in the scherzos. In true late romantic fashion, Bruckner's vast majestic peaks and deep valleys seem to completely engulf the human element.

The final set of symphonies (Nos. 7, 8, and 9) return again to the solemn procession and gravity of the earlier works. Thematic quotations from various earlier Bruckner sacred works abound in these, and in general the tone is very mystical and intense. This is especially true of the Ninth Symphony, which in its piercing, searing dissonance, angular themes, and deep sense of tragedy, points to Mahler and beyond—to the expressionistic school of Schoenberg.

Gustav Mahler

With the music of Gustav Mahler (1860–1911) we reach the end of the great movement that had inspired a century of unprecedented creativity in the arts. With monumental designs and unequaled profundity of subject matter, Mahler carried the late romantic idea of seeking the infinite to its ultimate conclusion. Using the forms of song cycle and symphony, Mahler attempted to make music a vehicle for projecting his thoughts about the nature of existence, life and death, and immortality. In a sense then, his compositions are a mirror of his soul, are spiritual autobiographies.

Although he is sometimes referred to as a post-romantic, it would perhaps be more appropriate to regard Mahler as the last important member of the late romantic group. Aside from exhibiting a high degree of originality, his intense sincerity toward his art and complete exemplification of romanticism in his music and life justifies a searching examination of Mahler's work and contributions to the movement. His designation as "last of the great romantics" is readily defensible when we look at succeeding romantic composers. Much of the romantic-styled music of Bruckner's and Mahler's successors (such as Strauss and Franck) seems, in contrast, artificial and highly melodramatic—indeed, as ineffectual strivings to recapture the spirit of romanticism.

In our haste to group everything under the heading of "German romanticism," the dominant trend in nineteenth-century arts, we should not underemphasize the fact that the movement in music was from beginning to end centered in Vienna. Such names as Beethoven, Schubert, Brahms, Bruckner and Mahler—practically all of the major figures of the romantic era—were closely affiliated with the musical life of this famous city. Here the representative forms of the romantic movement, the symphony, piano piece, and lied, first acquired their romantic cast. Of these, the romantic symphony was the most important contribution of the Viennese. Beethoven, especially in his Ninth, set the general pattern and character of the romantic symphony, Schubert contributed the characteristic lyricism, Brahms restored the classical principles, and then Bruckner gave the four-movement plan unequaled power and mysticism in the Baroque manner. And now the long history of the Viennese symphony comes to an end with Gustav Mahler, who sought to reconcile the essential romantic forms of symphony and song.

Life Sketch   Gustav Mahler was born into a family of poor Moravian Jews in 1860, one year after Wagner composed *Tristan und Isolde.* Mahler's musical education, pursued simultaneously with his private gymnasium studies, began at fifteen when he entered the Vienna Conservatory. Here he studied harmony, piano, and composition for three years, graduating with the diploma in 1878. After graduation he embarked on a conducting career. Beginning with small German opera houses, his appointments eventually included the Prague Opera, Budapest Opera, and the esteemed Vienna Royal Opera, where in his ten-year period (1897–1907) he became world renowned as a conductor and champion of the great works in the operatic repertoire, including the operas of Mozart, Gluck, and Wagner. In 1907 he accepted the conductorship of the Metropolitan Opera in New York, and in the fall of 1909 he took over the directorship of the New York Philharmonic Orchestra, a post he held until 1911, when he was forced to resign due to ill health.

Conducting was Mahler's chief occupation, but, as time went on, his great interest in composing gradually usurped more and more of his hours. His creative inspiration, which sprung from the lied, followed two basic directions, one being the song-cycle form (a *song cycle* is a group of songs based on poems usually by one poet and connected by a general idea) and the other the symphony. At first Mahler was occupied with large-scale song cycles, beginning in 1880 with *"Das klagende Leid"* (The Plaintive Song), for solo voices, chorus, and orchestra and based on the composer's adaptation of a text by the Grimm brothers. More song cycles followed, including *Lieder eines fahrenden Gesellen* (Songs of a Wayfarer), completed in 1885 and consisting of four song settings of a text by Mahler. His next cycle, *Des Knaben Wunderhorn* (The Youth's Magic Horn, 1889), was inspired by a gigantic collection of German folk poetry dating back to the sixteenth century. This collection, also entitled *Des Knaben Wunderhorn,* was compiled by the poets von Arnim and Brentano during the years 1806–1808. The pathetic-toned *Kindertotenlieder* (Songs on the Death of Children, 1904), is a cycle for solo voice and orchestra, set to the poems of Rückert. The high point in this phase of Mahler's creative work came with *Das Lied von der Erde* (The Song of the Earth, 1908), a song cycle based on ancient Chinese poems for tenor, contralto, and orchestra. This is generally regarded as Mahler's finest contribution.

Principles of Style   During the short span of time, 1888–1910 (a period of intensive conducting duties), Mahler turned out ten symphonies, the last of which was left uncompleted. As the final composer of the long line of illustrious Viennese symphonists, Mahler continued the essential outlines of the great classical form. However, his conception of the symphony, markedly different from his predecessors, was heavily influenced by three factors: (1) the far-reaching shadow of Wagner, (2) his own deep romantic roots in German folklore, and (3) his true romantic obsession for reflecting states of the soul. And particularly his penchant for a large performing body (reaching colossal proportions in the Eighth Symphony), along with his attempt to express through music the intangible, the infinite, the philosophical, and the metaphysical, indicates Mahler's roots in the Wagnerian world.

The fundamental characteristics of Mahler's art include an unusual mastery of orchestration: a unique "chamber style" in his symphonies, that is, his unusual deployment of a small number of instruments within the framework of the full orchestra; and the conscientious use of the German lied and folk elements. The spirit of Schubert is felt in Mahler's ingenious melodic lines, while the folk elements (folk poetry, march and dance tunes, and pastoral bird calls) stem from Mahler's extraordinary interest in German folklore, a major source of which was *Des Knaben Wunderhorn.*

The programmatic element is either expressly intended in his symphonies or strongly alluded to. For example, Redlich mentions that the Symphonies No. 2, 3, and 4 "represent a symphonic trilogy reflecting the composer's struggle for a lasting religious belief and ultimate finding of it in the victory of love and forgiveness over doubt and fear. . . ."[16] At the heart of each symphony emanates a religious message from *Des Knaben Wunderhorn,* which expresses Mahler's faith in resurrection and eternal life through love. As much as Mahler frequently spoke out against program music, he apparently relied heavily upon the technique for creative inspiration, according to Redlich. In a letter written in 1897, he makes the following statement in regard to his second symphony:

---

[16] *Bruckner and Mahler,* p. 185.

When I conceive a great musical organism I invariably arrive at a point where I feel compelled to call in the art of words as a carrier of my musical idea. . . . In the case of the last movement of my second symphony this went so far that I had to search through the whole world of literature, down to the Holy Bible in order to find the appropriate words.[17]

Mahler's personality—fiery temperament, hypertensiveness, and an inflexible will for perfection—shows itself throughout his music, and probably accounts for the strange juxtaposition of contrasting moods and feelings. The prominent position of his personality in his music is validated in his own words: "The act of creation in me is so closely bound up with all my experience that when my mind and spirit are at rest I can compose nothing." Here then, with this identification of art with personal emotion, is the true romantic, echoing Schumann, Beethoven, Wagner, and others.

Of the ten symphonies by Mahler, the Second, the "Resurrection" (1894), and the Eighth, the "Symphony of a Thousand" (1907), are best known. The Second is so called because of the poem, "The Resurrection" (by Klopstock), which serves as the program for the finale of the five-movement symphony. This work fully exemplifies the lofty, profound mysticism that prevails throughout most of Mahler's music. It is, according to Redlich, a deep-probing, soulful mysticism that generally reflects Mahler's thoughts on the Resurrection, the mystery of life, the tragedy of death, and evidently his own spiritual loneliness and longing for inner peace.

The Eighth Symphony or "Symphony of a Thousand," so named because of its huge body of performers, is a colossus of romanticism. It is scored for an immense orchestra, with auxiliary brass choir, two choruses, boys' choir, and seven vocal soloists. The program for the symphony, which is in two parts, is drawn from the hymn *Veni creator spiritus* and from portions of the second part of Goethe's *Faust.*

MAHLER, SYMPHONY NO. 8,
(SYMPHONY OF 1000)
TOTAL FORCES

WOODWINDS

Flutes 1,2,3,4
Piccolo
Oboes 1,2,3,4
E-flat clarinet
Clarinets in B-flat,
    1,2,3,
Bass Clarinet
Bassoons 1,2,3,4
Contrabassoon

BRASS

Horns 1,2,3,4,5,6,7,8
Trumpets 1,2,3,4
Trombones 1,2,3,4

PERCUSSION

Timpani
Bass Drum
Cymbals

---

[17] *Bruckner and Mahler,* p. 159.

ORGAN   *CHILDREN'S VOICES*

STRINGS   *MIXED CHOIR I*

Violin I   Soprano
Violin II   Alto
Viola   Tenor
Cello   Bass
Contrabass

                                     MIXED CHOIR II

VOCAL SOLOISTS
                                     Soprano
Sopranos 1,2   Alto
Altos 1,2   Tenor
Tenor   Bass
Baritone

In general, Mahler is more remote than any other romantic—more so than Bruckner, who seems closer to reality with his symphonies and masses, which evoke pastoral and liturgical associations on the part of the listener. Strangely, Mahler moves progressively away from reality, from folk-centered expressions in his early symphonies to a deep, gray-toned pessimism, reflecting, perhaps, increasing personal tension and religious unrest.

Romanticism has thus run its full course, beginning early in the movement with a renascence in the artistic representation of personal feelings, moods, and nature, and concluding with the contemplation of man's innermost and deepest thoughts. In his later works Mahler, like Bruckner, clearly points to *expressionism,* an important style period to be discussed under twentieth-century music.

REPRESENTATIVE WORKS IN THE HUMANITIES: THE ROMANTIC ERA (1800–1900)

MUSIC

Trends: The classic principles of balance and clarity give way to the language of feeling. Thus, musical creativity tends toward a wider range of emotional expression, greater freedom of form and highly individualistic styles. This was an age of marked advancement in instrumental construction and performance. Modern valves were added to the brass instruments, and new instruments were invented, such as the modern harp, contrabassoon, pedal timpani, and English horn. The romantic era also saw the rise of orchestral technique and the piano virtuoso. Early romanticism (to about 1850) generally stressed subtle, intimate expressions set in the short, lyrical forms of piano piece and art song. Late romanticism, with its huge symphonies and operas, tended toward a more profound, and grandiose, style.

PHILOSOPHY

In contrast to the eighteenth-century philosophers who explored the power of reason and applied it to general areas of man's existence (society, religion, morals), the nineteenth-century philosophers, led by the Germans Hegel, Schlegel, Schleiermacher and Schopenhauer, turned to the inner nature of man. In proclaiming the emotions as the fundamental seat of human nature (Schleiermacher), the freedom of self expression (Schlegel), and escape from world pessimism through the arts (Schopenhauer), these thinkers gave impetus to the romantic movement. Increasingly, attention was given to the nature and problems of art (under the discipline known as *esthetics*) throughout the romantic age.

1788 *Critique of Practical Reason*, Emmanuel Kant
1799 *Addresses on Religion*, Friedrich Schleiermacher
1819 *The World as Will and Idea*, Artur Schopenhauer
1859 *Origin of The Species*, Charles Darwin
1867 *Das Kapital*, Karl Marx
1876 *On Judging Works of Visual Art*, Conrad Fiedler
1896 *The Sense of Beauty*, George Santayana
1897 *What Is Art?*, Leo Tolstoy

LITERATURE

1730 *The Seasons*, James Thomson
1768 *Clarissa*, Samuel Richardson
1751 *Elegy Written in a Country Churchyard*, Thomas Gray
1760 *Fragments of Ancient Poetry Collected in the Highlands
         of Scotland*, James Macpherson
1762 *Fingal*, James Macpherson
1764 *Castle of Otranto*, Horace Walpole
1781 *Confessions*, Jean Jacques Rousseau
1785 *Ode to Joy*, Friedrich von Schiller
1788 *Egmont*, Johann Wolfgang Goethe
1791 *Marriage of Heaven and Hell*, William Blake
1798 *Lyrical Ballads*, Samuel Coleridge and William Wordsworth
1805 *Die Flegeljahre*, Jean Paul Richter
1808 *Faust, Part I*, Johann Wolfgang Goethe
1812 *Childe Harold's Pilgrimage*, George Byron
1817 *Manfred*, George Byron
1819 *Ode to the West Wind*, Percy Bysshe Shelley
1826 *The Last of the Mohicans*, James Fenimore Cooper
1830 *Hernani*, Victor Hugo
1831 *Notre Dame de Paris*, Victor Hugo

1850   *The Scarlet Letter*, Nathaniel Hawthorne
1851   *Moby Dick*, Herman Melville
1854   *Walden*, Henry David Thoreau
1866   *Crime and Punishment*, Feodor Dostoevski
1869   *War and Peace*, Leo Tolstoy
1880   *The Brothers Karamazov*, Feodor Dostoevski

ART

1781   *The Nightmare*, Henry Fuseli
1789   *Songs of Innocence*, William Blake
1805   *Mme. Rivière*, Jean Ingres
1814   *May 3, 1808*, Francisco Goya
1819   *The Raft of the Medusa*, Théodore Géricault
1821   *The Hay Wain*, John Constable
1822   *Dante and Virgil in Hell*, Eugène Delacroix
1824   *The Massacre of Scio*, Eugène Delacroix
1829   *Death of Sardanapalus*, Eugène Delacroix
1830–1831   *Interior of Petworth Castle*, Joseph Turner
1855   *Painter in His Studio*, Gustave Courbet
1865   *Olympia*, Edouard Manet

HISTORICAL EVENTS

1789–1794   French Revolution
1789   George Washington first president of the United States
1804   Napoleon crowned Emperor
1807   Steamboat invented by Fulton
1812   Napoleon retreats from Moscow
1819   First steamship crosses the Atlantic
1825   Opening of the Erie Canal
1830   First railroad, in England
1837   Morse telegraph
1838   Beginning of photography by Daguerre
1848   California gold rush
1861–1865   American Civil War
1869   First transcontinental railroad in America
1870   Germany defeated France in Franco-Prussian War
1876   Telephone invented by Bell
1877   Edison invented phonograph

9

IMPRESSIONISM
(1880–1918)

*ARTISTIC TRENDS, LATE
NINETEENTH CENTURY*

Everything stable and coherent is dissolved . . .
and assumes the character of the unfinished and
fragmentary.
        Arnold Hauser, *The Social History of Art*

Perspectives of the Arts and Style Movements   In our survey of the musical achievements of Western man we have tried to acquire a perspective of each epoch. Using the procedure of periodization (dividing the vast musical panorama into large, easily studied segments or movements) an attempt has been made to make music history more than a "large portrait gallery of composers,"[1] or, as Meyer writes, "more than a series of events strung like beads upon the slender thread of sequence."[2] Indeed, our thesis has been that the history of music is a history of musical styles,[3] which change in relation to the life and times of each epoch.

In trying to determine the boundaries of these music periods, we have observed that they rarely show decisive signs of their beginnings and endings. Certain monumental events or creations tend to accentuate the origins or high points, but generally the new style grows out of the old in a wavelike motion. That is, the main style gradually attains its

---

[1] Manfred Bukofzer, *The Place of Musicology in American Institutions of Higher Learning* (New York: The Liberal Arts Press, Inc., 1957), p. 30.
[2] Leonard B. Meyer, *Music, The Arts, and Ideas* (Chicago: The University of Chicago Press, 1968), p. 93.
[3] *The Place of Musicology in American Institutions of Higher Learning.*

293

peak and then slowly recedes, only to be replaced by a new wave representing a new creative ideal. Furthermore, the progression and recession of these style waves seem to be governed by the *Zeitgeist* (prevailing spirit) of the times.

This way of describing the phenomenon of style change indicates that there is no "scientific" advancement or perfection of art from one epoch to another, but merely a series of movements, some stronger and more powerful, that is, having deeper roots within the age and being more widely spread throughout the arts. Thus each period stands as an entity, possessing its own artistic profile and unique intellectual and spiritual soul—its values, ideals, and aspirations—which influence the directions, functions, forms, and content of its art.

Neoclassicism demonstrated a marked degree of similarity of style throughout the various arts. Romanticism, we found in contrast, even though largely generated by common principles in the arts, tended less toward a commonality of style and more toward multiplicity. Within the large movement of German romanticism, each artist, writer, and composer evolved a highly individualized expression, which, however, had its roots in the previous period. This point is important in our consideration of style change: the great artists, we have found, do not destroy their heritage but rebuild anew out of existing, accepted, or established esthetic concepts. In this regard we will find that in their rebellion against romanticism (as with Beethoven's confrontation with classicism), Debussy, Monet, and others did not destroy tradition (as is wont today among some circles) but exerted tremendous creative effort to extend, modify, and reconstruct the heritage of tonal and visual art.

We will find that the nearer we come to our present period the more difficult it is to discern the significant trends or stylistic "waves" in the great expanse of modern art that looms before us. It is as though we are closer to the waves, which come and go with great rapidity. Hence, lacking in our perceptive power is the vision or *perspective* furnished by historical time, which tends to bring into view, in some strange, unknowable way, only the most distinctive styles or trends and their most illustrious examples. This process of historical distillation is the result of extended periods of criticism by the connoiseur, the efforts of an untold number of practitioners, and a vast audience of listeners who nurture the style or trend.

A perspective of the arts, then, has more than an educational value in making the past come alive, and is more than an aid in differentiating the great achievements of man. It indicates, for each new generation, the need for the adoption of the philosophical point of view in dealing with the myriad styles and trends, novel as well as thoughtful, that are present in its contemporary scene and that have not as yet been subjected to the test of cultural heritage. All art—if it has any *form* (thereby permitting it to be studied, examined, and experienced again and again)—eventually passes to notoriety or oblivion on the basis of *human* taste and discrimination.

In summary, the orientation of the listener to the complexities of twentieth-century music involves more than what some music appreciation writers would have us believe, more than an intensive study of musical techniques and a priority given to the avant-garde. Furthermore, since modern music in general is prone to the constantly shifting winds of taste, it is essential that our outlook be tempered by value judgments based upon historical retrospect and a sympathetic understanding of the artist, his aims, and his times. These, then, are the premises upon which our survey of twentieth-century music will be made.

The Coming of Impressionism and Expressionism   The two major trends that announce the approaching modern era and that constitute the last major autonomous styles in music are *impressionism* and *expressionism.* The word *autonomous* refers here to a style system or common language embodying certain elements that keep recurring among a group of composers' works with considerable regularity.

As we move deeper into the twentieth century, we will observe that eclecticism and compulsion for experimentation become increasingly common, making the task of style definition and classification extremely difcult for the music historian. However, this problem has been in existence since Plato complained of the encroachments upon serious art by "modern" poet-musicians. He lamented that they "were ignorant of what was just and lawful in music, and being frenzied and unduly possessed by a spirit of pleasure, mixed dirges with hymns and paeans with dithyrambs . . . and blended every kind of music with every other." (*Laws*)[4] This description, which is analogous to our contemporary scene, points up the fact that the problem of reconciling the old and new will always be with us.

Of the many new musical streams that emerged shortly before 1900, impressionism and expressionism appear to have had the strongest and longest impact in the twentieth century. Impressionism is represented chiefly by the work of Claude Debussy (1862–1918) and expressionism by Arnold Schoenberg (1874–1951) and his followers. Since expressionism (including its derivative styles) has been one of the major continuing strains throughout much of the century, it will be discussed along with other trends in the next and final chapter, which focuses entirely upon music since Debussy.

Even though musical impressionism produced a small number of composers who adhered somewhat consistently to the basic elements of this style, the magic spell of the art of subtle tone-painting touched practically every twentieth-century musician to some extent. One of our basic objectives will be to outline the characteristics of impressionism as represented by the leading figure, Claude Debussy. But first, in order to make the esthetic goals and musical styles of Debussy and his successors clearer, let us briefly trace the origins of impressionism and discuss the stylistic relationships between music, art, and poetry.

[4] Plato, *The Laws*, R. G. Bury, ed., in the Loeb Classical Library, 2 vols., 1926, Vol. I, p. 245.

Paris: The Setting of the New Style   In the last decades of the nineteenth century, the cultural center of Europe shifted from Germany to France, and specifically to Paris, the mecca for artistic innovation since medieval times. Given impetus by a wave of prosperity following the French financial crash and depression of the 1870s, a social climate of opulence and luxury arose in Paris. Parisian artistic taste became permeated by a kind of sophisticated sensuality mixed with a cool, reserved intellectualism—important traits common to all of the French fine arts of the era. This period of affluence, which continued until the outbreak of World War I in 1914, marked the end of not only the old world but a way of political and social life. Artistically the era was headed by such important painters, musicians, and poets as Monet, Renoir, Debussy, and Mallarmé, whose work clearly signalized the approaching twentieth-century concepts of music and art.

We have noted throughout our survey of Western music that the cultural setting of the epoch has a direct relationship to the style and content of the arts. In this regard it is interesting to reflect upon the various phases through which French art has passed over the centuries: the religious-centered Gothic, the classical undertones of the court of Louis XIV during the French Baroque, the decorative logic of the rococo, and the revolutionary spirit that undergirded the arts of the romantic age. The period to be discussed, the impressionistic, covering the last decades of the nineteenth and opening of the twentieth centuries, is generally referred to as the *fin de siècle*; it could also be appropriately labeled the *sensate age* in French culture. It is in some respects a continuation of the romantic movement, especially in its pursuit of rich, luxuriant color effects in all of the arts. However, what immediately separates the two movements is the impressionists' interest in the small instead of the large and, especially, their substitution of sensualism for the romantics' love of conflict, drama, mystery, and passion.

A partial explanation for these characteristics of impressionism is to be found, as was intimated earlier, in the French life of the times. For example, the *fin de siècle* represents the epitome of an age, the climax in luxurious living and personal pleasure. It has been described by Hauser as an atmosphere of estheticism, characterized by "the passive, purely contemplative attitude to life."[5] In this hedonistic society people regarded the arts as a form of escape from reality, that is, from the practical and routine way of bourgeois life. The tendency was, in the words of Hauser, "to seek a higher, more sublimated and more artificial world than the previous romantics."

It is not difficult to understand why Wagnerism not only was emulated by noted French composers (Saint-Saëns and Franck) but was also established as a kind of cult in Parisian intellectual circles. Although its mammoth and heroic rhetoric was quite opposed to the emerging impressionistic mentality favoring the small and the casual, the sensuousness and dreamlike world of Wagnerian art appealed to many, including lead-

[5] *The Social History of Art,* Vol. IV, p. 180.

ing symbolist-poets such as Mallarmé, Verlaine, and Baudelaire. Indicative of the rising esthetic of the times is the statement by Dujardin, the founder of the new journal, *Revue Wagnérienne* (1885) who writes: "The new Wagnerian art recreates the complete feeling of reality by appealing to all the senses at once."[6] Debussy, who was early in his career an advocate of Wagnerism (later he completely rejected the style), mirrors the same esthetic of the times when he writes:

> Music should humbly seek to please: within these limits great beauty may well be found. Extreme complication is contrary to art. Beauty must appeal to the senses, must provide us with immediate enjoyment, must impress us or insinuate itself into us without any effort on our part.[7]

The real spirit of impressionism was, however, first evoked by the painters who left the romantic studio behind them and turned to the out-of-doors, to the boulevards and gardens to capture the transitory and fleeting moods and sensations. The earlier realists, led by the painter Gustave Courbet, prepared the way through their "rejection of romantic flights of imagination and academic glorification of the heroic past."[8]

THE NATURE OF IMPRESSIONISM: CHARACTERISTICS OF MUSIC AND ART

Roots of Impressionism in Painting The champions of the impressionistic style of painting include Édouard Manet (1832–1883), Claude Monet (1840–1926), Pierre Auguste Renoir (1841–1919), and Edgar Dégas (1834–1917). Their work was to some extent antedated by earlier French painters such as Charles François Daubigny (1817–1878) and Eugène Boudin (1824–1898); actually, the roots of the movement extend as far back as the English romanticist, Joseph Turner (1775–1851), in the 1830s.

Impressionism, as a fairly definite movement, came into focus in 1874, when the first impressionist exhibition was held in Paris. It was the critics of the first impressionists who called their works "impressionistic," using the term, of course, in a derogatory sense like so many style names we have noted in earlier periods. The word itself was derived from the picture *Impression: Sunrise*, exhibited by Claude Monet in the same showing of 1874, and which he referred to as "an impression of the sun rising through mist over the Thames."

[6] Jacques Barzun, *Darwin, Marx, Wagner* (New York: Doubleday and Company, Inc., 1958), p. 289.
[7] Peter S. Hansen, *An Introduction to Twentieth Century Music* (Boston: Allyn and Bacon, Inc., 1961), p. 11.
[8] *Arts and Ideas*, p. 481.

Time-Line: Impressionism

Year	Event
1894	Debussy: Prelude, *Afternoon of a Faun*
1899	Nocturnes for Orchestra; Ravel: *Pavane for a Dead Infanta*
1903	Ravel: String Quartet
1905	Debussy: *La Mer*
1908	Debussy: *Children's Corner* (piano)
1910	Debussy: Preludes, Book I (*The Engulfed Cathedral, Footsteps in the Snow*)
1912	Ravel: *Daphnis and Chloé*
1918	Death of Debussy
1920	Ravel: *La Valse*

The impressionistic movement was at its height from 1874 to 1886—the date of the last exhibition in Paris. Gradually, the style became more formalistic and mathematical and less casual and spontaneous, particularly in the work of Georges Seurat. His famous painting of 1886, *A Sunday Afternoon on the Island of the Grande Jatte*, marked the trend away from the naturalistic, representational mode toward the modern concept of non-representational art (abstract paintings bearing no lifelike imagery).

The impressionists' interest centered upon familiar, daily events and scenes, garden settings, still life, and seascapes. A spontaneous, almost accidental approach to the subject matter generally prevailed, the aim being to capture a feeling, emotion, mood, or atmospheric condition at a given moment.

In quite the opposite vein to the romantics, these artists generally depicted the lighthearted qualities of humans at play or work rather than the profound, tragic, and passionate experiences of life. The principal elements or qualities stressed in their paintings include much emphasis on the full spectrum of color, preferably the quiet tints rather than the brilliant, forceful colors of the romantics; a vagueness of form and outline; a tendency toward emotional neutrality (avoidance of extremes such as violence, despair, anger, and the like) and understatement of effect, that is, never quite filling in the details to make a concrete form. Many of these characteristics, we shall observe, are equally applicable to the music and poetry of the *fin de siècle*.

SOME LANDMARKS IN IMPRESSIONIST PAINTING

DATE	TITLE	ARTIST
1860	*Concert in the Tuileries Gardens*	Édouard Manet
1869	*La Grenouillère*	Claude Monet
1869	*Café Interior*	Claude Monet
1870	*Diligence at Louveciennes*	Camille Pissarro
1871	*Westminster Bridge*	Claude Monet
1872	*Impression: Sunrise*	Claude Monet
1873	*Monet Working in His Garden in Argenteuil*	Pierre Renoir
1874	*The Dancing Class*	Edgar Dégas
1878	*The Road Menders, Rue Mosnier*	Édouard Manet
1894	*Rouen Cathedral, West Façade*	Claude Monet
1903	*Waterloo Bridge*	Claude Monet

Unity of Ideals in the Arts: Impression over Description What connects Debussy's *La Mer*, Monet's *Rouen Cathedral, West Façade*, and Baudelaire's poem, "Correspondences"? Although all are of different subject matter and medium, the pastel tints, whispered, silvery tones, and veiled, sensuous words seem to evolve from a common attitude or spirit of the age. As with earlier periods, the affinity rests not upon a similarity in method but on a unity of ideals, and this unity of ideals we need to explore. Our point of departure will be from the general—that is, the expressive commonalty in the arts—to the specific—the distinctive musical techniques and devices that underly Debussy's art.

All of the impressionists—the painters, musicians, and the symbolist-poets—seemed to have shared one ideal: to suggest rather than describe or depict. They were essentially interested in presenting their impression of some object, scene, or event. Somewhat different in their approach, the symbolist-poets likewise refrained from stating the object in concrete fashion and instead, employed symbols that would evoke sensual feelings and other associations. The painters', poets', and musicians' creative path was the same—through the use of sensual elements, either in beautiful, shimmering hues, words carefully chosen for their "musical," poetic qualities, or lush-sounding melodies and harmonies.

Of the three forms of art, symbolism in poetry is generally more idealistic and intellectual, involving a complicated association of words, whereas in the visual and tonal arts the esthetic impact is more physical and immediate. The first key to understanding this style, then, is to recognize that the impression of the mood or feeling evoked by or associated with the object is more important than the actual description of the object itself.

The manner in which Debussy carries this idea out in music is actually a continuation of the programmatic principle. However, instead of telling a story (as in Wagner), using concrete themes and printed program (as in Berlioz), or depicting psychological depths of feeling (Mahler), Debussy prefers to evoke the simple, untroubled mood or atmosphere of an object or scene as designated by the title (*Footsteps in the Snow, Reflections in the Water,* and so on). Sometimes these impressions seem to take on realistic qualities resulting from the use of musical devices that imitate sounds of nature. However, a realistic depiction in the manner of a Richard Strauss tone poem is obviously not the intent. "Listening to Debussy's orchestral *La Mer,*" writes Otto Deri, "it becomes obvious that the composer's aim was not to portray the unique sound images of the sea, but to penetrate to the core, to the symbolic essence, of what the sea meant to him."[9]

Fusion and Intensification of Sense Impressions   The striving toward fusion in the arts, that basic romantic concept which we saw grow from the simple joining of words and tones in the art songs of Schubert and Schumann to the grand amalgamation of all the arts under Wagner, is perhaps the chief explanation for the pronounced degree of esthetic unity among the fine arts of the impressionistic era. However, whereas Wagner concentrated on the more objective fusion in the grand manner and setting of the stage, the impressionists approached the matter of fusion on a more subtle, subjective level, that is, from the inner essence of each of the fine arts. For example, the poets employing symbols placed emphasis on the *musical* (rather than the *rational*) elements of the art form: on color, tone,

[9] Otto Deri, *Exploring Twentieth-Century Music* (New York: Holt, Rinehart and Winston, Inc., 1968), p. 155.

and rhythm of words. Moreover, the poet was intrigued by the relationships that existed among the stimuli of the various senses. Words suggestive of various sensations—tactile, visual, aural, and so on—were frequently fused together in a highly sophisticated and abstract manner.
This is borne out in the following example of symbolist poetry by
Baudelaire:

CORRESPONDENCES

> Nature is a temple whose living colonnades
> Breathe forth a mystic speech in fitful sighs;
> Man wanders among symbols in those glades
> Where all things watch him with familiar eyes.
>
> Like dwindling echoes gathered far away
> Into a deep and thronging unison
> Huge as the night or as the light of day,
> All scents and sounds and colors meet as one.
>
> Perfumes there are as sweet as the oboe's sound,
> Green as the prairies, fresh as a child's caress,
> —And there are others, rich, corrupt, profound
>
> And of an infinite pervasiveness,
> Like myrrh, or musk, or amber, that excite
> The ecstasies of sense, the soul's delight.[10]

The musician also wished to translate into musical tones a wide
variety of sensual or physical impressions, as indicated by the very titles
of Debussy's works: *Les parfums de la nuit* (Perfumes of the Night), *Le vent
dans la plaine* (The Wind in the Plain), *Des pas sur la neige* (Footsteps in
the Snow), *La fille aux cheveux de lin* (The Girl with the Flaxen Hair), *Reflets
dans l'eau* (Reflections in the Water), and *Dialogue du vent et de la mer* (The
Play of the Wind and Sea). Although it is impossible to represent these
fundamentally tactile, aural and visual sensations in tone, Debussy clearly
wished to translate the essence of the experience into tonal patterns.
Shortly, we shall see what techniques Debussy used to carry out these
objectives.

The painter followed the same esthetic path. He reached beyond the
romantics in his attempt to intensify the sensual approach to his art—
almost to the point where the viewer may vicariously reach out to feel
the vibrant warmth of the sunlight and to touch the richly colored foliage
of a Renoir garden scene (for example, *Monet Painting in His Garden in
Argenteuil* by Renoir, 1873), or perhaps feel the empathy of a moving crowd
on a bustling French boulevard (Pissarro, *The Pont Neuf*, 1901), or sense
the damp, heavy fog that enshrouds many of Monet's scenes (*Westminster
Bridge*, 1871).

---

[10] Charles Baudelaire, *The Flowers of Evil*; translation of "Correspondences"
by Richard Wilbur (New York: New Directions, 1962) p. 12. Reprinted by permission.

Claude Monet, *Impression: Sunrise*, 1872. Oil on canvas, 19½ x 25″ Musée Marmottan, Paris. Photographie Giraudon

The Coloristic Urge In romantic music we found the chief concern of the composer to be the representation of emotion. In impressionistic music it seems to be the creation of a sensual effect. Debussy shows this propensity in his emphasis on richness of timbre, or *tone color*. Moreover, we might think of him as a highly refined and skilled painter of tone colors, rather than as a sculptor or architect of giant structures in the manner of Beethoven or Wagner. In this regard, Debussy's closest counterpart is unquestionably Chopin. Although he occasionally leaned toward the decorative at times, Chopin exhibited the same French sophistication and refinement in his art.

Just as the impressionists Monet and Renoir sought a fuller spectrum of colors and explored the broken-color technique, that is, the use of patches and dabs of color, so, too, did Debussy look beyond the romantic musicians' limited palette to a realm of kaleidoscopic tones and shadings. Furthermore, as Thomson writes, "he used the orchestral palette as impressionist painters used theirs, not for the accenting of particular passages [instrumental function] but for the creation of a general luminosity" [purely esthetic function].[11] Debussy likewise used what might be described as the *broken-color principle* in scoring, whereby instrumental tones are deployed on his "musical canvas" in small dabs and splotches for pure coloristic affect.

Generally speaking, we can designate three ways in which the leading tone-painter created color in his works: (1) shading or "coloring" of the fundamental scale tones through either chromatic alterations or adoption of exotic pentatonic and whole-tone scale patterns (melodic color); (2) combining of unusual dissonant tone combinations into complex chord structures (harmonic color); and (3) unusual methods of scoring for instruments (orchestral color).

Impressionists' Use of Color—"Exotic Scales"
(a) Whole-tone Scales
(b) Pentatonic Scale
(c) Ancient Mode (Dorian)

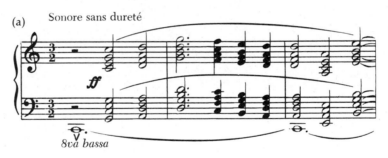

Impressionists' Use of Color—Harmony
(a) Debussy: "The Engulfed Cathedral"
Copyright owners Durand and Cie of Paris, Elkan-Vogel Co., Inc. Sole Agents
(b) Debussy: "Footsteps in the Snow"
Copyright owners Durand and Cie of Paris, Elkan-Vogel Co., Inc. Sole agents

---

[11] Virgil Thomson, *Music Reviewed* (New York: Vintage Books, 1967), p. 248.

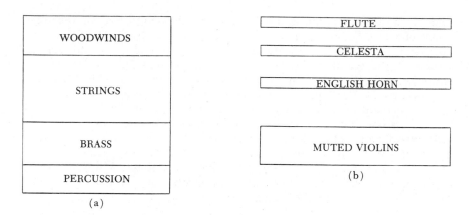

Comparison of Orchestral Color:
(a) Homogeneous blending of instruments into "thick" texture (late Romanticism)
(b) Heterogeneous blending of instruments into "thin" texture (Impressionism)

Other Points of Similarity in the Arts: Dissolution of Form   Another fundamental characteristic of impressionism is the tendency to dissolve form. With emphasis on the mood of the scene rather than the scene itself, the artists' canvases became bathed in shimmering light. Primary colors are frequently reduced to subtle gradations and solid outlines are dissolved into spots and dabs of colors.

In a similar vein, the symbolist poets glorified the fleeting rather than the permanent. Feeling replaced fact, with more being communicated "between the lines" than through the lines themselves. A corresponding dissolution of form resulted that at times is practically complete; witness the difficulty of comprehending (let alone translating) the complex poetry of this school.

The ethereal, drifting quality so prominent in Monet and Debussy is also fully manifested here. The aim "was not so much to communicate (the poet's) thoughts to others directly as to give them suggestions which will induce them to dream for themselves."[12]

The symbolists, like their counterparts in art and music, strove for a multisensory approach, using words symbolical of strange and exotic sounds, rhythms, odors, and colors, which were woven together in dreamy, ethereal forms.

Understandably, the romantics' heavy equipment of heros, epic themes, passion, pathos, power, sweeping forms, and gigantic frescos did not interest the symbolists, nor the painters and musicians. Mirroring

[12] Addison Hibbard and Horst Frenz, *Writers of the Western World* (Boston: Houghton Mifflin Company, 1954), p. 814.

their own age of opulence and estheticism, they preferred the enchantment of sensual colors and sounds and to escape from the dynamic problems of the world. The same trend is also found in late nineteenth-century drama, in the works of Chekhov, whose plays, according to Hauser, exemplify the esthetic of impressionism: a renunciation of all formal organization for fleeting, passing moods, passiveness of character portrayal, understatement of ideas, and negation of dramatic conflict.[13]

Debussy, too, dissolved the large tonal structures, heavy melodic lines and forms of the romantics into irridescent, shimmering, and vague splotches of harmony and melody. But, despite the seeming casual vagueness and transitory quality of Debussy's music, we will find that he, perhaps more than any other composer, strove for refinement and perfection down to the smallest detail.

Comparison of Impressionistic and Classical Thematic Style:
(a) Mozart: Piano Sonata in A Major
(b) Debussy: Theme from *Prelude, Afternoon of a Faun*
Copyright owners Editions Joubert of Paris, Elkan-Vogel Co., Inc. Sole Agents

CLAUDE DEBUSSY

Overview of Life and Work To merely review or catalog the details of a composer's life in an historical fashion is not the purpose of our study. What we are seeking in the picture of Debussy's life, as we sought in the other brief biographical sketches, is a key or clue to the composer's

[13] *The Social History of Art*, p. 209

musical personality. Although they were not easily discerned, we did generally find such "indicators" or clues to future musical directions in the personal sketches of many noted figures, for example, in Mozart's culture-centered childhood, in Beethoven's contempt for aristocratic oppression, in Brahms' youthful compulsion for perfection, in Wagner's megalomanic tendencies, and in Schumann's introspective and poetic nature. Likewise, Debussy's youthful confrontation with musical rule and personal taste left a legacy of music of unmatched style, beauty, and imagination.

The leading exponent of musical impressionism was born in 1862, in the town of St. Germain-en-Laye, a short distance from Paris. At eleven he entered the Paris Conservatoire, where he studied piano with Marmontel and theory and composition under Lavignac, Durand, and Massenet. His college experiences remind one of the rebellious Berlioz. Like his earlier compatriot, Debussy thrived on experimentation and innovation—forces that led to Berlioz's unusual orchestration and Debussy's unique harmonic language. To the consternation of his teachers, he would frequently improvise dissonant chord progressions at the keyboard, substituting personal taste for rules of harmony. An intensive interest in the harmonic aspect of musical invention eventually led to the formation of daring new tone combinations and unusual chord movement reminiscent of medieval organum.

Despite his general disinclination for the academic principles that lay behind musical art, Debussy won awards and prizes for piano, counterpoint, and fugue, and later the highest award of the Conservatoire, the Grand Prix de Rome. The award, won at twenty-two with his cantata *L'Enfant prodigue (The Prodigal Son)*, carried with it several years of study at the Villa Medici. However, like Berlioz, he left Rome before the completion of the term, returning in 1887 to his beloved Paris, where he took up residence as a professional composer.

Several events may be cited as important factors in the development of his musical style. Among these are the sojourns to Russia in 1882 and 1884 while in the employ of Mme. von Meck, Tchaikovsky's patroness. These excursions undoubtedly whetted his taste for the Russian color and exoticism so prominently displayed in his later musical compositions. He became further acquainted with the Russian style at the Paris Exposition of 1889, when he heard a series of concerts of Russian music conducted by Rimski-Korsakov, the master orchestrator whose influence extended to Debussy, Respighi, Ravel, Stravinsky, and others in the twentieth century.

While it is generally acknowledged that Debussy acquired his brilliant and exotic orchestral techniques from the Russians, especially Rimski-Korsakov, his impressionistic inclinations probably originated from his associations with the Parisian avant-garde. Mallarmé's home, where Thursday afternoon symposia were frequently held, was the main center for the exchange of ideas among the impressionist painters, musicians and symbolist-poets.

Debussy's close affiliation with the symbolists is mirrored in a number of songs composed in the 1890s. Some of these use texts by the leading symbolists, Baudelaire, Mallarmé, and Verlaine. Most of these light, wispy tone-paintings focus upon typical symbolist subject matter, such as reflections on nature and romance. Representative of this close affinity is Debussy's famous orchestral composition, *Prélude à l'après-midi d'un faune (Prelude to the Afternoon of a Faun)*, based on Mallarmé's poem written in 1876.

Debussy's experience in hearing Javanese music at the Paris Exposition of 1889 ranks perhaps as the second strongest influence in the shaping of the Debussyan characteristics. For example, his quaint, archaic-sounding melodic style, based largely on non-Western scale patterns such as pentatonic scales and whole-tone progressions, seems to have been derived from Oriental influences. His unprecedented lightness of effect, nonsymmetrical rhythms, and an all-pervasive "drifting" effect in harmony and melody may have been inspired by these Javanese musicians. Debussy, it should be pointed out, also collected Oriental art objects, which further substantiates his keen interest in Eastern cultures. There are also strong tinges of Spanish culture in his music, notably in the use of Spanish dance rhythms, the tango and the habañera (in *La Soirée dans Grenade, Iberia,* and *La Sérénade Interrompue.*)

To this long list of influences we must add the name of Wagner, whose freedom in the use of chromaticism, dissonant chord movement, and sensuous tone colors was also emulated by Debussy. However, the over-all tonal effect and underlying esthetic of these two composers are as different as night and day.

A partial listing of Claude Debussy's most celebrated works is as follows:

Cinq Poèmes de Baudelaire, songs (1889)
Fêtes galantes, song (1892)
String Quartet in G minor, (1893)
Prélude à l'après, midi d'un faune, symphonic poem (1894)
Nocturnes, symphonic poem (1899)
Pour le piano, suite (1901)
Pelléas et Mélisande, opera (1902)
Estampes, piano suite (1903)
La Mer, symphonic poem (1905)
Suite bergamasque, piano suite (1905)
Children's Corner, piano suite (1908)
Images, symphonic poem (1909)
Douze Préludes (Book I), piano preludes (1910)
Jeux, ballet (1912)
Douze Préludes (Book II), piano preludes (1913)
Sonata for Cello and Piano (1915)
Sonata for Flute, Viola, and Harp, (1916)
Sonata for Violin and Piano (1917)

DEBUSSY STYLE-CHART

Preferred Forms

symphonic poems	piano solos	ballets
5	24	3
songs	opera	chamber music
30	1	1 string quartet
		3 sonatas

MELODY

1. Short, fragmentary designs instead of complete themes as a rule
2. Melodies generally built upon exotic scales (pentatonic, whole-tone, and modal)
3. Melodic outlines vague, generally of a fleeting, amorphous quality; goals indistinct

HARMONY

1. Chiefly sevenths and ninths used
2. Dissonant level greater than the romantics; dissonance practically an end in itself
3. Parallel movement of chord tones in manner of medieval organum
4. Chord successions rather than progressions

TEXTURE

1. Generally homophonic
2. Usually thin and transparent vs the thick impasto of late romantics

RHYTHM

1. Strong tendency toward nonpulsatile expression
2. Irregular metrical and rhythmic patterns
3. Avoidance of strong rhythmic propulsion

EXPRESSION

1. Much care given to fine gradations and nuances in volume
2. Unprecedented attention given to softer level of volume (frequently referred to as "master of the musical whisper")

ORCHESTRATION

1. Discarded heavy, continuous full scoring of romantics
2. Favored lighter, thinner, noncontinuous method
3. Sought subtle color effects and shading (muted instruments)

OTHER MUSICAL IMPRESSIONISTS:
RAVEL

From the Sensual to the Rational   Maurice Ravel (1875–1937) occupies a position in music similar to Georges Seurat, the leading post-impressionist painter. Both were products of the impressionistic movement in France, and both took a similar path in seeking solutions to esthetic problems. Although they were essentially impressionists, their formalistic treatment of typical impressionistic subject matter and themes forecast one important artistic strain of the twentieth century, that of *classicism*. More of an attitude than a codified school or style, the classicistic strain is represented in several streams of art and music in the present century, notably in the early decades by the *cubists*—Cézanne, Picasso, and Braque —and in music by Satie and Stravinsky.

Both Ravel and Seurat evolved a more disciplined, formal approach to impressionism: Seurat in the 1880s (*A Sunday Afternoon on the Island of the Grande Jatte*, 1886) and Ravel beginning about 1899 with *Pavane pour une Infante défunte (Pavane for a Dead Infanta)*. Within the framework of the impressionistic view of reality (a shimmering, sensuous view of the world) they subtly brought the tonal configurations and visual forms into clearer focus, juxtaposing themes and painted figures into ordered, logical patterns and removing the drifting amorphous quality from their work. The concept of form in music and painting was again emphasized, resulting in more precise musical themes and melodic goals in the music of Ravel and in a kind of sculpturesque solidity in the painted human figures and forms of Seurat.

This stylistic leaning toward the classical or rational originated in Seurat's work as a stated reaction against the formlessness of Monet and other impressionists and in Ravel's music as a natural predilection, which became established early in his musical creativity. In essence, the casual, informal, and sensuous expressions of Monet and Debussy were supplanted by a preplanned, formal, and essentially rational expression—as a brief prelude to the stream of classicism that appeared with the cubists in the first decade of the century.

Ravel grew up in the same impressionistic atmosphere as Debussy, received the same academic training in music and created in the same musical forms. Since Ravel was active in composition well into the twentieth century, some automatically regard him as a successor of Debussy, while actually he was contemporary with his colleague. Interestingly, only a few years separate their Paris Conservatoire experiences and their first major compositions (Debussy composed the *Afternoon of a Faun* from 1892 to 1894, and Ravel's *Pavane for a Dead Infanta* appeared in 1899).

Most scholars believe that, even though there is a marked stylistic similarity, Ravel was not directly influenced by Debussy. Much of the stylistic affinity undoubtedly stemmed from the impressionistic environment in which Ravel matured as a musician, including his French descent (he was born in Ciboure in 1875), conservatoire background, and the very

Claude Monet, *Rouen Cathedral, West Façade, Sunlight.* 1894. Oil on canvas, 39½ x 26″.
Washington, National Gallery of Art. Chester Dale Collection.

Wassily Kandinsky, *Improvisation No. 30 (on a Warlike Theme)*. 1913. Oil on canvas, 43¼″ square. Art Institute of Chicago.

Georges Seurat, *A Sunday Afternoon on the Island of the Grand Jatte.* 1884–86. Oil on canvas, 6'9" x 10'6". Courtesy, Art Institute of Chicago

influential Parisian avant-garde movement. The attraction for the Russian style, as with Debussy, accounts for his unusual exotic coloring and brilliance in orchestration. His great skill in this area, which is so wondrously manifested in his orchestration of Mussorgski's *Pictures at an Exhibition,* is unquestionably the explanation for Ravel's continued popularity in the world's music halls.

Ravel's music is basically cast in the impressionistic vein, as demonstrated in his use of many of the same techniques common to Debussy: sensuous tone colors in melody and harmony, nature themes, emphasis on atmosphere and mood, and similar choice of musical forms (see listing below). And yet, despite these broad resemblances, there is a striking classicistic quality in Ravel's work: his themes are more straightforward and clearly outlined, his rhythms are more definite and rooted in real life (he uses many authentic rhythms, such as bolero, waltz, pavane, and habañera), and a more forceful, positive expression generally prevails. Note, for example, that the volume scale is tipped away from Debussy's soft and delicate expressions; Debussy intimates or suggests, whereas Ravel proclaims.

And finally we observe that rhythm seems to be the essence, the core of his art rather than tone color which is so much a part of Debussy's musical personality.

Below, in chronological order, is a listing of Ravel's most important contributions.

Pavane pour une Infante défunte, piano solo (1899*)
Jeux d'eau, piano solo (1901*)
Quartet in F, string quartet (1903)
Schéhérazade, song cycle (1903)
Sonatina, piano solo (1905)
Miroirs, piano solo (1905*)
Rapsodie espagnole, orchestral work (1907)
Gaspard de la nuit, piano solo (1908*)
Daphnis et Chloé, ballet (1912*)
Trois Poems de Stéphane Mallarmé, songs (1913*)
Le Tombeau de Couperin, piano solo (1917)
La Valse, orchestral work (1920*)
Orchestration of Mussorgski's *Pictures at an Exhibition* (1922)
Boléro, orchestral work (1928)
Concerto in D for Piano and Orchestra (1931)

(* indicates markedly impressionistic in style)

Summary

As with so many movements in the arts, impressionism developed as a reaction to the previous period, specifically to the powerful rhetoric of the late romantics. However, in many ways it seems to have been a continuation of romanticism. Another movement, concomitant with impressionism—expressionism—also seems to have been a continuation of the romantic stream. The dilemma of reconciling the two movements as offshoots of romanticism is resolved by suggesting or postulating that impressionism was a manifestation of the romantics' outer sensual life, while expressionism was indicative of the inner, psychological life.

REPRESENTATIVE WORKS IN THE HUMANITIES:
THE ERA OF IMPRESSIONISM (1880–1918)

MUSIC

Trends: Musical style develops in the opposite direction of late romanticism, from mighty pronouncements of profound themes to mere suggestion and intimation of mood and atmosphere. Melody and harmony have a purely esthetic function—used for sheer sensuous effect, rather than to convey thematic ideas. A series of mood impressions take the place of musical ideas in the traditional sense, resulting in vague melodic outlines and goals. Center of impressionism is France, its leading advocate Claude Debussy (1862–1918).

PHILOSOPHY

The prevailing philosophy or mental climate that permeates the arts of the impressionistic period is, according to Hauser, *estheticism.* "Its characteristic criteria, the passive, purely contemplative attitude to life, the transitoriness and noncommitting quality of experience and hedonistic sensualism, are now the standards by which art in general is judged."[14] The dominion of the moment over permanence, and the transitory, fleeting qualities so common to impressionistic music and art are, moreover, mirrored in the ideas of the leading philosopher of the age, Henri Bergson: "Intuition is a higher faculty than reason . . . existence is never static but a transition between states and movements of duration. Experience is a series of qualitative changes, which melt into and permeate one another without precise outlines."[15]

ART

1868	*The River,* Claude Monet
1871	*Westminster Bridge,* Claude Monet
1872	*Impression: Sunrise,* Claude Monet
1877	*The St. Lazare Station,* Claude Monet
1880	*Ile aux Fleurs,* Claude Monet
1881	*Luncheon of the Boating Party,* Pierre Renoir
1884–1886	*A Sunday Afternoon on the Island of the Grande Jatte,* Georges Seurat
1888	*The Sunflowers,* Vincent van Gogh (early expressionism)
1889	Eiffel Tower completed
1889	*The Thinker,* Auguste Rodin
1893	*The Cry,* Edvard Munch (expressionism)
1894	*Rouen Cathedral, West Façade,* Claude Monet
1903	*Waterloo Bridge,* Claude Monet

LITERATURE AND DRAMA

1876	*L'Après-Midi d'un Faune,* Stéphane Mallarmé
1880	*Nana,* Emile Zola
1883	*Treasure Island,* Robert Louis Stevenson
1884	*Huckleberry Finn,* Mark Twain
1887	*Der Vater,* August Strindberg
1890	*Hedda Gabler,* Henrik Ibsen
1892	*Pelléas et Mélisande,* Maurice Maeterlinck

[14] Arnold Hauser, *The Social History of Art,* (New York: Vintage Books, 1951), vol. 4, p. 180.

[15] William Fleming, *Arts and Ideas,* 3d ed. (New York: Holt, Rinehart and Winston, Inc., 1968), p. 500.

1893 *Adventures of Sherlock Holmes,* Conan Doyle
1894 *Candida,* George Bernard Shaw
1894 *The Jungle Book,* Rudyard Kipling
1897 *Cyrano de Bergerac,* Edmond Rostand
1900 *Lord Jim,* James Conrad
1904 *The Cherry Orchard,* Anton Chekhov
1913 *Pygmalion,* George Bernard Shaw
1913 *Sons and Lovers,* D. H. Lawrence
1914 *North of Boston,* Robert Frost
1914 *The Congo and other Poems,* Vachel Lindsay

HISTORICAL EVENTS

1880 Electric light invented by Thomas Edison
1883 First skyscraper in Chicago
1895 X-rays discovered by Röntgen
1896 Establishment of Nobel Prize
1898 Spanish-American War
1901 Theodore Roosevelt elected President of the United States
1903 First powered air flight, Wright brothers
1905 Revolution in Russia
1908 Henry Ford produces Model-T
1909 Peary discovers North Pole
1914 Panama Canal opened
1914 First World War begins

10

THE TWENTIETH CENTURY

THE SHAPING FORCES
OF TWENTIETH-CENTURY STYLES

> If break-up has been a vital part of their [modern
> artists'] expression, it has not always been a
> symbol of destruction . . . it has been used to
> examine more fully . . . to make more familiar
> certain aspects of life that earlier we were apt
> to neglect.
> Katherine Kuh, *Break-up: The Core of Modern Art*

The Arts as a Measure of a Civilization Stylistic change, eruption, and
fluctuation characterize the arts of the twentieth century. How do we
account for this state of flux? If art is a reflection of life—a contention basic
to this study—then we might seek our answers in the "great ideas" out
of which modern culture has been forged. An equally fruitful path would
be to examine the works of art themselves. There are many who believe
(even in our present highly materialistic age) that the spirit of the epoch,
its values and ideals, are projected into its fine arts—and rightfully so, for
obviously the writer, composer, and artist whose subject matter is generally
drawn or abstracted from life itself are most sensitive to the fluctuations
and changes in the pulse of society. No other period seems to have
demonstrated the phenomenon as graphically as ours.

The arts, then, are equally as valid a yardstick for determining cultural achievement as the formal ideas or theories generated by scientists,
mathematicians, and philosophers. Moreover, since painting, music, literature, and other forms of expression constitute the spiritual record or

313

conscience of the age, the arts—and more specifically the values derived from them—are the true measure of a culture. For "only in the realm of values do we depend upon the exercise of discrimination; history is proof that the values that a civilization accepts for itself determine whether or not that civilization will flourish or perish."[1]

Since the arts are "reflectors" as well as determinants of a culture, that is, they mirror life as well as affect it spiritually or esthetically, modern man should have considerable interest in contemporary trends. Thus it seems feasible and within the framework of this book to strive for a critical evaluation of present-day movements, even though, of course, a final answer is beyond our reach.

The Pulls of Optimism and Pessimism   *Disintegration, eruption, repudiation, tension* are terms that in a general way may define the unsettled or pessimistic state of mind. Such terms as *stability, control, wholeness of purpose,* and *resolution* seem to define a settled or optimistic state of mind. Both states have been found to dominate certain past periods of Western art and music. Therefore, since they may be regarded as artistic qualities that acquire meaning through common discourse by historians and critics, we can use them in our discussion to indicate poles to which styles may gravitate.

Furthermore, these qualities seem to be generated in the arts to a lesser or greater extent depending on the Zeitgeist of the age. Several examples, already discussed in our survey of music history, are readily brought to mind. The northern European artists of the sixteenth century, such as Dürer and Brueghel, seem to reflect the pessimism of their age, that is, the tensions and religious unrest caused by such movements as the Spanish Inquisition and the Protestant Reformation. On the other hand, the general well-being and assurance cast by Queen Elizabeth's rule was reflected in the most joyous and spontaneous flourish of music in England's history. The same comments would apply to the significant achievements in arts and ideas of fifth-century Greece under the rule of Pericles.

Concerning the romantics, even though they were often consumed with a passion for self-pity, melancholy, and intense dramatic effect, generally their works give off an aura of optimism. This is mirrored in their use of the conflict-resolution principle (the tendency to express release even after interminable conflict), their emphasis upon heroic figures and episodes in all of the arts, and their indomitable belief in the full range of human experience. Shining through, then, is their regard for the dignity of man. It is quite clear that these traits represent a positive or optimistic point of view in the arts.

What of the twentieth century? What has been the prevailing Zeitgeist in our arts and ideas? Has there been one particular gravitation or movement? How do the period's greatest minds regard our times and our artistic achievements?

[1] Mary Elizabeth Whitner, *Music in American Life Commission* (Washington: Music Educators National Conference, 1959), p. 13.

Being too close to our day, it is difficult to determine which of the several artistic trends is dominant. As to the forces that serve as well-springs for the arts, scholars generally cite several modes of thought that characterize our modern culture: *materialistic pessimism, Freudianism,* and the *plea for humanism.* The "big ideas," the formal reflections of contemporary philosophers and scientists, include *pragmatism, relativism,* and *existentialism.* The various informal and formal patterns of thought are to some extent reflected in the arts, serving in some cases as stimulus for the different streams of art and music that flow through the turbulent years of the twentieth century.

Critical Juncture in Civilization   Following the appalling carnage of the war of 1914–1918, men of good will thought that militarism, tyranny, and aggression had been crushed for all time and that lasting peace would be assured. Unfortunately, the dream was exploded in an even greater holocaust, the Second World War and other monstrous disorders of our time. In regard to the condition of man during the past fifty years, Henry Steele Commager writes:

> Ancient nations were overthrown, empires fragmented, principles of law subverted, and traditional standards of morality repudiated. The era which was to have seen the end of war ushered in instead the most terrible of wars, which rose to a climacteric in the most terrible of weapons; the era which was to have seen the triumph of democracy saw instead the triumph of tyranny; the era which was to have witnessed the triumph of science over inveterate ills heard instead the hoofbeats of the Four Horsemen of the Apocalypse.[2]

In essence, our entire civilization has been weakened by the gradual decline of optimism in the wake of a series of social and political paradoxes that have deeply disturbed the modern conscience. The first to disclose this conscience were the early twentieth-century writers, painters, and musicians, especially the expressionists, whose works clearly indicated a new trend: the depiction of harsh and painful reality.

Judging from still other veins of creativity running through twentieth-century art and music, optimism has not been completely removed. Few would deny, however, that its existence as of late has been profoundly threatened. Fortunately, then, the scale has not been completely tipped away from this key element of cultural achievement. This is not to say, of course, that only one vein of creativity exists, for indeed the opposing currents provide artistic variety and enrichment. But it does seem to point to the necessity of inspiration, inner purpose, and especially faith in oneself and humanity in striving for artistic excellence.

Actually, then, what we seem to be going through at this critical juncture of civilization is the supreme test of the human spirit. If we succeed, it could very well mean a renascence of man and his arts. Using

[2] Henry Steele Commager, "1918:1968—Is the World Safer for Anything?" *Saturday Review,* November 9, 1968, pp. 21–22.

past great ages as a standard, it would seem, therefore, that, aside from quantity and quality of work, an abundance of optimism—that is, spiritual well-being—is required to measure up to the Golden Age of Greece or the Italian High Renaissance.

The Strain of Pathos   The decline of optimism has followed a steady path, extending from the general world-weariness after the first world conflict to the total abandonment of optimism for the absurd and chaotic, as shown in some recent forms of painting, music, literature, and other of the arts. At its earliest stage the trend is symbolized in the work of the expressionists, and at its latest in the existentialists.

Born in the mood of rebellion against the futility of war and materialistic goals of society, the strain of pessimism became manifested in the arts as a form of social criticism. Members of the expressionist movement such as the painter Kirchner and the composer Schoenberg, turned to tragedy, pathos, and despair. Their power was not sought in beauty, but in tension, distortion, and anguish.

Schoenberg, working in Vienna during the first decade of the century, began experimenting with the free use of the twelve-tone scale, laying the foundation for a dissonant new language of the modern age called *atonality*[3] The first eruptive stage of twentieth-century art also saw the formation of the earliest expressionist group, called *Die Brücke* (The Bridge), founded in Dresden in 1905 by Heckel, Kirchner and Schmidt-Rottluff. Another group, called *Der Blaue Reiter* (The Blue Rider) and represented by the noted Kandinsky, among others, was established in Munich in 1911.

The primordial stirrings of expressionism actually go back to van Gogh (*Starry Night*, 1889) and Edvard Munch (*The Cry*, 1893). Their psychic and often gloomy depictions had a profound influence on the German expressionists. Expressionism and other avant-garde developments such as *futurism* were apparently influenced by Freud's work in psychoanalysis. An examination of expressionist paintings and musical scores (especially those with accompanying texts) discloses a striking affinity between Freud's probing into the recesses of the mind and the visual and tonal aberrations. The realm of the unconscious, hallucinatory visions, deep despair, and terrifying horror were prominently displayed. In short, the psychoneurotic became the dominant theme of the expressionists and their followers, such as the writers Strindberg and Kafka, the painters Kirchner and Kokoschka, and the musicians Schoenberg and Berg, to name but a few.

In attempting to mirror the dark and melancholy areas of the soul, the artists' emphasis was on extreme emotionalism executed with free use of distortion, nonnatural colors, violent postures, and exaggerated facial expressions. Negativism, gloom, and harsh physical violence, fre-

---

[3] *Atonality* refers to a system of composing in which all tones of the chromatic scale are used freely, that is, without regard for conventional keys, scales, and chords. Schoenberg's music composed after 1908 falls into this style.

Edvard Munch, *The Cry*. 1893. Lithograph on red paper. Museum of Fine Arts, Boston.
Mrs. S. W. Mosby—W. F. Warden Fund

quently for shock value (a trademark of expressionist esthetics), became their credo. Jagged melodic lines, jarring dissonances, strange eerie mixing of orchestral colors, and distorted rhythms prevail in expressionistic music, including such examples as Schoenberg's *Erwartung* (1909) and *Pierrot Lunaire* (1912).

There are many degrees of pessimism in twentieth-century arts. In literature, for example, extreme negativism began to emerge as early as Somerset Maugham's *Of Human Bondage* (1915), and found supreme statement in Jean Paul Sartre, the leading existentialist. His *Being and Nothing* (1943) and Albert Camus' *The Stranger* (1942) are essentially about nothingness, the futility and meaninglessness of all existence. "The existentialists deny the idea of God, and hence of any divine purpose inherent in the universe. The universe itself is an absurd and purposeless phenomenon."[4]

There has been no letup in the existential movement (Camus, however, later drastically altered his postion relative to humanism in *The Plague* in 1947). The continuation can be observed in certain examples of literature, drama, and music of today, such as Ionesco's *The Bald Soprano* (1950), Beckett's *Waiting for Godot* (1952), and Gunter Grass's *The Tin Drum* (1962), among others. Intensive interest in the ugly and the purely psychopathic is also characteristic of Allen Ginsberg's *Howl* (1955) and Roethke's *The Lost Son* (1948). Similar tendencies dominate the so-called *chance,* or *aleatoric,* experiments of John Cage in music, in which the principles of form and artistic communication are completely abolished.[5]

The Vein of Ethos   All has not been pathos or chaos in the tense period in which we live. The twentieth century has witnessed significant achievements in many fields of endeavor: medical advancements, space exploration, the establishment of the National Humanities Foundation, the coming of universal higher education in America, and numerous movements to correct social inequities.

It is little wonder, then, that in spite of seemingly overwhelming chaos within our society and our arts, many twentieth-century musicians, writers, and painters, working in different styles, have clung to their faith

[4] Neal M. Cross, Leslie Dae Lindon, and Robert C. Lamm, *The Search for Personal Freedom* (Dubuque: Wm. C. Brown Company Publishers, 1968) p. 414.

[5] Dadaism, a similar movement that originated in Paris at the end of World War I, rejected every moral, social, and esthetic code. John Canaday (in *The Mainstreams of Modern Art* [New York: Holt, Rinehart and Winston, Inc., 1966], p. 524) writes that "the esthetic of dada was that there is *no* esthetic, since an esthetic is built on reason and the world had demonstrated that it was without reason." There is a close relationship between the dadaists and present-day nihilistic tendencies such as those of John Cage in music. Cage claims "that as man has no control over nature he should give up his control over musical sounds." Thus, instead of communicating thoughts or feelings music should become "an unending process without any inherent design" (Otto Deri, *Exploring Twentieth Century Music* [New York: Holt, Rinehart and Winston, Inc., 1968], p. 491).

in humanity. Essentially, their creations tend toward integration rather than destruction, goal orientation rather than aimless drifting and resignation, and artistic integrity rather than negation.

Many works, of course, bear the twentieth-century stamp of a progress-oriented, materialistic society. Thus, constant regard for newness and innovation underlies much of the music and art of our time. Other artists work at a different pace and under a different personal philosophy; in fact, many of our leading composers have turned out their most significant compositions while working against the prevailing current (or fad) of the day.

Perhaps the one lesson that we are beginning to learn in the late twentieth century, after an almost ceaseless barrage of innovations (frequently for the sake of innovation), is that "legitimacy of one esthetic code does not rule out the legitimacy of another."[6] For some this has meant a discovery of the esthetic ideals and modes of another era (for example, the current renewal of interest in nineteenth-century romanticism, a period that was so heartily condemned not too long ago), and for others an exploration of ethnicism and nationalism for artistic inspiration, as represented in a great number of modern composers.

It should be understood, then, that not all music of the twentieth century springs from cynicism or pessimism; indeed, most seems to originate from what might be called imageries of rationalism and romanticism. Much of our contemporary music is closely aligned to rational procedures, ranging from attempts to capture the spirit of eighteenth-century classicism in pure orchestral sound (Piston and early Stravinsky, for example) to extremely complex forms of serial music (Boulez and late Stravinsky), which will be discussed in subsequent pages.

By far, the largest bulk of contemporary music is closely related to romantic imagery, that is, idioms, themes, subject matter, and sources of inspiration similar to nineteenth-century practices and ideals. Other works in this vein constitute striking modern adaptations of the romantic philosophy. For example, the most interesting aspect of twentieth-century romantic imagery has been the exploration of ethnic and nationalistic roots by Bartók, Copland, Shostakovich, Vaughan Williams, and others. Also prominent in twentieth-century romanticism is the eternal interest in adventure, mystery, romance, and mythology, presented in modern musical forms and language.

The same patterns of development just described—pessimism, rationalism, and romanticism—apply to contemporary art. The accompanying chart of the mainstreams of music and art shows the constant interest in these areas throughout the modern period—extending from Kandinsky and Kokoschka to de Kooning and Knaths in expressionism; from Picasso and Braque to Sheeler, Mondrian, and Saarinen in classical or rationalist imagery; and from Ryder and Homer to Hopper, Burchfield, and Wyeth in romantic or realist imagery.

[6] John Canaday, "Art and Ideals," *University Review,* State University of New York (Summer 1968), p. 26.

THE TURNING POINT
FROM ROMANTIC TO MODERN

Changing Esthetic Concepts   Among the many characteristics that separate music of the twentieth century from that of the nineteenth, the most prominent perhaps is *immediacy of effect*, as opposed to the romantic's *extension and expansion of effect*. The difference is largely due to the choice of material: central to the romantic mode is the literary-based idea (Liszt, Berlioz, Wagner), which involves a gradual unfolding of plot ending in a triumphant climax. And, even where the literary idea is not present, this same propensity exists. The modernist frequently forgoes narrative for abstract manipulation of tones, in which there is no "built-in" pattern or procedure provided by a text or story.

The romantic mind also dealt with the full range of life's experiences frequently couched in moral overtones (the pursuit of the good end, victory in conflict, glorification of the heroic, inner searching and so forth). Goals, then, became all important, to the extent that the pattern in many musical compositions may be described as a drive toward a climactic end through the overcoming of disturbances and blockages. These patterns are represented in tonal form (resolution of tense dissonant or rhythmic passages) and literary form (unfolding of complex plot or story), and are not only characteristic of the romantic drama and novel, but can also be observed in Beethoven's symphonies, the mammoth operas of Wagner, and the vast tonal edifices of Bruckner and Mahler.

Furthermore, the romantic committed to such ideals worked with a different time-span principle, one that involved spacious forms, longer themes, and delayed resolution of dissonance. Thus, time and contemplation were requisite. The modernist, on the other hand, represents the twentieth-century way of life: immediacy, speed, compression, motion, brevity, and directness prevail in many compositions, especially those of the expressionists and the classicists. The time span is decreased, impact is more direct and immediate, and resolutions are not delayed. In many modern styles resolutions are not only not required, but the traditional concept of dissonance is nonexistent.

Though all the various musical elements are important, the psychological impact of vivid harmonic tension and dynamic rhythm are essential to almost all mainstreams of twentieth-century music. However, the avant-garde in recent years (the serialists, for example, Boulez and Stockhausen), have discarded the emotive concept of music for pure cerebral manipulation of tones, substituting almost completely formalism for estheticism.

Historical Roots   As to the origination of the modern outlook, we find that both music and art seemed to have made the historical "turn" about the same time. When musicians and artists focused their attention completely on the substance of the medium itself, on the *effects* exclusive to it, they arrived at what may be considered the pivot point between the romantic and the modern age. In essence, in painting it was a "dis-

Marcel Duchamps, *Nude Descending a Staircase, No. 2.* 1912. Oil on canvas, 58″ x 35″.
Philadelphia Museum of Art (The Louise and Walter Arensberg Collection)

covery" of painting as an entity and in music a discovery of dissonance as an all-consuming element of interest.

When the post-impressionist Georges Seurat, through his formalistic approach to impressionist subject matter, placed the esthetic impact not on the representation of a scene or object but on the painting technique itself, he gave impetus to the autonomy concept in art. His contemporary, Paul Cézanne (1839–1906), the real founder of modern painting, took one more step away from reality, toward *abstraction,* the characteristic twentieth-century point of view. He demonstrated that a painting need not be confined to the representation of reality, for painting has values of its own, inherent in pure color, rhythmic movement of lines, and arrangement of forms.

The path thus blazed for succeeding artists led to three different types of abstract art; recognized imagery (life-related elements) was either (1) partially eliminated, as with the cubists Braque and Picasso; (2) completely obliterated but retaining personal expression through strong colors and free spontaneity (as with the abstract expressionists Kandinsky, Rothko, and de Kooning); or (3) completely obliterated via pure structural or geometricized patterns (Mondrian and Vasarely).

It is a curious fact that the extreme avant-garde of both the visual and tonal arts have followed the same general direction throughout the century. Since about 1950 a certain segment of artists and musicians have sought the ultimate in abstract expressionism, that is, a complete negation of human experience and imagery, as demonstrated in music by the "serialists" and "electronic experimenters" and in painting by the "geometricists." In later pages, further comparisons will be made between the arts of the contemporary era.

In regard to the roots of modernism in music, the sheer fascination with dissonance for the sake of esthetic satisfaction, so markedly demonstrated by Debussy, may be regarded as the turning point from old to new. Even though linked to romantic imagery, Debussy directed his attention to the "color" of tones, manipulating them in dissonant ways that broke the esthetic code of the romantic age. The evolution of this gradual shift to the element of dissonance as the primary focus is worth tracing momentarily.

Even though the dissonant level of the nineteenth-century romanticists was much greater than that of their classical predecessors, the romantic composer still followed the traditional rules in resolving discordant combinations. Wagner, who stands at the peak in the development of traditional harmony, raised the level of dissonance usage, stretched the limits of the "key" concept, and all but set chords free into complete "floating" motion. This process was completed by Debussy, whose chord movements were not regulated to conform to traditional progressions built around I IV V⁷ I or similar patterns. Instead, chord *streams* (chord tones all moving in the same direction) were permitted to flow with complete freedom, as mere successions, creating a suspended, drifting effect. Occasionally, chords were "grounded" from time to time by returning to the tonic key of the composition.

Umberto Boccioni, *Unique Forms of Continuity in Space.* 1913. Bronze, 3'7½" high.
Museum of Modern Art, New York (Acquired through the Lillie P. Bliss Bequest)

The trend, then, of music around 1900 was clearly toward the abandonment of the traditional ordering of tones and chords around a key center. If Debussy severed chords into a drifting state, Schoenberg and the expressionists set all of the tones of the chromatic scale free, resulting as we shall see in a complete negation of key concept and of all of the traditional principles of harmony and scales. Schoenberg's formulation of a "method of composing with twelve tones," completed about 1922, spelled the end of tonality as the dominant musical language and the establishment of atonality in the Western World.

Paradoxically, some composers of today (let us call them *abstract expressionists* or *serialists,* in attempting to follow the ideals of Schoenberg, have created such rigid, mathematical systems that they have enclosed themselves in a system that is more confining and limiting than the tonal system from which Schoenberg departed in the 1920s.

This kind of dismantling and reconstructing in different abstract forms, whether it be cubistic painting, avant-garde theater, serialist music, or electronic experimentation, is typical of our century. And here lies perhaps the chief difference between the nineteenth- and the twentieth-century artist. The romantic's ambition was to produce the "total work of art," which would appeal to all of the senses, emotions, and intellect. Hence, he put himself completely into his art and interpreted reality, the physical, natural world about him, in terms of art forms embodying continuity, wholeness, and completeness.

The twentieth-century artist, strongly influenced not by nature but by modern science, has gradually relinquished the image of *self* in his work and has interpreted reality in terms of isolated and fragmented phenomena. In fact, the history of music and art since about 1900 can be viewed as a steady movement from romantic "totality" to dissolution of form, beginning with the impressionists, including the cubists and surrealists, and finding complete embodiment in the abstract expressionists.

The nineteenth-century artist, being much less sophisticated, less self-conscious regarding "visibility" in the marketplace, and obviously much less influenced by the scientific world, was perhaps more interested in experiencing life in his art than in analyzing it.

Fragmentation of form and impersonalization of self, so characteristic of the music and art of our times, has not always been symbolical of disintegration or, at its extreme, artistic destruction. On the contrary, the expansion of our visual and auditory modes since about 1900 has opened up a whole new world of esthetic experience. Essentially, the twentieth-century artist and musician require us to see and hear with a "new" point of view, a new focus that takes us increasingly into the pure realm of art, away from the real to the abstract. And, at the same time, being given so little time for the enjoyment of the fruits of the greatest artists of our age, we are required by the proliferation of new styles and forms to be more selective and to separate the most meaningful and truly valuable from the insignificant.

THE MAINSTREAMS OF
TWENTIETH-CENTURY MUSIC

Designation of Movements: the Rationale   One of the major tasks of the music historian is to search for unity within the various periods, an endeavor that ultimately leads to the definition of the major styles and trends. Through the process of synthesis—that is, focusing upon the broad general movements rather than upon separate musical entities—the historian may communicate in a more meaningful way the over-all significance of the musical epoch.

Twenty years ago it would have been difficult if not impossible to identify the emerging currents of musical thought. Now, as we look back over more than two-thirds of the century, we note the outlines of several movements that lie at the core of the complex maze of styles and techniques comprising modern music (music since World War I, or since Claude Debussy).

The rationale for the derivation of these style movements rests upon the historical phenomenon that man's artistic nature, though changing with the times, remains basically concerned with his view of reality. The main periods of history have shown us that the artistic focus of each is essentially upon either an intellectualized interpretation of reality (rationalism or classicism) or an emotionalized interpretation (romanticism). The present century, perhaps because of its unusual state of instability caused by social and political tensions, has indicated that a third interpretation is indeed present in our arts—the psychological or expressionistic.

This latter category needs to be added to the traditional classic-romantic polarity first theorized by the nineteenth-century philosopher Friedrich Nietzsche. As has already been pointed out, there is ample evidence in the arts of the twentieth century that indicates an unprecedented movement in the psychological vein. None of the previous periods, with the possible exception of certain stages of Hellenistic art, sixteenth-century northern European art, and some phases of the romantic era, seem to have concentrated so heavily upon this view of reality.

The Quest for Form and Structure: Classicism   Seen through historical perspective, one avenue of creativity in both music and art has, since the romantic era, been moving steadily away from the real to the abstract, from life-oriented creations to pure intellectual designs, toward what we may call *classicism*, as found in much of the music of Stravinsky, Bartók, and Piston. In its extreme form we will label it *formalism*, or *structuralism*, as represented by present-day serialist composers.

Its main characteristic is the emphasis on structural principles and rational procedures over romantic feeling and emotion. Its rejection of romantic imagery as the nerve center of inspiration, and its alliance to formal, almost scientific "method," makes this mode more challenging for the listener, a fact especially true of "serial music."

The presence of the scientific attitude has had curious effects in our musical culture. Some composers since the beginning of the modern neo-classical trend (from about 1910) have found a balance between the art-science syndrome of our times. Others, turning away from art to technology for inspiration, have attempted to move music from the concert hall to the laboratory. Moreover, others, apparently in rebellion against this advancing "loss of self" mirrored in the computerization of music, have threatened the art with complete annihilation. Such outbursts are not new to the scene; as we mentioned earlier, they occurred among the dadaists during the First World War.

Resurgence of the Romantic Mind   Simultaneously with the trend toward the classic or formalistic point of view, there has been a continual interest in the "art of feeling" as expressed in folk idioms, mythology, nationalism, romance, dance, and religious idioms. This mode of creativity, rooted deeply in European and American tradition, we will call *romanticism*.

It is so named because of its continuation of the fundamental spirit behind the nineteenth-century movement, the belief that esthetic elements, ideas, and inspiration are to be derived from the rhythm of life's experiences. The central emphasis of this vast group—romantic imagery—provides a familiar ground for the listener. Romanticism, like the other two streams of contemporary music, classicism and expressionism, knows no geographical or national boundary.

Ironically, as much as the early twentieth century rebelled against the "art of feeling," there has been a strong, unremitting activity in this vein in all countries throughout the modern world, extending from Sibelius to Hanson, Harris, Shostakovich, and Copland of the present day (see chart of mainstreams of twentieth-century music: romanticism, page 366).

Looking from Within: Expressionism   Seemingly at the core of much of our modern music are strong tinges of cynicism and irony that seem to reflect the contemporary state of mind. When given full reign, this powerful strain of intense emotionalism, which began in the first decade and has continued into our present day, is generally regarded as *expressionism*. Since 1945 there has been the gradual development of an offshoot (via Anton Webern, disciple of Arnold Schoenberg), tending more toward the cerebral than the emotional.

In the following pages we will discuss the principal characteristics and leaders of the three mainstreams of twentieth-century music, beginning with expressionism.

QUEST FOR THE PSYCHOLOGICAL: EXPRESSIONISM

> A work of art can achieve no finer effect than when it transmits to the beholder the emotions that raged in the creator, in such a way that they rage and storm also in him.
>
> Arnold Schoenberg

Arnold Schoenberg (1874–1951)

New Spatial Concepts in the Arts   Arnold Schoenberg stands in the same light as two of his leading contemporaries: Pablo Picasso and Wassily Kandinsky. We might regard these three as the founders of the modern period of music and art, for they opened up new vistas that were followed by their successors.

The fact that the three made their initial mark about the same year indicates the scope of the artistic upheaval that occurred shortly before the First World War. Picasso's entrance into cubism began with his *Les Demoiselles d'Avignon* in 1907. One year later Schoenberg disclosed his impending break with tonality in his Second String Quartet. And in 1910 Kandinsky wrote his historic treatise on abstract art, *Concerning the Spiritual in Art.*

So significant are the concepts of these "prophets of the modern" that we should pause here to reflect upon their relationship to the emerging contemporary esthetic. Perhaps these concepts viewed collectively will provide insight into the enigmatic and austere style of the first "school" of modern composers, the expressionists headed by Arnold Schoenberg.

Picasso, first of all, was interested in a different way of interpreting objects: from several points of view at one time, from all sides, and from inside and out. For Kandinsky the search for the new meant a total negation of reality by replacing perspective and representational forms with pure form and color. And for Schoenberg it was also a rejection of reality —that is, *tonal reality* (traditional organization of music into keys and scales) —that had been known and practiced for several centuries. In its place he substituted *atonality*, in which tones were given a new *spatial* organization; that is, a central unifying series of twelve tones called the *twelve-tone row* were arranged in musical space in a horizontal and vertical fashion, as in the following example. (Numbers indicate the tones of the row.)

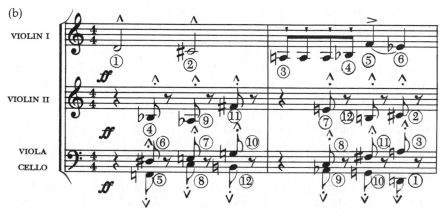

From String Quartet No. 4, Op. 37, Arnold Schoenberg
(a) The 12-tone row used for the quartet
(b) Distribution of the "row"

Schoenberg—Self-Portrait. Bettmann Archive

In summary, all three—Picasso, Kandinsky, and Schoenberg—shared a new focus, or actually a *multifocus*, which expanded the traditional modes of viewing and listening. In place of the familiar guidelines, such as perspective and representational forms in painting and tonality in music, there appeared about the end of the first decade, what we may call *simultaneity of expression*. In cubistic painting it is demonstrated by the presentation of several aspects of the object in simultaneous fashion; in Schoenberg's music by the weaving of musical ideas, or the twelve-tone row, on both the vertical and horizontal planes and in reverse and inverted directions; and in James Joyce's novels, for instance, it is manifested in the simultaneous juxtaposition of conscious as well as subconscious streams of thought. Quite obviously then, beginning about 1910, all of the arts began to take on greater complexity.

From this common esthetic ground there emerged the true artistic natures of the three leading avant-garde figures, as disclosed in the degree to which emotion or structure became dominant. Thus Picasso in his cubist phase (followed shortly after by Stravinsky) favored the rational, logical ordering of spaces, lines, and forms—the vein of ethos of which more will be said when we come to Stravinsky. Schoenberg and Kandinsky, favoring the psychic states of the soul, followed the vein of pathos, or expressionism.

Schoenberg: Life Sketch and Style   Vienna, the center and crossroads of so many musical styles throughout history, was the birthplace of the champion of expressionism in music. Schoenberg's training in music was

Oskar Kokoschka, *Webern*—Mrs. Annie Knize, New York

quite the opposite of most modern-day composers. Due to the insufficient economic resources of his family, a formal music education was not open to him. Thus, like a number of musicians before him, he acquired an unusual mastery of harmony and counterpoint through intensive self-study.

Actually, his only real teacher was Alexander von Zemlinsky, who instructed Schoenberg for a period of several months. Quite clearly, the penetrating studies of the contrapuntal-harmonic techniques of Bach, Beethoven, and Brahms molded the Schoenbergian esthetic: a predilection for highly abstract musical thought, which is so clearly stamped in almost all of his music, especially in the later atonal compositions.

Lacking a formal music education, Schoenberg found considerable difficulty in getting established in the professional musical world; however, Zemlinsky was very helpful in introducing the struggling Schoenberg to the Viennese musical circles. We learn from his biographers that the young Schoenberg, in a difficult financial position, turned to orchestrating popular music and operettas. Finally his first opus, a series of songs, was performed in Vienna in 1900. The event met with much hostile criticism, which Schoenberg later recalled by saying: "And ever since that day the scandal has never ceased."

Schoenberg's first phase of musical creativity, his "romantic period" is closely aligned to the styles of Wagner, Strauss, and Brahms. Included in this period (1896–1908) are such examples as *Verklärte Nacht* (*Transfigured Night*) (1899), the huge *Gurrelieder* (1901), and the String Quartet No. 2 (1908), which in its final movement announces the atonal style.

These "romantic" works are characterized by their post-Wagnerian profile: long, sentimental themes with the characteristically Wagnerian inflections provided by chromatics. A heavy, ponderous orchestration (*Gurrelieder*), thick harmony, and great time span reveal quite clearly the inspirational roots of this music. Uppermost is the penchant for romantic climaxes, use of literary sources for inspiration, and the presence of a chromatically saturated tonality as the main organizing force in composition. And yet throughout this music one senses a strong compulsion to compress, to concentrate, and to cut away all but the bare essentials (the *Chamber Symphony*, for example), as a prelude to the atonal Schoenberg.

The second period of creativity, the "free-atonal period," which extends from about 1908 to 1912, was the time of Schoenberg's strong attraction to the expressionists. In fact, it was during this time that we learn of a little-known facet of Schoenberg's artistic nature: his keen interest in painting as evidenced by exhibitions of his works in Vienna (in 1910), Munich, and Berlin. Indeed, during this period the struggling musician thought of turning to painting on a professional scale to augment his meager income.

Schoenberg's self-portrait (1910) is presented here with a painting of another atonalist, Anton Webern, done by a leading expressionist, Oskar Kokoschka. In general, as we have already discussed, many of the expressionistic paintings stress psychological feelings, deep despair, and pathos, frequently bordering on the neurotic. Indeed, as one writer pointed out they seem to be "case studies of tensions, fear and inner conflict."

The same expressionistic traits prevail in Schoenberg's music of this period, including: *Das Buch der hängenden Gärten* (*The Book of the Hanging Gardens*) (1908), *Three Piano Pieces* (1908), *Erwartung* (*Expectation*) (1909), *Five Pieces for Orchestra* (1909), *Pierrot Lunaire* (*Moonstruck Pierrot*) (1912), and *Die glückliche Hand* (*The Lucky Hand*) (1913). Frequently convulsive, disjunct, hypertensive, and permeated by maximum and constant searing dissonance (especially in *Pierrot Lunaire* and *Erwartung*), these works constitute the apex of musical expressionism.

Schoenberg's texts in these works provide further indication as to their psychoneurotic intent. For example, in the monodrama *Erwartung*, the plot centers around a woman who, in the dark of night, sets out to find her husband in a forest. States of anxiety and terror are portrayed as she looks in vain. Finally, she slumps down with exhaustion, only to sense the presence of a human form by her feet. The discovering of her husband's corpse touches off feelings of psychoneurosis and eventual overt pathological reactions.

In *Die glückliche Hand*, another "nightmare" opera as Peter Hansen describes it, Schoenberg again concentrates on terror, as indicated in the stage directions for the opening scene:

> The stage is almost dark. Towards the front lies the man with his face to the floor. On his back sits a fantastic cat-like animal (hyena with large feather wings) which apparently has bitten the man's neck.[7]

[7] Peter S. Hansen, *An Introduction to Twentieth-Century Music* (Boston: Allyn and Bacon, Inc., 1961), p. 69.

The "Sick Moon" from *Pierrot Lunaire* by Arnold Schoenberg. Used by permission of Belmont Music Publishers, Los Angeles, and Universal Edition, Vienna.

Aside from the highly expressionistic qualities of this period, Schoenberg developed many of the features common to his later works and those of his disciples in the expressionistic school, Berg and Webern. These include the exploitation of unusual color effects seldom if ever used before, such as flute flutter-tonguing, pointillism (fragmentation of the orchestration into bits and scraps of tonal fabric that are assigned to instruments in rapid succession), use of extensive muting, extreme "stratospheric" ranges of instruments, and harmonics.[8]

Above all, we note in this middle period the typically modern penchant for tightness of structure, sparseness of orchestration, motivic manipulation, and especially the tendency toward brevity. Themes, moreover, are disjunct and angular, involving jagged leaps of not only an octave but intervals of greater compass. Also, the modern trait of *athematic melody* is strongly evident (melodies do not have the traditional sound and structure of phrases and cadences). Clearly, as one writer commented, a state of *intrasubjectivity* has begun to enter musical thought.

Schoenberg's famous twelve-tone system, which constitutes the main achievement of his third and last period, had its nascent beginnings in the second period. During these years of his intensive expressionistic creativity, the composer became friends with the leading figure of the German "Blaue Reiter," and one of the founders of nonobject expressionism, Wassily Kandinsky. In later years Schoenberg reflected upon the inspiration he gained from Kandinsky's theories: "With great joy I read Kandinsky's book, *On the Spiritual in Art,* in which the road for painting is pointed out."[9]

As was mentioned earlier, the "modern" directions for painting and for music were strikingly similar: both turned away from the traditional point of view. For Schoenberg the essential problem was to find a substitute for tonality as a unifying force, and for Kandinsky it was the search for a substitute for perspective and representational forms.

Schoenberg's Third Period: The Twelve-Tone System   During an interim of comparative silence, roughly from about 1912 to 1923, Schoenberg gradually worked out his complex theory of musical composition known as the *twelve-tone method.* This system or procedure forms the foundation for approximately thirty compositions composed in the final period (1923–1951). These works are much more cerebral and detached than the earlier pieces, and therefore relatively unknown in the concert hall.

Before discussing these, let us briefly outline some of the principles of the twelve-tone method:

1. The first step is to construct a "row" (theme) of twelve tones selected arbitrarily from the chromatic scale.
2. The twelve tones of the chosen row are to be treated equally, being related to each other rather than to a central tone or key center as in tonality. Therefore, the magnetic attraction of the tonic both as to melody and chords is eliminated.

[8] High-pitched, artificial tones, produced by certain techniques in fingering.
[9] Arnold Schoenberg, *Style and Idea* (New York: Philosophical Library, 1950), p. 5.

3. Traditional principles of consonance and dissonance are discarded. Dissonance, then, is completely emancipated, not requiring resolution or preparation.
4. Unity is not to be found in traditional methods such as key relationships, scales, and chord progressions, but in a structural set or series of twelve tones woven throughout on two planes: the horizontal (melody) and vertical (simultaneous sounding of the row or its parts).
5. There are forty-eight possible forms of a given twelve-tone row: its basic form, its inversion form (in reverse pitch placement), its retrograde form (backwards), and retrograde inversion (both backwards and inverted). In addition, there are eleven transpositions of the basic row to the remaining degrees of the chromatic scale. Needless to say, an almost infinite number of twelve-tone series or rows may be devised by the composer.

The highly cerebral works from this final period include: *Serenade* (1923), Wind Quintet (1924), String Quartet No. 3 (1926), *Variations for Orchestra* (1928), String Quartet No. 4 (1936), Piano Concerto (1942), and *A Survivor from Warsaw* (1947). Among the salient features of these works taken as a whole is their lack of gloom and neuroses; indeed, they are much more optimistic and rational than the compositions of the preceding period. However, the dry, abstruse style—actually a highly calculated mathematical style—makes these works quite inaccessible for the general listener. Strangely, Schoenberg at times softens or, shall we say, mellows in his senior years, and occasionally introduces devices of tonality such as triads and even traditional cadences. Two of the most successful compositions among these later works are the *Theme and Variations for Band* (1943) and the Piano Concerto (1942).

Alban Berg (1885–1935)

Following Schoenberg's invention of the twelve-tone method, two of his most celebrated pupils, Alban Berg and Anton von Webern, further developed and refined the new mode of composition. The directions the two devoted disciples took were, however, quite different from the path blazed by the founder of musical expressionism.

Though arranged into the familiar classic molds such as the concerto and string quartet, Schoenberg's twelve-tone music is essentially arid and relentlessly abstruse. Berg's we will find is much more "humanized," and therefore more readily understood by the average listener. Employing narrative-based ideas as in his most important work, the opera *Wozzeck*, and a flexible use of the twelve-tone system, Berg commanded the largest listening audience. In effect, he proved that the twelve-tone style could be made accessible to those accustomed to hearing music based on traditional scales and keys.

Webern's approach to the twelve-tone system is, on the other hand, more cerebral and mathematical, thus placing his music somewhat out of reach for many listeners. However, Webern's music has had a strong influence on present-day musicians, much more so than any other composer (a spell of reverence that has also touched Stravinsky in the past decade). Since most of Webern's important contributions fall into the rational or structural style, we will postpone the discussion of Webern until we consider the classicistic strain of the twentieth century.

The reader, understandably, might tend to regard Berg and Webern as successors to Arnold Schoenberg. Quite the contrary—their atonal works began to appear soon after their esteemed teacher broke the boundaries leading into the twelve-tone method (1908–1912). As Schoenberg rejected the post-Wagnerian style for atonality, so did his pupils, reflecting, however, a different personal esthetic from that of the master expressionist.

Life Sketch   In contrast to Schoenberg, Alban Berg was born into a family of considerable means and strong cultural interests. And again, in marked contrast to the dynamic, forceful Schoenberg, Berg was highly emotional, nervous, and introverted. Frequently given to states of depression, the sensitive musician attempted suicide in 1903 over a failing grade in a humanities exam.

In 1904—about the time that expressionism in art was coming to the fore in Germany and Austria—Berg began studying composition with Schoenberg. The student–teacher relationship continued for about six years, until 1910. Webern, the third member of this Viennese triumverate, was also a student of Schoenberg during this period.

Originating in the twilight era of romanticism, it is understandable that Berg's first musical explorations would mirror the lush melodic and harmonic trends of the day. However, with the approaching prewar years, his music reflected his teacher's gradual negation of tonality, a tendency we find in Berg's String Quartet, Op. 3 (1910), Five Songs for Voice and Orchestra, Op. 4 (1912), and *Three Orchestral Pieces,* Op. 6 (1914).

Berg, like so many expressionists, was deeply troubled by the outbreak of World War I in 1914. Despite considerable health problems, he was called into the service and subsequently placed in the War Ministry in Vienna. During this period, which saw the most horrible violence in the history of mankind, Berg laid the foundations for his most important work, the opera *Wozzeck,* which was finally completed in 1921. This composition brought international acclaim to Berg almost overnight. In the year 1925 the opera was performed eleven times in Berlin, indeed, an unprecedented record for a modern opera.

Whereas Schoenberg passed from expressionism to what might be called abstract expressionism (if we may compare his later work to Kandinsky's style of painting), Berg clung to expressionism in the few compositions that followed *Wozzeck.* The unusually small output noted in Berg's catalog is typical of the three leading figures in twelve-tone music, Schoenberg, Berg, and Webern. Of the three, Schoenberg wrote the most (however, a tiny fraction of the output of the earlier classicists and romanticists), while Webern wrote the least. The urge for brevity and small output was evidently predicated by the twelve-tone style, which, because of its constant high dissonance rate, demanded a short time span—at least until composers created new techniques or, like Berg, devised interesting ways of combining old and new.

Wozzeck It is a supercharged expressionistic opera of three acts, divided into five scenes each. Cast into the tragic framework and reinforced by a twentieth-century setting and atonal dissonance, the ageless theme of *Wozzeck* stands as a mirror of modern, war-torn society, and especially of the aberrations engendered by the spirit of chaos.

The entire fabric of this work—its general type of text and musical style—stem directly from Schoenberg's most bizarre expressions, *Pierrot Lunaire* and *Erwartung*. Much more listenable and successful in the music hall than the Schoenberg works, *Wozzeck* has been acclaimed as one of the leading examples of twentieth-century opera.

The opera was adapted from material by George Büchner, a nineteenth-century German author. The action centers around a poor, ridiculed soldier, Wozzeck, and his unfaithful wife, Marie. In the first act, the full gamut of the expressionistic spirit is displayed: the violent captain's deriding of Wozzeck for his stupidity and the illegitimate child born unto Wozzeck's wife, Marie; haunting, frightening visions of Wozzeck's neurotic nature; Marie's flaunting of sexuality before the handsome drum major; and the military doctor's obsessive interest in Wozzeck's mental disorders.

In the third act, the tension between the principal characters finally snaps. Accompanied by a piercing, ear-splitting crescendo and incessant beating of a bass drum, Wozzeck, in a state of mad frenzy, stabs Marie and later commits suicide by drowning. At the opera's close, Wozzeck's child is seen alone on stage playing with a hobby horse, adding another element characteristic of the twentieth century: irony in deepest tragedy.

The success of *Wozzeck* can be attributed, not only to the skillful musical setting of the story (one that was assured to interest the audience), but especially to Berg's full grasp of the potentialities of atonality and the twelve-tone system in enhancing the dramatic action. No other modern opera has achieved this effect with such directness and compression of elements.

Actually, *Wozzeck* is a mixture of tonality and atonality. In this regard, Berg, the humanist of the Schoenberg group, proved that a composition embodying the twelve-tone system could be successfully created. His combining of tonality and atonality also indicated the compatibility of the two systems, a pattern later composers would frequently follow.

Berg's style is much more closely related to traditional techniques than is that of either Schoenberg or Webern. Lush, romantic-sounding sections are frequently heard intermingled with the strident dissonances so characteristic of the expressionist mentality. This is true of not only *Wozzeck* but of the four major works that followed: the *Kammer Konzert* (1925), *Lyric Suite for Strings* (1926), the opera *Lulu* (1935), and the Violin Concerto (1935).

The Violin Concerto The concerto was commissioned by the noted violinist Louis Krasner and dedicated to Manon Gropius (the daughter of Alma Mahler, to whom Berg was closely attached), who died suddenly at age eighteen. In essence, the concerto is a kind of requiem for the deceased girl, a fact that may help us to understand the fundamentally pathostoned piece of music.

The concerto consists of two separate movements, each divided into two sections as follows: I Andante, Allegretto; II Allegro, Adagio. Some writers have interpreted the lyrical and delicate first movement as a musical portrait of the lovely Manon, and the searing, dissonant edifice of the second as a depiction of her death. The closing Adagio seems to represent "the search for consolation in religious belief," manifested in a strange, celestial calm.

One accustomed to the aridity and concision of late Schoenberg is immediately impressed by the clarity and beauty of Berg's orchestral writing, and especially the successful reconciliation of tonal and twelve-tone techniques. Note below that the instrumentation of the concerto is similar to the conventional nineteenth-century orchestra (with the exception of the alto saxophone).

Flutes (and piccolos)
Oboes (and English Horns)
Clarinets
Bass clarinet
Alto saxophone
Bassoons
Contrabassoons
Horns
Trumpets
Tuba
Strings
Percussion

Berg's twelve-tone row, which serves as the foundation for the concerto, is a mixture of several ingredients that are strongly related to tonality, namely, a series of minor and major thirds, concluding with a whole-tone scale.

Tone Row, Violin Concerto by Alban Berg

Summary Berg had more romantic inclinations than the others in the twelve-tone group. In his scores the traditional beauty of melodic line, sonority, and orchestration were continued, whereas Schoenberg attempted to negate these principles. Like Schoenberg (and unlike the mature Webern, as we shall observe) Berg gave the twelve-tone row and its arrangement a highly emotional romantic tempering which closely aligned him with the nineteenth-century German movement in the arts.

Musical expressionism did not die out with Berg and Schoenberg. In the United States, through the teachings of Schoenberg (at the University of California from about the mid-1930s to 1944) and Ernst Křenek and others, the spirit and method of expressionism touched many composers, among them are Roger Sessions, Carl Ruggles, Wallingford Riegger, and Hugo Weisgall to name but a few representatives of the late twentieth century.

THE QUEST FOR MYSTERY, ROMANCE, AND FOLKLORE: THE TWENTIETH-CENTURY ROMANTICS

I love the mysterious sounds of the fields and forests, water and mountains. It pleases me greatly to be called a poet of nature, for nature has truly been the book of books for me.

Jean Sibelius

Scope and Definition of Modern Romanticism   Strange as it may seem, the powerful waves of stylistic change, first expressionism and later neoclassicism, did not smother the romantic inclination in twentieth-century musical art. In fact, it seems almost paradoxical that in our highly materialistic and computerized existence there has been a continuous interest in the nineteenth-century romantic tradition. Even as we observe the increasing attention being given to the purely scientific approach to music (serialism and electronic experiments), the legions of modern romantics have continued to remain strong well into the last decades of the century.

What, then, is modern romanticism, and how does it differ from the German movement of the last century? In brief, we might state that the twentieth-century brand of musical romanticism is fundamentally of the same outlines and content of the preceding era: it is realistic, traditional, and generally nationalistic or folkloristic in character.

Other elements are common to this vein of creativity, namely the dominance of the narrative principle and the rhetorical style. Following the path of the early romantics, many of our moderns have based their works on a story, drama, or what we may simply refer to as *narrative*. As with the earlier romantics, sometimes only short, fragmentary program notes or descriptive titles are provided as a guide for the listener. Also characteristic of both present and past romantics is the use of the *rhetorical style:* the tendency to couch musical ideas in lengthy, elaborate statements rather than in the highly compressed and concise assertions common to neoclassicism and expressionism. The rhetorical style also implies patterns of conflict and resolution, the heroic, and strongly emotive melodic lines.

Also closely identified with the romanticism of today and yesterday is the *principle of expectation.* A particular mode of listening has prevailed throughout our history of music in Western Civilization; that is, as a piece of music is performed, certain melodic ideas, chords, and the like are heard and identified. As the work unfolds they are brought to mind or recalled and related to what has gone on before. Of course, much of the esthetic enjoyment derived from this mode of listening comes from both expectation and surprise.

This principle underlies all modern romantic music, and, even though much less obvious in expressionism, it is nonetheless present (although the emancipation of dissonance has removed much of the element of surprise). In avant-garde idioms of "total serialism" and electronic music, such a principle is nonexistent, making the music quite meaningless to the average listener. The trend away from *process* (development or working out of themes involving goals and climaxes) to the static manipulation of tones is characteristic of our times, beginning with the frozenlike forms of the Picasso–Stravinsky era and extending to the complete fragmentation of tonal patterns, as in Webern and the later serialists.

Modern Romanticism vs Expressionism   How does modern romanticism differ from expressionism? A general comparison reveals that romanticism constitutes a much more positive view of man and the world. Expressionism, which focuses almost entirely upon man's darker side, covers a limited range of experience. Romanticism, on the other hand, is much broader in scope, encompassing the full sweep of human existence. The expressionist tends to turn away from outer life; the romanticist revels in its many glories. For example, themes of love, passion, drama, mystery, folk, and nationalism abound in the romanticism of today almost as much as they did in the nineteenth century. The subject matter and even the molds are much the same; the musical ideas are, of course, garbed in twentieth-century-styled harmony and melody.

The decisive difference between romanticism and expressionism can be found in the primal sources of creative energy. The expressionist derives his esthetic power or impact from extreme psychic disturbance (musically manifested in bizarre textual material and in jagged melodic lines and convulsive, piercing dissonances). The modern romanticist derives his strength, his inspiration, not from the subterranean regions of the soul but from a compulsion to recreate or interpret human experience (musically manifested in subject matter or themes drawn or abstracted from folk, national, historical, legendary, or popular sources). Also, if the expressionist examines the dark unknown regions of the psyche, the romantic explores man and the world about him.

What of the romantic's musical language? As a rule we will find that the romantics of our time are not the great upsetters of the period. For most, the syntax and musical vocabulary of their predecessors interspersed with or modified by characteristic modern devices meet their creative requirements. Some romantics, such as Copland, Barber, Vaughan Williams, Orff, and others, have greatly extended and expanded the art of music through innovation and the absorption and distillation of folk elements.

Most of the romantics compose in a quasi-tonal style. Even though the romantic may frequently make use of the expressionistic twelve-tone system, the resulting effect is strikingly different, for the romantic cannot, like the expressionist, hide his true identity or musical personality. A good case in point is Aaron Copland and his recent atonal works, but we see this especially in the great neoclassicist Stravinsky, who during the past two decades has adopted the twelve-tone system. His classic countenance seems to be stamped indelibly into every piece, whether tonal or atonal.

Summary   Modern romanticism is characterized by the following: (1) an obligation to reality, that is, a need to relate musical ideas to life experiences; (2) frequent use of indigenous (folk, ethnic, national) material; (3) dominance of feeling and emotion; (4) adherence to the nineteenth-century symphonic medium and rhetorical style; and (5) a programmatic basis stated or implied.

Three Romantics of the Twentieth Century: Sibelius, Shostakovich, and Copland

The listing of modern romantics is extensive, covering a wide variety of individual styles and regions. For our discussion, three names have been chosen because of their different approach to romanticism. They are Jean Sibelius, Dmitri Shostakovich, and Aaron Copland.

Jean Sibelius   Sibelius (1865–1957), active in the first quarter of the century, is famous for his nature tone paintings. Shostakovich (1906–   ), the leading representative of social realism in musical art, is cited for his romanticized treatment of Soviet themes. Aaron Copland (1900–   ), whose musical evolution has crossed several contemporary style movements, is the foremost spokesman of the American heritage.

Although markedly different as to style and social and geographical background, the three are closely connected with the modern romantic movement. The affinity becomes even more apparent when we place these figures against those representing the more abstruse analytical stream of neoclassicism and especially its antithesis, the dark pathos of expressionism.

Jean Sibelius may be regarded as the father of modern romanticism. He was born in the town of Tavastehus, Finland, at the time when Europe was in the midst of Wagnerism. Thus it was perhaps inevitable that the essence of his art would be colored by the bold, sweeping romantic, gesture. Furthermore, by the time of Sibelius' tone poem *Finlandia* and his First Symphony (both 1899), the music world had witnessed still other famous giants of the epic statement, Bruckner and Mahler. From them Sibelius undoubtedly inherited his penchant for the bold and massive, and perhaps from Beethoven and Brahms a particular predilection for musical logic; a third trait, a kind of austere, almost primitive earthiness, seems to be distinctly Sibelian, traceable to no other composer.

For a time Sibelius studied law at the University of Helsingfors in Helsinki, but at twenty-one he left to pursue a music career. In 1889, the young musician went to Berlin, and the following winter to Vienna, where he became familiar with the work of Brahms and Bruckner. At this time a strong feeling of Finnish nationalism was beginning to emerge as a result of the oppressive measures taken by the Russian czarist government. The change of postal and monetary systems from Finnish to Russian, the establishment of military conscription, and the restriction of Finnish newspapers gave impetus to Finnish political and cultural independence.

Sibelius came to prominence during this period, the 1890s, by giving a strong musical voice to the growing nationalistic spirit through such works as the symphonic poem *Kullervo* (1892), a huge composition for orchestra, chorus, and soloists based on material drawn from the national folk epic, the *Kalevala* (somewhat equivalent to the German romantics' valuable source, *Des Knaben Wunderhorn*). The strongly patriotic and heroic tone poem *Finlandia* (1899) won the popular favor of the masses. Soon after, Sibelius achieved national recognition by being awarded an annual stipend, which permitted him to put his full energy to musical creativity.

Although Sibelius composed in many forms, including the chamber, symphonic, choral, song, and piano idioms, his most important contributions lay in the symphonic realm, specifically seven symphonies and five symphonic (or tone) poems, as follows:

SYMPHONIES

Symphony No. 1 in E minor (1899)
Symphony No. 2 in D major (1901)
Symphony No. 3 in C major (1907)
Symphony No. 4 in A minor (1911)
Symphony No. 5 in E flat major (1915)
Symphony No. 6 in D minor (1923)
Symphony No. 7 in C major (1924)

TONE POEMS

En Saga (1892, revised 1901)
The Swan of Tuonela (1893)
Finlandia (1899, revised 1900)
Pohjola's Daughter (1906)
Tapiola (1925)

Stylistically, the Sibelius symphonic masterpieces stand quite apart from any other twentieth-century compositions. The truth of this statement becomes immediately evident when one brings to mind the noted works of his contemporaries. For example, the post-World War I excitement over the abstractions of Schoenberg and Stravinsky did not interest the Finnish tone-poet, who preferred the austere, mysterious solitude of nature.

Sibelius' large, expansive tone canvases generally suggest a scene rather than describe or narrate an event. As one writer remarked, they are "filled with imagery of northern landscape and musings on man, nature and fate." As with Bruckner and other tone-painters of the grand manner, whose works have generally been associated with similar extra-musical meanings, such subjective insights exist only in the imagination of the listener.

Following his First Symphony, which bears definite traces of Tchaikovsky, the foremost Finnish composer embarked on the gradual evolution of a highly personal style, characterized by basically powerful and elemental effects mixed with shifting moods of somberness and jubilation. The high point of this entire development is the Fourth Symphony, completed in 1911 and generally acclaimed as his chief masterpiece.

Instead of using complete melodies, Sibelius worked with motivic combinations somewhat in the manner of Beethoven. As did Bruckner, Sibelius built to a magnificent climax and used the overwhelming power of full ensemble. Unlike the late romantic, however, the nature tone-painter concentrated on transparency rather than opacity of orchestral texture. Ending passages, of course, were painted with the full, heavy romantic touch. Instrumental colors possessing the characteristic romantic pastoral effect (English horn, French horn, oboe, and deep, heavy brass) were carefully arranged to bring out the brooding, austere qualities we have come to associate with Sibelius' Northern forests, fjords, and mountains.

To be sure, the standard romantic rhetorical equipment is in full evidence: long, studied crescendos, bold, dynamic themes, and towering climaxes. Never does one feel overcome by sentimentality; Sibelius is too strong, too much like Beethoven for this effect to get in the way of his art. Indeed, the human element seems quite insignificant alongside the great peaks and valleys of the Northern romantic tradition.

Dmitri Shostakovich (1906–   ) An obligation to social reality serves as a cornerstone for much of Shostakovich's music. In place of Sibelius' visions of nature and northern landscapes, the leading Russian composer seems to derive his musical motivation from the Soviet world via historical, political, and folk sources. Uppermost is his regard for the simplicity and comprehensibility of musical thought, which stems from his conviction that musical art should communicate to the masses. Thus, unlike Sibelius, who worked with austere, somber themes, Shostakovich prefers more colorful, sentimental themes, themes that are easily grasped by the public.

This particular approach to much of his music stems in large measure from the esthetic view called *socialist realism* that was held in official quarters during the years 1930 to about 1958. The official line of thought stressed the basic emotional appeal of the arts and the importance of communicating with the people of the nation. Nikolai Shamota writes that under this view

> art is the individual expression of social tastes and predilections. . . . Art can exert its influence only if it is based on the broader esthetic likes of the people, which have resulted from all their social experiences. . . . Society's views on art indicate to art what its place in the life of the people is and determine what its subject matter should be. . . . The viewpoint of the workers and peasants becomes the viewpoint of art. . . .[10]

Additional insight into the Shostakovich esthetic is to be gained from the following:

> I am a Soviet composer, and I see our epoch as something heroic, spirited and joyous. Music cannot help having a political basis—an idea that the bourgeoisie is slow to comprehend. There can be no music without ideology. The old composers . . . most of them . . . were bolstering the rule of the upper classes. We as revolutionists have a different conception. . . . Lenin himself said that 'music is a means of unifying great masses of people.' . . . Good music lifts and heartens, and lightens people for work and effort. It may be tragic, but it must be strong. It is no longer an end in itself, but a vital weapon in the struggle.[11]

This was written in a letter to the *New York Times* in 1931, when the composer was in favor among the Soviet cultural leaders. However, in 1936 he underwent a scathing attack for his opera *Lady Macbeth*, which had run for two years to packed audiences in Leningrad. *Pravda*, the official Soviet news organ, had this to say:

> The author of *Lady Macbeth* was forced to borrow from jazz its nervous, convulsive and spasmodic music in order to lend passion to his characters. While our music critics swear by the name of socialist realism, the stage serves us, in Shostakovich's work, the coarsest kind of naturalism. The music quacks, grunts and growls and suffocates itself in order to express the amorous scenes as naturalistically as possible. And 'love' is smeared all over the opera in the most vulgar manner.[12]

---

[10] Nikolai Shamota, "On Tastes in Art," *Soviet Literature*, 1957. Reprinted in *Aesthetics Today*, edited by Morris Philipson, New York, 1961, pp. 27–30.

[11] Donald N. Ferguson, *Masterworks of the Orchestral Repertoire* (Minneapolis: University of Minnesota Press, 1958), p. 528.

[12] Joseph Machlis, *Introduction to Contemporary Music* (New York: W. W. Norton and Company, Inc., 1961), p. 285.

In 1937, with the premiere of his Fifth Symphony Shostakovich's name was restored to good standing with the Soviet party. *Pravda* praised the "grandiose vistas of the tragically tense Fifth Symphony, with its philosophically seeking." Shostakovich gained still further honor from the official party with the Piano Quintet, which brought him the Stalin Prize of one hundred thousand rubles in 1940.

What was it that restored Shostakovich to good standing with the proletariat? What was the musical standard? Apparently the criterion remains in obscurity, to the dismay of both composer and listener, although we can gain some insight from the structure and content of the Fifth Symphony and other works.

The Fifth Symphony was written according to the traditional four-movement plan: I Moderato, II Allegretto (Scherzo), III Largo, and IV Allegro non troppo. Note, however, that the scherzo is second rather than third. No program accompanies the score, other than this brief statement made by the composer:

> The theme of my symphony is the stabilization of a person-
> ality. In the center of this composition, which is conceived lyrically
> from beginning to end, I saw a man with all his experiences. The
> finale resolves the tragically tense impulses of the earlier movements
> into optimism and the joy of living.

As one would expect, the rhetorical style plays a prominent role, particularly evident in the juxtaposition of large, expansive mood settings and the gradual building of tension, which finally reaches its goal in the final movement. No doubt simplicity of structure forms a part of socialist realism, evidenced by the use of the clear-cut, phrase-structured themes that pervade the composition, and also shown in the easily followed sonata form of the first movement.

In matters of orchestration, Shostakovich achieves typical Russian brilliance through octave scoring, string and brass unisons, and xylophone figures doubled with other percussion instruments and muted brass. The instrumentation he uses is basically the same as that of the late romantics: strings; large brass group; standard woodwinds, including piccolo, E-flat clarinet, and contrabassoon; and an expanded percussion section of timpani, snare drum, tamtam, cymbals, two harps, xylophone, celesta, and piano.

Shostakovich's Seventh Symphony, the "Leningrad" (1941) is a programmatic work that deals with the events of war-torn Russia. The general spirit and character of the symphony is indicated in the composer's statements as reported by the *New York Times*. The symphony commences with a theme intended to describe the existence of

> ordinary people—people not distinguished by any special features or
> talents—just good, quiet people, going about their daily life. After
> this preliminary theme I introduce the main theme, which was
> inspired by the transformation of these ordinary people into heroes
> by the outbreak of the war. This builds up into a requiem for those
> of them who are perishing in the performance of their duty. . . .

> The fourth movement can be described by one word, victory . . . as the victory of light over darkness, of humanity over barbarism, of reason over reaction.[13]

Aaron Copland (1900–   )   Romanticism runs deep in American music, chiefly because of our musical heritage, which is firmly rooted in nineteenth-century practices. Also, the newness of our musical art (and especially the constant shadow of European superiority) has caused many American composers to turn to the romantic point of view for inspiration and wide-ranging subject matter.

In striving to develop a truly indigenous American style, many composers have turned for inspiration and ideas to the cultural roots of our land, including folk melody, dance, patriotic elements, early hymnody, jazz, and ethnic historical subject matter. Among the American composers who have followed this vein to some extent are Charles Ives (1874–1954), Roy Harris (1898–   ), Howard Hanson (1896–   ), and Aaron Copland (1900–   ).

Although these composers may be regarded as romantics, it should be stated that such a style label, as with other labels, is applicable in only a general way, designating certain phases or works usually regarded as romantic. While it is possible to put fairly definite labels on composers of earlier periods, it is obvious that the living moderns cannot be treated categorically, since the musical style of these figures tends to vary from one period or decade to the next, reflecting the trends of the times. Hence modern romanticism, like neoclassicism and expressionism, differs by degree from one composer to another. Of the above listing, those who have shown the strongest leaning toward the romantic view are Harris, Hanson, and Copland, especially in his works of the 1930s and 1940s.

One of the most distinguished representatives of twentieth-century music, Aaron Copland has been rightfully called "the dean of American music." Born in Brooklyn in 1900, Copland, like another famed American —Howard Hanson—has done much to champion the cause of modern music and the works of the younger generation of composers. Thus, through a steadfast conviction in composing music of true contemporaneity and artistic value, Copland has helped to raise American music to a high level of quality and dignity. As an active proponent of the modern, he has lectured at leading educational institutions, guest-conducted major orchestras, and has written several books, including *What to Listen for in Music* (1939), *Our New Music* (1941), *Music and Imagination* (1952), and *Copland on Music* (1960).

Particular significance is to be attached to Copland's large catalog of music, which covers many idioms and styles. His use of jazz elements and folk material in a truly artistic fashion marks the most successful attempt to integrate national American idioms. While some like to regard

---

[13] *Masterpieces of the Orchestral Repertoire,* pp. 530–531.

Charles Ives as the first "modern," the real start of the modern American movement as such actually dates from Copland's first compositions of the 1920s. The reader might assume an earlier beginning, but it should be born in mind that America's art music, largely based on the German romantic tradition, did not really come into being until the last decades of the nineteenth century.

Other major American figures contemporary with the young Copland (in the 1920s) were Charles Ives, the first avant-garde composer in America[14] and George Gershwin (1898–1937), the foremost song writer of the early twentieth century and important for his attempts at combining jazz and the symphonic medium (*Rhapsody in Blue* [1924] and Concerto in F [1926]).

Following a period of European music study at Fontainebleau in the summer of 1921, and two years of study under a Guggenheim Fellowship (1925–1927), Copland returned to America, where he entered upon his first creative phase. Largely influenced by Stravinsky (through his Paris studies under the noted Nadia Boulanger), but especially by the jazz craze, which hit in the 1920s, Copland's first works exhibit a combination of Stravinskyian neoclassicism and elements of Negro blues (*Music for the Theatre* [1925], Piano Concerto [1926], and *Symphonic Ode* [1929]).

Copland's second period, strongly romantic in character and during which his best-known works originated, began in the mid-1930s, when the nation was in the throes of the great depression. Feeling the necessity to close the gap that existed between the listener and much modern music, Copland initiated a marked change in his style by turning to folk and nationalistic material. Picturesque elements, local color, folk dance and melody, expressly Americanistic themes and subject matter, were incorporated into such works as the ballets *Billy the Kid* (1938), *Rodeo* (1942), and *Appalachian Spring* (1944); the orchestral suite *El Salón México* (1936); and the composition for narrator and orchestra, *A Lincoln Portrait* (1942).

In his third period, Copland returned to a more abstract and austere style, still imbued, however, with traces of the folk expression. This is particularly true of the noted Third Symphony, completed in 1946 under a commission by the Koussevitzky Foundation. The symphony represents a radical departure from the more functional ballets and typically romantic works of his previous period. Melodies of wide range, dissonant counterpoint, asymmetrical rhythms, and stress on form indicate a marked shift to the abstract point of view. Other works in this vein include the Violin Sonata (1943) and the Clarinet Concerto (1948).

Since the 1950s the composer has, like Stravinsky, incorporated twelve-tone techniques into his music; such works include the *Twelve Poems of Emily Dickinson* (1950), the Piano Quartet (1950), the Piano Fantasy (1957), and *Connotations for Orchestra* (1962).

[14] His "modern" techniques of polyharmony, polyrhythm, and strident, atonal dissonance predate their general acceptance by a decade or more.

THE QUEST FOR FORM AND STRUCTURE:
THE NEOCLASSIC ORIENTATION

> What is important for the lucid ordering of the work—for its crys-
> tallization—is that all the Dionysian elements . . . must be subjugated
> . . . and must finally be made to submit to the law: Apollo de-
> mands it.
>
> Igor Stravinsky, *Poetics of Music*

A belief in the power of restraint, order, and lucid simplicity has
been the conviction of a multitude of artists, musicians, and writers for
more than two thousand years. We have observed that certain epochs
characterized as "classical" such as those of the Italian High Renaissance,
seventeenth-century France, and late eighteenth-century Europe as a
whole, generally followed the precepts of ancient Greece and Rome.
However, what they emulated was the ancients' classic spirit adapted to
contemporary forms of literary, artistic, and musical expression.

The same holds true of the neoclassical strain in twentieth-century
music. Although Stravinsky's "classicism" differs in form from Mozart's,
the rational approach remains the same.

There are, of course, varieties of classicism in the contemporary
period, ranging from the interjection of modern content into Mozartian
forms (as with Prokofiev and Piston), and the adaptation of ancient Greek
and biblical themes (Stravinsky), to an almost mathematical manipulation
of tones (Webern and the modern serialists). As we approach the more
abstruse music of Webern and late Stravinsky, the formal considerations
seem at times to outweigh the expressive. Therefore, the term *abstract
classicism* would probably be more appropriate to designate a heavy concentration on analytical, calculative procedures in composing.

Rise of Modern Ethos   In view of France's long association with rationalism, it was perhaps only natural that the Parisian avant-garde would
become the champions of a taste diametrically opposed to romanticism
and its offshoot, expressionism. The neoclassical movement in music is
generally thought of as beginning about 1920, with Stravinsky's new works
in this vein. However, the way was prepared in the preceding years by a
circle of Parisians, including the musician Erik Satie (1866–1925) and the
writer Jean Cocteau. (1891–   ). In seeking to restore the Apollonian
ethos of order and structure, they rejected the vagueness and dreaminess
of Debussy and the sentimentalizing of the postromantics.

Satie, about the time Paris was reveling in estheticism, turned to
simplicity, wit, and directness of expression in such piano compositions
as *Gymnopédies* (1888), *Three Pieces in the Form of a Pear* (1903), and *Desic-
cated Embryos* (1913). The lightness, humor, and economy of means so
characteristic of Satie's music were soon to be adopted by another composer, Igor Stravinsky.

Jean Cocteau added verbal fuel to the neoclassic explosion in his little book of 1918 entitled *Coq et Arlequin (Cock and Harlequin)*, containing a series of pungent aphorisms attacking impressionists and romanticists alike; some of these are as follows:

> Wagner's works are long works which are long and long drawn out, because this old sorcerer looked upon boredom as a useful drug for the stupefaction of the faithful.
> Debussy missed his way because he fell from the German frying pan into the Russian fire. Once again the pedal blurs rhythm and creates a kind of fluid atmosphere congenial to *short sighted* ears. Satie remains intact. Hear his "Gymnopedies" so clear in their form and melancholy feeling. Debussy orchestrates them, confuses them, and wraps their exquisite architecture in a cloud.[15]

The growing atmosphere of classicism was enhanced by other noted figures who gathered in Paris at the close of the war, including the author and avid proponent of modernism, Gertrude Stein; the famed teacher and advocate of neoclassicism in music, Nadia Boulanger; the musical giant of modern classicism, Igor Stravinsky, who became a French citizen; and the originators of cubism, Pablo Picasso and Georges Braque.

Igor Stravinsky (1882–   )

Stravinsky, Picasso, and Neoclassicism   Igor Stravinsky's creative life is usually divided into several periods: the first is his romantic phase (1910–1918), including the famous ballets *The Firebird* (1910), *Petrushka* (1911), and *The Rite of Spring* (1913). The second, the time of his emerging neoclassical style, covers approximately the years 1918 to 1950. The period from 1950 to the present may be called *abstract classicism*.

As we have already noted, the drawing of parallels between music and art is particularly helpful in determining the underlying esthetic in contemporary music. Earlier, for example, we mentioned that Schoenberg's excursion into atonality paralleled Kandinsky's move into the uncharted regions of nonobjective or abstract expressionist art.

A similar relationship exists between Picasso, the prime mover of the classical or structuralist point of view in painting, and Stravinsky the originator of modern neoclassicism in music. In contrast to the radical departure of Kandinsky and Schoenberg, the two classicists retained objective reality: Picasso through recognizable *visual imagery*, Stravinsky through recognizable *musical imagery* (tonality). And, quite opposed to their expressionist predecessors, they exalted design and logic rather than the ironic and psychic.

---

[15] Jean Cocteau, *Cock and Harlequin,* translated from the French by Rollo Myers (London: The Egoist Press, 1921), pp. 4 ff.

Pablo Picasso, *Three Musicians*. 1921. Oil on canvas, 6'8" x 6'2". Philadelphia Museum of Art
A. E. Gallatin Collection

In Picasso's the *Three Musicians* (1921), for example, the emphasis is not upon romantic feeling and emotion but upon the formal arrangement of lines, cubes, colors, and planes. The subject matter, in this case three masked musicians, is discernible but there is a calculated rearrangement of the figures. Clearly, there is a subordination of natural relationships and appearance for manipulation of volume, space, planes, and colors into geometrical patterns, which cross and merge. As John Canaday writes, whether or not the artist presents a good profile or a good full face by representational standards is not the crux of the matter.

> The cubist is not interested in visual, representational standards. It is as if he were walking around the objects he is analyzing, as one is free to walk around a piece of sculpture for successive views. But he must represent all of these views at once.[16]

Beginning about 1918, a dominance of formalism also characterizes Stravinsky's music. Well-known compositions from the second period include the ballet *L'Histoire du Soldat (The Soldier's Tale)* (1918), the Octet for Wind Instruments (1923), Symphonies for Wind Instruments (1920), *Oedipus rex* (1927), the *Symphony of Psalms* (1930), and the Symphony in C (1940).

Interesting similarities can be noted between such examples as Picasso's *Three Musicians* and Stravinsky's Symphonies for Wind Instruments, both completed about the same time, 1921 and 1920 respectively. For instance, Stravinsky's neat, clean-cut melodic lines are similar to Picasso's clear, uncluttered outlines; and Stravinsky's pitting of one clearly delineated sound mass against another is similar to Picasso's juxtaposition of one plane against another; too, the almost frozen, motionless musical architecture of the *Symphonies* relates to Picasso's frozen, stationary cubes.

Absent in both are questing, impetuous romantic lines; instead, angular, pointing lines meet the eye and the ear. Absent, too, is the melodramatic emphasis, the literary subject, moral statement, and grand climax. Moreover, the impersonal, detached, abstract sounds of Stravinsky are matched by Picasso's expressionless figures; and the subdued hues of the painting are mirrored in Stravinsky's muted tone colors and restrained orchestration. In both examples a kind of cool, precise, calculated outlook seems dominant—a point of view quite removed from the melodramatic, sentimental esthetic of the postromantics.

Eric Salzman summarizes very nicely the Picasso-Stravinsky esthetic:

> Just as cubism is a poetic statement about objects and forms, about the nature of vision and the way we perceive and know forms, and about the experience of art and the artistic transformation of objects

---

[16] John Canaday, *The Mainstreams of Modern Art* (New York: Holt, Rinehart and Winston, Inc., 1966), p. 458.

and forms, so is Stravinsky's music a poetic statement about musical objects and aural forms, about the way we hear and the way we perceive and understand aural forms . . .[17]

Opening Measures, *l'Histoire du soldat* by Igor Stravinsky. Used by permission of G. Schirmer, Inc.

Abstract Classicism Stravinsky's preoccupation with the classical ideals continued into his third period, which dates from about 1950. Even though during this period the composer has become increasingly preoccupied with the twelve-tone system—regularly since 1958—the Schoenberg method has not affected his fundamentally classical outlook. As a true artist he has bent the twelve-tone system to his creative will, so to speak, producing some of the most interesting music in this vein since Berg's humanization of the Schoenberg theories.

Some examples from this period include *In Memoriam Dylan Thomas* (1954) for tenor, string quartet, and four trombones; *Canticum sacrum* (1956) for tenor, baritone, and orchestra; *Agon* (1957); *Threni* (1958); *Movements* (1959); *The Flood* (1962); *Variations for Orchestra* (1964); and *Requiem Canticles* (1966).

[17] Eric Salzman, *Twentieth-Century Music: An Introduction* (Englewood Cliffs, N.J.: Prentice-Hall, Inc., 1967), p. 49.

Pablo Picasso, *Stravinsky*. Sketch, 1917. Picture Collection, New York Public Library.

Ingrained in most of these works is the fundamental spirit of modern classicism, with its emphasis on logic, compression, and purity of design, and colored, of course, by the incisive, biting dissonance of the twelve-tone system. Other ingredients have been added or reaffirmed: a religious, ceremonious quality, a veneration of medieval mysticism, and a preference for a static harmonic style reminiscent of the Gothic composers. Above all, the master's music exhibits a greater degree of austerity and concision, which probably stems from his admiration of Anton Webern, whom he calls "the discoverer of a new distance between the musical object and ourselves and therefore, of a new measure of musical time. . . ."[18]

Béla Bartók (1881–1945)

As we near the final phase of our discussion of twentieth-century music, it would be well to reflect upon the great pathfinders and molders of modern musical thought. Several names, already discussed, immediately come to mind: Claude Debussy, who is to be cited for the unique harmonic innovations he contributed to the impressionist movement; Arnold Schoenberg, for the theories which have largely shaped the atonal music of our day; Igor Stravinsky, for his distinctive renewal of the classical spirit; and the last composer to be discussed, Béla Bartók, for his successful fusion of the folk element with musical art. Other names, some affiliated with the avant-garde, might yet become truly perceptible in the contemporary scene.

Few composers of the first half of the century possess such a dynamic and clearly marked style as Béla Bartók. His sensitive, impetuous musical personality seems to permeate the entire fiber of practically every piece he composed, seemingly in the same undefinable way that Beethoven, Mozart, Leonardo da Vinci, and Delacroix personally inscribed their works.

All of the elements employed in the creative process—melody, rhythm, harmony, and form—bear the inimitable Bartók imprint. In our attempt to define musical greatness, it would seem that this characteristic, combined with originality and a mastery of medium, constitute the chief marks of a superior artist. In fulfilling these requirements, Bartók ranks with the leading masters.

Every composer of stature has a particular imprint or musical signature: with Beethoven it is a robust rhythmic vitality, with Mozart an ingratiating melodic line, and with Stravinsky a precise, crystal-clear delineation of musical elements in the true classical manner. The Bartók trademark is his stylized treatment of the Central European folk spirit, which he transformed into powerful, driving rhythmic figures and exotically colored melodic lines.

The characteristic Bartókian mannerisms, which are manifested in such outstanding examples as his six string quartets (dating from 1908 to 1939), Concerto for Orchestra (1943), and *Music for Strings, Percussion,*

---

[18] Igor Stravinsky and Robert Craft, *Conversations* (New York: Doubleday and Company, Inc., 1963), p. 97.

Béla Bartók. Hungarian National Office for Tourism, 1939

and Celesta (1936), began to evolve as early as 1904, when the young musician discovered the intrinsic character and expressive power of folk dance and melody. Possessed with a good deal of nationalistic pride, Bartók and a fellow composer named Zoltán Kodály, set out to revive the musical heritage of their native Hungary.

Bartók's zeal for folk song study and collection led him on numerous journeys to various parts of Hungary and later to North Africa (1913) where he investigated the music of Arabic tribes. The lifelong association with this branch of music study (called *ethnomusicology*) continued even into his later years. In 1940, following the collaboration of Hungary with Nazi Germany, Bartók moved to America. For a time he held an appointment in the department of music at Columbia University, and he continued to compose until his death in 1945.

The Neoclassicism of Bartók   Since Bartók's creative interests covered a variety of different techniques, forms, and influences, it is very difficult to classify his style. Actually, Bartók seems to have been the most eclectic of the composers active in the first half of the century. Never plagiaristic, he assimilated elements of the major trends past and present: expressionism, the classical chamber style, jazz, Hungarian and Romanian folklore, impressionism, and elements of the Stravinsky art.

If we choose to place Bartók in one of the three main categories of twentieth-century music, it will become evident to the listener that expressionism is not akin to the composer's basically optimistic nature. He is much too inspired by the outer world to be set alongside Schoenberg and Berg.

Some music historians list him among the modern romantics because of his concentration on folk elements and strong emotionalism. However, a closer examination shows Bartók to be nearer the classical point of view, as evidenced in his preponderant use of classical forms such as the suite, divertimento, concerto, quartet, and sonata—genres based upon pure patterns of tone rather than romantic narrative.

This, then, his penchant for manipulation of pure sound into logically organized designs, is perhaps the first key to understanding Bartók. A second key, and one perhaps of even greater importance, is his abstraction of folk elements, which clearly stamps his work as classic in style.

Abstraction in Tonal and Visual Arts   The term *abstract* means basically the same in the visual and tonal arts: to take or extract from a subject some phase of its characteristics and to shape it into a new entity. In effect, the new adaptation stands as a symbol more or less like the original. For example, in a cubist painting by Picasso, abstraction becomes a kind of "tampering with visual truths," where parts of the human anatomy are transformed into solid geometrical masses. A good illustration is Picasso's *Nude in the Forest* (1908), in which the figure's limbs are depicted as planklike forms.

Abstraction in modern music works much the same way. For example, when Bartók the classicist employs folk material, he is likewise attracted to the possibilities of treating the element intellectually. Thus, he takes delight in reshaping or fragmenting some or all of the elements into unusual patterns—in short, in abstracting the original material. In Bartók's scores abstraction takes two major forms: melodic and rhythmic.

According to Otto Deri, the most characteristic interval in Hungarian and other East European folk songs is the perfect fourth. In the two examples that follow, observe the fourths (bracketed) in the original Hungarian folk song and their abstraction in Bartók's Third Quartet. Other melodic intervals common to Slovak folk songs are used by Bartók, such as the augmented fourth (tritone), to be noted in the following:

Hungarian Folk Song

String Quartet No. 3, first movement, mm. 87–91, Béla Bartók. Copyright 1929 by Universal Edition; renewed 1956. Copyright and renewal assigned to Boosey and Hawkes, Inc. for the U.S.A. Reprinted by permission.

Slovak Folk Song

String Quartet No. 2, second movement, opening, Béla Bartók. Copyright 1920 by Universal Edition; renewed 1948. Copyright and renewal assigned to Boosey and Hawkes, Inc. for the U.S.A. Reprinted by permission.

Rhythmic abstraction of folk tunes also occupies a prominent position in Bartók's art, chief of which are the asymmetrical groupings of beats (5, 7, etc.) and fluctuating meters (as opposed to the consistent use of one meter throughout, as in earlier periods). Changing metric patterns, for example $\frac{4}{4}$ $\frac{2}{4}$ $\frac{3}{4}$ $\frac{5}{8}$ $\frac{3}{8}$ so common to Hungarian and Romanian folk song, appear regularly in Bartók. Compare the following original folk example with Bartók's usage:

Hungarian Folk Song

From Concerto for Orchestra by Béla Bartók. Copyright 1946 by Hawkes and Son (London) Ltd. Reprinted by permission of Boosey and Hawkes, Inc.

Principles of Style   Bartók's style development encompassed essentially three periods: first period (1905–1920), absorption of folk elements from East European cultures; second period (1920–1930), application and abstraction of folk elements; and third period (1930–1945), final synthesis. Below is a chronological list of Bartók's major works by period.

FIRST PERIOD (1905–1920)

Twenty Hungarian Folksongs, for voice and piano (1905)
Two Portraits for Orchestra (1908)
Fourteen Bagatelles, for Piano (1908)
String Quartet No. 1 (1908)
Duke Bluebeard's Castle, one-act opera (1911)
Allegro barbaro, for piano (1911)
The Wooden Prince, ballet (1916)
Suite for Piano (1916)
Five Songs, for voice and piano (1916)
String Quartet No. 2 (1917)
The Miraculous Mandarin, pantomime (1919)

SECOND PERIOD (1920–1930)

Sonata No. 1 for Violin and Piano (1921)
Sonata No. 2 for Violin and Piano (1922)
Sonata for Piano (1926)
Concerto No. 1 for Piano and Orchestra (1926)
String Quartet No. 3 (1927)
Rhapsody Nos. 1 and 2 for Violin and Piano (1928)
String Quartet No. 4 (1928)
Twenty Hungarian Folksongs (1929)
Concerto No. 2 for Piano and Orchestra (1931)
Cantata profana (1930)

THIRD PERIOD (1930–1945)

String Quartet No. 5 (1934)
Music for Strings, Percussion, and Celesta (1936)
Sonata for Two Pianos and Percussion (1937)
Mikrokosmos, 153 pieces for piano (1926–1937)
Contrasts for Violin, Clarinet, and Piano (1938)
Concerto for Violin and Orchestra (1938)
Divertimento for String Orchestra (1939)
Concerto for Orchestra (1943)
Concerto No. 3 for Piano and Orchestra (1945)

To cover the many facets of Bartók's musical language would go beyond the scope of this book; however, his significant innovations in each of the main aspects of musical composition may be lightly touched upon.

Rhythm, characteristically incisive, bold, and dynamic, seems uppermost in Bartók's art. In addition to asymmetrical groupings of beats and changing meters, Bartók's unusual rhythmic style is characterized by an intensive motoristic drive. This powerful kinetic movement is propelled by irregular meters, ostinato figures, and offbeat accents. Also characteristic is the employment of polymetric schemes whereby different meters are heard simultaneously: for example, one instrument or section in duple and another in triple, thus setting up unusual cross-accents.

Bartók's harmony, though fundamentally organized tonally and covering a wide range of expression, is usually intense and strident. These qualities result both from his use of chords constructed of fourths and major and minor seconds and from the simultaneous juxtaposition of two or more different streams of harmony *(polyharmony).* Contrapuntal techniques involving imitation and canon play an important part in such works as the *Mikrokosmos* (consisting of 153 graded piano pieces), the first movement of *Music for Strings, Percussion, and Celesta* and the first and last movements of the Concerto for Orchestra.

In summary, Grout writes, "The guiding thread through all Bartók's work is the variety and skill with which he integrated the essence of his national folk music heritage with the highest forms of Western musical art."[19]

Undoubtedly Bartók's highly original style, with its ever-present invention, freshness, and spontaneity derived from the folk realm will assure the composer a lasting position in the history of music.

Anton Webern (1883–1945)

Toward Fragmentation and the Mathematical If music strove for the condition of poetry in the nineteenth century, it has become increasingly evident in the late twentieth century that it seeks the condition of mathematics. In the former, communication through the emotions was paramount. In the cerebral world of pure mathematics there is no emotion or feeling, since there is no connection with life.

For good or bad, music of the avant-garde (serialists and electronic experimenters) has become less an art of feeling and more of an art of calculation. Such terms as *synchronization, computation, manipulation, mutation, filter, splice, thinned, reverberation, decibel scale,* and *sinusoidal tones* have replaced traditional concepts. Working with highly sophisticated electronic equipment and computers, these progressive composers may be regarded perhaps more correctly as tonal engineers than as tonal artists. The trend that we are speaking of began about 1950—a short time after the end of the Second World War and a few years after the death of Anton Webern.

Up to about a decade and a half ago, the music of Anton Webern was labeled "expressionistic" and grouped accordingly with that of his twelve-tone compatriots, Schoenberg and Berg. In recent times, as a result of musical research, increased performances (and belated recordings, which finally appeared in the mid-1950s), a more accurate assessment has been made of Webern's style. To be sure, Webern was a champion of the twelve-tone technique; however, his mature musical style is diametrically opposed to that of his teacher, Arnold Schoenberg.

Schoenberg's style is essentially romantic, with deep, probing tones of pathos and despair. Webern, in his mature phase (1920s to 1945), is more of a modern-day classicist—or shall we say structuralist?—striving for the summit of form rather than emotion. Obviously, classicism here does not refer to the methods and techniques of the eighteenth century, but rather, as was mentioned earlier, to a creative attitude.

By sliding the esthetic scale more toward the rational side, with its concern for structure and design, Webern, though employing the expressionists' twelve-tone language, set into motion what was to become a major trend (since 1945 or so) in late twentieth-century musical thought. Specifically, this is a tendency to extend the traditional classic ideals of form and structure into rarified and abstruse regions in which tones

[19] Donald J. Grout, *A History of Western Music* (New York: W. W. Norton and Company, Inc., 1960), p. 617.

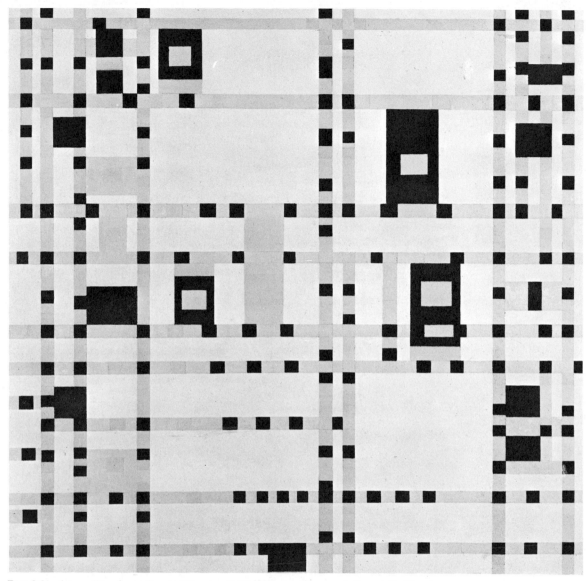

Piet Mondrian, *Broadway Boogie Woogie.* 1942. Oil on canvas, 4'2" x 4'2". The Museum of Modern Art, New York

are "engineered" with mathematical precision—first with Webern and then with the serialists and electronic experimenters.

The initial impact of the technological and materialistic Zeitgeist of the twentieth century is perhaps most completely and graphically manifested in the music of Webern and in the paintings of Mondrian. Both were occupied with the same basic esthetic during the years 1920–1944; the one may be regarded as a kind of "tonal engineer" and the other as a "pictorial engineer."

Mondrian's art, like Webern's, emphasizes a cool, geometrical precision and the constructionist's method of creating. "The new style," said Mondrian, "will spring from the metropolis." He was fascinated with the patterns offered by crisscrossing streets, skyscraper design, and architects' blueprints. Furthermore, Mondrian believed "the new art would not be individual, but collective, impersonal and international. All references to the 'primitive animal nature of man' should be rigidly excluded in order to reveal 'true human nature' through an art of 'balance, unity and stability.' "[20]

Poles apart from the romantics and most classicists of our age (much more abstruse and far out than Stravinsky's earth-bound expressions), Webern, like Mondrian, is not concerned with the passions of man but, rather, is withdrawn into the ethereal realms of pure tonal design—designs that have no relation to the earlier patterns of symphony, sonata, or concerto.

In Webern's use of the twelve-tone technique, each tone is weighted esthetically, as opposed to the more feelingful, gestaltlike melodic patterns of Schoenberg. No actual melodies per se are to be heard; thus his music is called *athematic*. Instead, flashes and bursts of tonal nebulae are projected in a kaleidoscopic fashion.

TRUMPET HARP	VIOLA CELESTA HARP	FLUTE HARP	GLOCKENSPIEL	CELESTA	CLARINET	FLUTE HARP STRINGS

"Progressive Disclosure" of Theme assigned to various instruments in rapid succession, from Five Pieces for Orchestra Op. 10, by Anton Webern. Universal Edition A.G., Vienna; Theodore Presser Company, Bryn Mawr.

Webern's high degree of sensitivity to sound produced unprecedented subtleties and orchestral effects, which stretch the performers' range and technique to the absolute limit (rehearsals of such music become less ensemble endeavors and more intensive individual tutorials). Cerebral sounds flood the air, mixed with periods of dramatic silence and barely audible dynamic levels. And the crystal-clear delineation of every tone, executed with almost surgical precision, leaves the listener with the feeling that everything has been wrung out, condensed, and compressed, resulting in transistorlike musical forms; some of Webern's pieces are less than half a minute in length). Representative examples by Webern include:

Passacaglia for Orchestra, Op. 1 (1908)
Five Movements for String Quartet, Op. 5 (1909)
Five Pieces for Orchestra, Op. 10 (1913)
Six Bagatelles for String Quartet, Op. 9 (1913)
Songs, Op. 12, Op. 19 (1914–1926)
String Trio, Op. 20 (1927)
Symphony, Op. 21 (1928)

[20] William Fleming, *Arts and Ideas*, rev. ed. (New York: Holt, Rinehart and Winston, Inc., 1963), p. 746.

Quartet for Violin, Clarinet, Tenor Saxophone, and Piano, Op. 22
   (1930)
Concerto for Nine Instruments, Op. 24 (1934)
Das Augenlicht, for mixed chorus and orchestra, Op. 26 (1935)
Variations for Piano, Op. 27 (1926)
String Quartet, Op. 28 (1938)
First Cantata, Op. 29 (1940)
Variations for Orchestra, Op. 30 (1940)
Second Cantata, Op. 31 (1943)

In the past decade Pierre Boulez and Karlheinz Stockhausen, following the Webern creed, have carried the serial technique (twelve-tone principles) to all aspects of music, including, in addition to pitch, note duration, rhythm, meter, dynamics, and articulation. The resulting music is regarded as being "totally organized," or serialized.

Electronic Experimentation   The logical step in the evolution of what Sypher calls "the loss of self"—so characteristic of the modern avant-garde—has been toward complete depersonalization of music. This has been achieved by the simple elimination of the human performer.

Beginning in the 1950s, electronic music studios developed chiefly in Cologne and subsequently in the United States (Otto Leuning, Vladimir Ussachevsky, and others). Electronic music derives its sound material from electronic devices (frequency oscillator). A piece of music is constructed by re-recording these sound fragments at higher or lower pitches, faster or slower speeds, louder or softer volumes, or backwards or forwards, and playing them through loudspeakers. A similar area of experimentation, *musique concrète* (initiated in Paris about 1948 by Pierre Schaeffer), makes use of a variety of natural sounds re-recorded onto tape.

It is not our intention to go into a detailed examination of these experimental areas; however, it is possible to relate these developments to the history of Western music and perhaps speculate as to what directions these avenues will lead. Our main concern with electronic music, then, is philosophical rather than technical, since it hinges upon esthetic trends in the contemporary world.

The Pros and Cons   When the first experiments in electronic music were carried out in Cologne in 1950, two basic reasons were cited for the scientific control of sound: first, totally organized (serialized) music had gone beyond the capabilities of the human performer; second, conventional instruments were not capable of producing the greater range of tones and timbre gradations envisioned through synthetic production.[21]

In addition, those who speak for the medium point out that it eliminates the middleman, the performer, and enables direct communication between the composer and the audience. The tonal range can be extended to an unlimited degree, and an infinite number of sounds,

[21] *Exploring Twentieth-Century Music,* p. 137.

rhythms, and total regulated control of these new elements achieved. Furthermore, rhythmic complexities formerly regarded as impossible for the human performer can now be realized.

As to its disadvantages, we note the following criticisms by leading performers and musicologists: the medium creates the problem of a gigantic amoeba because of its lack of order, its codified procedures and its constant additive method; it reaches beyond the threshold of human perception (in contrast to the composer-created forms, which remain within human limits); the stress is on the manipulation of artificially produced tones rather than on the art of creation. Also, and this seems to be the most cogent argument:

> mechanized music lacks the spontaneity of individual human performance in which each performance illuminates a work from a slightly different angle. Of more subtle effect is the unvarying regularity of mechanical rhythm which tends to destroy the elements of anticipation and surprise that the human performer instills in each successive phrase of a piece.[22]

Needless to say, electronic experiments have created a great fervor, resulting in the establishment of electronic studios in many university centers with supporting grants from public and private sectors. Perhaps if the electronic movement had occurred several decades earlier the favorable reactions would have been less visible. However, with the recent technological revolution the pattern of the life of man has completely changed.

The effect of the movement on music has of course already become noticeable, producing both positive and negative results that the practicing musician, and not the scientist, will need to reconcile.

In effect, we are on the edge of a new esthetic that will, apparently (if present trends continue), reverse the normal pattern of art in the Western world by adapting musical creativity to the scientific ideology of our age. Never before has this problem existed, that of science establishing an esthetic. In previous epochs musical art grew out of diffuse practices involving the personal tastes and efforts of numerous musicians in various regions, guided and influenced from time to time by certain private and public interests, social movements, and improvements in instrument construction. By and large, however, music was individual and personal and essentially art with a capital "A."

Very much aware of the present trend, the noted musicologist Paul Henry Lang has written that "electronic composers create a false relationship between acoustics and music, between objective nature and subjective art." And still further he states:

[22] Arthur Edwards and W. Thomas Marrocco, *Music in the United States* (Dubuque: Wm. C. Brown Company Publishers, 1968), p. 139.

For the core of the musical process, of the creative process in music, is subject neither to physics, physiology, nor mathematics but is an artistic thought process, a musical logic, virtually independent of the natural sciences. We are not dealing with physics but with music, not with science but with art; it is the human element that is decisive.[23]

Hence, whether or not electronic music will continue to grow and develop beyond its present background function in films into a recognized art form, depends on its successful fulfillment of the timeless requirement of art: that it be expressive and communicative. And in order for this to take place in the framework of the Western tradition, there must be what Luigi Nono calls "a reciprocal penetration of mind and matter and the conscious, responsible perception of the material element through the human spirit."[24] Music, then, in the words of Nono, is a testimony of man. It cannot be otherwise.

REPRESENTATIVE WORKS IN THE HUMANITIES: CONTEMPORARY PERIOD

MUSIC

Trends: Beneath the surface of change and fluctuation in style lie three main currents that characterize musical art in the twentieth century: (1) *romanticism,* which includes ethnic and nationalistic tendencies (representative composers include Jean Sibelius [1865–1957], Ralph Vaughan Williams [1872–1958], Dmitri Shostakovich [1906–   ], Aaron Copland [1900–   ]); (2) *expressionism* (Arnold Schoenberg [1874–1951], Alban Berg [1885–1935], Roger Sessions [1896–   ]); and (3) *classicism* or *structuralism* (Anton Webern [1883–1945], Igor Stravinsky [1882–   ], Serge Prokofiev [1891–1953], Béla Bartók [1881–1945], Walter Piston [1894–   ], and Pierre Boulez [1925–   ]).

PHILOSOPHY

Three major intellectual movements underscore the life and times: *pragmatism, relativism,* and *existentialism. Pragmatism,* an American movement founded by Charles Peirce and William James and further expounded in educational philosophy by John Dewey, is chiefly

[23] "Introduction," *Problems of Modern Music,* edited by Paul Henry Lang (New York: W. W. Norton and Company, Inc., 1962), p. 16.

[24] Luigi Nono, quoted by Karl H. Worner in "Current Chronicle," *The Musical Quarterly,* April, 1960, p. 271.

identified by the idea that "the meaning of conceptions is to be sought in their practical bearings."[25] Thus, the traditional idea of truth as something final, eternal and permanent, was substituted by a philosophy of practicality.

The twentieth-century idea of relativism, which is popularly known in its cliché form: "nothing is permanent except change itself," stems from profound changes in society and from the theories of Albert Einstein. His theory of relativity, which appeared in 1905, marked a drastic change in the concept of reality that had prevailed since Isaac Newton. In essence, Einstein held that "the true nature of the universe is forever unknowable, it lies beyond the farthest reach of man's mind. The statements which we call 'natural law' are creations of our mind, and are 'true' insofar as they explain the phenomena of which we are aware . . ."[26]

The *existentialists*, whose chief spokesman is Jean Paul Sartre, "deny the idea of God, and hence of any divine purpose inherent in the universe. The universe itself is an absurd and purposeless phenomenon; simply a vast group of dead celestial bodies wheeling through empty space . . . all of the history of this life on earth is without plan or purpose or meaning or sense."[27]

1905 *Special Theory of Relativity*, Albert Einstein
1916 *General Theory of Relativity*, Albert Einstein
1916 *Democracy and Education*, John Dewey
1916 *The Psychology of the Unconscious*, Carl Jung
1922 *The Decline of the West*, Oswald Spengler
1925 *Art and Nature*, John Dewey
1925 *Science and the Modern World*, Alfred North Whitehead
1934 *Art as Experience*, John Dewey
1942 *Philosophy in a New Key*, Susanne Langer
1943 *Being and Nothing*, Jean Paul Sartre
1947 *Existentialism and Human Emotions*, Jean Paul Sartre
1953 *Feeling and Form*, Susanne Langer
1953 *Philosophical Investigations*, Ludwig Wittgenstein

ART

1907 *Les Demoiselles d'Avignon*, Pablo Picasso
1911 *Man with Hat*, Pablo Picasso
1913 *Self Portrait*, Oskar Kokoschka
1914 *Winter*, Wassily Kandinsky

[25] *Webster's Third New International Dictionary* (Springfield, Mass.: G. & C. Merriam Co. Publishers, 1966), p. 1781. Definition of *pragmatism* (4b in part).
[26] Neal M. Cross, Leslie Dae Lindou, and Robert C. Lamm, *The Search for Personal Freedom* (Dubuque: Wm. C. Brown Company Publishers, 1968), p. 318.
[27] *The Search for Personal Freedom*, p. 414.

1921   *Painting No. 1,* Piet Mondrian
1921   *Three Musicians,* Pablo Picasso
1930   *The Mocker Mocked,* Paul Klee
1931   *The Persistence of Memory,* Salvador Dali
1931   *Classic Landscape,* Charles Sheeler
1932   *Girl before a Mirror,* Pablo Picasso
1940   *Willis Avenue Bridge,* Ben Shahn
1942   *Broadway Boogie Woogie,* Piet Mondrian
1948   *White Cockatoo,* Jackson Pollock
1950   *A Crow Flew By,* Andrew Wyeth
1952   *Woman I,* Willem de Kooning
1957   *Cassiopée,* Victor Vasarely
1965   *Corona,* Richard Anuszkiewicz

LITERATURE

1915   *Of Human Bondage,* Somerset Maugham
1920   *Main Street,* Sinclair Lewis
1922   *The Waste Land,* T. S. Eliot
1922   *Ulysses,* James Joyce
1925   *The Trial,* Franz Kafka
1926   *The Sun Also Rises,* Ernest Hemingway
1928   *Decline and Fall,* Evelyn Waugh
1929   *Look Homeward Angel,* Thomas Wolfe
1931   *Sanctuary,* William Faulkner
1932   *Brave New World,* Aldous Huxley
1939   *The Grapes of Wrath,* John Steinbeck
1946   *Deaths and Entrances,* Dylan Thomas
1947   *Streetcar Named Desire,* Tennessee Williams
1947   *Dr. Faustus,* Thomas Mann
1947   *The Plague,* Albert Camus
1949   *Nineteen Eighty-four,* George Orwell
1950   *The Cocktail Party,* T. S. Eliot
1950   *The Bald Soprano,* Eugene Ionesco
1952   *Waiting for Godot,* Samuel Beckett
1956   *The Fall,* Camus
1962   *The Tin Drum,* Gunter Grass

HISTORICAL EVENTS

1918   End of First World War
1924   Joseph Stalin, dictator in Russia
1927   Charles Lindbergh flies the Atlantic
1933   Hitler Chancellor of Germany
1933   Franklin D. Roosevelt inaugurated
1936   Spanish Civil War
1939   Second World War begins
1941   United States enters war
1944   Allies invade Germany

MAINSTREAMS OF MUSIC AND ART

Timeline: 1900 — 1910 — 1920 — 1930 — 1940 — 1950 — 1960 — 1970

EXPRESSIONISM

	1900	1910	1920	1930	1940	1950	1960
MUSIC:	Mahler	Schoenberg Berg	Webern	Ruggles Krenek	Sessions	Weisgall	
ART:	Munch Kokoschka	Kandinsky	Kirchner	Roualt	Rattner Shahn	de Kooning	Knaths

FOCUS: Intense Emotion, Objective Imagery

Surrealists: Dali, Miró, Tanguy

Abstract Expressionists: Pollock, Knaths, (Union of nonobjective imagery with Expressionist Techniques)

CLASSICISM

	1900	1910	1920	1930	1940	1950	1960
MUSIC:	Ravel Busoni	Satie	Stravinsky Webern	Prokofiev	Bartok Hindemith	Piston Boulez	Powell
ART:	Seurat Cezanne	Picasso	Braque Gris	Brancusi	Sheeler Mondrian	Arp LeCorbusier	Saarinen Vasarely

FOCUS: Structure
Objective or non-objective Imagery

ROMANTICISM

	1900	1910	1920	1930	1940	1950	1960
MUSIC:	Bruckner Sibelius	Vaughan Williams	Hanson	Harris	Orff	Shostakovich Britten	Barber Copland
ART:	Böcklin Ryder	Glackens Bellows	Sloan Hopper	Burchfield	Berman Levi	MacIver Dickenson	Wyeth

FOCUS: Romantic Imagery

1945   Atomic bomb, Hiroshima
1950   Korean War begins
1953   Death of Stalin
1957   Russian "sputnik" launched
1958   Krushchev premier, U.S.S.R.
1959   Castro takes over Cuba
1961   Peace Corps established
1961   Manned space flights begin
1963   Assassination of John F. Kennedy
1968   Rev. Martin Luther King, Jr. killed
1969   Richard M. Nixon inaugurated
1969   First moon landing

Conclusion

The dominant presence of the three ideologies—pragmatism, relativism, and existentialism—tends to emphasize one factor in twentieth-century life: the mutability of man. Modern art and music, with their ever-changing styles, tastes, and "isms," seem, to mirror the constant flux of our relativistic world.

The problems of reconciling these changes, tensions, and upheavals through the artistic medium—that is, to attempt "to bring order to the chaotic material of human existence"—has been most challenging to the contemporary musician. Whether to adopt the idea of innovation itself as a point of departure or to work from inspiration (or at least "ideas") has been the critical choice—and one that seems to separate the great from the inconsequential in our contemporary scene. Thus, it is not a matter of which pole to choose—ethos or pathos—since these have been the essence of art and music for centuries, but rather one of philosophy. For those who have been most communicative, and thus most successful in our age, it is one of deep conviction in the artistic process and derivative values. Even the most expressionistic composers and the most cerebral of the classicists have something to communicate when it is a statement of one's self.

At no other time, with the exception of the earlier dadaists, has there been such a strong, obsessive desire to repudiate and destroy. Happily, the modern era is represented by a considerable number of composers of stature who have not lost touch with humanity. These then, are the leading figures of the period, and it is upon their work that emphasis has been placed. As with all periods, it is not the extreme avant-garde who set the trends but the vanguard, imbued with artistic integrity and inspired by humanity and the challenge of the art medium itself.

BIBLIOGRAPHY

GENERAL *(References, Histories, Anthologies)*

Apel, Willi   *Harvard Dictionary of Music.* Cambridge, Mass., rev. 1969.

Barnes, Harry Elmer   *An Intellectual and Cultural History of the Western World.* 3 vols., 3d revised edition, New York, 1965.

Blom, Eric, (ed.)   *Grove's Dictionary of Music and Musicians,* London, 1954.

Canaday, John   *Keys to Art,* New York, 1963.

Columbia University.   *Introduction to Contemporary Civilization in the West,* 2 vols., New York, 1950.

Copland, Aaron   *What to Listen for in Music,* rev. ed., New York, 1957.

Cross, Neal M., Leslie Dae Lindou and Robert C. Lamm   *The Search for Personal Freedom,* 2 vols., Dubuque, 1968.

Davison, Archibald T. and Willi Apel, (eds.)   *Historical Anthology of Music,* Vol. I: Oriental, Medieval, and Renaissance Music; Vol. II: Baroque, Rococo, and Pre-Classical Music, Cambridge, Mass., 1950.

Donner, Morton, (ed.)   *The Intellectual Tradition of the West,* 2 vols., Glenview, 1968.

Fleming, William   *Arts & Ideas,* New York, 1968.

Gleason, Harold, (ed.)   *Examples of Music before 1400,* New York, 1946.

Grout, Donald J.   *A History of Western Music,* New York, 1960.

Harman, Alec and Wilfrid Mellers   *Man and His Music,* New York, 1962.

Lang, Paul Henry   *Music in Western Civilization,* New York, 1941.

Lerner, Edward R.   *Study Scores of Musical Styles,* New York, 1968.

Meyer, Leonard   *Emotion and Meaning in Music,* Chicago, 1956.

Myers, Bernard S.   *Art and Civilization,* New York, 1957.

Parrish, Carl and John F. Ohl (eds.)   *Masterpieces of Music Before 1750,* New York, 1951.

Read, Sir Hubert   *Encyclopaedia of the Arts,* New York, 1966.

Russell, Bertrand   *A History of Western Philosophy,* New York, 1964.

Sachs, Curt   *The Commonwealth of Art,* New York, 1946.

Schering, Arnold   *Geschichte der Musik in Beispielen* (History of Music in Examples), New York, 1950.

Sewall, John Ives   *A History of Western Art,* New York, 1961.

Starr, William J., and George F. Devine   *Music Scores Omnibus*, Parts 1, 2, Englewood Cliffs, 1964.

Strunk, Oliver (ed.)   *Source Readings in Music History*, New York, 1950.

Westrup, J. A., and F. Ll. Harrison   *The New College Encyclopedia of Music*, New York, 1960.

ANCIENT AND ORIENTAL

Anderson, Warren D.   *Ethos and Education in Greek Music*, Cambridge, Mass., 1966.

Boardman, John   *Greek Art*, New York, 1964.

Bowra, Cecil M.   *The Greek Experience*, New York, 1957.

Durant, Will   *The Life of Greece*, New York, 1966.

Fox-Strangways, A. H.   *The Music of Hindustan*, London, 1914.

Hamilton, Edith   *The Greek Way to Western Culture*, New York, 1942.

Hauser, Arnold   *The Social History of Art*, vol. 1, New York, 1951.

Horizon Book of Ancient Greece, New York, 1965.

Horizon Book of Ancient Rome, New York, 1966.

Lippman, Edward A.   *Musical Thought in Ancient Greece*, New York, 1964.

Malm, William P.   *Music Cultures of the Pacific, the Near East and Asia*, Englewood Cliffs, 1967.

Sachs, Curt   *The Rise of Music in the Ancient World, East and West*. New York, 1943.

Strong, Donald E.   *The Classical World*, New York, 1965.

MIDDLE AGES

Apel, Willi   *Gregorian Chant*, Bloomington, 1958.

Brantl, Ruth (ed.)   *Medieval Culture: The Image and the City*, New York, 1965.

Dawson, Christopher   *Religion and the Rise of Western Culture*, New York, 1950.

Durant, Will   *The Age of Faith*, New York, 1950.

Kidson, Peter   *The Medieval World*, New York, 1967.

Mâle, Emile   *The Gothic Image*, New York, 1958.

Morey, Charles R.   *Medieval Art*, New York, 1942.

Reese, Gustave   *Music in the Middle Ages*, New York, 1940.

Seay, Albert   *Music in the Medieval World*, Englewood Cliffs, 1965.

Steuart, Dom Benedict   *The Development of Christian Worship*, New York, 1953.

RENAISSANCE

Artz, Frederick   *From the Renaissance to Romanticism*, Chicago, 1962.

Berenson, Bernard   *The Italian Painters of the Renaissance*, New York, 1957.

Blume, Friedrich   *Renaissance and Baroque Music,* New York, 1967.
Burckhardt, Jacob   *The Civilization of the Renaissance in Italy,* New York, 1960.
Durant, Will   *The Renaissance,* New York, 1955.
Einstein, Alfred   *The Italian Madrigal,* Princeton, 1949.
Martindale, Andrew   *Man and the Renaissance,* New York, 1966.
Newman, Joel   *Renaissance Music,* Englewood Cliffs, 1967.
Pater, Walter   *The Renaissance,* New York, 1961.
Reese, Gustave   *Music in the Renaissance,* New York, 1959.
Sypher, Wylie   *Four Stages of Renaissance Style,* New York, 1955.

BAROQUE

Bazin, Germain   *Baroque and Rococo Art,* New York, 1966.
Bukofzer, Manfred   *Music in the Baroque Era,* New York, 1947.
David, Hans and Arthur Mendel, eds.   *The Bach Reader,* New York, 1945.
Forkel, J. N.   *J. S. Bach,* New York 1920.
Geiringer, Karl   *The Bach Family,* New York, 1959.
Hutchings, A. J. B.   *The Baroque Concerto,* New York, 1961.
Kirkpatrick, Ralph   *Domenico Scarlatti,* Princeton, 1953.
Kitson, Michal   *The Age of the Baroque,* New York, 1966.
Lang, Paul Henry   *Handel,* New York, 1966.
Palisca, Claude   *Baroque Music,* Englewood Cliffs, 1967.
Pincherle, Marc   *Vivaldi: Genius of the Baroque,* New York, 1948.
Spitta, J. A. P.   *Life of Bach,* New York, 1951, 2 vols.
Terry, Charles Sanford   *The Music of Bach,* New York, 1963.

ROCOCO AND CLASSICAL

Einstein, Alfred   *Mozart, His Character, His Work,* New York, 1962.
Friedlaender, Walter   *From David to Delacroix,* Cambridge, Mass., 1952.
Geiringer, Karl   *Haydn, A Creative Life in Music,* New York, 1947.
Kimball, F.   *The Creation of the Rococo,* Philadelphia, 1943.
Newman, William S.   *The Sonata in the Classic Era,* Chapel Hill, 1963.
Pauly, Reinhard G.   *Music in the Classic Period,* Englewood Cliffs, 1968.
Robbins-Landon, H. C.   *The Symphonies of Joseph Haydn,* London, 1955.
Scholes, Percy A.   *The Great Dr. Burney; His Life, His Travels, His Works,
    His Family and His Friends,* 2 vols., London, 1948.
Schönberger, A. and H. Soehner   *Age of the Rococo,* London, 1960.
Smith, Preserved   *The Enlightenment, 1687–1776,* New York, 1962.
Sypher, Wylie   *From Rococo to Cubism,* New York, 1963.

ROMANTICISM AND IMPRESSIONISM

Barzun, Jacques   *Classic, Romantic and Modern,* New York, 1961.
Brion, Marcel   *Romantic Art,* New York, 1960.

Brion, Marcel   *Schumann and the Romantic Age*, New York, 1956.
Burk, John N.   *The Life and Works of Beethoven*, New York, 1946.
Chissell, Joan   *Schumann*, New York, 1962.
Courthion, Pierre   *Romanticism*, Geneva, 1961.
Demuth, Norman   *Ravel*, London, 1947.
Einstein, Alfred   *Music in the Romantic Era*, New York, 1947.
Lockspeiser, Edward   *Debussy*, London, 1963.
Longyear, Rey   *Nineteenth-Century Romanticism, in Music*, Englewood Cliffs,
     1969.
Newton, Eric   *The Romantic Rebellion*, New York, 1962.
Peckham, Morse (ed.)   *Romanticism, The Culture of the Nineteenth Century*,
     New York, 1965.
Pool, Phoebe   *Impressionism*, New York, 1967.
Redlich, Hans F.   *Bruckner and Mahler*, New York, 1963.
Thayer, Alexander W.   *Life of Beethoven*, Princeton, 1964.

TWENTIETH CENTURY

Austin, William   *Music in the Twentieth Century*, New York, 1966.
Canaday, John   *The Mainstreams of Modern Art*, New York, 1966.
Davidson, Robert and Sarah Herndon, et al.   *The Humanities in Contem-
     porary Life*, New York, 1961.
Deri, Otto   *Exploring Twentieth-Century Music*, New York, 1968.
Freedman, Leonard (ed.)   *Looking at Modern Painting*, New York, 1961.
Hansen, Peter S.   *An Introduction to Twentieth Century Music*, Boston, 1961.
Johnson, Harold E.   *Jean Sibelius*, New York, 1959.
Kuh, Katherine   *Break-up, The Core of Modern Art*, New York, 1965.
Lang, Paul Henry   *Problems of Modern Music*, New York, 1966.
Langer, Susanne   *Philosophy in a New Key*, Cambridge, Mass., 1967.
Meyer, Leonard   *Music, The Arts, and Ideas*, Chicago, 1967.
Mitchell, Donald   *The Language of Modern Music*, New York, 1963.
Newman, Dika   *Bruckner, Mahler and Schoenberg*, New York, 1947.
Read, Sir Herbert   *A Concise History of Modern Painting*, New York, 1959.
Redlich, Hans F.   *Alban Berg, the Man and His Music*, New York, 1957.
Salzman, Eric   *Twentieth-Century Music: An Introduction*, Englewood Cliffs,
     1967.
Schwartz, Elliott and Barney Childs   *Contemporary Composers on Contem-
     porary Music*, New York, 1967.
Stevens, Halsey   *The Life and Music of Béla Bartók*, New York, rev. ed.
     1964.
Stravinsky, Igor   *Poetics of Music*, Cambridge, Mass., 1947.
Sypher, Wylie   *Loss of the Self in Modern Literature and Art*, New York,
     1962.
Vlad, Roman   *Stravinsky*, London, 1960.

PRONUNCIATION GUIDE

MUSICIANS, ARTISTS, TERMS AND STYLES

A

A cappella   *Ah*-cuh-*pel*-luh
Accelerando   Ah-*chel*-er-*ahn*-do
Adagio   Ah-*dah*-zho
Agnus Dei   *Ahn*-yoos-day-ee
Albéniz   Al-*bayn*-ith
Alberti   Al-*bair*-tee
Allegro   Ah-*lay*-gro
Allemande   *Al*-mahnd
Amati   Am-*ah*-tee
Amiens   *Ahm*-ee-ahn
Andante   Ahn-*dahn*-tay
Appoggiatura   Ap-poj-ya-*too*-ra
Aquinas   Ak-*wye*-nass
Arezzo   Arr-*rets*-so
Aria   *Arr*-yah
Arpeggio   Arr-*peh*-djo
Ars Antiqua   Ars An-*teek*-wah
Assai   Ahs-*sah*-ee
Aulos   *Ow*-los

B

Bach   Bahck
Ballade   Bal-*lahd*
Ballata   Bahl-*lah*-ta
Baroque   Ba-*rowk*
Bartók   *Bar*-tock
Basso continuo   *Bass*-o can-*tee*-noo-o

Beethoven — Byrd

Beethoven   *Bay*-toe-ven
Berg   Bairrg
Berlioz   *Bairrl*-yohz
Bernstein   *Burn*-styne
Binchois   Ban-*shwa*
Bizet   Bee-*zay*
Boccherini   Bock-er-*reen*-ee
Boethius   Boh-*eeth*-yus
Borodin   Boh-roh-*deen*
Bosch   Bos (Bahss)
Botticelli   Bot-ti-*chell*-ee
Boucher   Boo-*shay*
Boulez   Boo-*lez*
Bourrée   Boo-*ray*
Braccio   *Brah*-cho
Braque   Brock
Bruckner   *Brook*-ner
Brueghel   *Broo*-gl
Buffo   *Boof*-fo
Buxtehude   *Books*-ta-who-dah
Byrd   Bird

C

Caccia   *Cawch*-ya
Caccini   Cat-*chee*-nee
Cantabile   Can-*tahb*-ee-lay
Cantata   Can-*tah*-ta
Canzona   Cant-*soh*-na
Canzoni   Cant-*soh*-nee

Caravaggio Car-a-*vod*-jo
Celesta Che-*les*-ta
Cembalo *Chem*-bal-oh
Cézanne Say-*zahn*
Chaconne Shah-*kon*
Chambonnières Sham-bon-yair
Chanson Sha-*son*(g)
Chardin Char-*dan*
Chartres Shart(r)
Chiesa Kee-*ay*-za
Chopin Show-pan
Chorale Ko-*rahl*
Coda *Coh*-duh
Clavier Kla-*veer*
Corelli Core-*ell*-ee
Concertante *Con*-chair-*tahn*-teh
Concerti grossi Con-*chair*-tee gross-ee
Concertino *Con*-chair-*tee*-no
Concerto grosso Con-*chair*-toh *gross*-oh
Couperin *Koo*-pear-ahn
Courante Coo-*rahnt*
Courbet Coor-*bay*
Credo *Cray*-do
Crescendo Creh-*shen*-do
Cui Kwee

D

Da Capo Dah-*cah*-po
Dali *Dah*-lee
Daphnis and Chloë *Daf*-nis and *Clo*-ay
Daubigny Doe-*bee*-nyee
Daumier Doh-me-ay
David, Jacques Louis *Dah*-veet
Davidsbündler *Dah*-veets-*buin*-dler
Debussy Deh-bue-*see*
Degas D-*gah*
Delacroix Del-a-*crwah*
Des Prez Deh-*pray*
Dichterliebe *Dikh*-ter-*lee*-bah
Dies Irae *Dee*-ace-*ee*-ry
Diminuendo Dih-*min*-you-en-do
Dolce *Doll*-chay
Doryphoros Dor-*if*-or-us
Duccio *Du*-che-O
Dufay Du-fah-ee

Dufy Dew-fee
Dukas Dew-kah
Dürer Dure-er

E

Eine kleine Nachtmusik *Ein*-(ah) *klein*(ah) *Nakt*-moo-*zeek*
Empfindsamer stil Emp-*find*-zamer shtil
Erwartung Ayr-*vahr*-toong
Estampie *Ehs*-tahm-pee
Esterházy *Est*-ter-*hah*-zee
Etude *Ay*-tewd
Eyck, Jan van Ike, yon van

F

Falla Fah-ya
Fauré Fo-ray
Ficino Fah-chee-no
Fin de siècle Fon de syekl
Fine Fee-nay
Forte For-tay
Fortissimo For-tees-ee-mo
Fragonard Frag-o-nar
Franck Frahnk
Frauenliebe und leben Frow-en-leeb oont lay-ben
Fugato Foo-gah-to

G

Gauguin Go-gan
Gabrieli Gahb-ree-ell-ee
Galliard Gal-yard
Genre Zhon-ruh
Gericault Zhay-ree-co
Gesualdo Jeh-zhoo-al-do
Ghirlandaio Gear-lon-*die*-o
Gigue Zheeg
Giorgione George-*o*-nay
Giotto *Jot*-toe
Glissando Glis-*sahn*-do
Gluck Glook
Goethe *Gu(r)*-teh
Gogh Go
Götterdämmerung, Die *Gurt*-ter-*dem*-er-oong

Gounod *Goo*-noh
Grave *Grah*-vay
Greco *Greck*-oh
Gris Greece
Grosz Gross
Guernica *Gware*-nee-ca
Guido Goo-*ee*-doh
Guillaume Ghee-*yahm*

H

Hammerklavier *Hahm*-er-klah-veer
Handel Handle
Hautbois Oh-*bwah*
Haydn *Hy*-den
Heine *Hy*-neh
Hindemith *Hin*-de-mit
Histoire du soldat, L' *Lees*-twahr du sol-dah
Homme armé, L' Home ar-may
Homophonic *Hoh*-mo-*fon*-ic
Homophony Hoh-*mof*-o-nee
Honegger *Oh*-neh-gair

I

Ibert Ee-*bair*
Idée fixe Ed-*day* feeks
Ingres Ang-r
In Nomine In *Nom*-ee-nay
Issac Ee-zahk
Isorhythm I-so-rhythm

J

Jannequin Jahn-neh-can
Jongleur Zhong-gleur
Josquin *Zhohs*-kan

K

Kandinsky Can-*din*-skee
Karajan *Cah*-ra-yun
Khatchaturian *Kah*-cha-tour-ree-an
Kinderscenen Kin-der-*tsay*-nen
Kindertotenlieder Kin-der-toten-*lee*-der
Kithara *Kith*-a-ra
Klavier Klav-*eer*

Klee Clay
Kodaly *Koh*-dah-ee
Kollwitz Call-vits
Kreutzer *Croyts*-er
Kuhnau *Koo*-now
Kyrie *Keer*-e-ay

L

Laocoon Lay-*ock*-oh-on
Landini Lan-*dee*-nee
Lassus *Lah*-soos
Legato Lah-*gah*-to
Leitmotiv *Light*-mo-teef
Leonardo da Vinci Lay-o-*nar*-doe da *Vin*-chee
Léonin *Lee*-oh-nin
Lied Leet
Liebeslieder *Lee*-bes-leeder
Lied von der Erde Leet von dair air-deh
Liszt List
Lully *Loo*-lee
Lydian *Lid*-e-an

M

Machaut Ma-*show*
Mallarmé *Mah*-lahr-may
Manet Mah-nay
Mantegna Mon-*tayn*-yah
Marcellus Mass, Pope Mar-*chel*-us
Masaccio Mah-*sotch*-oh
Masque Mask
Matisse Ma-*teess*
Medici *May*-dee-chee
Mendelssohn *Men*-dell-sohn
Messe de Notre Dame Mess de Noh-tr Dahm
Mezzo piano (mp) *Met*-zoh pee-*ah*-noh
Mer, La Lah mayr
Michelangelo Mee-kul-*ahn*-jel-loh
Minnesinger Min-ne-zing-er
Milhaud Mee-yoh
Modigliani Moh-dil-*yahn*-ee
Moliere Moh-lyair
Mondrian *Mon*-dree-ahn
Monody *Mon*-o-dee

Monet   Moh-*nay*
Monophonic   *Mon*-o-fon-ic
Monophony   Mon-*off*-o-nee
Motet   Moh-tet
Mussorgski   Moo-*sorg*-skee
Monteverdi   Mon-tuh-*vair*-dee
Mozart   *Mo*-tsart
Munch   Munk

N

Nachtmusik   *Nakt*-moo-zeek
Neumes   Newmz
Nibelung (Ring of the Nibelung)
   Nee-be-loong

O

Ockeghem   *Ok*-e-ghem
Odo de Cluny   Aw-do de Clee-nee
Opera buffa   Opera *boo*-fah
Orfeo   Or-*fay*-oh
Organum   *Or*-ga-num
Orozco   Oh-*ross*-coh
Ostinato   Os-tee-*nah*-toh

P

Pachelbel   *Pahk*-a-bel
Palestrina   Pal-ess-*tree*-nah
Passacaglia   Pass-a-*cahl*-ya
Pavane   Pah-*vahn*
Peri   *Pay*-ree
Pérotin   *Pear*-oh-tin
Petrarch   *Pet*-rark
Petrucci   Pet-*troo*-chee
Phyrgian   *Fridg*-ian
Piano   Pee-*ah*-noh
Pianissimo   Pee-uh-*nees*-ee-moh
Picasso   Pee-*cahs*-oh
Pisano   Pi-*sahn*-noh
Pizzicato   Pit-see-*kah*-toh
Polyclitus   Polly-cly-tus
Polyphony   Po-*lif*-o-nee
Poussin   Poo-san
Praxiteles   Prack-*sit*-uh-lees
Primavera, La   *Pree*-ma-vair-ah
Prokofiev   Pro-*kof*-fee-ev
Purcell   *Per*-sel

Puccini   Poo-*chee*-nee

R

Rameau   Ram-*oh*
Raphael   *Raf*-ee-ul
Ravel   Rah-*vell*
Recitative   *Ress*-i-ta-teev
Renoir   Ren-*wahr*
Respighi   Res-*peeg*-ee
Rheims   Reems
Ricercare   Ree-chair-*cah*-ray
Rienzi   Ree-*en*-zee
Rimsky-Korsakov   Rim-skee-kor-
   suh-kof
Ripieno   Ree-pee-*ay*-noh
Ritornello   Ree-tor-*nel*-lo
Rococo   Ro-*co*-co
Rodin   Roh-dan
Rouault   Roo-oh
Rouen   Roo-on
Rousseau   Roo-*soh*
Ryder   Ri-der

S

Sarabande   Sar-a-bahnd
Sartre   Sart
Satie   Sah-tee
Scarlatti   Skar-lah-tee
Schoenberg   Shirn-berg
Scherzo   Skairts-oh
Schubert   *Shoo*-bert
Schumann   *Shoo*-mahn
Schütz   Shoots
Scriabin   Skree-*ah*-bin
Seurat   Sir-*ah*
Sforzando   Tsfor-*tsahn*-doh
Shostakovich   *Shahs*-tah-ko-vitch
Sibelius   See-*bayl*-yus
Sinfonia   Seen-fo-*nee*-ah
Sonata da camera   Son-*ah*-ta da
   cah-meh-rah
Sonata da chiesa   Son-*ah*-ta da
   kee-*ay*-za
Sprechtstimme   *Spreckts*-shtim-eh
Stadtpfeifer   *Shtat*-fife-er
Stamitz   *Shtah*-mits
Stile (Ital.)   *Stee*-leh

Stockhausen   *Shtock*-how-zen
Style galant (Fr.)   Steel gal-*anh*
Subito   *Soo*-bee-toh
Sweelinck   *Svay*-lingk
Szell   Sell

T

Tannhauser   *Tahn*-hoy-zer
Tartini   Tar-*tee*-nee
Tchaikovsky   Chy-*koff*-skee
Timbre   *Tám*-br (*tahm*-br)
Titian   *Tish*-n
Toulouse-Lautrec   Too-*looze*-lo-trek
Trouvères   Troo-*vair*
Tutti   *Too*-tee

V

Varèse   Var-ez

Verdi   *Vair*-dee
Vermeer   Ver-*mair*
Victoria (Span.)   Vee-*toh*-ree-uh
Vielle   *Vee*-yel
Viola da braccio   *Braht*-cho
Viola da gamba   Vee-*o*-la dah *gahm*-bah
Virelai   *Veer*-e-lay
Vivace   Vee-*vah*-chay
Vivaldi   Vee-*vahl*-dee

W

Wagner   *Vahg*-ner
Walküre   Vahl-keer-reh
Watteau   Wah-*toh*
Weber   *Vay*-ber
Webern   *Vay*-burn
Wolf   Vulf
Wozzeck   Vote-sek

GLOSSARY

A cappella   Sung without accompaniment.

Accent   Stress or emphasis on one tone or chord.

Accidental   A sharp, flat, double sharp or double flat, or natural, prefixed to a note in a passage of music.

Adagio   A slow tempo.

Aerophones   Instruments in which the sound is generated by a vibrating air column (for example, trumpet).

Agnus Dei   "Lamb of God." The last part of the musical setting of the Ordinary of the Mass (see Mass), concluding with a three-fold repetition of "Lamb of God, who takest away the sins of the world, have mercy upon us," and ending with *"dona nobis pacem"* (grant us peace).

Alberti bass   Broken chord accompaniment in piano music of the late eighteenth century.

Allegro   A lively, brisk tempo.

Allemande   A dance in moderate tempo, in duple meter; of late Renaissance and Baroque periods.

Answer   The subject of a fugue sounded or imitated a fourth or, more commonly, a fifth higher.

Alto   Second highest part in choral music.

Antiphony   The exchange of musical phrases or passages between two or more soloists or groups.

Appoggiatura   A dissonant tone that occurs on the strong beat and resolves up or down by half or whole step. Also a Baroque ornament consisting of a small added note (♪ ♩) played on the beat.

Arco   Designates the use of the bow (for violin, cello, and so on).

Aria   An elaborate song with instrumental accompaniment. First introduced in seventeenth-century opera.

Arpeggio   The tones of a chord played consecutively; also called a broken chord.

Ars Antiqua   Latin-ancient art; designation for music of the late twelfth and thirteenth centuries.

Assai   Very

Asymmetrical rhythm   Irregular patterns involving either successive changes in meter, accents, or tones of different duration.

377

Athematic   Melody which is not written in the traditional manner (does not have phrases, climax, or progressive flow of tones to a particular goal or cadence).

Atonality   (Atonal). The absence of key feeling; used generally in conjunction with the 12-tone technique of Schoenberg and modern "serialists" in which all 12 tones of the chromatic scale are treated equally; traditional scales, chords, key-centers are avoided.

Augmentation   Refers to lengthening of time values of notes.

Ballade   A type of medieval poetry and music of the thirteenth and fourteenth centuries; prominent in France among the trouvères. Also designation for dramatic piano pieces of the nineteenth century.

Ballata   (plural, ballate) A type of fourteenth-century Italian poetry and music.

Bar line   A vertical line through the staff which separates one measure from another.

Baroque   See *periods* of music and art.

Beat   The unit of measurement in music; a felt pulsation.

Binary form   A type of musical structure in which there are two distinct sections or themes, usually designated by A B.

Bourrée   A lively dance in duple meter; of French origin and used in the suites of the Baroque period.

Broken-color technique   Refers to method of scoring for instruments in which melodic fragments (as opposed to complete passages) are assigned to a succession of instruments of varied tone color or timbre. Common to the impressionists Debussy and Ravel.

Burgundian School   A group of composers affiliated with the court of the Dukes of Burgundy at Dijon, first half of the fifteenth century; representatives: Dufay (c.1400–1474) and Binchois (c.1400–1467).

Cadence   The ending portion of a melody or section of music. Different types of cadences, derived from a particular arrangement of melody-tones and/or chords, provide a kind of musical punctuation in which the musical flow is completely stopped (full cadence) or momentarily suspended (incomplete cadence).

Cadenza   An elaborate improvisatory passage played by a solo instrument in the concerto; usually occurs near the end of the first movement.

Canon   The exact imitation of one musical part by another.

Cantabile   Expressive term used to indicate a "singing" style of performance; smooth and flowing.

Cantata   An extended vocal form (with instruments in supporting role); those of J. S. Bach usually employed a sacred text, small orchestra, chorus, vocal soloists, and were arranged into a series of short movements or "verses."

Cantus firmus   A borrowed melody used as the basis of a polyphonic composition; common to vocal music of the Renaissance.

Canzona A sixteenth- and seventeenth-century instrumental form, for organ or ensemble; derived from the sixteenth-century chanson; in its later stages of development consisting of several contrasting sections.

Celesta Small percussion instrument with keyboard mechanism which produces light bell-like tones.

Chamber music Instrumental ensemble music (more than one instrument) with one player to a part; includes string quartets, quintets, violin sonatas, flute sonatas.

Chordophones Instruments plucked and/or bowed, such as instruments of the modern stringed family (violin, cello [violincello], bass, viola) and earlier forms such as the lute and viol.

Chorale A short hymnlike form for voices; usually written for four voice parts and in metrical rhythm; common to German Protestant music.

Chord Three or more tones sounded simultaneously.

Chorus Refers to a group that sings choral music; also the choral sections (parts sung by full choir) of a cantata, oratorio, or opera.

Chromatics Tones foreign to the key of the music, indicated by a flat, sharp, or natural sign.

Classical See *periods* of music and art.

Clef Sign written at the beginning of each staff which designates the pitches of the lines and spaces; the treble clef (𝄞) for example circles the pitch "g" (second line of the staff).

Coda An added section or concluding statement at the end of a movement in the symphony or sonata and other forms.

Concerto An orchestral composition either for one soloist (*solo concerto*) and accompanying body of instruments, or, for several soloists, usually two to three (*concerto grosso*) and supporting orchestra.

Concerto grosso A multimovement form (normally three movements) featuring a solo group of instruments (two to three) against the full orchestra.

Concertino Name given to the solo group in the concerto grosso.

Conductus Latin songs, secular or sacred of the twelfth and thirteenth centuries; in metrical rhythm and either polyphonic or monophonic.

Conjunct Refers to step-wise melodic movement.

Consonance A musical effect resulting from a particular arrangement of tones (usually in terms of harmony or chords) that provides a feeling of repose, balance, stability.

Con sord Abbreviation for *con sordino,* meaning: to be played with the mute (a small wooden piece attached to the strings of a violin, for example; or a plastic or metal device fitted into the end of a brass instrument).

Continuo (Also known as *basso continuo.*) A keyboard instrument which with one other instrument (normally a cello) provided the nucleus of Baroque music. The term *continuo* may also refer to the bass melody and numbers (indicating types of chords to be filled in) played by the keyboard instrument in the Baroque period.

Counterpoint The technique of combining two or more lines of melody;

synonomous with polyphony. As an adjective (contrapuntal) it refers to a piece of music or section written in counterpoint.

Courante   A lively dance in triple meter; of French origin and used in Baroque suites.

Credo   The third part of the Ordinary of the Mass. Begins: I believe in one God the Father almighty, maker of heaven and earth, and of all things visible and invisible . . .

Crescendo   Expressive term indicating a gradual increase in volume or loudness; abbreviated *cresc.,* or indicated by two diverging lines ⟨

Development   The working out or elaboration of thematic material by rhythmic, harmonic or contrapuntal techniques. Generally appears in the second phase of the *sonata form* where an important feature of the melody such as a rhythmic or melodic figure is elaborated upon.

Diatonic   Describes any melodic or harmonic movement that uses only the tones of the given key of the composition.

Disjunct   Refers to a melody that progresses mainly by skips, that is, large intervals between each of the melody tones.

Discant style   Term applied to music in which all the parts move in the same rhythm.

Dissonance   Combinations of tones in harmony or melody that produce a state of tension and unrest.

Dominant   The fifth tone of the scale, or the chord built on the fifth tone of the scale.

Dynamics   Terms and abbreviations that indicate degrees and changes in volume or loudness:

pianissimo	pp	very soft
piano	p	soft
mezzo piano	mp	moderately soft
mezzo forte	mf	moderately loud
forte	f	loud
fortissimo	ff	very loud

crescendo = gradual increase in volume
decrescendo or diminuendo = gradual decrease in volume
sfz = strongly accented

Eleventh chord   A chord of six different tones, spaced an interval of a third apart; common to certain styles of twentieth-century music such as Impressionism.

Empfindsamer stil   "Sensitive style" common to the music of the preclassicist Carl Phillip Emanuel Bach; characterized by sudden changes in volume and rhythmic movement, and highly personal quality.

Enharmonic   Refers to a note that has the same pitch (but different spelling) as another note, for example F♯ and G♭.

Equal temperament   A system of tuning that came into musical practice during the time of the Baroque in which all tones of the scale are tuned equally, thus permitting use of all major and minor keys (notably demonstrated in J. S. Bach's *The Well-Tempered Clavier*).

Exposition   The first phase or part of the *Sonata form,* in which the main themes are announced or presented.

Expressionism   See *periods* of music and art.

Flemish School   The composers active in Flanders (northern France and southern Belgium) following the Burgundians Dufay and Binchois, are commonly referred to as the Flemish School. Beginning about mid-sixteenth century such composers as Josquin des Pres (c. 1450–1521), Johannes Ockeghem (c. 1430–1495) and Jacob Obrecht (c. 1453–1505) greatly influenced the musical thought of the Renaissance.

Form   Refers to the structure or pattern in which musical ideas or themes are presented and arranged. Vocal forms include the oratorio, cantata, mass, motet and so on; common instrumental forms include: sonata, fugue, symphony, concerto, and symphonic poem.

Fugue   A musical form in which a single theme called the *subject* is stated in one key by a particular part and then imitated or *answered* by a second part in a different key; a series of successive statements and answers involving all of the parts (four usually) constitutes the over-all design of the fugue. Fuguelike sections called *fugatos* (short fugues) are commonly used in larger works, such as in the "Eroica" Symphony of Beethoven (last part of the second movement).

Gavotte   A dance in fairly lively tempo, quadruple meter, introduced by Lully in seventeenth-century French operas and ballets.

Gigue   A baroque dance of English origin (Jig); in $\frac{6}{8}$ meter and very lively.

Glissando   Sliding between pitches.

Gloria   "Glory," the second part of the Ordinary of the Mass, begins: "Glory be to God on high, and on earth peace to men of good will. We praise thee, we bless thee, we adore thee, we glorify thee."

Grace note   An ornamental note (appoggiatura) which is played very quickly; written as a very small note. In the Baroque and Classic periods it is played *on* the beat; after Beethoven, just *before* the beat.

Harmonics   High-pitched artificial tones produced by either overblowing (on the flute, for example) or using certain bowing and finger positions (on the violin, for example).

Harmonic rhythm   Rhythm created by chord changes or progressions.

Harmony   The technique of combining tones into chords and chord progressions.

Heterophony   A pseudo form of part singing in which the voices sing spontaneously at their natural level.

Hocket   Literally "hiccup" in which the melodic line is broken up by alternating the melodic notes between two or more parts.

Homophony   A type of musical texture in which emphasis is upon a single melody and supporting chords.

Impressionism   See periods of music and art.

Imitation   The echoing of one part by another is referred to as imitation; if carried throughout the composition it is referred to as a *canon*.

Interval   The distance between one pitch and another, measured in scale steps.

Key   A grouping of notes in which a piece of music is composed. Traditional keys have seven different tones.

Key signature   The sharps or flats (or complete absence of these as in C major which has none) designate a particular key. They are grouped together on the staff at the beginning of each line of music.

Kyrie   The first part of the Ordinary of the Mass: *Kyrie eleison* (Lord have mercy), *Christe eleison* and *Kyrie eleison,* are each repeated three times in succession.

Largo   Italian term designating the slowest tempo.

Landini cadence   A cadence in which a tone (sixth degree of the key) is inserted between the leading tone (seventh degree) and the final tone (octave). Named after Francesco Landini (1325–1397).

Ländler   Austrian folk dance, triple meter with strong emphasis on first beat of each measure.

Legato   Smooth, connected fashion.

Lento   Slower than Adagio; just above Largo.

Libretto   The text of any dramatic vocal work such as opera.

Madrigal   A secular vocal form popular in Italy and England during the sixteenth century; also the name of a secular fourteenth-century Italian form. The sixteenth-century English madrigal was usually written in a polyphonic texture of four or five parts and of free form, whereas the fourteenth-century Italian type was generally in two or three parts and based on strict poetic form.

Major, Minor   Refers to two basic types of scales differentiated by their third interval (in the C-major scale there is a major third between C and E, in the C-minor scale, there is a minor third, C to E-flat).

Mass   Refers generally (in a musical context) to a setting of the Ordinary of the Mass consisting of the Kyrie, Gloria, Credo, Sanctus and Agnus Dei, in which the texts are invariable. The Proper of the Mass, composed of texts which vary according to the occasion, include these items: Introit, Gradual, Offertory, and Communion.

Measure   The space between two bar lines.

Melody   The succession of meaningful tones; also called melodic line.

Meter   The regular grouping of pulses or beats into either *duple* (1–2, 1–2), *triple* (1–2–3, 1–2–3), *quadruple* (1–2–3–4, 1–2–3–4), or compound combinations (more than four beats).

Minor   See major.

Minuet   A French dance of moderate tempo and triple meter, reputedly introduced as a formal dance by Lully about 1650. Used in some baroque suites and widely employed in the classical symphony (late eighteenth century) as the third movement.

Modality   The period of musical practice from the Greek civilization to the end of the Renaissance, in which the ancient modes (Dorian, Phrygian, Lydian, and so on) were used as the basis for musical composition.

Modulation   The technique of passing from one key to another in the course of a musical composition.

Monophony   A type of musical texture in which only one part is sung or played by one or more performers.

Mordent   A three-note ornament that consists of a principal note, the note next below it in the scale, and followed by the principal note.

Motet   A vocal musical form which arose in thirteenth-century France; although derived from sacred vocal music (organum) it was also adapted by French secular instrumentalists of the Gothic period. Characteristics include the simultaneous use of different texts (sacred or secular), a rather rigid rhythmic movement and three-part texture. In the late Renaissance (1450–1600), the term motet denoted a setting for unaccompanied voices of a sacred Latin text, composed in the imitative style (after 1500).

Motive   The smallest musical idea consisting of several notes.

Musical form   The mold or pattern into which musical ideas or themes are organized.

Musicology   A discipline devoted to research in all phases of musical endeavor; in general historically oriented.

Ninth chord   A chord of five different tones, for example, G B D F A.

Note   The written symbol for a specific pitch and its time duration.

Opera   A drama set to music, staged with scenery and costumes, and usually based on a secular theme; includes orchestra, chorus, and soloists.

Opera buffa style   Refers to the bright, scintillating effect generally attributed to Italian opera of the eighteenth century; imitated by symphony composers of the classical era.

Opus   The chronological number given to a composition; abbreviated Op.

Oratorio   A drama, usually of a sacred nature, set to music with a narrator, soloists, chorus and orchestra. Those of late Baroque (Handel, for example) are without scenery and costumes.

Organum   The collective name given to all music, involving several parts, of the medieval period.

Ornament   Refers to decorative figures applied to the melodic lines of seventeenth and eighteenth century music. See mordent, grace note, turn and trill.

Ostinato   A repeated melodic or rhythmic idea, usually placed in the bass.

Parallel motion   An early type of medieval organum in which all of the parts or voices ascend and descend in the same motion. Also common to the Impressionistic style of Debussy of the twentieth century.

Part   A single line of notes to be played or sung; the printed music designated for an instrument or voice.

Pentatonic scale   A five-note scale common in the Orient; an equivalent: C D F G A.

Periods and movements in music and art   These are generally given as follows:

Greek 1200–146 B.C.	Romantic 1800–1900
Roman 146 B.C.–A.D. 500	Impressionism 1880–1914
Romanesque 250–1150	Expressionism 1900–
(or sometimes 1000–1150)	Neoclassicism 1918–
Gothic 1150–1400	Neoromanticism 1900–
Renaissance 1400–1600	Abstract expressionism 1945–
Baroque 1600–1750	Structuralism 1950–
Rococo and Classical 1725–1800	

Phrase   Denotes a melodic division in traditional music. Much of the music of the classical and romantic periods is based on melodies having two phrases, each of four measures, the first ending with an incomplete cadence and the second, a complete cadence.

Pizz   Abbreviation for *pizzicato,* meaning the plucking of the strings on the violin, for example.

Plateau dynamics   Definite gradations of volume as used in the Baroque concerto.

Pointillism   Technique in which the melodic passage is divided up among various instruments in rapid succession, creating a kaleidoscopic effect of tone colors.

Polyphony   The technique of combining two or more melodic lines; also known as counterpoint.

Proper   See mass.

Pulsatile   Possessing a definite beat feeling.

Recitative   A type of singing in a speechlike manner; common to opera of the Baroque and Classical periods.

Recapitulation   The third and last phase or part of the sonata form; the re-statement, in whole or part, of the Exposition section.

Register   The level or range of the musical sound denoted by the general classifications: *treble clef* for high pitched instruments or voices, and *bass clef* for low pitched.

Renaissance   See *periods* of music and art.

Resolution   Refers to the progression of tones from a point of dissonance (marked by a feeling of tension) to consonance (feeling or state of repose, stability). In classical period compositions, dissonant chords had to be resolved according to accepted practices of the age. In the late romantic period, such dissonant chords were treated with increasing freedom, eventually leading to the abandonment of traditional concepts of dissonance and consonance by Schoenberg and the expressionists, early in the present century.

Rhythm   The regular, constant feeling of forward motion or propulsion in music achieved by the repetition of a beat or pulse and a particular pattern of note values.

Ricercar   A sixteenth- and seventeenth-century instrumental form (particularly for the organ), written in imitative counterpoint and derived from the sixteenth-century motet.

Ritornello   A recurring theme common to the baroque concerto.

Ripieno   The full orchestral portion of the baroque concerto grosso; sometimes referred to as *tutti.*

Rococo   See periods of music and art.

Root position   The fundamental note of the chord (C for example in the chord C E G) is placed as the lowest part of the chord; *first inversion* of the chord denotes the placement of the third (E, for example in the C chord) in the lowest position.

Romantic, Romanticism   See periods of music and art.

Round   A short vocal canon in which one part imitates another at the same pitch level or at the octave (eight steps higher or lower).

Sanctus   The fourth part of the Ordinary of the Mass, which begins: Holy, Holy, Holy, Lord God of Hosts. Heaven and earth are full of Thy glory. Hosanna in the highest . . . .

Saraband   A dignified, slow dance, in triple meter; common to the baroque suite.

Scale   A series of successive tones placed in order from low to high; also, a particular key written out in ascending order of tones: C D E F G A B C.

Scherzo   A musical joke or jest.

Score   The notation of music in printed form with all parts (instrumental or vocal) indicated in full.

Semitone   A half-tone, for example C to C-sharp. Synonomous with half-step.

Seventh chord   A chord of four different tones, for example: C E G B-flat.

Sinfonia   Italian for symphony; predecessor of the classical symphony.

Sonata   This word has at least two meanings: it may refer either to a musical genre or form (for example, piano sonata) having three or four movements, or, to a type of musical structure having three sections or divisions common to the classical symphony: exposition, development, recapitulation. (See separate entries of these terms.)

Staff   The five parallel lines upon which music is written.

Subdominant   The fourth degree of the scale, or the chord built on it.

Subito   Suddenly; sudden change, for example loud to soft.

Symphonic poem (also known as tone poem)   A programmatic work (based on an extramusical idea such as a poem, story, painting, historical event) for orchestra, in one extended movement.

Symphony   A large-scale composition for orchestra having several movements.

Style, musical   Refers to the distinguishing features of a composition or of music representative of a particular school or group of composers, such as certain melodic, harmonic, and rhythmic characteristics.

Style galant, or *rococo style*   Designates the style of music composed by musicians of the rococo period (such as François Couperin) and is characterized by its lightness, excessive ornamentation, and homophonic texture.

Tablature   A type of notation used for the lute in which numbers (instead of notes) are written on staff lines; numbers indicating finger placement on lute strings.

Ternary   Three-part form: A B A.

Texture, musical   The manner in which tones are woven or arranged in musical space. See *monophony, polyphony* and *homophony.*

Timbre   The characteristic tone quality or tone color of an instrument or voice.

Toccata   A brilliant, virtuosic piece in free form; common during the Baroque period and usually composed for the organ.

Tonality   A period of musical practice from about 1600 to 1900 in which music was composed in major and minor keys.

Tone   A musical sound of definite pitch.

Tonic   The name of the central chord (or scale-tone) to which all other tones or chords gravitate; common to the period of tonality, 1600–1900.

Triad   Usually thought of as the simplest type of chord having three different tones: C E G.

Trill   The rapid alternation of two adjacent tones, indicated by the abbreviation *tr.*

Trio   The second division of the minuet, originally played by three instruments.

Trio Sonata   One of the Baroque forms of the sonata, for two violins and cello (or bass) and a continuo (keyboard instrument). Thus, actually four instruments took part. A Baroque solo sonata called for solo instrument and a continuo.

Turn   A rapid embellishment, usually a group of four notes, indicated by this sign: ∾

Unison   The sounding of the same note either in exact pitch or at an octave lower or higher, by two or more players or singers.

Vibrato   A wavering of the tone.

Whole-tone scale   Each tone is separated by a whole step or whole tone, for example: C D E F# G# A# C; common to impressionism.

INDEX

Italicized numbers denote pages on which black-and-white illustrations or diagrams appear; underscored numbers indicate color plate on facing page; boldface numbers locate songs or musical excerpts.